Navegando 1B

Annotated Teacher's Edition

James F. Funston

Contributing Writers

Rolando Castellanos

Paul J. Hoff

Keith Mason

EMCParadigm Publishing, Saint Paul, Minnesota

MIDDLE SCHOOL EDITION

Navegando 1A and *Navegando 1B* are two textbooks in the new *Navegando* series that have been specifically designed for use in middle school. *Capítulos 1–5* appear in *Navegando 1A* for students in their first year of Spanish in middle school; *Capítulos 6–10* appear in *Navegando 1B* for students in their second year of Spanish in middle school. Support materials for *Navegando 1A* and *1B* that are designed for the age-specific needs of middle school students are *Middle School Resources A* and *B*. Since middle school students have unique interests and abilities, they need varied learning situations for exploration, extension, and application of their knowledge; chances to express their creativity with hands-on learning activities; and opportunities to develop social skills, share thoughts, and experience success and recognition. Teachers can provide for such differences by using these two resource materials. They contain activity sheets to reinforce and expand upon the vocabulary, structures, and culture introduced in the *Navegando 1A* and *1B* textbooks. Activities focus on communication skills (surveys, paired, and information gap activities), hands-on projects, and games. In addition, the *Middle School Bridge Program* thoroughly reviews both the vocabulary and grammar covered the previous year in *Navegando 1A*. All the new structures in *Navegando 1A* are reintroduced before they are practiced in a variety of new activities. Other distinctly middle school support materials include the *Navegando 1A* and *1B* workbooks.

ISBN 0-8219-2831-7

© 2005 EMC Corporation

Published by EMC/Paradigm Publishing
875 Montreal Way
St. Paul, Minnesota 55102
800-328-1452
www.emcp.com
E-mail: educate@emcp.com

Printed in the United States of America
1 2 3 4 5 6 7 8 9 10 XXX 08 07 06 05 04

CONTENTS

Scope and Sequence

Capítulo 6 En casa

 Venezuela **Colombia**

	Objectives	Topics	Dialog	Cultura viva
Lección A	• identify items in the kitchen and at the dinner table • express obligations, wishes and preferences • talk about everyday activities • state an opinion • discuss food and table items • point out people and things • describe a household • tell what someone says • say how someone is doing	objects in a kitchen table setting and cleanup foods Venezuela at the dinner table	¿Me vas a ayudar? ¿Te gusta la sopa?	Explorando Venezuela Las arepas venezolanas
Lección B		rooms and floors of a house describing a home Colombia how someone is doing	La casa de Elisa Tengo mucho calor	Colombia ¡Hogar, dulce hogar!

Tú lees: Estrategia: *Using graphics to understand a reading*
La casa de mis sueños

Tú escribes: Estrategia: *Connecting phrases*

Capítulo 7 El tiempo libre

 Argentina **Chile**

	Objectives	Topics	Dialog	Cultura viva
Lección A	• talk about leisure-time activities • discuss sports • say what someone can do • discuss length of time • describe what is happening • talk about the seasons and weather • indicate order	leisure-time activities entertainment sports Argentina time expressions	¿No quieres jugar al ajedrez? Quiero alquilar una película	Argentina Che, bailá conmigo...
Lección B		seasons weather sports leisure-time activities Chile ordinal numbers	¡Vamos a esquiar! ¿Qué temperatura hace?	Chile ¿Farenheit o centígrados?

Tú lees: Estrategia: *Previewing*
El mundo de los deportes

Tú escribes: Estrategia: *Questioning*

Idioma	Estrategia	Oportunidades	¡Extra!	Readings
Expressing obligations with *tener que* and *deber* Stem-changing verbs: $e \to ie$ Pointing out someone or something: demonstrative adjectives		¿Piensas viajar a otro país?	Más comida	Una deliciosa tradición
Telling what someone says: *decir* Expressing wishes with *querer* or *gustaría* *Repaso rápido:* regular present-tense verbs Stem-changing verbs: $e \to i$	Recognizing words in context		Altos y bajos Las palabras *e* y *u* Con permiso y perdón	Grupo musical La Ola

Idioma	Estrategia	Oportunidades	¡Extra!	Readings
Stem-changing verbs: $o \to ue$ and $u \to ue$ Expressions with *hace* Saying what is happening: present progressive *Repaso rápido:* direct object pronouns Using the present progressive with direct object pronouns	Clarifying meaning by asking questions	El español y los deportes	La fiebre del gol ¿Damas en los baños? Comparando inglés y español	El juego del pato
Verbs that require special accentuation Present tense of *dar* and *poner* Describing people using *-dor* or *-ista* Using ordinal numbers			¿Cuándo es verano?	Grupo musical La Ola

Capítulo 8 Mis quehaceres

 España

	Objectives	Topics	Dialog	Cultura viva

Lección A	• talk about household chores
	• say what just happened
	• ask for and offer help
	• talk about the past
	• identify and describe foods
	• discuss food preparation
	• make comparisons
		household chores
		Spain
			¿Me ayudas?
			Hay mucho por hacer
				España: país
				  multicultural
				Los quehaceres en una
				  casa española

Lección B		foods
		shopping in a market
		comparisons
		preparing *paella*
		eating in Spain
			¿Qué nos hace falta
			  comprar?
			Comprando chorizo
				La paella
				¡Cómo se come en
				  España!

Tú lees:	Estrategia: *Gathering meaning from context* Ir de tapas y a merendar			
Tú escribes:	Estrategia: *Using graphic organizers*			

Capítulo 9 La ropa

 Panamá   **Ecuador**

	Objectives	Topics	Dialog	Cultura viva

Lección A	• describe clothing
	• identify parts of the body
	• express disagreement
	• talk about the past
	• discuss size and fit
	• discuss price and payment
		clothing
		shopping in a
		  department store
		parts of the body
		Panama
		bargaining
			¿Cuál prefieres?
			Un vestido de seda
				Panamá, el cruce del
				  mundo
				También se dice

Lección B		shopping in a
		  department store
		gift ideas
		jewelry
		size and fit
		Ecuador
		at the cash register
			Busco un regalo
			¿Cómo va a pagar?
				Ecuador, país de
				  maravillas naturales
				De compras en
				  Guayaquil

Tú lees:	Estrategia: *Using visual format to predict meaning* La tienda por departamentos Danté			
Tú escribes:	Estrategia: *Indicating sequence*			

Idioma	Estrategia	Oportunidades	¡Extra!	Readings
Repaso rápido: direct object pronouns Indirect object pronouns Saying what just happened with *acabar de* Present tense of *oír* and *traer* Talking about the past: preterite tense of *-ar* verbs	Increasing your vocabulary	Estudiante de intercambio	El verbo *colgar* El uso de *vosotros* El cambio de $g \rightarrow j$	¿Quién lo hace?
Making comparisons *Repaso rápido:* preterite tense of regular *-ar* verbs Preterite tense of *dar* and *estar*			*Hacer falta, importar* y *parecer* ¿Cuánto pesa? El euro	Grupo musical La Ola

Idioma	Estrategia	Oportunidades	¡Extra!	Readings
Adjectives as nouns Talking about the past: preterite tense of *-er* and *-ir* verbs Preterite tense of *ir* and *ser* Affirmative and negative words	Developing language survival skills: *regatear*	Regatear	¿Recuerdas?	Las molas: símbolo de la cultura kuna
Diminutives Preterite tense of *leer, oír, ver, decir, hacer* and *tener* *Repaso rápido:* prepositions Using prepositions			En otras palabras	Grupo musical La Ola

Capítulo 10 Un año más

 Perú  **Guatemala**

	Objectives	Topics	Dialog	Cultura viva
Lección A	• discuss past actions and events • talk about everyday activities • express emotion • indicate wishes and preferences • write about past actions • talk about the future • make polite requests • describe personal characteristics	school likes and dislikes Peru travel	Fue un año divertido	El Perú, centro del imperio inca
Lección B		plans for the future vacations Guatemala careers	¿Adónde van de vacaciones?	Guatemala, tierra maya

Tú lees: Estrategia: *Applying your skills*
Es sólo una cuestión de actitud

Tú escribes: Estrategia: *Defining your purpose for writing*

INTRODUCTION

Navegando is a comprehensive Spanish language series that was designed and written to make teaching and learning Spanish an exciting and rewarding experience. The 21st century is a time of innovation and change in which knowledge of a world language is more important than ever before. Information-based technologies and an international marketplace require a workforce with specific competencies and knowledge in the area of interpersonal communication. Such a dynamic environment calls for a global mind-set, cultural understanding and a personal commitment to ongoing self-development to participate effectively with diverse populations.

The series was created to support and advance the vision of the National Standards for Foreign Language Learning. *Navegando* combines the five Cs of communication, cultures, connections, comparisons and communities with interesting content, varied and effective methodology, interactive activities and an ongoing discussion of the wealth of opportunities available to students through the study of Spanish. The program empowers students to learn to speak, read, write and comprehend Spanish and to do so in a culturally authentic manner. Chapter activities and readings motivate students to look beyond the classroom at real life in the Spanish-speaking world. Clear and concise grammar explanations guide students to understand and use Spanish with increasing accuracy, while communicative activities allow students to use Spanish in meaningful, everyday situations. In addition, the many text-related photographs and illustrations provide attractive, authentic visual support for the thematic content.

The extensive components of the series that complement the textbook are described in this Annotated Teacher's Edition (ATE) and have been carefully developed to provide instructors with an effective and flexible program for teaching students to communicate in Spanish. Whether a teacher wants to provide Web-based learning, listening practice, additional grammar and vocabulary activities, video, CD-ROM software or some other means of addressing student learning, materials are available to reinforce, recycle and expand upon the textbook content, thus allowing the teacher to decide which components and activities to use in a given lesson.

One of the greatest challenges that educators face today is the need to reach a large number of students, each with individual interests and learning styles. *Navegando* is a comprehensive, flexible instructional program that allows teachers and students to meet the challenge together. The series offers exciting opportunities to address the multiple intelligences, career skills, critical thinking, cross-curricular learning, creative problem solving and the ability to work effectively with others. With *Navegando*, students will enjoy using Spanish in meaningful ways while becoming familiar with the fascinating cultures of the Spanish-speaking world.

PHILOSOPHY AND GOALS

Learning a language has always meant more than merely memorizing words and structures and then putting them together with the hope of actually being able to communicate. Just as language is inseparable from culture, so is it inseparable from the authentic communication of thoughts and emotions. The culture of the Spanish-speaking world varies from moment to moment and from one place to the next. Language and culture cannot be segmented and learned out of context if students are ever going to become proficient. As students use *Navegando 1B,* they will have exciting opportunities to learn about culture and to use language for obtaining and communicating information. In *Navegando 1B,* students will cross several disciplines and will use a wide variety of resources, including the Internet, newspapers, magazines and libraries, for obtaining and sharing information, ideas and feelings. These authentic learning experiences will introduce them to and expand their knowledge of language, math and science, social sciences and the arts and humanities. In *Navegando 1B,* students will learn not only academic skills but also problem solving, survival and employment skills, so that when they walk out of the classroom, they will be able to communicate confidently using authentic Spanish.

Navegando 1B is a reflection of extensive research and the work of many dedicated professionals in foreign-language education and related fields. Focus-group research and extensive feedback from teachers have been applied to every component to make it better. In addition, a variety of important initiatives in language teaching and learning influenced the writing and design of the series. Many of the key principles and guiding forces in the creation of both the textbook and the supplemental materials are summarized on the following pages.

NATIONAL STANDARDS

The *Goals 2000: Educate America Act* of 1994 provided funding for improving education. One result of this funding was the establishment of content standards in foreign-language education as determined by a K–12 Student Standards Task Force. The task force represented people involved in various languages, levels of instruction, geographic regions and curricular models. They defined a national framework of content standards in foreign-language education, which was published in 1996. This document was revised and expanded in 1999. The new framework, *Standards for Foreign Language Learning in the 21st Century including Chinese, Classical Languages, French, German, Italian, Japanese, Portuguese, Russian, and Spanish,* includes information about standards application in specific languages. An executive summary of the National Standards can be obtained from the American Teachers of Foreign Languages, a collaborator in the project, at www.actfl.org. Following are the main points of the National Standards.

Communication

Communicate in Languages Other Than English

Standard 1.1: Students engage in conversations, provide and obtain information, express feelings and emotions and exchange opinions.

Standard 1.2: Students understand and interpret written and spoken language on a variety of topics.

Standard 1.3: Students present information, concepts and ideas to an audience of listeners or readers on a variety of topics.

Cultures

Gain Knowledge and Understanding of Other Cultures

Standard 2.1: Students demonstrate an understanding of the relationship between the practices and perspectives of the culture studied.

Standard 2.2: Students demonstrate an understanding of the relationship between the products and perspectives of the culture studied.

Connections

Connect with Other Disciplines and Acquire Information

Standard 3.1: Students reinforce and further their knowledge of other disciplines through the foreign language.

Standard 3.2: Students acquire information and recognize the distinctive viewpoints that are only available through the foreign language and its cultures.

Comparisons

Develop Insight into the Nature of Language and Culture

Standard 4.1: Students demonstrate understanding of the nature of language through comparisons of the language studied and their own.

Standard 4.2: Students demonstrate understanding of the concept of culture through comparisons of the cultures studied and their own.

Communities

Participate in Multilingual Communities at Home and around the World

Standard 5.1: Students use the language both within and beyond the school setting.

Standard 5.2: Students show evidence of becoming lifelong learners by using the language for personal enjoyment and enrichment.

PERFORMANCE ASSESSMENT

A standards-based instructional program is characterized by meaningful communication in the target language as opposed to simply learning about the language. Given that it is important to test not only what we teach but also how we teach, two logical implications of the National Standards for Foreign Language Learning are that assessments should be meaningful in terms of content and purpose and that they should be a reflection of regular classroom practices. For example, the activities in each chapter of *Navegando 1B* offer numerous opportunities for communicative performance assessments that engage students in the interpersonal, interpretive and presentational modes. Through such assessments students can showcase their abilities and also gain an appreciation of the many practical purposes for which they can use the target language.

CROSS-CURRICULAR LEARNING

The National Standards for Foreign Language Learning illustrate that the foreign-language classroom provides a powerful opportunity for connecting language study with other academic disciplines. Such connections make language learning interesting and meaningful via relevant topics and a wide variety of resources for obtaining and sharing information. Students can understand and enjoy the real-life application of their language learning as they relate the study of Spanish to art, geography, history, literature, mathematics, music, social studies and science.

Navegando 1B offers many activities for connecting Spanish with other disciplines. The student textbook includes cross-curricular activities titled *Conexión con otras disciplinas* and the margins of the ATE provide cross-curricular activities titled "Connections."

CAREER AWARENESS/ WORKPLACE READINESS SKILLS

In the Spanish classroom it is important to develop an awareness of the many benefits of learning another language. For example, today there are more opportunities than ever to apply language skills on the job and elsewhere outside the classroom. The global economy has made it more important than ever for graduates from high schools and colleges in the United States to develop their language skills to be able to compete in the international marketplace. Moreover, the growing Hispanic population in the United States has created the need for employees with Spanish proficiency in a wide variety of jobs.

Navegando 1B uses a strand approach to career awareness to address employment opportunities. While students are learning the skills and knowledge that are necessary for them to become proficient in Spanish, they also explore how Spanish language skills can be beneficial when looking for employment. Career awareness is integrated regularly through the *Oportunidades* features in *Navegando 1B*. Activities for introducing students to this significant benefit of learning another language also can be found in the margins of the ATE.

SERVICE LEARNING/ MENTOR PROGRAMS

Service learning and mentor programs are avenues through which students can contribute to their communities and utilize their Spanish skills in real-life settings. Service learning is volunteering one's time to learn about an organization, gain experience and make a positive contribution. A mentor is a person with considerable experience who is willing to work with and help a student learn about an organization. Young people benefit by gaining firsthand experience while learning about themselves, certain types of organizations and their communities. The organization and the community benefit by involving future leaders, saving resources and generating new ideas.

Educators interested in promoting such programs should encourage students to talk with their parents about their desire to volunteer in the community. For example, students may wish to work with an organization where they are able to use Spanish with customers, such as at a library or a museum. Brainstorm with the class other ways students might participate in community service or find a mentor.

Teachers can offer certain practical suggestions to students who would like to pursue service learning opportunities or mentor programs for school-aged volunteers: 1) Explore the available options; 2) select a job that is interesting; 3) talk with people in several possible organizations to obtain additional information; 4) be realistic about the time available to volunteer; 5) consider whether transportation to the site will be a problem; 6) visit the organization and talk with its members to answer concerns; 7) make a decision.

PARENTAL INVOLVEMENT

Parental involvement in a student's education is a topic of considerable interest. The benefits of having students, parents, teachers and the community involved in supporting one another are undeniable. Teachers can do many things to encourage parents to take on a positive role in their child's education, both in and beyond the classroom. The margins of the *Navegando 1B* ATE and accompanying ancillaries offer suggestions for encouraging parental support for classroom learning, for strengthening communication and for improving parental awareness of student progress and goals.

SPANISH FOR SPANISH-SPEAKING STUDENTS

One result of the growing Hispanic population in the United States is that it is increasingly common to have students who are native or heritage speakers of Spanish in the Spanish classroom. These students may present special needs as they formally study a language that they already have acquired or experienced to varying degrees. At the same time, such students can be a positive presence and a unique resource for other students in the classroom. To address these realities, the *Navegando 1B* ATE includes a variety of activities and suggestions for teaching Spanish to Spanish-speaking students.

THE MULTIPLE INTELLIGENCES

Many factors affect learning. For years, classroom teachers have recognized that intelligence, social environment and motivation all need to be considered when teaching. All students do not learn in the same way and students' diverse learning styles need to be addressed in different ways to maximize individual potential.

Research on how the brain works has provided language teachers with additional information about intelligence and the learning process. One study that has drawn wide attention is Howard Gardner's theory of multiple intelligences. The theory suggests that people have different abilities in many different areas of thought and learning, and that these varying abilities affect their interests and how quickly they assimilate new information and skills. This pluralistic view of intelligence suggests that all people possess at least eight different intelligences, which operate in varying degrees depending on each person's individual profile. The eight intelligences identified by Gardner are the following: bodily-kinesthetic, interpersonal, intrapersonal, linguistic, logical-mathematical, musical, naturalist and spatial (visual) intelligence.

The general characteristics associated with each of these intelligences are described below, along with suggested teaching strategies:

- **Bodily-Kinesthetic:** Students who are athletic may demonstrate bodily-kinesthetic intelligence. They learn best by doing what they enjoy, want to learn through movement and touch and express their thoughts with body movement. They are good with hands-on activities such as woodworking, dancing, athletics and crafts.

  Teaching Strategies:
  Perform an activity as directed by a classmate or the teacher (TPR)
  Create artwork that represents some aspect of the Spanish-speaking world
  Act out a part from a play
  Perform a dance from a Spanish-speaking country
  Build a housing structure that is reminiscent of one that appears in the textbook

- **Interpersonal:** Students with interpersonal intelligence are natural leaders. They communicate well, empathize with others and often know what someone is thinking or feeling without having to hear the person speak.

Teaching Strategies:
Lead a discussion
Debate an issue
Organize and direct a survey
Role-play
Negotiate a settlement

- **Intrapersonal:** People with intrapersonal intelligence may appear to be shy. They are self-motivated and are very aware of their own thoughts and feelings about a given subject.

  Teaching Strategies:
  Create a list of favorite activities
  Write a poem expressing feelings
  Write answers to questions about personal life
  Prepare a written plan for a career path
  Determine the pros and cons of an issue

- **Linguistic:** This type of student demonstrates a strong appreciation for and fascination with words and language. People who display linguistic intelligence enjoy writing, reading, word searches, crossword puzzles and storytelling.

  Teaching Strategies:
  Write to a key pal on the Internet
  Tell a story
  Summarize a magazine or newspaper article
  Discuss the meaning of a song
  Write a poem
  Do a crossword puzzle

- **Logical-Mathematical:** This type of student likes establishing patterns and categorizing words and symbols. Students with logical-mathematical intelligence enjoy mathematics, experiments and games that involve strategy or rational thought.

  Teaching Strategies:
  Tabulate the total cost of a shopping trip
  Calculate the temperature in degrees
      Fahrenheit and in Celsius equivalents
  Figure changes in ingredient amounts to
      double or triple a recipe
  List the reasons why something happened
  Write an analysis of an event

- **Musical:** These students can be observed singing or tapping out a tune on a desk or other object. They are discriminating listeners who may be able to hear a song once and then play or sing the tune. Students who demonstrate musical intelligence catch what is said the first

time, whereas others around them may need to hear the same thing repeated a number of times.

  Teaching Strategies:
  Perform a song
  Write a song
  Identify musical styles from the
      Spanish-speaking world
  Listen to and describe a musical piece
  Prepare a comparison of the music of two or
      more musicians

- **Naturalist:** Students with naturalist intelligence might have a special ability to observe, understand and apply learning to the natural environment. For example, students with naturalist intelligence might collect data about environmental conditions for a particular place and instinctively know what crop would grow best there.

  Teaching Strategies:
  Draw or photograph nature scenes
  Present to the class an object found in nature
  Collect and categorize objects from the
      natural world
  Do research and present findings about a
      wildlife protection project
  Keep a notebook of observations of nature
  Go on a nature hike or field trip

- **Spatial (Visual):** These students think in pictures and can conceptualize well. They often like complicated puzzles and may be seen drawing a picture, constructing something from the objects that surround them or daydreaming. They are able to imagine how something would look from a verbal description.

  Teaching Strategies:
  Write a description or comparison of two
      paintings
  Compare the artistic styles of two painters
  Draw the ideal house
  Design a building
  Identify a shape based on a classmate's
      description
  Prepare a Cad-Cam design

Benefits of Using the Multiple Intelligences:
All students possess different combinations of intelligences. The multiple intelligences theory reflects a way of thinking about people that allows for both similarities and differences. It fosters inclusion, increases opportunities for enrichment, builds self-esteem and develops respect for individuals and

the gifts they bring to the classroom. Teachers who utilize multiple intelligences research create an environment that allows all students to learn through their strengths and to share their abilities with others.

Gardner's research has provided important information and a clear message: Educational designers should develop teaching materials that motivate a greater number of students and, in turn, teachers should select teaching and assessment materials that are geared to maximizing student potential. To this end, *Navegando* has been created to address the benefits of teaching to students' multiple intelligences.

COMPONENTS

Navegando consists of a comprehensive three-level Spanish-language program. The *Navegando 1B* program includes the following components:

- Textbook
- Annotated Teacher's Edition (ATE)
- ATE on CD-ROM
- Program Manager
- Workbook
- Workbook Teacher's Edition
- Middle School Bridge Program
- Middle School Resources B
- Grammar and Vocabulary Exercises Manual (includes answer key)
- Listening Activities (includes Listening Activities Manual, Listening Activities Manual answer key and Listening Activities Audio CDs)
- Testing/Assessment Program (includes Quizzes with answer key, Test Booklet, Portfolio Assessment and Listening Comprehension Audio CDs)
- Test Generator
- Audio CD Program (includes manual)
- Video/DVD Program (includes manual)
- Overhead Transparencies
- Communicative Activities Manual
- TPR Storytelling Manual
- Activities for Proficiency Manual
- *Materiales para hispanohablantes nativos*
- Spanish Reader
- CD-ROM Software (includes program guide)
- EMC/Paradigm Web site (includes Internet Activities, i-Catcher Video and News Ticker)

TEXTBOOK

The textbook consists of a front section providing maps and the Table of Contents, five numbered chapters and a handy reference section at the end of the book consisting of appendices, a Spanish–English and English–Spanish glossary and an index. Each thematic chapter is divided into four parts: the two-page chapter opener with objectives, *Lección A, Lección B* and *¡Viento en popa!* The chapters all are structured in a similar manner so that students will become accustomed to the various sections and, therefore, know what to expect. Chapter 10 is intended as a review chapter. It contains no new vocabulary or grammar. Teachers may select from the interesting and varied review activities and readings the chapter offers or may skip the chapter if they choose. **Note:** Instructions for activities in *Navegando* are given in the *tú* form. By requiring that students use the *usted* form of verbs with you and by suggesting that they use *tú* with their peers, you will increase students' exposure to both formal and informal forms. The subject pronoun *vosotros* is introduced, but students are not required to actively use the *vosotros* form of verbs. If you decide to teach using *vosotros,* modify activities to include practice with both *ustedes* and *vosotros.*

Two-page Chapter Opener

Each chapter of *Navegando 1B* opens with two photo-illustrated pages that visually prepare students for the cultural and communicative content of the thematic lessons that follow. Each chapter opener depicts life in the distinct Spanish-speaking places featured in that chapter. Functional and communicative objectives that students will be learning in the chapter are also listed here.

Lección A and Lección B

Both lessons follow the same organizational pattern:

Vocabulario I—Lessons begin with a contextualized, colorful two-page presentation of new and review vocabulary and grammatical structures in a meaningful context. New active vocabulary is presented only in *Vocabulario I* and *II.* Inform students that they are responsible for learning the new words and expressions on these pages and that they should try to guess the meaning of the new vocabulary based on visual cues. You may wish to add that any words they do not recognize can be found in the Spanish–English vocabulary list that appears at the end of each chapter and in the glossary at the end of the book. Accompanying activities help students learn the new words and expressions right where they are first introduced. Vocabulary is recycled in subsequent lessons to further improve student mastery of the material. **Note:** The first activity after *Vocabulario I* (and *Vocabulario II*) is always a listening comprehension activity. The recorded activity is included both in the Listening Activities Program and in the Audio CD Program. (The ATE margins provide icons indicating which components offer additional supporting activities for the contents of the students' textbook.) Reproducible answer sheets for these activities are located at the end of the Audio CD Program Manual.

Diálogo I—Lessons continue with a short thematic dialog that uses new vocabulary and expressions in interesting and authentic depictions of everyday life in the Spanish-speaking world. The people involved in the conversations represent a cross section of age groups, although the emphasis is on the lives of young people. The dialog is followed by three activities: One checks comprehension of the content of the dialog *(¿Qué recuerdas?);* a second serves as a realistic and natural motivation for students to apply the vocabulary and content of the dialog to their own lives by answering open-ended personalized questions *(Algo personal),* while concentrating on the communicative aspect of offering opinions and solving problems in Spanish; the third is an additional listening comprehension activity. **Note:** This last recorded activity is included both in the Listening Activities Program and in the Audio CD Program. Reproducible answer sheets for these activities are located at the end of the Audio CD Program Manual.

Cultura viva—The *Cultura viva* section expands the cultural theme of the lesson and provides historical, geographical and political information about the country or countries featured in the chapter. These interesting narratives are intended to heighten

students' appreciation of the target culture and to provide insight into daily aspects of Hispanic life. Additional ideas for expanding on the core content may be suggested in the accompanying activities or annotations that appear in the margins of the ATE. The section often presents the opportunity for creative out-of-class projects. Topics covered in the *Cultura viva* include history, geography, nonlinguistic behavioral cues, the arts and culture—relevant information that students will find appealing and useful.

Idioma—The *Idioma* section summarizes the main grammatical points of *Navegando 1B,* which are presented as individual *Estructuras.* The clear and concise explanations (often with the addition of colorful charts for easy reference) are followed by activities that increase in difficulty and scope from mechanical to meaningful to communicative. These activities practice key grammatical structures and vocabulary and are categorized as either *Práctica* or *Comunicación.* In addition, the activities allow for maximum flexibility because they may be done orally or in writing. For easy identification, activities with answers recorded on the audio CD are indicated in the ATE by a compact disc icon.

Vocabulario II—Lessons continue with a second two-page presentation of new and review vocabulary followed by activities.

Diálogo II—A second thematic dialog in the lesson provides additional exposure to authentic Spanish.

Cultura viva—A second, more personal, *Cultura viva* follows, offering a glimpse into some aspect of everyday life in the Spanish-speaking world and providing balance to the more historical *Cultura viva* in the first half of the lesson.

Idioma—A second *Idioma* section follows. Breaking the grammar content for the lesson into two manageable chunks makes it easier for students to digest the information.

Lectura cultural—*Lección A* concludes with a Spanish reading titled *Lectura cultural,* in which students learn about life in the Spanish-speaking world. *Lección B* concludes with a Spanish reading titled *Lectura personal,* in which members of a singing group *(La Ola)* reflect on their surroundings and experiences as they travel throughout the Spanish-speaking world. These personalized readings are written to appeal to the interests and abilities of students. Both readings are followed by comprehension questions *(¿Qué recuerdas?)* and open-ended personalized questions in Spanish *(Algo personal)*.

¿Qué aprendí?—The end-of-lesson feature *¿Qué aprendí?* offers students an opportunity to reflect upon what they have learned in the lesson. The section provides a self-test covering important content from the lesson, giving students the opportunity to review the content before having to take the lesson test. Students can access activity answers to the *Autoevaluación* by visiting the EMC/Paradigm Web site at **www.emcp.com**. The section also provides a list of active vocabulary from the lesson in *Palabras y expresiones*. The list of active vocabulary includes only the words that students must be able to speak, read, write and understand. Words from the list are included in other components of this Spanish program (workbook, testing/assessment, videos, etc.).

Make sure students understand how to use the *Vocabulario*. They may review the list, quizzing themselves to see how many words and expressions they recall. The list also helps teachers hold students accountable for their own learning. English translations are not given here since the list is for reference only. English equivalents may be found in the *Vocabulario* at the end of the chapter and in the glossary at the end of the textbook.

¡Viento en popa!

Tú lees—The end-of-chapter section *¡Viento en popa!* (Full speed ahead!; literally, Wind to the stern!) begins with a formal opportunity for students to improve their ability to read in Spanish. There are a variety of possible techniques for teaching the section. For example, you might wish to begin by having students read the *Estrategia* that accompanies every *Tú lees* in *Navegando 1B*. Then have students complete the warm-up activity titled *Preparación*. Next, you may might want to play the audio CD recording of the first paragraph of the reading. As an alternative, you might choose to read the first

paragraph yourself. Read the paragraph again, with students following along in the book. Give students a moment to look over the paragraph silently on their own and to ask questions. Ask for a student to volunteer to read the paragraph aloud. Continue in this way for subsequent paragraphs. Choose the technique that is most effective.

Explain to students that it is not essential to understand every word to read in Spanish. Equivalents for most unknown words have been provided to help students enjoy the content of the readings without having to look up important but passive vocabulary. **Note:** All footnoted vocabulary within the reading is intended to expand student receptive skills and is not intended for active use at this point.

The reading is followed by two activities: One checks comprehension of the content of the reading *(¿Qué recuerdas?)* and the second encourages students to connect the content to their own lives by answering open-ended personalized questions *(Algo personal)*.

Tú escribes—The section *Tú escribes* consists of a writing strategy, which is followed by an activity that encourages students to apply what they learned in the chapter. The *Tú escribes* provides a formal opportunity for students to improve their Spanish skills by providing developmental practice in creative writing.

Proyectos adicionales—This section consists of projects that you may choose to use or not, depending on your needs and your students' needs. Many of the activities involve cooperative learning, in which students work in pairs or small groups to accomplish a task. Other activities allow students to work independently. Projects address the five National Standards (see the section on the National Standards in this ATE Introduction) and provide additional opportunities for students to use technology. Furthermore, the *Proyectos adicionales* feature helps students develop their ability to use the functions, grammar, vocabulary and cultural content of the preceding lesson in a manner that is consistent with the instructional intent of the textbook.

Consider using some of the activities from the *Proyectos adicionales* as a quiz or for prescriptive testing to determine deficiencies in student understanding of the lesson content. This allows for remediation before end-of-lesson testing/

assessment. The section also may be used in place of, or along with, the Testing/Assessment Program as part of a portfolio for end-of-lesson summative assessment. (See the Testing/Assessment Program description in this ATE Introduction for information about portfolio assessment.)

Repaso—The section *Repaso* consists of a checklist of the communicative functions taught in the chapter, along with additional objectives that students can use as a self-check to evaluate their own progress. Before beginning a chapter, have students read the list of objectives in the chapter opener. Then, after completing the chapter, have students review what they have learned by reading the *Repaso*.

Trabalenguas—The *Trabalenguas* (tongue twister) is intended as a lighthearted and fun activity to challenge even the best students.

Vocabulario—The *Vocabulario* provides students with an easy-to-find reference in Spanish with English equivalents for all new active vocabulary that students must know from the chapter. Word meaning is confined strictly to the context in which the words are used in that particular chapter. Explain to students that the vocabulary listed in the sections *Palabras y expresiones,* and again in the *Vocabulario,* is vocabulary they need to know for tests, for subsequent chapters of the textbook and for becoming fluent Spanish speakers.

Additional Sections and Special Activities

Conexión con otras disciplinas—These cross-curricular activities (highlighted in blue in the student textbook) require students to apply Spanish skills while focusing attention on another curricular area (mathematics, geography, music, art, history, culinary arts, etc.).

Estrategia—This section offers strategies for learning. Included are pointers on topics such as how to be successful learning Spanish vocabulary and how to improve skills in reading, speaking, writing and listening.

¡Extra!—The *¡Extra!* section provides additional related vocabulary, notes, tips and suggestions to help students feel successful. The section gives students extra information, much like the side notes for teachers in the ATE. The content of the *¡Extra!* features is not required and thus is not addressed in the accompanying Testing/Assessment Program.

Oportunidades—To make learning real for students, teachers try to show how knowledge learned in the classroom translates to real life. The section titled *Oportunidades* provides thoughtful insights about the advantages students will have because they know Spanish and are familiar with the cultures of the Spanish-speaking world. The section addresses issues such as careers, travel, college and lifelong study in the field of languages and cultures.

Repaso rápido—This section offers a quick review of previously taught grammar. The abbreviated explanations are followed by an activity that practices the content of the *Repaso*. You may skip the section anytime you feel students do not need the extra practice.

Appendices

Grammar Review—The grammar introduced in the textbook has been summarized in this end-of-book section for convenient reference.

Verbs—This reference tool offers a summary of the verb conjugations presented in chapters of the textbook.

Numbers—This appendix summarizes the numbers for quick reference.

Syllabification—Syllabification is explained here for teachers who may wish to introduce students to the concept.

Accentuation—This summary is provided for teachers who may choose to teach how words are accentuated in Spanish.

Vocabulary—All active words introduced in the textbook appear in this end glossary. The number and letter following an entry indicate the lesson in which an item is first actively used. Additional words and expressions are included for reference and have no number. Obvious cognates and expressions that occur as passive vocabulary for recognition only have been excluded from this end vocabulary.

Index—The Index lists grammar presented in the textbook, along with an easy reference to where the point was introduced.

ANNOTATED TEACHER'S EDITION (ATE)

This Annotated Teacher's Edition, or ATE, contains a front section and an annotated version of the student textbook. The teacher's notes serve as a guide for using the textbook and accompanying ancillaries, including the following.

ATE Introduction—This ATE Introduction contains a scope and sequence chart for each chapter; the philosophy and goals of the series; a description of all components; a summary explanation of the methodology used in the textbook; a section on using video; a section on using the Internet and computers; a section offering teaching suggestions; a comprehensive section providing suggestions for additional activities and games; a list of useful classroom expressions; and a transcript of the recorded listening comprehension activities that appear in the student textbook, for teachers who wish to read the activities aloud instead of using the recorded version in the Audio CD Program.

Margin Icons—The ATE is an annotated, reduced-size version of the student textbook. Located at the top of each page of the ATE, the following icons denote additional ancillaries that support the contents of that page.

 Activities for Proficiency Manual

 Audio CD Program

 CD-ROM Software

 Communicative Activities Manual

 Grammar and Vocabulary Exercises Manual

 Listening Activities

 Materiales para hispanohablantes nativos

 Overhead Transparencies

 Quiz

 Spanish Reader

TPRS **TPR Storytelling Manual**

 Video/DVD Program

 Workbook

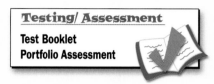

Testing/Assessment
Test Booklet
Portfolio Assessment

Margin Notes—Bottom margins of ATE pages provide additional teaching suggestions and cultural notes that expand on the lesson content.

Margin Activity Answers—The left- and right-hand margins of the ATE contain answers to close-ended activities.

Margin Activities—Activities described in the left- and right-hand margins of the ATE pages offer additional opportunities to address individual learner needs. Each of the activities falls into one of the following categories:

- **Communities.** These activities connect students to the community through Spanish and provide students with suggestions on how they may participate in service learning.
- **Connections.** Cross-curricular activities included here are opportunities to use Spanish in conjunction with other subject areas.
- **Cooperative Learning.** These activities offer students additional opportunities for cooperative learning beyond the textbook content. The activities require students to cooperate with one another in pairs or small groups, using Spanish for authentic communication.
- **Critical Listening.** These activities promote listening comprehension. They require that students learn not only the sounds of the language, but also the meaning behind them.

Ultimately, students will reach a point where they are able to correct their own errors.

- **Critical Thinking.** These activities enhance higher-order thinking skills. Critical thinking is an essential part of the total academic development of students. *Navegando 1B* includes a thorough and systematic program of higher-order thinking activities that address comprehension, application, analysis, synthesis and evaluation.
- **Expansion.** Expansion activities offer enrichment opportunities. They allow students' personal interests and creativity to take over, empowering them to discover a wealth of information about the language and the cultures studied in *Navegando 1B*.
- **Language through Action.** These activities require students to combine Spanish-speaking or listening skills with physical movement. The suggestions enhance student learning while relieving the teacher of the time required to prepare such activities.
- **Multiple Intelligences.** The multiple intelligences are addressed through activities focused on the eight areas identified by brain research: linguistic intelligence, logical-mathematical intelligence, spatial intelligence, bodily-kinesthetic intelligence, musical intelligence, interpersonal intelligence, intrapersonal intelligence and naturalist intelligence.
- **Prereading Strategy.** These questions about the subject matter prepare students for what they are about to read. Students might be asked to look at an illustration and guess what the theme of that dialog is. Students are encouraged to guess the meanings of words they do not recognize and are taught that they need not understand all the vocabulary to discern the main theme of an activity.
- **Pronunciation.** These activities allow students to practice pronunciation. Have students break down sentences into individual words and sounds and then have them use the words you have practiced in meaningful sentences. In addition, after presenting the initial dialog (or other expository material) and accompanying activities, have students work in pairs practicing the activity and focusing on the new pronunciation point. Circulate and assist with pronunciation and intonation.
- **Spanish for Spanish Speakers.** These activities are designed especially for students who are native speakers of Spanish. They allow students to examine their cultural heritage and to increase their Spanish skills.
- **Students with Special Needs.** These activities are for students who need extra help. They allow students to practice areas in which they are having difficulty and facilitate the acquisition of new skills and the comprehension of various subject matters.
- **Technology.** These activities require students to use the Internet, e-mail or another electronic medium in combination with their knowledge of Spanish to complete an activity.
- **TPR.** These activities involve Total Physical Response (TPR). Whereas many teachers have used TPR either extensively or on a limited basis, these activities often require an extra effort on the part of the teacher to prepare for and use TPR in the classroom.

ATE ON CD-ROM

The complete Annotated Teacher's Edition on CD-ROM offers a convenient alternative medium for displaying the wealth of information contained in the ATE. It also contains pop-up versions of the ancillaries indicated by icons in the ATE margins.

PROGRAM MANAGER

The Program Manager provides suggestions for using *Navegando 1B* and the program ancillaries in day-to-day instruction. Refer to the content for helpful hints that will help you determine which content you wish to include in lessons and which activities you wish to omit due to your particular circumstances and time limitations. The end-of-chapter section *¡Viento en popa!* (consisting of the reading section *Tú lees,* the writing activity *Tú escribes,* the national standards and technology projects, the *Trabalenguas* and the reference section *Vocabulario*) is optional, thus offering you additional flexibility in matching content to the needs, interests and curriculum requirements of your own particular situation.

Dialogs, narratives and many activities from the textbook have been included as audio recordings. This gives you additional choices about how to present or review chapter content. For example, you may choose to have students listen to a recorded activity before going to the textbook, or you may choose instead to use the audio CD as additional reinforcement after having completed the activity in the textbook. Recorded activities are indicated by icons in the margins of the ATE, according to the activity type.

In addition, the many ancillaries described in this ATE Introduction can be used to supplement the textbook. These program components provide an abundance of textbook-related activities to enable you to customize your teaching to the many and varied learning styles and needs of your students.

Because every teacher has his or her own approach to the subject of homework, and because of the extensive variety offered by the *Navegando 1B* support materials, specific homework assignments are not provided in the Program Manager. However, suggestions for including activities from the accompanying ancillaries have been offered to give you an idea of the possible variations the teaching program offers. You should try to include an assortment of different activities, choosing some from the textbook and others from the ancillaries (such as the Workbook, the ATE, etc.).

WORKBOOK

The Workbook activities reinforce and expand student understanding of the functions, grammar, readings and cultural points presented in the textbook. Interesting written activities emphasize both communication and structural production. The Workbook includes a variety of practice in several different formats to maintain student interest. The level of difficulty of the activities ranges from rote practice of vocabulary and basic activities emphasizing receptive skills in reading to more challenging, open-ended items that emphasize productive writing skills.

Reading, writing, grammar, vocabulary and culture are all given thorough attention in the Workbook. Specifically, the Workbook presents an assortment of activities: reading passages taken from actual newspaper and magazine articles with follow-up questions and exercises; sentence-completion exercises; guided compositions; matching activities; practice in geography in mapping activities; word searches; crossword puzzles; and more.

WORKBOOK TEACHER'S EDITION

The Teacher's Edition of the Workbook includes an overprint that provides answers to close-ended activities in the Workbook.

MIDDLE SCHOOL BRIDGE PROGRAM

The *Middle School Bridge Program* thoroughly reviews both the vocabulary and grammar covered the previous year in *Navegando 1A*. All the new structures in *Navegando 1A* are reintroduced before they are practiced in a variety of new activities.

MIDDLE SCHOOL RESOURCES B

This manual of additional activities is specifically designed for middle school students in their second year of Spanish. More than 100 activities reinforce and expand upon the vocabulary, structures and cultural material presented in *Navegando 1B*. Included are communication skills activities (surveys, paired, and information gap activities) and hands-on projects. There are also word searches, crossword puzzles, graphic organizers, Internet projects, grammar worksheets, and forms to be used for playing various games.

GRAMMAR AND VOCABULARY EXERCISES MANUAL

These blackline masters offer additional written practice in basic structures and topics. The activities are correlated to the textbook presentation of grammar and vocabulary. Grammar activities are each preceded by a summary explanation of the new structures introduced in the textbook. Vocabulary activities consist of word games, puzzles and other practice that will help students assimilate new words and expressions that are taught in the textbook. Both grammar and vocabulary sections offer excellent practice for quizzes and tests and provide a solid foundation for continuing in Spanish. An answer key is provided at the end of the Grammar and Vocabulary Exercises Manual.

LISTENING ACTIVITIES

- **Listening Activities Manual.** The Listening Activities Manual provides worksheets to be used in conjunction with audio CDs. The activities offer additional listening comprehension practice using the structures and vocabulary of corresponding textbook lessons. Using the activities will help students improve their listening skills and, therefore, their ability to communicate in Spanish. In addition, the activities serve as an excellent preparation for the listening comprehension and oral-proficiency portions of the Testing/Assessment Program. The answer key is included at the end of the manual.
- **Listening Activities Audio CDs.** These audio CDs have been recorded by native speakers and are to be used with the Listening Activities Manual.

TESTING/ASSESSMENT PROGRAM

A proficiency-based curriculum requires testing or assessing an individual's attainment of specific objectives. The *Navegando* Testing/Assessment Program offers comprehensive means for evaluating student performance. Elements of the Testing/Assessment Program are available as a part of the Test Generator for teachers wishing to format customized assessment. The basic program consists of the following components.

- **Quizzes.** Quizzes provide a convenient and flexible means of ongoing written assessment. Ranging in number from ten to thirteen per lesson, quizzes determine the level of student comprehension of the vocabulary, grammar and cultural content of the textbook. They may be used individually, point by point throughout each lesson or combined as a test after completing an entire lesson.
- **Test Booklet.** Tests evaluate students' listening, writing, reading and speaking skills. Each chapter of the booklet contains two sections: 1) the student answer sheets for the listening comprehension and written portion of the test; 2) a separate section that evaluates oral

proficiency. For convenience and ease of scoring, each section is worth 100 points. The tests should be given after each chapter. Students use the answer sheets while listening to the audio CDs, which direct them step by step through specific tasks. The tests include true/false, multiple choice, matching and fill-in-the-blank questions based on the recorded material. Wherever appropriate, picture cues further assist students in selecting their answers as directed by the speakers.

The written tests are intended to measure students' understanding of the language and cultural content of each chapter. They allow students to demonstrate their ability to read and write with accuracy. The oral-proficiency section of each chapter test can be used in an informal and flexible manner and includes three kinds of activities: communicative interaction between teacher and student, paired activities calling for student-to-student interaction and illustrations with related questions students must answer orally in Spanish.

The Test Booklet contains tests for each chapter of *Navegando 1*. In addition, there are comprehensive midyear and year-end achievement tests. The answers to all the tests are included in the back of the manual.

- **Listening Comprehension Audio CDs.** The listening portion of the *Navegando* Testing/Assessment Program has been recorded by native speakers and is included on audio CDs.
- **Portfolio Assessment.** Intended as an alternative to traditional evaluation tools and as an extension of the Testing/Assessment Program, the Portfolio Assessment includes a variety of activities for monitoring student progress. The communicative objectives that appear on the first pages of each chapter can be used as goals against which the students' progress can be measured. This manual provides valuable tips and guidance for evaluating student performance.

TEST GENERATOR

The Test Generator has several benefits. It allows teachers to test exactly what they have taught, allowing for differences in instructional emphasis, teaching approaches and student learning styles. The teacher can select and modify sections from the existing Testing/Assessment Program, including quizzes and chapter tests, to generate tests that reflect what has been taught. The Test Generator also allows teachers to add their own test questions, as well as edit existing questions. Finally, the Test Generator allows teachers to create A and B versions of tests.

AUDIO CD PROGRAM

The Audio CD Program is an integral part of *Navegando 1B*. It exposes students to a variety of native speakers' voices with different accents and variations in pronunciation and intonation. All content that has been recorded on audio CDs is indicated in the ATE by a compact disc icon. Although the text for many of these activities is contained in the textbook itself, a separate manual provides an exact transcript of the recordings, many of which have been modified so they are more appropriate for speaking and listening practice.

In addition, activities located after *Vocabulario I, Vocabulario II, Diálogo I* and *Diálogo II* that are indicated in the student textbook by the icon 🔊))) have been recorded specifically for listening comprehension practice and are part of the Audio CD Program. For teacher convenience, reproducible answer sheets have been provided for these activities and can be found at the end of the Audio CD Program Manual. The recording transcript of all the listening comprehension activities is provided at the end of this ATE Introduction for teachers wishing to read the activities instead of using the audio CDs.

VIDEO/DVD PROGRAM

Coordinated with each chapter of the *Navegando* textbooks, the three-level Video/DVD Program— titled *El cuarto misterioso*—is an exciting and motivational tool for recombining and reinforcing the content of the series. The mystery was filmed on location in various parts of the Spanish-speaking world using professional actors. The ten episodes, which vary in length from five to eight minutes per chapter, consist of a continuous story line that is carefully coordinated with each chapter of the textbook. The videos depict native speakers in authentic situations that reflect the content of

textbook chapters, thus allowing students to see and hear Spanish used in a carefully controlled but realistic and enjoyable context. The few unknown words that are used can be easily understood by the context (motion, action, gestures, background). Available either as a videocassette or as a DVD, *El cuarto misterioso* allows students to follow along and identify with the characters as they solve the mystery.

Video Program Manual. An accompanying Video/DVD Program Manual contains a transcript of the videos, notes about using the program and numerous pre- and post-viewing activities.

OVERHEAD TRANSPARENCIES

A set of sixty-eight full-color overhead transparencies, coordinated with the chapters, is available for use with *Navegando 1*. The transparencies can be used for a variety of activities, including rote vocabulary and grammar review, map identification of featured countries and conversation over comprehensive scenes that encourage creative self-expression. Use the transparencies to review and expand on the cultural content, grammar, vocabulary and functions that are presented in the textbook and to encourage students to apply their knowledge of Spanish and the Spanish-speaking world.

COMMUNICATIVE ACTIVITIES MANUAL

Effective communicative activities are integral to the success of a Spanish-language program. The Communicative Activities Manual is designed to provide additional communicative practice for students. The manual provides information gap activities and situation cards that promote student-to-student interaction, a communicative functions checklist that reviews the functions introduced in each chapter and postcards that develop writing skills.

TPR STORYTELLING MANUAL

The TPR Storytelling Manual has everything teachers need to incorporate this movement-oriented technique in their classrooms. First, teachers are instructed to present new vocabulary (provided in the manual) through gestures. Then students practice this vocabulary in short situations before finally using it to tell and act out a story. The front portion of the manual explains the TPR Storytelling philosophy and teaching techniques for instructors who have little or no experience with this strategy. Then step-by-step instructions guide teachers through the presentation of basic and advanced stories, one of which is correlated to every chapter in the textbook. Gestures are given for new words and phrases to help teachers convey meaning as they present the situation and the stories. Numerous illustrations guide students as they re-create the stories. Additional teaching suggestions, strategies and assessment options are also provided for each story.

ACTIVITIES FOR PROFICIENCY MANUAL

This manual contains general forms facilitating games, mapmaking, and activities that can be used throughout the year. Also included are chapter-by-chapter blackline masters with supplemental activities that correspond to the content of the chapters. The activities in this manual are fun and engaging, and expose students to a variety of real, everyday language.

MATERIALES PARA HISPANOHABLANTES NATIVOS

The *Materiales para hispanohablantes nativos* manual expands upon the content of *Navegando 1B.* The manual offers additional opportunities for native speakers of Spanish to improve their language skills and knowledge in classrooms in which the majority of students are learning Spanish as a second language. Although the manual is intended to increase student success in class, it also may serve as an independent skill-building activity book that provides opportunities for portfolio assessment, at the discretion of the teacher.

Activities in the manual give native Spanish-speaking students an opportunity to demonstrate their abilities and knowledge in Spanish using the vocabulary, structures and cultural themes in the textbook. In addition, excerpts have been included

from the classic Spanish novel *Marcelino pan y vino,* by José María Sánchez-Silva, which students will enjoy reading while improving their skills.

The Appendices at the end of the manual offer additional reinforcement of essential skills. For example, Appendix A offers a list of suggestions for projects requiring students to think creatively and to apply what they learned while reading. Appendix B is a guide for students to use to improve their skills in studying, researching, speaking, reading and writing. Appendix C provides forms to facilitate student and project evaluation.

The activities contained in this manual may be used beginning on the first day of class. Schools may purchase copies for individual students or photocopy pages as they are needed. Native Spanish-speaking students then may read the introductory pages and begin to work on activities that are appropriate to their needs and that are related to the content of the lessons in the textbook. In this way, they will be able to affectively and cognitively connect with the content.

The activities and suggestions contained in the *Materiales para hispanohablantes nativos* offer both students and teachers an alternate means of assessment. Simultaneously, the manual will challenge native Spanish-speaking students to improve their skills and knowledge by offering them interesting and worthwhile practice using their native language.

SPANISH READER

A Spanish reader, *La familia Miranda/El viaje a Guatemala,* is available for teachers wishing to increase student reading opportunities. The first episode, *La familia Miranda,* is coordinated with *Navegando 1A,* and the second episode, *El viaje a Guatemala,* is coordinated with *Navegando 1B.*

CD-ROM SOFTWARE

This interactive adventure in multimedia is designed to enhance language acquisition within a functional and cultural context. As publishing interns, students enter a futuristic world where they must solve problems using technology and their Spanish-language skills. In each module, students are faced with the challenge of communicating with colleagues throughout the world, using an online atlas, dictionary and encyclopedia.

Included are learner and teacher reports that are used to assess student progress and to determine promotions. The program contains authentic video clips in which native Spanish speakers interact verbally with students on a variety of topics. Students will enjoy applying the vocabulary, grammar and cultural content they are learning to the real-life problems they face in the business world. An abundance of geographic, historic and cultural information further expands the students' understanding of the Spanish-speaking world.

EMC/PARADIGM WEB SITE

Internet Activities—The *Navegando* Internet Activities Web site features activities that are constantly updated to provide students with practice that expands the cultural content of the textbook chapters. These interesting and enriching activities are based on current events, up-to-the-moment information and research data. There are three activities for each chapter of *Navegando.* Students practice using their language skills as they explore authentic realia in Spanish and read contemporary information about Hispanic culture. They combine the use of technology and Spanish in real-life situations as they develop their Internet research skills. Students are carefully guided through the various links to complete each activity. Teachers receive a password to allow them to access all

the activities' answers. To view these activities, visit www.emcp.com and follow the on-screen menus and links until you reach the activities.

News Ticker—The News Ticker features five scrolling news articles every day in Spanish. Students click on these articles to read about current events throughout the Spanish-speaking world, chosen to appeal to teenagers. An audio feature allows students to hear the articles recorded by professional native speakers. These articles are archived so that they are accessible by date or by topic. Reach the News Ticker by visiting www.emcp.com and follow the on-screen menus and links.

i-Catcher—These interactive Internet video clips in Spanish showcase young adults who talk about and demonstrate their interests and hobbies. One young Spanish speaker is featured each month. Students can choose the subtitled version to check their listening comprehension skills. The site promotes real-life communication through a monthly monitored chat with the video star simply by logging on. Not only is the site fun, but it has a strong educational foundation. The i-Catcher offers another opportunity for students to check their listening skills with an on-line multiple-choice comprehension quiz. Students develop their writing skills with related Internet links and Web-based activities. Access i-Catcher by going to www.emcp.com and following the on-screen menus and links.

METHODOLOGY

Language-teaching methodology has undergone significant changes over the years. One of the most dramatic changes has been the shift from a sometimes rigid focus on *what* and *how* an instructor would teach to a more flexible and varied approach that focuses on what students can *do* with the language. The *Standards for Foreign Language Learning* are a clear manifestation of this important change. It is exciting to see the increased emphasis on improving students' abilities to use authentic language in real-life contexts.

The methods and techniques found in *Navegando 1B* reflect this student-centered approach to teaching and the authors' commitment to providing the best possible Spanish program to meet the needs of teachers and students in the 21st century. As teachers deal with an

ever more diverse student population, there is a greater demand for teaching materials that address varied learning styles and interests. There also is an ever-increasing need for educational materials that enable students to function using Spanish in a variety of practical situations. By presenting meaningful content and by putting students in real-life contexts, *Navegando 1B* creates a positive learning spiral. The activities are structured to allow students to apply immediately what they have learned. The resulting feeling of accomplishment leads them back into the textbook, where they acquire more skills and information and are then able to draw upon their own personal experience to communicate information, ideas, feelings and opinions.

The following methods and techniques reflect the approaches to language instruction found in *Navegando 1B* and will help maximize the effectiveness of both the textbook and ancillary materials.

Learning Styles—Students learn through three main modes: visual, auditory and kinesthetic. Whereas many students learn through a combination of these modes, some students learn mainly through one mode. For example, a visual learner likely benefits from seeing the written language in the textbook, on the board and on an overhead, and also by seeing pictures or a video. Auditory learners benefit from hearing the language spoken by the teacher, by other students and in audiovisual media including music and song lyrics. Kinesthetic learners benefit from making handicrafts such as Mexican paper folding, creating a floor plan of a house or playing games.

Another approach to learning styles, known as 4MAT, outlines four types of learners based on left- and right-brain dominance.

- **Type 1.** Innovative ("why?") learners are mainly interested in personal meaning. This includes connecting new information to personal experience and making it useful in daily life. A number of strategies work with Type 1 learners, such as cooperative learning, brainstorming and integrating content areas (interdisciplinary learning).

- **Type 2.** Analytic ("what?") learners enjoy acquiring facts to deepen their understanding of concepts and processes. They learn best from lectures, independent research, expert commentary and analysis of data.

- **Type 3.** Commonsense ("how?") learners want to know how things work. They enjoy rolling up their sleeves and trying. Concrete and experiential activities are preferred: hands-on tasks, kinesthetic experiences and demonstrations.

- **Type 4.** Dynamic ("if") learners are primarily interested in self-directed discovery. They rely on intuition and enjoy teaching themselves and others. Independent study, simulations, role-plays and games are ideal for dynamic learners.

Knowledge of learning styles helps teachers plan lessons that accommodate all students. Projects, in particular, support learning styles because of the infinite variety that may be used over time to better develop the five Cs of the National Standards: communication, cultures, connections, comparisons and communities. Project types include the following:

Visual and Performing Arts	Media/Technology	Hands-on/Kinesthetic
artwork	advertisement	collage
cartoon	commercial	collection
dance	computer graphic	construction
greeting card	computer program	craft
jewelry	filmstrip	demonstration
mask	infomercial	diorama
mural	magazine	environmental study
music	marketing campaign	field trip
pantomime	movie	flash card
photograph	news report	floor plan
poster	newsletter	game
pottery	newspaper	invention
puppet show	opinion poll	learning center
role-play	radio program	model
sculpture	slide show	sewing
skit	television show	sport
song	video	tool
weaving	Web home page	treasure hunt

VIDEO IN THE CURRICULUM

Using Video

Video in the language curriculum offers opportunities to visit other lands and locales and to learn about interdisciplinary themes tied to language and culture. Technological advances and expanded cable programming provide teachers in all fields with a variety of special programs to use with students. Educators of world languages are no exception, as more and more programs focusing on target countries and cultures are debuting all the time. It can almost be a full-time job to find and choose educational programming for integration in the foreign-language curriculum. Indeed, the careful selection of video segments in language learning can be a gargantuan task. Fortunately, such efforts can be well worth it. High-quality video selections used in the classroom can become a platform for many successful content-based activities and projects. Video also offers opportunities for curricular enrichment that does not rely solely on teachers.

Advocates of interdisciplinary curriculum initiatives support exposing students of one subject area to related subject matter in other disciplines. Because Spanish-speaking people, countries and cultures have contributed greatly to humanity in so many areas, quality programming has been produced that explores these contributions. From art to cuisine, from music to automobiles, from cinema to fashion, today's cable and public television programming allows people and themes of the target culture to shine in the spotlight.

The National Standards for Foreign Language Learning promote the five Cs: Communication, Cultures, Connections, Comparisons and Communities. All five Cs can be supported by the use of videos and video-inspired activities, especially Connections. The National Standards for the English Language Arts promote "viewing" as a worthy educational goal. While students benefit greatly from viewing high-quality video programs, teachers can fully exploit video viewing through related activities, projects and units.

English versus Target Language—Videos are available with language dialog and narration in English or in Spanish. Some programs offer English with occasional dialog in the Spanish language with English subtitles. Some educators might question the use of "in English" videos in language classes. However, segments in English can be effective learning tools, especially when they encourage Spanish-language activities, projects, discussions or writing or promote the target culture. For example, students of Spanish can watch a segment in English about the Andes that enriches a chapter about a South American Andean nation and then do one or more activities in the target language, such as a collage, a written summary, a handout, an oral report, a discussion, or a reading in the target language about a similar topic. Of course, a balance between videos in English and in Spanish is key. Both English and Spanish videos can be educationally beneficial. Videos in the target language must not be too difficult, following Stephen Krashen's i + 1 theory. He theorized that the level must not be more than one level above students' current level of ability, or frustration and lack of comprehension among students will result. Foreign films often have subtitles, which help compensate for comprehension challenges.

Videos: A Variety from Which to Choose—The following types of videos can be used to enrich language instruction:

- **Movies.** Both Spanish-language films with subtitles and traditional native-language films can be used to support the goals of your curriculum. Musical films such as *Man of La Mancha, Evita* and *Selena* can enhance topics such as Don Quixote de la Mancha, Argentina and the Mexican-American singer, respectively. School plays or musicals can be utilized as well to enhance language learning through projects tied to the school's cast and crew, as well as themes, characters, settings and music from the stage plays. Full-length films can be analyzed as literature is analyzed, by discussing plot, setting, characters, conflicts and themes in the target language.
- **Music Specials.** It can be useful to expose students to concerts or other music specials by

artists who sing in Spanish. If time is limited, one or a few song performances could be utilized. Students could dig deeper by finding out more about a specific song (e.g., "La Bamba"). Documentaries about a specific genre of music such as Spanish flamenco, Caribbean salsa or Spanish zarzuela could also enhance learning. Select chapters in *Navegando 1B* feature vocabulary and readings tied to target-culture music and names of musical instruments. This could be an ideal time to utilize music-related videos.

- **Documentaries and Travel Segments.** Information-based segments describing background about a topic can be interesting and educational. A segment about Spanish architecture, for example, is ideal. Other possible topics include ecotourism in Costa Rica, archaeological digs in Peru and railroad development in central Mexico.
- **Cooking Shows.** Segments that detail the cuisine, ingredients, cultural aspects of food and actual food preparation can easily enhance the study of cuisine in Spanish-speaking cultures.
- **Visual and Decorative Arts Programs.** Target-culture art including painting, sculpting, architecture, ceramics, glassblowing and woodworking are of interest. Segments from Home and Garden Television feature appropriate programs such as *The Best of Spanish Design* or *The Best of Mexican Design* that can easily complement a unit treating the rooms and appliances of the house.
- **Biographies.** Segments about famous actors, musicians, authors, politicians, scientists and historical figures can enrich the curriculum. Well-known individuals help make up popular culture, an area supported by curriculum integration. Reacting to the facts about these individuals' lives can also help promote students' social and emotional learning.
- *Navegando* **Video/DVD Program.** The ancillary video materials that accompany the *Navegando* series are also valuable educational tools, linking video stories to the material in the textbooks. They offer appropriate materials that can enhance comprehension for both visual and auditory learners.

Activities and Projects

Create a Video—Students can create their own video, making a commercial, preparing a skit using the current chapter's theme and vocabulary, recording a news story about your school or developing a documentary about the sports or drama program. Students could interview other students in Spanish or in English, providing a dubbed translation or subtitles with the translation as is done on television and in movies.

A Movie Review—Students can view a film and write a review of it in Spanish. Students could also do the review orally, live or on videotape.

Art-based Project—Students can create a calendar, brochure or collage about a topic featured in a video that they viewed.

TV/Cable Guide—Students can create a television guide that gives blurbs about various programs tied to Spanish. They can include a magazine cover and even several feature articles about a few of the programs. This project could easily be completed using technology and could be done as a cooperative effort.

Learning Scenarios for Video-Inspired Lessons

Political Issues—Students view the film version of *Selena* and learn about the southwestern United States, Mexican Americans and Tejano music. They explore the U.S.–Mexico border issue historically, learn about Chicano social issues, explore the cuisine of the region and learn more about Selena and her genre of music, Tejano.

Biographies—Another video-inspired activity involves viewing a biography segment about a Spanish-speaking celebrity or historical figure. The students could then read an article about the individual and write a summary of the article. Students could also discuss the segment orally, thus gaining speaking and listening practice.

Foods—You might consider having students view a segment about Spanish, Latin American or Caribbean desserts. Students then replicate one recipe in

Spanish, prepare it and sample it. Students could also create their own menu, do a role-play in a Spanish restaurant or café or create a collage about desserts in the Spanish-speaking world.

Homes—Have students view a video about house design in one of the Spanish-speaking countries and then create a floor plan of their own home, with rooms and objects labeled in Spanish. Students could also learn about how to decorate their homes for holidays.

Arts and Crafts—Students might enjoy viewing a segment about a well-known artist or artisan and then create a work of art or a piece of pottery with the help of the art teacher. If this is not feasible, students could create a drawing that is reflective of an artist's work and color it by hand.

Summary

Videos vary in length, and it is not always necessary to show an entire video. For example, if the textbook features a specific recipe, you could find a cooking segment and use just the part about that recipe. A video segment can be a few seconds to a few class sessions in length, depending on your goals.

Video can enrich your curriculum. Activities, lessons and units can be implemented by the creative teacher to explore themes from videos. You can carefully select programming that will bring many topics and people to life for your students. Such programming can accommodate both visual learners, who must see to learn, and auditory learners, who must hear to learn. Hands-on projects inspired by video segments can also accommodate students who learn through touch.

Tips for Selecting Video Formats—Videotapes and DVDs cannot be played on all types of equipment. VHS videos will not play on European PAL systems and vice versa. Additionally, six DVD zones exist throughout the globe, making DVDs from one zone unplayable in the other five zones. The United States and Canada comprise zone one. Multizone players have been made available over the Internet to provide flexibility. In comparison to videotapes, DVDs and laser discs have several advantages: they generally have superior sound and picture quality and are easier to use in terms of finding a specific scene, because they are encoded in chapters. Many DVDs and laser discs include additional footage or documentaries about the making of the film and frequently have alternate sound tracks, some in Spanish or other languages.

USING THE INTERNET: SUGGESTIONS AND IDEAS

Because of its widespread and instantaneous nature, the Internet holds much promise as a tool for teaching and learning. In foreign-language instruction, the Internet can help teachers meet the challenge of providing students with materials that are up to date and culturally authentic. With scarcely a trace of lag time, information from the target culture can be accessed and utilized in a variety of ways. For example, in a lesson about Madrid, you and your students can:
- visit online museums and see famous paintings
- obtain news from Spanish newspapers
- participate in discussion groups on Spanish culture and civilization
- obtain current weather information and forecasts
- access city and subway maps

- view photographs of major landmarks of the city
- locate tourist information
- exchange e-mail correspondence

By using the Internet as a supplement to *Navegando 1B*, you will create exciting new opportunities for students. Internet-related activities are limited only by your imagination. What follows are sample activities and a variety of supplementary materials that illustrate the vast possibilities of the Internet.

E-MAIL PROJECTS

Consider arranging e-mail (electronic mail) exchanges to complement the use of *Navegando 1B*. For example, have students participate in a number of exchanges that allow them to apply the concepts, vocabulary and cultural information studied in a given lesson. Sample exchanges include the following:

1. After studying weather, students write a weather report for their state/city and send it to a collaborating class or key pals. They also inquire about the weather and climate in the region where the collaborating class is located or where the key pals live. Subsequent exchanges could deal with:
   - sports and activities related to different seasons of the year
   - outdoor activities that the students enjoy
   - the school calendar and how the local climate may affect it
   - weather conditions in different Spanish-speaking countries

2. In relation to a food unit, students develop an e-mail exchange sharing the following information about their culture/family:
   - a typical meal schedule at home
   - a traditional meal schedule in their country
   - a menu for a typical day and for a special celebration

3. After learning about leisure-time activities, students share with their collaborating partners what they do on a typical weekend or during vacation.

4. Students write a description of a well-known individual in sports, music, politics or movies. Send the description to your collaborating classroom with an invitation to guess who the person is.

5. Students conduct surveys to explore cultural comparisons. Topics of interest include:
   - the amount of independence given to adolescents
   - the access and admittance to dance clubs
   - the legal age for driving
   - the number of students who work
   - the minimum wages paid to adolescents who work

6. Examples of other possible exchange topics include school, daily life, family, friends, travel, sports, clothing and popular music. More complex topics of interest might include current events, politics, household rules, curfew and educational aspirations.

A Model Unit for an E-Mail Exchange: Mi familia

This unit allows students to share information about their families and learn about the families of their classmates and key pals. Whereas the unit is appropriate for learners at various levels of proficiency, teacher expectations and student performance will vary accordingly.

Academic Goals—Students will be able to:
1. Use vocabulary related to the family.
2. Use possessive and descriptive adjectives and appropriate verb structures.

Social Goals—Students will be able to:
1. Share information about their families.
2. Find out about the families of their key pals.
3. Recognize similarities and differences between families in the United States and families in cultures where Spanish is spoken.

Procedures for a Beginning Language Class

1. Teach and practice specific vocabulary pertaining to family members. For example, the teacher shows pictures and begins by describing his/her real family or a fictitious family in terms of members, roles, names, ages, likes, dislikes and professions. After the description, the teacher checks to see what students are able to remember. This questioning gives students a chance to use basic expressions.

2. The next step is for students to describe their own families. As preparation for class, students prepare notes about their families (real or imagined) according to the specifications given in advance.

3. After further practice in class, students write descriptions of their families. Possible information includes:
   - family name
   - number of people in the family (family makeup)
   - description of each member of the family (name, age, occupation, personality)
   - family activities and traditions

4. Once the documents are completed and revised using peer editing and student/teacher editing,

the descriptions are sent to collaborating classes abroad and students wait for the responses from their key pals describing their families. When the correspondence is received, students compare families in both cultures and find similarities and/or differences.

Locating Collaborating Colleagues and Key Pals

Possible collaborating partners can be found in the same school building or district, in another city or around the world. Here are some strategies for locating key pals:

- Place ads in professional organization newsletters and journals.
- Attend professional conferences and technology workshops to network with colleagues.
- Search the Internet for Collaborating Classrooms, Cultural Classroom Connection or Exchanges.
- Post messages in Spanish news groups.
- Subscribe to listservs pertinent to Spanish or countries where Spanish is spoken.
- Check related WWW home pages or Internet Guides (a listing is included in the section titled Teacher Resources on the World Wide Web).
- Write to American Schools Abroad (a listing may be obtained from the Department of State in Washington, D.C.).

Tips for Using E-Mail

- Have students avoid tabs and foreign characters unless both groups are using compatible software.
- Write your introductory remarks for the collaborating teacher and then paste the letters of each student/group after your message. Separate each individual message using a line, a symbol or a character. This will make it easier for your collaborating teacher to separate the messages and distribute them to his/her students.
- Specify the font and size to use on a project.
- Clearly specify project checkpoints and deadlines.
- Give clear directions for minimum length and content to be included.
- Explain how you will evaluate a project.
- Explain how and where to save a project, including how to name it before saving.

E-Mail Projects: Overcoming E-Mail Limitations

Hardware Limitations—When a limited number of computers are available, students can work in pairs, or individual students can access computers at other times (for example, while others in class are working on an assignment, after completing a test or during lunch periods, study hall or before and after school). Assignments made well in advance of their due date will allow students to manage their work time and produce final products of high quality.

Time Limitations—When computer lab time is limited, schedule individuals or groups in such a way that at least one exchange can be completed per quarter, trimester or semester.

Access Limitations—If you have only one computer with a modem and access to the Internet, get the project ready and transmit it when the line is available. A designated student can be the mailer. If there is no access in school, a teacher or student who has access to the Internet can be the mailer for the group.

Students with computers at home can do their work on their own time. Today's computers allow texts created on one platform to be read by computers on another. For example, using Microsoft Word 5.0 or later, you can open just about any type of text file. In addition, software programs such as Access PC and PC Exchange allow the exchange of files written using computers of different platforms.

INTERNET SEARCH

To search the Internet, use the latest version available of the Web browser of your choice. Web browsers provide a harmonious interface for text and graphics.

You have different options for search engines. Some of them search titles or headers of documents, others search the documents themselves, and still others search indexes or directories. The following are some popular and powerful search engines:

Google	http://www.google.com/
Lycos	http://www.lycos.com/
Overture	http://overture.com/
Yahoo	http://www.yahoo.com/
Yahoo Español	http://espanol.yahoo.com/

Sample Internet Activity—The Internet can be used for research and activities limited only by your imagination. One popular activity is a virtual city tour. Students use a search engine to find information on a city of their choice. They can locate maps of the city, identify sites of interest and look at pictures of those sites, learn about transportation in the city, research brief historical facts about the city, find airlines and/or trains serving the city, look for weather data and find out about typical cuisine.

Some Spanish-speaking cities have virtual tour Web sites that you may want to use.

Madrid, Spain
http://www.visualware.es/guiamad/index.htm
Mallorca, Spain
http://www.mallorcaservice.com/nueva/
Valencia, Spain
http://www.upv.es/cv/valbegin.html
Alicante, Spain
http://www.upv.es/cv/alibegin.html
Mar del Plata, Argentina
http://www.todomardelplata.com/360/
San Diego, California
http://www.sandiego360.com/
Ciudad de México
http://www.mexicocity.com.mx/
Cancún, México http://www.cancun.com/
select Mexico cities
http://www.mexconnect.com/
MEX/mxc/tour.index.html
multi-city sites http://www.virtualtourist.com
http://www.lonelyplanet.com

Alternatives for this activity include the following:
- Place students in small groups. Each small group "visits" a different section of the city. They determine which sites to visit during a 48-hour period on a given budget. For example, one group may visit several museums; another may travel to a park to see sculptures and attend a cultural event.
- Each group visits a different city in the same country. After groups have processed the information on the cities, they give a class presentation to highlight the attractions of the various cities.
- In small groups, students design a travel brochure about their city.

Cultural/Historical Studies and Presentations

Students work in small groups to become "experts" on a country where Spanish is spoken. The objectives of the activity are to help students get acquainted with the history, geography, economics, climate, attractions and current events of the target country and culture. Working in groups, students search for information pertaining to a country that is assigned or chosen. Once the search is completed, the groups summarize the information and present it to the class.

The search starts by selecting the name of the country and browsing through the results. Once a site with relevant information is found, it may be possible to do searches within that site. The information found may differ from country to country and from site to site, but suggest to students information that should be included in their presentation. Such content may include:
- geography
- maps
- history
- climate/weather
- major cities and tourist attractions
- popular events
- airlines serving the country
- economic activity and exchange rate
- major newspapers (include a copy of recent headlines)

In addition to sharing their findings with the class, students should submit to you the following:
1. A printed copy of the material found and used for the presentation.
2. A copy of the final presentation.
3. A reading/listening comprehension quiz prepared by the group and based on the presentation. The quiz should also include a key with the correct responses. To complete the quiz, the class does either a listening comprehension exercise while the presentation is given or a reading comprehension exercise at the conclusion of the presentation when printed copies of the presentation are made available to the class.

Virtual Museums and Works of Art

When teaching colors, emotions, description and even history, works of art may be downloaded to teach, illustrate and reinforce a variety of concepts. For example, students may be assigned to search for works of given artists to illustrate the concepts and/or vocabulary studied in class. Students also may be assigned to give a presentation on a given artist that includes the following:

- country of origin
- biographical information about the artist
- period of time in history when the artist lived
- style of work
- colors and shapes used by the artist
- feelings and aspects of life represented by his/her work
- examples of his/her work

Radio Broadcasts

The Internet offers access to radio broadcasts. Students can improve their listening comprehension skills and awareness of culture by listening to music originating from Spanish-speaking parts of the world and talk shows that are broadcast in Spanish.

Weather Reports

Weather reports, including satellite and infrared maps, are available on the Internet. When teaching about weather and weather conditions, have students access weather reports from Spanish-speaking countries and regions of the United States. The students then use this information to give weather reports or forecasts to the class. If used throughout the year, such information can be included in different units of the curriculum to link weather conditions with seasons, clothing, sports, outdoor activities and other topics.

As with other projects, the ability level of the students will be a factor in assigning specific tasks and content. For example, beginning students may give simple weather reports, including temperatures and precipitation, whereas advanced students may explore the relationship between weather conditions and lifestyle, tourism and the economy.

Newspapers and Magazines

The many newspapers and magazines on the World Wide Web are another outstanding resource for students and teachers in the language classroom. One possible activity involves these steps:

1. Locate appropriate newspapers and magazines from countries where Spanish is spoken.
2. Familiarize yourself with their format and content.

3. Divide the class into small groups.
4. Assign a content area to each member of the group or allow the students to choose an area of interest. Possible areas include international news, national news, politics, entertainment, weather and sports.
5. According to the number of groups in class, the level and the time allotted, develop a schedule that allows each group to present news from its newspaper or magazine on a regular basis. For example, a different group can do this at the beginning of class every day, or you may want to identify a day of the week for several group presentations. However done, the activity should not take more than five to ten minutes per group. It is helpful to give specific instructions about the content, length and depth you expect of the presentations and to post a calendar of presentation dates in the classroom.

A variation of this activity is to divide students into small groups and have them summarize the school newspaper in Spanish. Once done, the newspaper and/or summary are sent via e-mail to a collaborating class with which you have contact. Such an exchange of news can be an activity done throughout the year.

ASSESSING INTERNET PROJECTS

The following guidelines may be helpful when developing and assessing e-mail and Web projects:

1. Give specific instructions in writing about the project.
2. Post a calendar or time line corresponding to the project.
3. Remember that some flexibility may be necessary if students encounter difficulties (for example, with access or printing).
4. Develop clear criteria for grading and evaluation. Being specific about how student work will be evaluated will make it easier to assign a grade at the end of the project. Depending on the project, factors to consider may include:
   - whether students meet guidelines for content, length, etc.
   - whether the project is completed on time
   - the quality of the presentation and/or written assignment(s)
   - participation

TEACHER RESOURCES ON THE WORLD WIDE WEB

(**Note:** These addresses may change at any time. Visit sites to verify they are active before using them in class.)

Travel and tourism
http://www.embassyworld.com/
http://www.embassy.org
http://www.virtualtourist.com/
http://www.towd.com/
http://cityguide.lycos.com/
http://www.lonelyplanet.com
http://travel.discovery.com/destinations/main.html
http://www.lycos.com/travel/

Radio and television broadcasting
http://news.bbc.co.uk/hi/Spanish/news/
http://www.voanews.com/Spanish/
http://www.radio-locator.com/
http://www.univision.com/

Suggested sites for e-mail projects
http://www.epals.com/
http://www.linguistic-funland.com/penpalpostings.html/
http://www.worldwide.edu/index.html

Weather
http://cnnespanol.com/tiempo/
http://cnn.com/weather/
http://www.espanol.weather.com/
http://www.intellicast.com/

Newspapers and magazines
http://www.editorandpublisher.com/editorandpublisher/index.jsp
http://libraries.mit.edu/guides/types/flnews/spanish.html
http://yahoo.com/news/
http://cnnespanol.com/

Culture
http://www.lanic.utexas.edu/las.html
http://www.recetario.com/

http://www.mcu.es/agenda/index.html
http://www.lacultura.com.ar/lacultura/index.shtml

Education and teaching ideas
http://www.worldwide.edu/index.html
http://web66.coled.umn.edu/schools.html
http://www.lanic.utexas.edu/las.html
http://www.clta.net/lessons/topspanish.html
http://www.actfl.org

Language Professionals
The Foreign Language Teaching Forum is an integrated service for language teachers. The organization includes an Internet site (FLTEACH.com), e-mail (FLTEACH@listserv.buffalo.edu) LISTSERV Academic Discussion List, archives and the FLNEWS server at the State University of New York College at Cortland. The sites facilitate networking and dialog among language professionals. Topics include language teaching methods, school/college articulation, training of student teachers, classroom activities, curriculum and syllabus design. To subscribe to the list, send the following message: SUBSCRIBE FLTEACH [first name] [last name] to: LISTSERV@UBVM.CC.BUFFALO.EDU.

POLICY AND GUIDELINES FOR COMPUTER USERS

It is essential to create an acceptable use policy before allowing student access to the Internet. The development of such a policy should include all interested parties, such as school administrators, faculty, students, parents and members of the school board. The following policy and guidelines are an example created by one school. They were presented as a "working document" to allow for revisions and additions.

Acceptable Use Policy

The major school rules provide the basic structure for the Acceptable Use Policy. All users must be honest and respectful of others. Their work must meet the schoolwide guidelines for appropriate language and subject matter; it must not violate the school's harassment policy.

All use of the computers must be within the law. Copyright laws must be observed. Only software licensed to the school may be put in school computers. Copyrighted files cannot be sent from or received by school computers without permission of the copyright owner.

Users may access only their own files and programs or those intended for their use. Access to another's account or files without authorization is forbidden. Students must not attempt to access administrative files.

Those using the school's computing resources for classroom use and school-related projects have priority for use of the lab and/or equipment. School facilities may not be used for commercial purposes. Individuals are expected to use the resources thoughtfully. Use that unnecessarily slows access to the network, wastes storage or wastes other resources is forbidden.

Students who violate these policies will be subject to the school's disciplinary process.

Students will be asked to read and sign a list of additional guidelines before being given access to the school's computers. These guidelines will give students additional information about safe and respectful use of the school's computing resources.

Guidelines for Computer Users

Permission to use the school's computing facilities is granted to those who agree to use them thoughtfully and respectfully. The following guidelines should be followed:

All use of the school's computers must be consistent with the school's Acceptable Use Policy. You are expected to be honest, respect others, follow the school's rules about harassment and do nothing illegal.

Access only those files for which you are authorized. You must not use or attempt to use any other person's files or programs without permission. Attempting to access administrative files, even for fun, will be viewed as a serious offense.

Do not use offensive language, which includes both vulgar or insulting language and derogatory language.

Do not monopolize the use of the equipment. Users working on class-related projects have priority for the use of the facilities.

Do not give your home address or phone number over the Net. If you need to give someone an address or phone number, use the school's. If in doubt, check with a teacher.

Be a positive member of the school's computer-using community. Be helpful to those less knowledgeable than you. Avoid activities that earn some computer users bad reputations: Do not "hack," "spam," "flame," introduce viruses and so on.

Keep the system running legally and efficiently. Get rid of unwanted programs, files, and e-mail that take up valuable storage. "Unsubscribe" from mail lists that no longer interest you. Do not use illegal software. Do not store your own personal software at school.

Student use of the Internet is limited to the computers in the student computer lab unless they are working under the supervision of a faculty member.

TEACHING SUGGESTIONS

Navegando is a flexible program that allows teachers to cover material in the textbooks and ancillaries to suit their individual needs. This allows you to cover the various sections of a lesson with the degree of thoroughness suggested by your students' needs, your time and personal teaching style and your school's resources. In general, try to vary your presentations by using as many different resources as possible. Recombine similar materials for your students' diverse learning styles. For example, the Listening Activities offer comprehension practice; the Video/DVD Program allows students to observe native speakers using Spanish in contexts that require skills your students are learning; the CD-ROM tutorials and games individualize and personalize instruction; overhead transparencies offer visual support of spoken Spanish and can serve both to practice rote material and to provide situational contexts for conversations; activities in the textbook and Workbook and the Communicative Activities Manual offer additional writing practice.

The Program Manager offers day-by-day suggestions on using components of the series. Depending on the needs and time limitations set by individual circumstances, some activities may be skipped. The reading section titled *Tú lees* is optional, thus offering you additional flexibility in matching content to the needs, interests and curriculum requirements of your own particular situation.

Opening vocabulary spreads, dialogs, other narrative material and many activities in the textbook have been recorded and thus offer you additional choices about how to present or review the chapter content. For example, you may choose to have students listen to a recorded activity before going to the textbook, or you may choose instead to use the audio CD as additional reinforcement after having completed the activity in the textbook. Recorded activities are indicated by icons in the margins of the ATE, according to the activity type.

In addition, many ancillaries already discussed in this ATE Introduction supplement the textbook. These program components provide an abundance of textbook-related activities and teaching formats that will enable you to customize your teaching to the many and varied learning styles and needs of your students.

Every teacher has his or her own approach to teaching. Suggestions for including activities from the accompanying ancillaries have been offered in the margins of the ATE and in the Program Manager to give you an idea of the possible variations the teaching program offers. You should try to include an assortment of different activities, choosing some from the textbook and others from the ancillaries (the Workbook, the ATE, etc.), according to your needs.

ADDITIONAL ACTIVITIES AND GAMES

ACTIVITIES

The following activities and games offer additional avenues through which to enrich and supplement the lessons in the textbook. The ideas support skill development, cooperative learning, critical thinking, multiple intelligences and Total Physical Response (TPR). Pick and choose from the wide variety of activities and games as needed.

Skill Development

Listening—Before a dialog or other listening passage, have students use cues from accompanying illustrations to make an educated guess about what they are about to hear. Students may be able to determine such things as how many people are speaking, whether the speakers are young or old, male or female. Have students try to determine if they are hearing questions or statements. Then play the audio CD as students listen with their books closed.

Encourage students to learn to become good listeners by asking follow-up questions to listening activities: What are the speakers talking about? How are they feeling? What are their plans? Play the audio

CD again with books open, having students read along silently. Have students repeat after you as you read the content in short phrases. You may choose to act out or paraphrase the meanings of words and expressions, avoiding word-for-word repetition.

Reading—Prepare students for the content of a reading by asking some general questions on the reading topic, such as the questions found in the section *Preparación*. You may choose to read the first paragraph yourself as students follow along in the book. Give students a moment to look over the paragraph silently on their own and then have them ask questions. Ask for a student to volunteer to read the paragraph aloud. Continue in this way for subsequent paragraphs. After the reading, discuss the principal ideas and themes, secondary ideas and themes, cultural practices, etc.

Research—Assign projects that allow small groups of students to research aspects of the fascinating cultures of the Spanish-speaking world. Possible topics can involve history, art, architecture, government, social customs and cultural traits, for example.

Dictionary—Show students the glossary in the back of the book. Then teach some important dictionary skills by having them find the meanings of two or three new words. This activity can be done in any lesson, as often as you like. As an alternative, have students identify several infinitives in a Spanish dictionary. (The textbook glossary can serve as the dictionary.)

Mapping—Teach mapping skills on a regular basis. For example, use the map transparencies to practice pronouncing the names of countries and capitals in the Spanish-speaking world. Ask students *¿Cómo se llama?* while pointing to one of the countries on a map transparency; students should answer with *Es* (name of the country).

To integrate cultural information, use a wall map or an overhead transparency of the maps in the book. Have individual students go to the map (*Ve* or *Camina*

al mapa) and touch (*Toca*) or point to (*Señala*) the items you mention: *Toca un país donde se puede esquiar en julio; Toca un país que produce mucho café;* and so forth.

Cooperative Learning

When students finish school and enter the workforce, the knowledge they will have acquired will be complemented by the socialization skills they have learned. The following activities are designed to help students work cooperatively to solve problems in Spanish.

Concentric Circles—Students form two concentric circles. Students in the inner ring pair up with students in the outer ring, each student asking the other for information (for example, his or her name and how it is spelled). Students in the outer ring move one student to their right and begin the process again.

Information Exchange—1) Have students gather information about other students in class by pairing up or working in small groups, asking and answering questions about one another's lives. They should then share the information with the class. 2) Have students write a description of themselves in Spanish, including information about where they live and their interests. Then photograph each student with an item showing a hobby or interest. Number each of the photos and have the class try to match the descriptions to the photo. As an extension of the activity, mail the descriptions and photos to a partner school for them to read and match. If the schools are connected by Internet, follow-up communication could include the correct matchup and any additional questions and information to establish long-term communication between the students of the different schools.

Critical Thinking

It is important for students to develop a variety of skills that go beyond the four basic skills of listening, speaking, reading and writing. As students move into the workplace, they will need to think critically and solve problems. Some possible activities for developing critical thinking skills include the following:

Analysis: Comparing and Contrasting—Have students pick out names that are unlike names they know in English: *Maite, Nuria* and so forth. Then have students select several names that are similar to names they know in English, while pointing out any spelling differences: *Susana*—Susan.

Analysis: Distinguishing—Have students identify the letters in the Spanish alphabet that are not in the English alphabet—*ñ, rr*—and differences in punctuation between English and Spanish.

Evaluation: Concluding, Comparing, Appraising—Discuss student conclusions about Hispanic cultures based upon the cultural information they learn in *Navegando 1B* (gestures, physical contact when greeting others or saying farewell, etc.). Then have students tell how the culture they are learning about is similar to or different from their own culture. Finally, ask how students feel about the similarities and/or differences.

Multiple Intelligences

Educators have long agreed that not everyone learns in the same way, nor is everyone intelligent in the same way. For example, one person might have verbal or mathematical ability, whereas another may demonstrate musical ability. These different intelligences must be developed so that students can achieve their full potential. Activities that address the multiple intelligences include the following.

Logical-Mathematical Intelligence—After students have studied the days and months, ask the class some questions that require students to do some calculations with the days and months of the year. Call on a student to answer each question. Then, to keep everyone involved, call on another student to confirm whether the answer given was correct and to give the correct answer if it was not. Begin with some of the following questions: *¿Cuántos minutos hay en un cuarto de hora?; ¿Cuántos días hay en una semana?; ¿En tres semanas?; ¿Cuántos minutos hay en seis horas y media?; ¿Cuántos segundos hay en doce minutos?; ¿Cuántos meses hay en cinco años?; ¿Cuántos meses hay en tres siglos?; ¿Cuántos meses hay en cinco siglos?* This activity involves critical thinking and will develop your students' logical-mathematical intelligence.

Spatial Intelligence—Have students prepare maps of the Spanish-speaking world in Spanish, adding any details they wish to borrow from the color maps at the beginning of the textbook or from an atlas.

Total Physical Response (TPR)

Plural Commands—Practice recognition of the *Uds.* form of commands by having the entire class perform certain actions or gestures as you say them aloud in Spanish. The commands should be presented in logical thematic groups *(lean, escriban, borren; escuchen, hablen, repitan).* Practice the action or gesture two or three times with students, then repeat the pair of commands one or two times with no actions or gestures.

Singular Informal Commands—After students are adequately familiar with the *Uds.* commands, you may want to use the *tú* form of a few verbs for TPR activities. Ideally, the *Uds.* and the *tú* forms should be presented on separate days. Before proceeding to the familiar commands, briefly review the *Uds.* form of the verbs you plan to use by having students perform several actions. Examples include: *Abran Uds. los libros; Cierren Uds. los libros; Toquen Uds. los libros.* Then select several students to react to the informal commands of the corresponding verbs: *Abre el libro; Cierra el libro; Toca el libro.* Vary the commands slightly to further check for comprehension: (student's name), *abre el libro*; (student's name), *abre el cuaderno.* Perform the action or use gestures only if a student does not respond.

Colors—Combine the teaching of colors with teaching or reinforcing common commands. For example, say *Toca algo azul (rojo, verde,* etc.) and observe to see that students respond appropriately. Then broaden the activity to include clothing (or other objects). You may choose to bring in a bag of old clothing, especially clothing that is out of style, awful colors, unusual sizes and so forth as a humorous way to allow students to find and point out colors and items of clothing that you name or describe.

GAMES

The following games can be modified to suit the needs of your students or to support your particular approach to teaching.

Concentration—This game can be used for practicing numbers or for reviewing or practicing verbs. The same rhythm is maintained: students tap the tops of their desks twice, clap their hands twice and snap their fingers twice—words may be called out only during the snapping of fingers. For verb practice, for example, the first student in each row gives an infinitive *(hablar)* on the first snapping of fingers, the next student gives a subject pronoun *(tú)* on the second, and the third student must respond with the appropriate answer *(tú hablas)* on the third snapping of fingers. Students who make an error move to the end of the row and the other students move up. Try to have an uneven number of students in each row so that every student will have an opportunity to match the subject pronoun and verb ending. All the students in each row monitor each other for errors. You also may have the entire class participate rather than play the game by rows. In this case, you may want to point to students for a verb infinitive, subject pronoun and response.

El detective—This game may be played with a number of different objectives: to help students get to know one another, to practice specific vocabulary, to practice different verb tenses, and so on. Make a number of lists with five to ten different items on each list. If the object is for students to get to know each other, include items such as *le gusta el fútbol, el béisbol,* etc. (a different sport on each list); *come pollo, ensalada, hamburguesas,* etc. (a different food on each list); *mañana va a la playa, al concierto, al cine,* etc. (a different place on each list); and so on. Include an unusual category to make the activity more interesting. Copy the lists to equal the number of students you have, so that each member of a group (of five, for example) has the same list and different groups have different lists. *El detective* must fill in his or her list by asking fellow students if certain categories apply to them, and if so, they sign the list by the appropriate category. Students will practice the *tú* form while asking classmates questions *(¿Juegas al fútbol?),* and may practice the third-person singular by reporting the findings to the class after all students have completed the activity.

Dibujos—This game is designed to review vocabulary while allowing students to use their artistic abilities.

The class is split up into teams. Give one member of each group a word or phrase. The team member with the word or phrase then draws clues for his or her team members. Each team has one minute to guess the word or phrase from the drawn clues. Award points to the fastest team and continue with different vocabulary and artists until a team reaches a point total determined in advance.

¿Dónde está?—(directional vocabulary and commands)—Choose a small object such as a piece of chalk, show it to the students and ask them to hide it somewhere in the room. Go out of the room for a few minutes while they hide the item. When you return, they will help you find it by giving you directional commands or indicating direction *(Doble a la derecha, está cerca, mire en el suelo,* etc.). Next, divide the class into groups of four or five, choose one person from each group to leave the room and then repeat the game, this time with familiar commands.

Hot Potato—This simple game will help beginning students gain confidence in speaking because it occupies students with a physical activity while they are conversing in Spanish, thus reducing their inhibitions about making an error. Hot Potato is played as follows: Students stand in a circle in the classroom. One student, who is holding a soft rubber ball, asks a question of another student in the circle and then calls the student by name. The first student then carefully tosses the ball to the second student, who must answer the question. Allow students ten to fifteen seconds to answer each question. The student who catches the ball and answers a question then asks a question and passes the ball to another student and so on. The game continues until all students have had at least two chances to answer a question. Questions can be based on chapter vocabulary and grammar, cultural topics or a textbook story. The teacher serves as the moderator.

Vary the game by restricting the amount of time a student can hold the ball. For example, tell students they cannot hold the ball for more than twenty seconds before beginning to ask or answer a question, or they will have to sit down. The last person standing wins the game.

The game eliminates a student's natural inclination to think in English before saying something in Spanish so that thinking in Spanish becomes a natural reflex. An added benefit is that all students actively participate in the activity since they are not just responding to the teacher's questions while passively sitting at their seats.

I Spy—Have students work in pairs to play guessing games. Students take turns describing an object they see (being certain to describe the colors, the size, what it is made of), mentioning one clue at a time while the partner guesses what the object is.

Jeopardy—This game is especially good as a general review before an exam, but it can be used at almost any time in many different ways. Similar to the television game show, it involves writing a series of categories horizontally on the board. Write the numbers ten through fifty by tens under each category. Prepare questions in advance. Unlike the television game show, students need not respond with a question. Questions may be completions, synonyms or antonyms, translations, direct questions, matching, and so forth. Divide the class into three or four teams and tell students that each person on the team must make a buzzer sound to indicate they are able to answer. (You may wish to locate an actual buzzer.)

To determine which team will go first, ask a question that may be answered by any student. The first student who sounds the buzzer gets a chance to answer. The team that correctly answers the opening question has the opportunity to choose a category and a dollar amount. Read the question, allowing that team to respond within a time limit (ten or fifteen seconds). If not answered within the specified time limit, the question is open to the entire class, but buzzers must be used; that is, students should not randomly blurt out answers.

Prepare several *Daily Double* questions, as well. Use these when enthusiasm for the game wanes. Whatever the dollar amount in the chosen category is at that moment, double it. These questions may be answered by any team, not just the team that chose the category.

When a question is answered correctly, write the answer in the space left by the erased dollar amount as you keep score. This will provide students with visual reinforcement of the material. When the entire board is filled with answers, total the scores. You may wish to offer prizes as an incentive.

El mensaje—This enjoyable activity is useful for reviewing vocabulary and reinforces listening, writing, reading and speaking skills. In advance, provide students with a list of the names of all the students in class. The list can be in alphabetical or in random order. As you hand out the list of names, inform students that they will be leaving phone messages with one another in Spanish and should hold on to this phone list to know whom to call with messages. Then, on a day when you would like to review vocabulary (or just to vary the routine), start several phone calls by whispering to several students a word or expression in Spanish that they must write down and then whisper to the next student on the list. Give students a set time when you will be collecting all phone messages (five minutes, for example). Compare what the final person wrote down to the "phone message" you whispered to the first person for each vocabulary word or expression.

Stop the Clock (vocabulary review)—Make up a series of small cards with pictures on one side and their Spanish definitions on the other, and distribute them to the class. Divide the class into two groups and choose one person to be "it" for each group (you will have two games going at once). The rest of the students sit on their desks (or stand in front of them) in a circle, holding their cards with the picture facing out. The person who is "it" stands in the center.

To begin the game, pick one student in each group. Each of those students must say the name in Spanish of the object pictured on the card he or she is holding and the name of the picture on another student's card. (It makes it harder on the person who is "it" to not be looking at the person whose card is named. Thus, you may wish to advise students to name a second card that is to the side of or behind the person who is "it.") The person in the center of the circle must find the second person and point at the corresponding picture, thus "stopping the clock," before the second student can name both his or her picture and another person's picture. Make sure the person in the center is accurately pointing at, or preferably touching, the picture. If someone's clock is stopped, that person is then "it."

Streetcar (vocabulary review)—Prepare file cards with the words you want to practice in Spanish on one side (it may be helpful to indicate infinitives with an asterisk and include articles with nouns) and in English on the reverse side. You may extend this game by using synonyms and antonyms. Your list could be based on the active vocabulary words listed at the end of each lesson. Decide whether you want the students to produce the English or the Spanish. Students should study the vocabulary before playing Streetcar. The object of this game is to get all the way back to one's seat. Every time a student answers correctly, he or she moves forward one seat. The teacher may direct the game or have a student do it.

Begin on the left side of class with the first row. The first student stands up next to the second, who remains seated. Show a card to these students while saying the word. The first student to respond correctly moves on to compete with the third student. Whoever answers correctly stands next to the third student. So if the second student wins the round, he or she moves on to the third student and the first student sits down in the second student's seat. If neither of the first two students can answer after five seconds, the third student is given an opportunity to respond. If there is still no answer, use the card as a free review, ask the class to define the problem word and choose a new card. This should be a relatively fast-paced game. By saying the target word as you show it, students practice assigning sound to visual cues as well.

Teatro—Students prepare a short list of action verbs, which they must act out in front of the class. Classmates then try to guess which Spanish verbs are being dramatized. Limit the time to encourage presenters to act out the list as quickly as possible.

CLASSROOM EXPRESSIONS

Use Spanish in the classroom beginning on the first day of class, and increase its use throughout the year. Although this may seem difficult at first, margin notes and activities and the model lesson plan included in the ATE Introduction offer suggestions, activities and tips for teaching that make using Spanish on a daily basis not only possible, but quite simple.

Be sure to let students know what your expectations are in advance. Although Spanish should serve as the primary means of communication, explain to students that you will paraphrase, use gestures or act out expressions to convey meaning and that you will avoid overusing English. Setting this tone will make your students aware of your expectations that they use the target language. You may choose, however, to note that important information about homework assignments, structures and other topics will be given or repeated in English as necessary.

Encourage students to respond to directions and give answers in Spanish. Initially, they may feel frustrated by their limited Spanish skills, so you may need to explain that people often use one-word answers and incomplete phrases to communicate in their native language. (Give some examples in English for comparison purposes.) Point out that the more students use Spanish, the more natural it will become as a means of communication. In addition, you may wish to introduce the following frequently used classroom expressions early in the year so that students have a communicative foundation on which to build:

Abre (Abran Uds.) el libro/cuaderno en la página....   Open your book/workbook to page....
Apunta/Señala (Apunten Uds./Señalen Uds.)....   Point at....
Borra (Borren Uds.) la pizarra.   Erase the board.
Cierra (Cierren Uds.) el libro/cuaderno.   Close your book/notebook.
Contesta/Responde (Contesten Uds./Responden Uds.).   Answer.
Continúa/Sigue (Continúen Uds./Sigan Uds.).   Continue.
Copia (Copien Uds.)....   Copy....
Cuenta (Cuenten Uds.)....   Count....
Da (Den Uds.) la vuelta.   Turn around.

Dibuja (Dibujen Uds.)....	Draw....
Dime (Díganme Uds.)....	Tell me....
Empieza (Empiecen Uds.) ahora.	Begin now.
Escoge (Escojan Uds.)....	Choose....
Entrégame (Entréguenme Uds.) la tarea.	Hand in your homework to me.
Escribe (Escriban Uds.)....	Write....
Escribe (Escriban Uds.) a máquina....	Type....
Escucha (Escuchen Uds.).	Listen.
Estudia (Estudien Uds.)....	Study....
Formen Uds. grupos de....	Form groups of....
Habla (Hablen Uds.) en español.	Speak in Spanish.
Inserta (Inserten Uds.) el diskette en la computadora.	Insert the diskette into the computer.
Levanta (Levanten Uds.) la mano (para contestar).	Raise your hand (to answer).
Lee (Lean Uds.)...en voz alta.	Read...out loud.
Levántate (Levántense Uds.).	Stand up.
Llévate (Llévense Uds.)....	Take...with you.
Mira (Miren Uds.)....	Look....
Oye (Oigan Uds.).	Listen.
Para (Paren Uds.).	Stop.
Pasa (Pasen Uds.) a la pizarra.	Go to the board.
Piensa (Piensen Uds.).	Think.
Pon (Pongan Uds.)....	Put/Place....
Presta (Presten Uds.) atención a....	Pay attention to....
Pronuncia (Pronuncien Uds.)....	Pronounce....
Recoge (Recojan Uds.)....	Pick up....
Recuerda (Recuerden Uds.)....	Remember....
Repite (Repitan Uds.).	Repeat.
Revisa (Revisen Uds.)....	Review....
Quita (Quiten Uds.) todo de encima de sus pupitres.	Take everything off the top of your desks.
Saca (Saquen Uds.) una hoja de papel/un bolígrafo/ un lápiz.	Take out a sheet of paper/a pen/a pencil.
Siéntate (Siéntense Uds.).	Sit down.
Toca (Toquen Uds.)....	Touch....
Trabajen Uds. en parejas en....	Work in pairs on....
Trae (Traigan Uds.)....	Bring....
Trata (Traten Uds.).	Try.
Ve (Vayan Uds.) a....	Go to....
Ven (Vengan Uds.) aquí.	Come here.
Muy bien.	Very good.
Excelente.	Excellent.
Para mañana....	For tomorrow....
Más alto/bajo.	Louder/Softer.
Silencio.	Quiet.
Otra vez.	Once more.
Vamos a tener una prueba/un examen.	We're going to have a quiz/a test.
¿Quién sabe (la respuesta)?	Who knows (the answer)?
¿Alguien?	Anyone?
Todos juntos.	All together.

¿Hay preguntas?	Are there any questions?
¿Cómo se dice...(en español)?	How do you say...(in Spanish)?
¿Cómo se escribe...?	How do you write...?
¿Qué quiere decir...?	What does...mean?
No sé.	I don't know.
No comprendo/entiendo.	I don't understand.
No recuerdo.	I don't remember.
Tengo una pregunta.	I have a question.
Bueno (Pues, Este)....	Okay (Well, Um)....
Yo creo/pienso que....	I believe/think that....

TRANSCRIPT FOR TEXTBOOK LISTENING ACTIVITIES

Listening Comprehension Activities in *Navegando* are indicated by the icon 🔊))). These activities are recorded and are available in the Audio CD Program. For teacher convenience, reproducible answer sheets have been provided for these activities and can be found at the end of the Audio CD Program Manual. The following section contains a transcript of the recorded activities for teachers who wish to read the activities aloud instead of using the recorded version in the Audio CD Program.

CAPÍTULO 6 (LECCIÓN A)

1. ¿Qué tenemos que hacer en la cocina? Selecciona la ilustración que corresponde con lo que oyes.
   1. ¿Por qué no enciendes el lavaplatos?
   2. Debes cerrar la puerta del refrigerador.
   3. ¿Por qué no enciendes la lámpara del comedor?
   4. Debes poner la mesa del comedor con aquellos platos.
   5. ¿Por qué no enciendes la estufa?
   6. Debes poner la mesa con aquellas servilletas.

5. ¿Qué hacen para ayudar? Mira las palabras de la lista. Di la que corresponde con lo que oyes.
   1. Tu cuarto tiene buena luz.
   2. Tu comida está fría aquí.
   3. Tu comida está caliente aquí.
   4. Tus platos están limpios aquí.
   5. Tu plato con comida está aquí.
   6. Tu refresco está aquí.

15. ¿Qué necesitas? Di lo que necesitas para hacer lo que oyes.
   MODELO Para tomar sopa.
   1. Para poner mantequilla en el pan.
   2. Para tomar agua.
   3. Para comer el postre.
   4. Para tomar café o té.
   5. Para comer la ensalada.
   6. Para tomar jugo.

21. Yo necesito.... Selecciona la letra de la frase que completa lógicamente cada oración que oyes.
   1. Para comer pescado y una ensalada, voy a necesitar un....
   2. Para la sopa, necesito....
   3. No quiero café, gracias. Prefiero un vaso....
   4. Por favor, pásame las....
   5. Voy a poner los platos en....
   6. Voy a poner un poco de mantequilla....
   7. Necesito la pimienta y la....
   8. Para la mesa voy a necesitar un....

CAPÍTULO 6 (LECCIÓN B)

1. Dictado. Escucha la información y escribe lo que oyes.

Hola papás,

¿Qué tal? Escribo desde Cartagena. Cartagena es una ciudad muy bonita e interesante. Cada día le gusta más a Daniela la idea de vivir aquí, pero también le gustaría vivir con Uds. en Caracas.

La casa del primo Julián es muy cómoda. Aquí va el dibujo de la casa donde vive él. Entramos en la casa por una puerta en el patio. El cuarto de Daniela está al lado de la cocina. Tiene unas ventanas pequeñas. Yo estoy en el cuarto de Julián. Cuando yo estoy aburrido, voy a la sala a ver televisión. Por las noches siempre comemos en el patio.

El tío dice que en dos semanas vamos a ir a Barranquilla. Vamos a pasar siete u ocho días allí en la casa de su tía Isabel. Allá vamos a aprender a montar a caballo. Tenemos muchas ganas de ir.

A Daniela no le gusta escribir cartas. Entonces, ella los va a llamar por teléfono en estos días.

Un abrazo,
Santiago

7. ¿Está en la casa, en el colegio o en el parque? Di dónde están las siguientes personas según lo que oyes.

1. Veo televisión en la sala con mis padres.
2. Rodrigo habla con su profesora de historia, en la planta baja.
3. Mi profesor de español lee un libro en el cuarto de su hija.
4. Allí patina sobre ruedas Esperanza con sus amigas todos los sábados.
5. La Sra. Durán prepara la comida en la cocina al lado del garaje.
6. Pedrito juega con su perro en el patio que está al lado de la piscina.
7. Natalia toma un refresco en la cafetería del primer piso.
8. Rafael limpia el baño del cuarto de sus padres.

18. ¿Cierto o falso? Di si lo que oyes es cierto o falso, según la información en el *Vocabulario II*. Si es falso, di lo que es cierto.

1. Nicolás no tiene sueño.
2. Mateo tiene ganas de correr.
3. El abuelo dice que tiene calor.
4. Los tíos dicen que tienen frío.
5. Verónica tiene mucha hambre.
6. Cristina tiene prisa.

22. ¿Qué tienen? Selecciona la ilustración apropiada que corresponde con lo que oyes.

1. Ellas tienen frío.
2. Tienen hambre.
3. Ella tiene calor.
4. Él tiene ganas de correr.
5. Tengo sed.
6. ¿Tienes sueño?

CAPÍTULO 7 (LECCIÓN A)

1. ¿Qué actividad es? Identifica la actividad que oyes.

1. Vamos a jugar al básquetbol.
2. Vamos a jugar al fútbol americano.
3. Vamos a jugar al ajedrez.
4. Vamos a jugar al béisbol.
5. Vamos a jugar a las cartas.
6. Vamos a jugar al voleibol.

5. ¿Qué comprendiste? Di si lo que oyes es cierto o falso, según el diálogo *¿No quieres jugar al ajedrez?*

1. Luz quiere jugar al tenis.
2. Hugo mira una telenovela en la televisión.
3. Hugo no quiere jugar al ajedrez.
4. Luz no recuerda cómo jugar al ajedrez.
5. Los chicos juegan a videojuegos.

13. El tiempo libre. Selecciona la ilustración que corresponde con lo que oyes.

1. Es tarde.
2. Está durmiendo.
3. Hace una hora que está viendo televisión.
4. Quiere alquilar una película nueva.
5. ¿Jugamos ajedrez?
6. Es casi mediodía.

17. Dictado

Escucha la información y escribe lo que oyes.

HUGO: ¿Estás durmiendo?

LUZ: No. Estoy viendo televisión. ¿Por qué?

HUGO: Porque quiero ir a alquilar una película.

LUZ: ¿Ahora mismo?

HUGO: Sí, quiero ir antes de comer. ¿Quieres ir?

LUZ: Un segundo.... Ya voy.

LUZ: No quiero ver las mismas películas otra vez.

HUGO: ¿Cuánto tiempo hace que no ves una película?

LUZ: ¡Uy! Hace mucho tiempo. Casi dos meses.

HUGO: ¡Entonces no vas a ver las mismas películas!

CAPÍTULO 7 (LECCIÓN B)

1. Las estaciones. Escoge la estación correcta, según lo que oyes.

1. Hace frío y puedes patinar sobre hielo.
2. Hay flores por todos lados y llueve mucho.
3. Hace sol y mucho calor.
4. No hace mucho calor.

5. ¿Qué actividades puedes hacer? Escucha la información y di qué actividad o actividades puedes hacer.

MODELO Es el otoño y hace sol.

1. Es invierno y hace mucho frío.
2. Es verano y hace mucho calor.
3. Es primavera y llueve.
4. Es otoño y no hace calor.
5. Es primavera y hace sol.

16. ¿Quién es? Selecciona la foto de la persona apropiada.

1. Soy tenista.
2. Soy futbolista.
3. Soy esquiadora.
4. Soy patinador.
5. Soy corredora.
6. Soy jugadora de fútbol.

21. ¿Qué tiempo hace? Selecciona la ilustración que corresponde con lo que oyes.

1. Hace calor.
2. Está nublado.
3. Hace viento.
4. Llueve mucho.
5. Hay neblina.
6. Nieva ahora.

CAPÍTULO 8 (LECCIÓN A)

1. ¿Qué tienen que hacer? Write the names Julia and Enrique. Next, listen and list under each of their names what chores each of them has to do. Then circle any items on the lists that they both have to do. The first one has been done for you.

1. Tengo que adornar la sala para la fiesta de cumpleaños de mi tía.
2. Tengo que cocinar el pollo.
3. Tengo que trabajar en el jardín.
4. Tengo que hacer mi cama.
5. Tengo que limpiar la cocina.
6. Tengo que adornar la sala para la fiesta de cumpleaños de mi tía.
7. Tengo que preparar la ensalada.
8. Tengo que doblar la ropa.
9. Tengo que hacer mi cama.
10. Tengo que limpiar la cocina.

6. ¿Me ayudas?

Mira las tres fotos que van con el diálogo y di si lo que oyes va con la primera, la segunda o la tercera foto.

MODELO La Sra. Zea está hablando con Inés y Víctor.

1. Inés le dice a la Sra. Zea que la cocina está limpia.
2. Víctor dice que está haciendo unos quehaceres.
3. Inés está colgando su abrigo.
4. La cocina ya está limpia.
5. Víctor le dice a Inés que tiene que terminar de limpiar la casa.

19. Los quehaceres. Selecciona la foto de la persona que corresponda con lo que oyes.

1. Pasa la aspiradora.
2. Arregla el cuarto.
3. Barre.
4. Lava las ollas.

23. ¿Vais a hacer un quehacer o un deporte? Las siguientes personas van a hablar de sus actividades de hoy. Di si lo que oyes es *un quehacer* o *un deporte.*

1. Hola. Me llamo Tomás. Voy a jugar al fútbol hoy.
2. Soy Ramón. Tengo que pasar la aspiradora por la sala hoy.
3. Me llamo Roberto. Voy a lavar las ollas esta noche para ayudar a mis padres.
4. Hola. Yo soy Verónica. Voy con unos amigos a esquiar.
5. Me llamo Margarita. Voy a buscar leche y pan en la tienda hoy.

CAPÍTULO 8 (LECCIÓN B)

1. En el supermercado. Selecciona la ilustración que corresponde con lo que oyes.

1. Los aguacates parecen muy maduros.
2. Los tomates están frescos.
3. Aquellos son los mejores pimientos.
4. Necesitamos el ingrediente más importante, el ajo.
5. Éstos son los peores guisantes.
6. Voy a llevar un kilo de pescado.

5. ¿Qué les hace falta? Di la letra de la ilustración que identifica lo que les hace falta comprar a las siguientes personas, según lo que oyes.

1. Ayer compré el pollo. Me hace falta comprar un kilo de arroz.
2. A nosotros nos hace falta comprar unas cebollas.
3. Yo necesito comprar una lechuga para la ensalada.
4. A mi madre le hace falta comprar unos pimientos y una lata de tomates.
5. Yo tengo todas las verduras, sólo me hace falta comprar un pollo.

20. En el mercado. Selecciona la ilustración que corresponde con lo que oyes.

1. Les di las mejores manzanas.
2. ¿A qué precio tiene las habichuelas?
3. Ayer estuve en el mercado y compré fresas.
4. Las zanahorias están a un euro el kilo.
5. Éstas son las mejores naranjas.
6. Este maíz es tan bueno como aquel maíz.

25. ¿Qué comprendiste? Escucha lo que dicen las personas del diálogo *Comprando chorizo* y di si lo que oyes es cierto o falso. Corrige lo que no es cierto.

1. Ayer estuve con Víctor en el supermercado.
2. Compramos los ingredientes para hacer una ensalada.
3. Quiero comprar queso.
4. El chorizo del supermercado no me gusta.
5. Este es el peor supermercado de la ciudad.
6. El chorizo está a € 4,00 el kilo.

CAPÍTULO 9 (LECCIÓN A)

1. Comprando ropa. Selecciona la ilustración que corresponde con lo que oyes.

1. Quiero una blusa de seda rosada.
2. Busco una corbata morada.
3. Necesito unas botas marrones.
4. Busco un traje de baño anaranjado.
5. Quiero un pijama de algodón azul.
6. Necesito un vestido verde.

6. ¿Cuál prefieres? Selecciona la letra de la ilustración que corresponde con lo que las siguientes personas prefieren.

1. Prefiero el traje negro.
2. El negro no me gusta. Prefiero el marrón.
3. Prefiero los zapatos bajos.
4. Prefiero la camisa morada.
5. La morada no me gusta ni un poquito. Prefiero la anaranjada.
6. Yo prefiero los zapatos de tacón.
7. Prefiero el vestido rosado.
8. Prefiero las medias azules.

20. ¿Qué es? Escribe el artículo de ropa que oyes.

MODELO Me gustó el sombrero rojo.

1. Preferí los guantes negros.
2. Quiero comprar un abrigo de lana.
3. Voy a buscar una chaqueta nueva.
4. Necesitas un impermeable porque va a llover.
5. ¿Llevas tu suéter de algodón?
6. Escogí el pantalón verde.

25. ¿Cuándo? Listen carefully to statements made by several people. Indicate whether each sentence you hear is in the past *(pretérito)* or in the present *(presente)*.

1. ¿Te conté que ayer fui a una tienda por departamentos?
2. Puedes comprar ese abrigo nuevo, si quieres.
3. No me queda ninguno de lana.
4. Te prometí llevarte al centro comercial ayer, ¿verdad?
5. Te compré algo nuevo.
6. No quiero ni la chaqueta ni el impermeable.
7. Es un suéter para tus vacaciones.

CAPÍTULO 9 (LECCIÓN B)

1. ¿Qué les gustaría recibir de regalo? Selecciona la letra de la ilustración que corresponde con lo que oyes.

1. A mí me gustaría recibir una billetera.
2. A mí me gustaría recibir una pulsera de oro.
3. De regalo, a mí me gustaría recibir un paraguas.
4. Yo quiero recibir de regalo unos aretes de plata.
5. Yo quiero recibir un cinturón de cuero.
6. A mí me gustaría recibir un anillo de oro.

6. Bueno, bonito y barato. Selecciona la letra de la ilustración que corresponde con lo que buscan las siguientes personas.

1. Busco un bolsito de material sintético barato.
2. Busco una bufanda larga para usar todos los días.
3. Busco un paraguas bueno, bonito y barato.
4. Buscamos unos pañuelos de seda.
5. Busco un collar y unos aretes de perlas.
6. Buscamos una chaqueta de cuero corta.

18. ¿Cuál es la respuesta correcta? Escoge la letra de la respuesta correcta a lo que oyes.

1. ¿Cómo va a pagar?
2. ¿Quieres venir conmigo a la tienda?
3. ¿Qué necesito para cambiar este paraguas?
4. ¿Cuánto es mi cambio?
5. ¿Te gusta la calidad de la blusa?
6. ¿Es caro el collar?

22. ¿Sí o no? ¿Son lógicos los diálogos? Corrige lo que no es lógico.

1. ¿Cuánto cuesta el perfume?
   Cuesta veinte dólares.
2. ¿Está en oferta el perfume?
   Sí, es muy caro.
3. ¿Cómo va a pagar?
   Voy a pagar con recibos.
4. Aquí tiene su recibo y dos dólares de cambio.
   No, no lo voy a cambiar.
5. ¿Cómo puedo ahorrar dinero?
   Puedes ahorrar dinero si compras lo barato.

CAPÍTULO 10 (LECCIÓN A)

3. ¡Fue un año divertido! Di si lo que oyes es cierto o falso, según el Diálogo I. Si es falso, corrige la información.

1. Silvia dijo que el año fue muy aburrido.
2. Mario dijo que le gusta la historia.
3. Silvia dijo que le gusta la geografía.
4. Mario dijo que no le gusta la biología.

CAPÍTULO 10 (LECCIÓN B)

3. ¿Quién dijo qué? ¿Quién dijo lo siguiente, Inés o Luis?

1. Tuve que ayudar a mis padres.
2. Vamos a ir a las ruinas de Tikal.
3. Fui a Tikal el año pasado.
4. Me gustaría ir a California.
5. Pienso que debes ir a California.

Navegando 1B

Authors

James F. Funston

Alejandro Vargas Bonilla

Contributing Writers

Belia Jiménez Lorente

Karin Fajardo

Rolando Castellanos

Consultants

Paul J. Hoff
University of Wisconsin—Eau Claire
Eau Claire, Wisconsin

Anne Marie Quihuis
Paradise Valley High School
Phoenix, Arizona

Heidi Oshima
Parsippany High School
Parsippany, New Jersey

Anna Watson
Henrico High School
Richmond, Virginia

Marne Patana
Middle Creek High School
Apex, North Carolina

Nancy Wrobel
Champlin Park High School
Champlin Park, Minnesota

EMCParadigm Publishing, Saint Paul, Minnesota

CREDITS

Editorial Consultants
Judy Cohen
Lori Coleman
David Thorstad
Sarah Vaillancourt

Readers
Pat Cotton
Mónica Domínguez
Barbary Forney
Daniela Guzmán
Charisse Littiken
Barbara Peterson
Roy Sweezy
Beth Verdin

Proofreaders
Susana Petit
Mercedes Roffé
Gilberto Vázquez

Illustrators
Kristen Copham
Len Ebert
Tune Insisiengmay
Susan Jaekel

Nedo Kojic
Paul Mirocha
Hetty Mitchel
D.J. Simison

Photo Research
Jennifer Anderson

Design
Interior Design: Tina Widzbor,
Monotype Composition
Cover Design: Suzanne Montazer and
Ken Croghan, Monotype Composition

Cover Photo
Mónica Béjar Latonda

Production
Precision Graphics
Matthias Frasch, scan technician

We have attempted to locate owners of
copyright materials used in this book.
If an error or omission has occurred,
EMC/Paradigm Publishing will acknowledge
the contribution in subsequent printings.

ISBN 0-8219-2830-9

Published by EMC/Paradigm Publishing
875 Montreal Way
St. Paul, Minnesota 55102
800-328-1452
www.emcp.com
Email: educate@emcp.com

Printed in the United States of America
1 2 3 4 5 6 7 8 9 10 X X X 08 07 06 05 04

¡Saludos!

You are about to embark on a journey that will take you to many countries and that will open doors you may never have imagined. Whether you are drawn to Spanish because of your interest in travel or your desire to learn how to communicate with others, this year offers you rewarding possibilities as you navigate your way through the Spanish-speaking world. This sense of real-life adventure and travel is reflected in the covers of the *Navegando* series.

Learning a language has always meant more than merely memorizing words and grammar rules and then putting them together, hoping to actually be able to communicate. Just as language is inseparable from culture, so is it inseparable from the authentic communication of thoughts and emotions. The culture of the Spanish-speaking world varies from one country to another. In *Navegando,* you will navigate your way, learning about others while at the same time learning how to share your ideas and feelings. These real-life learning experiences will introduce you to and expand your knowledge of language, geography, history and the arts. In *Navegando* you will learn not only fascinating information, but also problem-solving, survival and employment skills so that when you leave the classroom you can step right into the real world.

Are you ready to learn to use Spanish in the real world? Experience the authentic: *Navegando.*

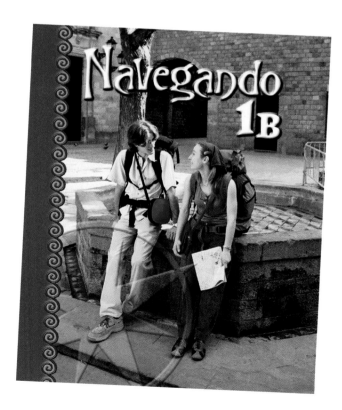

Contents

Groenlandia
(Din.)

ISLANDIA

NORUEGA

SU

Alaska
(EE.UU.)

REINO UNIDO

DINAMARCA

IRLANDA

ALEMANIA

CANADÁ

FRANCIA

ESTADOS

Denver   Chicago   Nueva York

PORTUGAL   ESPAÑA   Andorra
la Vella

ANDORRA

ITAL

Madrid

OCÉANO

Los Ángeles
San Diego

UNIDOS

MARRUECOS

TUNICIA

San Antonio

ATLÁNTICO

I. Canarias

ARGELIA

LIB

Miami

BAHAMAS

Trópico de Cáncer

Sahara
Occidental

La Habana

MÉXICO

CUBA

REPÚBLICA
DOMINICANA

MAURITANIA

MALI

NÍGER

C. de México

BÉLIZE

HAITÍ

Puerto Rico (EE. UU.)

CABO VERDE

GUATEMALA   Belmopán
Guatemala   HONDURAS
EL SALVADOR   Tegucigalpa
San Salvador   Managua
COSTA RICA   NICARAGUA
San José   Panamá   PANAMÁ

JAMAICA   Santo
Domingo

3

2   4

Caracas

TRINIDAD Y TOBAGO
Puerto España

SENEGAL
GAMBIA

BURKINA
FASO

GUINEA-BISSAU   GUINEA

NIGERIA

COSTA
DE
MARFIL

GHANA

TOGO

BENIN

VENEZUELA

SIERRA LEONA

CAMERÚN

OCÉANO

Santa Fe
de Bogotá

GUYANA

SURINAM

LIBERIA

Malabo
GUINEA ECUAT.

Ecuador

COLOMBIA

Guayana Francesa (Fr.)

SANTO TOMÉ
Y PRÍNCIPE

GABÓN

REP.
POP.
CONGO

Quito

0°

Is.Galápagos
(Arch. de Colón)
(Ec.)

ECUADOR

160°

Is. Hawai
(EE. UU.)

PERÚ

BRASIL

OCÉANO

ANG

20°

Lima

ATLÁNTICO

La Paz

PACÍFICO

BOLIVIA

Sucre

NAMIB

PARAGUAY

Asunción

C H I L E

A R G E N T I N A

Santiago

URUGUAY
Montevideo
Buenos Aires

SUD

MAPA

La lengua españ

I. Malvinas

OCÉANO   GLA

Nº	PAIS	Nº	PAIS
1	ST. CRISTÓBAL Y NEVIS	20	ALBANIA
2	SAN VICENTE	21	LÍBANO
	Y LAS GRANADINAS	22	JORDANIA
3	DOMINICA	23	LESOTHO
4	BARBADOS	24	SWAZILANDIA
5	PAÍSES BAJOS	25	BAHREIN
6	BÉLGICA	26	ESTONIA
7	LUXEMBURGO	27	LETONIA
8	REP. CHECA	28	LITUANIA
9	AUSTRIA	29	MOLDAVIA
10	SUIZA	30	GEORGIA
11	MÓNACO	31	ARMENIA
12	SAN MARINO	32	AZERBAIDZHAN
13	LIECHTENSTEIN	33	KIRGUIZISTÁN
14	HUNGRÍA	34	TADZHIKISTÁN
15	ESLOVENIA	35	ESLOVAQUIA
16	CROACIA	36	DJIBOUTI
17	BOSNIA-HERZEGOVINA	37	RUANDA
18	YUGOSLAVIA	38	BURUNDI
19	MACEDONIA		

AN

©edigol ediciones,s.a.

160°   120°   80°   40°   Oeste de Greenwich   0°   Este de Greenw

GLACIAL ÁRTICO

Alaska (EE.UU.)

R U S I A

KAZAJSTÁN

MONGOLIA

UCRANIA

BIELORRUSIA

BULGARIA

TURQUÍA

CHIPRE

SIRIA

ISRAEL

IRAK

IRÁN

UZBEKISTÁN

TURKMENISTÁN

AFGANISTÁN

PAKISTÁN

REP. POP. CHINA

COREA DEL NORTE

COREA DEL SUR

JAPÓN

OCÉANO PACÍFICO

40°

EGIPTO

ARABIA SAUDITA

KUWAIT

QATAR

EMIRATOS ÁRABES UNIDOS

OMÁN

NEPAL

BHUTAN

INDIA

BANGLA-DESH

BIRMANIA

LAOS

VIETNAM

TAIWÁN

SUDÁN

ERITREA

YEMEN

THAILANDIA

CAMBOYA

Manila

FILIPINAS

REP. DE PALAOS

REP. CENTRO-AFRICANA

ETIOPÍA

SOMALIA

BRUNEI

MALASIA

SINGAPUR

SRI LANKA

MALDIVAS

REPÚBLICA DEMOCRÁTICA DEL CONGO

UGANDA

KENYA

TANZANIA

SEYCHELLES

OCÉANO ÍNDICO

I N D O N E S I A

PAPÚA-NUEVA GUINEA

SALOMÓN

MALAWI

ZAMBIA

MOZAMBIQUE

COMORES

MAURICIO

ZIMBABWE

BOTSWANA

MADAGASCAR

AUSTRALIA

Trópico de Capricornio

REP. AFRICANA

NUEVA

ZELANDA

40°

Línea internacional de cambio de hora

MUNDI

ñola en el mundo

GLACIAL ANTÁRTICO

	Países donde el español es la lengua oficial o co-oficial	**Madrid** Ciudad de más de 1 millón de hab.
		Panamá Ciudad de 100.000 a 1 millón de hab.
	Zonas donde el español es hablado por una parte de la población	*Malabo* Ciudad de menos de 100.000 hab.
		▪—▪ Límite de Estado
		▪ Capital de Estado
		● Otras ciudades

ANTÁRTIDA

Greenwich

40°

80°

120°

160°

160°

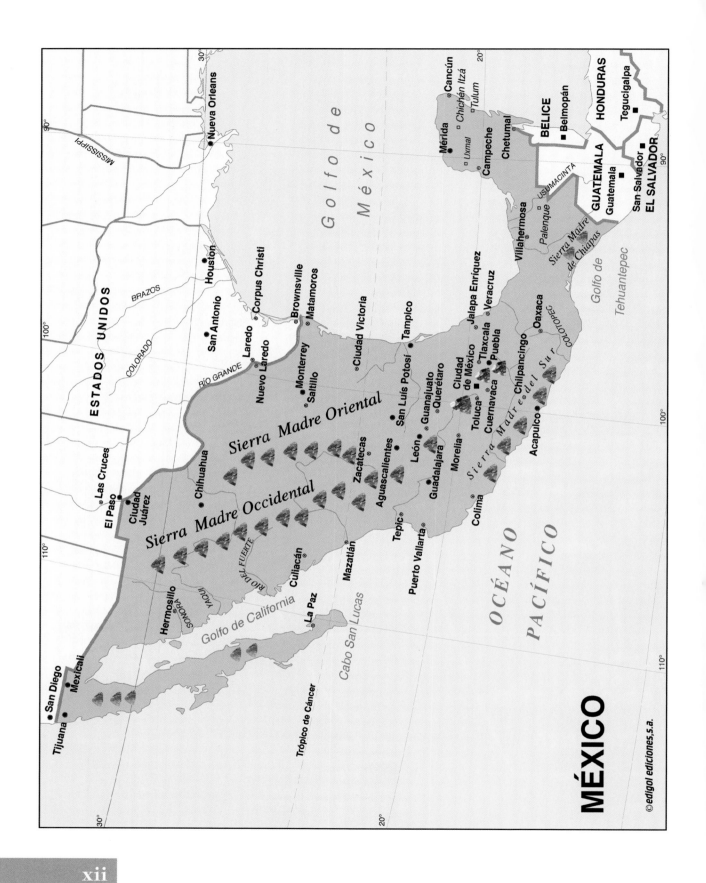

MÉXICO

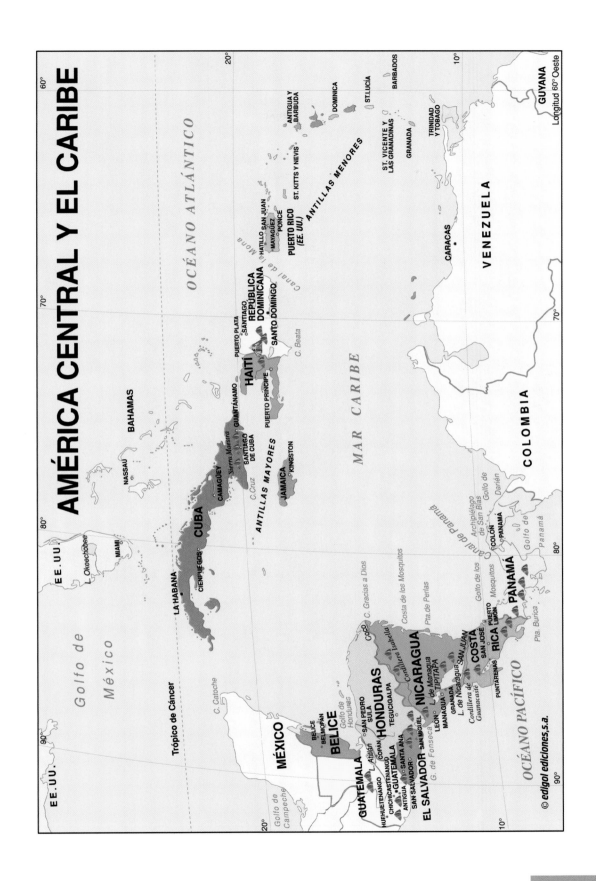

AMÉRICA CENTRAL Y EL CARIBE

EE. UU.

EE. UU.

Golfo de México

L. Okeechobee

MIAMI

Trópico de Cáncer

OCÉANO ATLÁNTICO

60°

70°

80°

90°

20°

Golfo de Campeche

C. Catoche

BAHAMAS

NASSAU

LA HABANA

CIENFUEGOS

CUBA

CAMAGÜEY

Sierra Maestra

SANTIAGO DE CUBA

GUANTÁNAMO

C. Cruz

ANTILLAS MAYORES

JAMAICA

KINGSTON

MAR CARIBE

PUERTO PLATA

HAITÍ

PUERTO PRÍNCIPE

REPÚBLICA DOMINICANA

SANTO DOMINGO

C. Beata

Canal de la Mona

HATILLO SAN JUAN

MAYAGÜEZ

PONCE

PUERTO RICO (EE. UU.)

ANTIGUA Y BARBUDA

DOMINICA

ST. LUCÍA

BARBADOS

ST. KITTS Y NEVIS

ANTILLAS MENORES

ST. VICENTE Y LAS GRANADINAS

GRANADA

TRINIDAD Y TOBAGO

CARACAS

VENEZUELA

GUYANA

20°

MÉXICO

C. Catoche

Golfo de Honduras

BELICE

BELICE

BELMOPÁN

SAN PEDRO SULA

HONDURAS

TEGUCIGALPA

COPÁN

HUEHUETENANGO

CHICHICASTENANGO

GUATEMALA

GUATEMALA

ANTIGUA

SANTA ANA

SAN MIGUEL

L. Atitlán

SAN SALVADOR

EL SALVADOR

G. de Fonseca

LEÓN

MANAGUA

L. de Managua

TIPITAPA

GRANADA

L. de Nicaragua

Cordillera Isabelia

Cordillera de Guanacaste

NICARAGUA

Coco

C. Gracias a Dios

Costa de los Mosquitos

Pta. de Perlas

Golfo de los Mosquitos

SAN JUAN

PUNTARENAS

SAN JOSÉ

COSTA RICA

PUERTO LIMÓN

Pta. Burica

Archipiélago de San Blas

Golfo de Darién

COLÓN

PANAMÁ

PANAMÁ

Canal de Panamá

Golfo de Panamá

COLOMBIA

OCÉANO PACÍFICO

10°

10°

70°

80°

90°

© edigal ediciones, s.a.

Longitud 60° Oeste

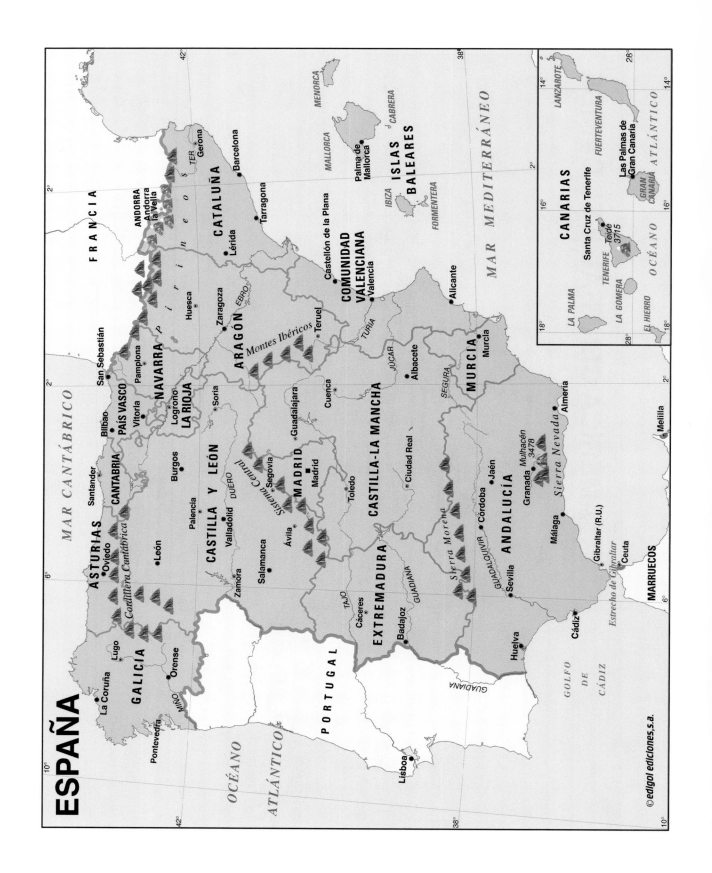

ESPAÑA

AMÉRICA DEL SUR

MAR CARIBE

G. de Venezuela

BARRANQUILLA
CARTAGENA
MARACAIBO CARACAS
L. de
Maracaibo
MÉRIDA
VENEZUELA
Delta del
Orinoco

OCÉANO
ATLÁNTICO

BUCARAMANGA
ARAUCA
ORINOCO
GEORGETOWN
PARAMARIBO
GUYANA
SURINAM
GUAYANA
FRANCESA
(Fra.)
CAYENA

MEDELLÍN
SANTA FE
DE BOGOTÁ
CALI
VILLAVICENCIO
MAGDALENA

PASTO
QUITO
COLOMBIA
CAQUETÁ

Estuario del
Amazonas

Ecuador

ECUADOR
Cotopaxi
5896
Chimborazo
6267
GUAYAQUIL
Golfo de
Guayaquil
CUENCA
IQUITOS
AMAZONAS
AMAZONAS

FORTALEZA

Pta. Negra
PERÚ
CHICLAYO
TRUJILLO
Los Andes

B R A S I L

RECIFE

SAN FRANCISCO

CALLAO
LIMA
Machu Picchu
ICA
CUZCO
JULIACA
L. Titicaca
LA PAZ
BOLIVIA
COCHABAMBA
L. de Poopó
SUCRE
POTOSÍ

ARICA

PARAGUAY

BRASILIA

SALVADOR

BELO HORIZONTE

SÃO PAULO
RÍO DE JANEIRO

OCÉANO

PACÍFICO

Trópico de Capricornio
ANTOFAGASTA

CHILE

Gran Chaco
PARAGUAY
CONCEPCIÓN
PILCOMAYO
Itaipú
Cataratas
del Iguazú
ASUNCIÓN
PARAGUAY

Los Andes
Aconcagua
6959
SAN MIGUEL
DE TUCUMÁN
ARGENTINA
RESISTENCIA
CORRIENTES
URUGUAY
PARANÁ

IS. JUAN FERNÁNDEZ
(Chile)

CÓRDOBA
SAN JUAN
PARANÁ
SALTO
URUGUAY

VIÑA DEL MAR
VALPARAÍSO
SANTIAGO
DE CHILE
TALCA
MENDOZA
SALADO
ROSARIO
BUENOS
AIRES
LA PLATA
Pampas
URUGUAY
MONTEVIDEO
RÍO DE LA PLATA

OCÉANO

ATLÁNTICO

CONCEPCIÓN
COLORADO
BAHÍA BLANCA
MAR DEL PLATA
Pta. Norte

VALDIVIA
NEUQUÉN
NEGRO

PUERTO
MONTT
SAN CARLOS DE
BARILOCHE
Los Andes

Patagonia

C. Tres Puntas

Golfo de Penas
Bahía
Grande
Estr. de Magallanes
ISLAS MALVINAS (R.U.)
PUERTO STANLEY

GEORGIA DEL SUR (R.U.)

PUNTA ARENAS
USHUAIA
TIERRA DEL
FUEGO
Cabo de Hornos

Estr. de Drake

Teacher Resources

TPRS *Capítulo 6*

 Capítulo 6

Connections with Parents

Involve more parents and guardians in their children's school lives. Ask for volunteers to assist in class; assign activities that require students and their parents or guardians to interact; have the parents or guardians sign homework. The benefits of increased parental and guardian involvement in student learning are undeniable.

Capítulo 6

En casa

Objetivos

- ❖ identify items in the kitchen and at the dinner table
- ❖ express obligations, wishes and preferences
- ❖ talk about everyday activities
- ❖ state an opinion
- ❖ discuss food and table items
- ❖ point out people and things
- ❖ describe a household
- ❖ tell what someone says
- ❖ say how someone is doing

Visit the web-based activities at www.emcp.com

Notes Be sure to review the communicative objectives that are provided on this page in order to give students an idea what they will be able to do after completing the chapter. A list of the functions appears at the end of the chapter on page 42 so students can do a self-check to evaluate their progress.

Venezuela
Nombre oficial: **República de Venezuela**
Población: **23.917.000**
Capital: **Caracas**
Ciudades importantes: **Maracaibo, Valencia, Barquisimeto**
Unidad monetaria: **el bolívar**
Fiesta nacional: **5 de julio, Día de la Independencia**
Gente famosa: **Simón Bolívar ("El Libertador"); Rómulo Gallegos (escritor)**

Colombia
Nombre oficial: **República de Colombia**
Población: **43.071.000**
Capital: **Bogotá**
Ciudades importantes: **Medellín, Cali, Cartagena**
Unidad monetaria: **el peso**
Fiesta nacional: **20 de julio, Día de la Independencia**
Gente famosa: **Fernando Botero (pintor); Gabriel García Márquez (escritor)**

Activities

Connections
Ask students to name some cities in Venezuela and Colombia. Then ask if anyone in class has visited or knows someone who has visited either country. Ask if students can tell the class any interesting information about these countries.

Notes The cultural focus of this chapter combines the South American countries of Venezuela and Colombia. The two countries have had many connections over the years. They remain connected today due in part to the disputes about oil reserves located between the two countries.

Students will find it interesting that Venezuela is named after Venice due to its extensive waterways; Colombia is named for Christopher Columbus.

The small photograph on the opposite page is of a house in Colombia. The large photograph depicts a typical family in their home.

> **Content reviewed in *Lección A***
> - family
> - express courtesy
> - discuss food
> - the verb *tener*

Activities

Expansion
Use overhead transparencies 40 and 41 to introduce the new words and expressions in *Vocabulario I*. Begin by showing students transparency 40. Point to one of the objects in the kitchen and identify it in Spanish. Students should repeat after you. Continue on to the next item and repeat the process. As a second step, show students transparency 41. Once again identify the objects in Spanish, allowing students to see how each word is spelled.

Prereading Strategy
Play the audio CD recording of the vocabulary and have students repeat the words while showing them overhead transparency 40.

Notes The verb *poner* is presented here as new vocabulary in the expression *poner la mesa*. Students will not learn all forms of *poner* until *Lección 7B*. For the time being, however, they are able to use all present-tense forms of this new verb except for the first-person singular form *pongo*. Page 211 of the Appendices contains a chart with the present-tense forms.

Tell students that *poner* is also used with appliances to mean **to turn on**: *poner la televisión.*

2

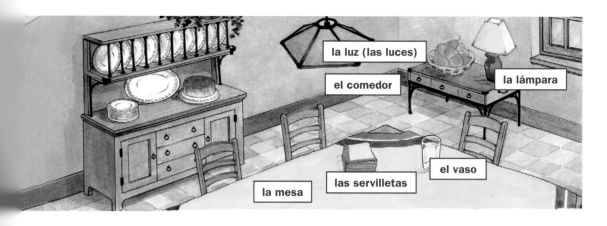

la luz (las luces)

el comedor

la lámpara

el vaso

las servilletas

la mesa

1 ¿Qué tenemos que hacer en la cocina?

Selecciona la ilustración que corresponde con lo que oyes.

A   **B**   **C**   **D**   **E**   **F**

2 ¿Adónde llamo?

Imagine you live in Caracas, Venezuela, and several appliances in your home are broken. Decide whom you would call to come and have them fixed.

ELÉCTRICOS GALAXIA

¡Los mejores técnicos en reparación de electrodomésticos en Caracas!

Todas las marcas: estufas, lavaplatos, fregaderos y triturador de desperdicios, lavadoras, secadoras, aspiradoras, planchas. Garantía total, domicilios, Av. Junín, llámenos hoy: 614-22-64.

A

CENTRALES

Somos especialistas en la reparación de microondas, refrigeradores, lavaplatos, licuadoras, tostadoras, procesadores de comida. Servicio a domicilio. Venta de repuestos. 40 años sirviendo a Caracas. Servicio las 24 horas del día. Línea directa: 215-58-78.

B

1   **2**   **3**   **4**   **5**

Teacher Resources

 Activity 1

 Activity 1

 Activity 1

Answers

1 1. E
   2. F
   3. B
   4. A
   5. D
   6. C
2 1. A
   2. B
   3. A, B
   4. B
   5. A

Activities

Prereading Strategy
Have students look at *Vocabulario I* and identify cognates and other words they recognize. Then ask students to summarize what each box on page 2 says.

Pronunciation
Model the pronunciation of several words and phrases from *Vocabulario I* for students to repeat.

Students with Special Needs
Help students with the two advertisements on page 3. Then give a model for activity 2.

Notes Select ancillaries listed under Teacher Resources at the top of pages 2 or 3 for introducing and reinforcing the new content on these pages. For example, you may wish to introduce vocabulary using overhead transparencies 40 and 41 or you may prefer to use the audio CD. Written activities for practicing the new vocabulary are available in the Workbook and in the Grammar and Vocabulary Exercises Manual. Choose support items that help you accomplish your goals.

Diálogo I

¿Me vas a ayudar?

JULIO: ¿Qué haces, mamá?
MAMÁ: Hago la comida. ¿Me vas a ayudar?
JULIO: ¿Qué debo hacer?

MAMÁ: ¿Por qué no enciendes el lavaplatos?
JULIO: ¿Qué más?
MAMÁ: ¿Por qué no limpias el refrigerador?

JULIO: No, ¡el refrigerador no! Prefiero otra cosa mamá.
MAMÁ: Bueno, ¿por qué no pones la mesa?
JULIO: ¡Sí, cómo no!

3 ¿Qué recuerdas?

1. ¿Qué hace la mamá de Julio?
2. ¿Va a ayudar Julio a su mamá?
3. ¿Qué hace Julio primero?
4. ¿Julio va a limpiar el refrigerador o prefiere hacer otra cosa?

4 Algo personal

1. ¿Ayudas en la cocina en tu casa?
2. ¿Qué cosas haces para ayudar en la cocina?
3. ¿Qué cosas hay en la cocina de tu casa?

5 ¿Qué hacen para ayudar?

Mira las palabras de la lista. Di la que corresponde con lo que oyes.

el refrigerador	la lámpara	la estufa
el vaso	la mesa	el fregadero

4 *cuatro*

Lección A

4

Explorando Venezuela

When European explorers came to the shores of Lake Maracaibo, they named the area Venezuela (meaning "Little Venice") because the homes that were located along the shores of the lake reminded them of Venice, Italy. Venezuela is a land of varied geography, with wonderful beaches *(Playa Medina, Playa Colorada)*, mountains

Caracas, Venezuela.

(Andes), plains and deserts *(Médanos de Coro)*. One of the most sensational natural attractions found in the country is Angel Falls *(el Salto del Ángel)*, the highest waterfall in the world. Venezuela also has big industrialized cities, such as Caracas, the capital and economic and political center of the nation. Other large cities include Maracaibo, known for its petroleum production, Mérida, a cultural and intellectual center, and Puerto Cruz, a very popular destination for tourists from all over the world.

At one time Venezuela had one of the highest standards of living in South America due to its many natural resources, especially the vast abundance of oil *(el petróleo)* found near Lake Maracaibo. The country is one of the world's principal producers of oil and an important member of OPEC (in Spanish, *OPEP*, or *Organización de Países Exportadores de Petróleo*). Venezuela is also known for its pearl industry. In addition to exporting big quantities of oil and pearls *(las perlas)*, the country is one of the world's largest exporters of cocoa beans *(el cacao)*, the basic ingredient for chocolate.

When Venezuelans gather, they enjoy talking, laughing and sharing good food, such as *arepas, ropa vieja* and *cachapas.* Investigate this fascinating South American country. You may be surprised by what you find!

Venezuela exporta petróleo, perlas y cacao.

6 Explorando Venezuela

Completa las siguientes oraciones sobre Venezuela.

1. *Venezuela* quiere decir...
2. Dos playas famosas en Venezuela son...
3. Una de las atracciones más importantes de Venezuela es...
4. La capital de Venezuela es...
5. Tres productos de exportación de Venezuela son...
6. Tres comidas famosas de Venezuela son ropa vieja, cachapas y...

Capítulo 6   *cinco* 5

Notes *Ropa vieja*, literally **old clothes,** is a hearty stew-like dish of shredded meat and vegetables that is served over rice or in a warm flour tortilla. *Cachapas* are similar to corn cakes. They can be eaten with cheese, whipped cream or butter.

The acronym OPEC stands for the Organization of Petroleum Exporting Countries.

New words that students may not recognize include the following: *exportadores* (exporters); *petróleo* (oil).

Teacher Resources

 Activity 2

 Activity 3

Answers

6 1. Little Venice.
2. Playa Medina y Playa Colorada.
3. el Salto del Ángel.
4. Caracas.
5. petróleo, perlas y cacao.
6. arepas.

Activities

Expansion
Ask students to use the Internet and/or library to learn more about a topic they find interesting in the *Cultura viva*. They should then list in Spanish three or four interesting facts they found and share the information with the class.

Technology
Have students search the Internet for Web pages advertising trips to Venezuela. Are any of the sites written in Spanish? Students should print information from a Spanish-language site, skim it for phrases that they recognize and then share it with the class.

Teacher Resources

 Activity 8

 Activity 3

 Activity 4

 Activity 2

 Activities 2–3

Answers

7 Possible answers:
1. Debo
2. Tengo que
3. Debo
4. debo
5. Tengo que
6. Tengo que

8 1. Ellos deben ayudar a su madre
2. Mi hermana debe llamar....
3. Tengo que poner....
4. Debes cerrar siempre....

Activities

Cooperative Learning
Have students write three sentences stating they have to do something when they should be doing something else. Then have students work in small groups correcting one another's sentences and making appropriate changes. Inform students that groups have five minutes to make any necessary corrections, after which time you will select students from each group to read aloud their sentences. Example: *Sé que debo ayudar en la cocina, pero tengo que tocar el piano.*

Idioma

Estructura

Expressing obligations with *tener que* and *deber*

Use the expressions *tener que* (+ infinitive) and *deber* (+ infinitive) when you wish to express what someone is obligated to do. Whereas *tener que* (+ infinitive) indicates what someone has to do, *deber* (+ infinitive) implies more of a moral obligation or what someone should do.

Tengo que poner la mesa.	**I have to** set the table.
Debo ayudar a mi madre.	**I should (ought to)** help my mother.

 Práctica

7 *¿Debo o tengo que?*

Complete the following sentences with the correct form of *deber* or *tener que* as appropriate.

1. Mi padre tiene mucho que hacer en la cocina. __ ayudarlo.
2. __ comer todos los días para vivir.
3. Los refrescos están calientes y me gustan fríos. __ ponerlos en el refrigerador.
4. Para comer la comida caliente rápidamente __ usar el horno microondas y no la estufa.
5. Mañana hay un examen de historia. __ estudiar mucho hoy.
6. El fin de semana viajo a Colombia. __ tener un pasaporte.

8 *¿Deben hacerlo o tienen que hacerlo?*

Create sentences using the following cues and adding the appropriate form of either *deber* or *tener que*, according to what fits logically.

MODELOS lavar los platos mañana (Pedro)
Pedro tiene que lavar los platos mañana.

estudiar primero y hacer deportes después (los estudiantes)
Los estudiantes deben estudiar primero y hacer deportes después.

1. ayudar a su madre (ellos)
2. llamar a nuestra abuela (mi hermana)
3. poner los platos sucios en el lavaplatos (yo)
4. cerrar siempre la puerta del refrigerador (tú)

Los estudiantes deben estudiar.

Notes Point out that *deber* is a regular *-er* verb.

Students have already learned the various forms of *tener* in *Capítulo 5*. Do a quick review of the forms of *tener* at this time. Explain that the verbs *tener* and *venir* have this same stem change *e → ie*, except for the *yo* irregular forms of these two verbs *(tener: tengo; venir: vengo)*.

Remind students that when two verbs appear together (e.g., *tener que* + verb), the first is conjugated and the second must remain an infinitive.

 **Comunicación**

 9 Nuestras obligaciones

First, create a list of at least two things you must do and two things you should do this week. Then, in small groups, talk about your schedules and obligations.

MODELO   A: El jueves tengo que ir de compras.
         B: Por las tardes yo debo estudiar.

Estructura

Stem-changing verbs: e → ie

The verb *pensar* (to think) requires the spelling change e → ie in all forms of the present-tense stem except for *nosotros* and *vosotros*. Note, however, that this stem change does not affect the regular verb endings (*o, as, a, amos, áis, an*).

pensar (ie)	
pi**e**nso	pensamos
pi**e**nsas	pensáis
pi**e**nsa	pi**e**nsan

When combined with other words, *pensar* has several different uses:

- When followed immediately by an infinitive, *pensar* indicates what someone plans or intends to do.

  Pienso ir *a Venezuela.*   I plan to go to Venezuela.
  ¿Cuándo **piensas ir?**   When do you intend to go?

- When combined with *de*, *pensar* is used to ask for an opinion. Use *pensar* followed by *que* to express your opinion or thoughts.

  ¿Qué **piensas de** *los platos nuevos?*   What do you think of the new plates?
  Pienso que *son bonitos.*   I think they are pretty.

- *Pensar* may be combined with *en* to indicate whom or what someone is thinking about.

  ¿En qué **piensas?**   What are you thinking about?
  Pienso en *mi tarea de español.*   I am thinking about my spanish homework.

Pensar (ie) is just one of many e → ie stem-changing verbs. (The letters in parentheses after the infinitive are to help you identify these verbs and to indicate the change that occurs in the stem.) Others include the following: *cerrar (ie), empezar (ie), encender (ie), preferir (ie), querer (ie)* and *sentir (ie)*.

Note: The verb *empezar* is used with *a* when an infinitive follows, as in *Empiezo a estudiar* (I am beginning to study).

Notes   Explain to students that the letters *ie* shown in parentheses after infinitives listed in *Navegando 1B* serve as a help for students to remember how these verbs are formed: *cerrar (ie)*.

Note for students that the verbs *tener* and *venir* have this same stem change e → ie except for the *yo* irregular forms.

Comparisons. Note the distinction between *pensar* (to think) and *creer* (to believe). Tell students that the equivalent in Spanish for **I think so** is *Creo que sí* (I believe so). Likewise, to say **I don't think so**, they should use *Creo que no* (I don't believe so).

Teacher Resources

 Activity 4

 Activities 5–8

 Activity 3

 Activities 4–9

Answers

9 Creative self-expression.

Activities

Expansion
After completing activity 9, have a member of each group summarize the information for the class as a way of practicing the plural forms. *Dos personas en nuestro grupo tienen que hacer....; Todos nosotros debemos estudiar*, etc.

Students with Special Needs
Review the conjugation of -*ar* verbs before introducing the stem change e → ie.

Activities

Multiple Intelligences (spatial)
Make memory models to assist in learning the concept of the stem-changing verb. Divide the class into groups and assign each group to make a visual representation of the concept of the stem-changing verbs indicating which forms have the spelling change and which do not. (For example, draw a line around the forms that change and you see the shape of a shoe; then call it a **shoe verb**.)

Students with Special Needs
Have students write out the conjugation of several *e → ie* verbs.

✳ Práctica

◀ 10 ¿Qué piensan hacer?

Tell what these people are planning to do, using words from each column and the appropriate form of *pensar*. Verb forms may be repeated.

A	B	C
Juan y Raúl	pienso	hacer un almuerzo especial
unos amigos y yo	piensas	hacer arepas
yo	piensa	comer en el comedor
una amiga	pensamos	buscar los platos de todos los días
Ana y Eva	piensan	poner la mesa
tú		ayudar en la cocina

◀ 11 Un almuerzo especial

Completa el siguiente párrafo con la forma correcta de los verbos indicados entre paréntesis.

Paco y Aurora *1. (pensar)* hacer un almuerzo especial para su amiga María. Ella va a estudiar a Colombia por un año. Aurora *2. (pensar)* hacer unas arepas y Paco *3. (querer)* hacer un pollo con mole y una ensalada. Ellos *4. (empezar)* a hacer la comida muy temprano. Otros amigos *5. (pensar)* venir al almuerzo. Rafael *6. (venir)* y Carmen y José *7. (pensar)* venir también. Graciela lo *8. (sentir)* mucho, pero no *9. (venir)* al almuerzo porque tiene que estudiar. Pedro *10. (deber)* ayudar a sus padres en la casa y *11. (preferir)* venir después del almuerzo. Él *12. (querer)* decirle "adiós" a María. Y tú, ¿qué *13. (pensar)*? ¿*14. (venir)* al almuerzo?

◀ 12 ¡Somos diferentes!

Use the cues that follow to create sentences that compare and contrast how different Sara and Julio are from their parents.

MODELO empezar a oír música / empezar a leer
   Si nosotros empezamos a oír música, ellos empiezan a leer.

1. querer nadar en la playa / querer caminar en la playa
2. pensar ir al parque / pensar ir a un museo
3. encender el reproductor de CDs / encender el televisor
4. tener que hacer la tarea / tener que lavar los platos
5. querer comer en un restaurante / querer hacer arepas y comer en casa otra vez
6. cerrar la puerta / abrir las ventanas
7. preferir ir al cine / preferir ver un DVD en casa
8. empezar a mirar la televisión / empezar a escuchar la radio

¿Prefieres nadar o caminar en la playa? (Los Roques, Venezuela.)

Notes Although students have already seen the expression *lo siento,* in this chapter they are learning how to conjugate the entire present-tense conjugation of *sentir* and other stem-changing verbs.

Remind students that when a verb like *pensar* is followed by another verb, the second verb must be an infinitive.

13 Una fiesta

In pairs, take turns asking and answering questions about what your family and friends are thinking about, according to the illustrations, as you all prepare for a holiday dinner.

MODELO tu madre

A: ¿En qué piensa tu madre?
B: Mi madre piensa en la comida.

1. yo   2. Gloria   3. tus hermanos

4. Andrés y Camila   5. nosotros   6. tú

✦ Comunicación

14 Pensamos hacer mucho

In small groups, talk about some things you are planning to do next summer or at some time during your life. Be creative. You might also discuss what you think of each person's aspirations. Then decide what your remarks have in common. One student should report the results of your discussion to the class.

MODELO A: Pienso viajar a otro país. Quiero ir a Venezuela el verano que viene.
B: En el verano yo pienso ayudar a mis padres en casa y leer cien libros.
C: Pienso cantar con JLo en un concierto.

¡Oportunidades!

¿Piensas viajar a otro país?
Do you enjoy travel? Have you ever wondered what it might be like to live in another country? What if you were transferred to Venezuela to work? Do you think you would enjoy the experience? Do any members of your family live in another country? Would you like to visit them if they did? Can you think of any benefits your language skills might afford you while traveling?

Capítulo 6   *nueve* 9

Notes Spot-check student conversations for activities 13 and 14 for the appropriate forms of *pensar* and *querer*.

Note for students that the verb *querer* may mean **to want** or **to love**. Context will help make an intended message clear. Also,

remind students to use the *a personal* when using *querer* to refer to people: *Quiero **a** mis abuelos.*

Have students make a list of verbs with the stem change *e → ie*.

En la mesa

 Activity 5

 Activities 42–43

 Activities 9–11

 Activity 4

 Activities 10–12

Activities

Expansion

Use overhead transparencies 42 and 43 to introduce the new words and expressions in *Vocabulario II*. First, using transparency 42, point to the objects on the table and identify them in Spanish one at a time. Ask students to repeat after you. Then, using transparency 43, identify each vocabulary item in Spanish, allowing students to see how each object is spelled. As an alternative, use an actual table setting to introduce the new dinner-table vocabulary *(el plato, la taza, el tenedor,* etc.).

Vocabulario II
En la mesa

10   *diez*

Lección A

Notes Introduce the new vocabulary and reinforce the content of pages 10 and 11 by using overhead transparencies 42 and 43, the audio CD recording of *En la mesa* and other ancillaries listed under Teacher Resources at the top of these two pages. You can evaluate student progress using Quiz 4.

15 ¿Qué necesitas?

 Di lo que necesitas para hacer lo que oyes. *(Say what you need in order to do what you hear.)*

> MODELO Necesito una cuchara.

16 A la hora de comer

Completa las siguientes oraciones, según las ilustraciones.

> MODELO Pásame un <u>tenedor</u>, por favor.

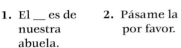

1. El __ es de nuestra abuela.

2. Pásame la __, por favor.

3. Necesito la __.

4. Pásame el __, por favor.

5. Me gusta la __ bien caliente.

6. Quiero más __ para la ensalada.

7. Necesitan unas __ para el postre.

8. Son las __ de los días especiales.

9. Quiero un __ de agua fría.

10. Los __ son muy bonitos.

17 ¿Qué vemos en el comedor?

 Working in pairs, take turns asking what your partner needs while you point to an item shown in the illustration *En la mesa*. Your partner then must ask you to pass the item to him or her.

> MODELO **A:** ¿Qué necesitas? ¿Qué quieres?
> **B:** Pásame el pan, por favor.

18 ¿Qué buscamos?

Create a drawing similar to the one in the illustration *En la mesa*, but with three items missing. Then, in pairs, take turns asking each other questions about which objects are missing (or not) from your illustration. List in Spanish the objects missing from your partner's illustration. Check to see if you guessed which objects were missing.

Capítulo 6

once 11

11

Answers

19 1. Julio quiere una cucharita.
2. Sí, le gusta.
3. La sopa necesita un poco más de sal.
4. No tiene una cuchara.
5. Le gusta la arepa.
20 Answers will vary.
21 1. C; 2. G; 3. A; 4. E; 5. D; 6. F; 7. B; 8. H

Activities

Expansion
Additional questions *(¿Qué recuerdas?)*: *¿Dónde están Julio, Sara y sus padres?*; *¿Quién es Sara?*

Additional questions *(Algo personal)*: *¿Come tu familia mucho en el comedor?*; *Si no comen en el comedor, ¿dónde comen Uds.?*

Prereading Strategy
Ask students to list things typically found in a kitchen and at the dinner table. Then instruct them to cover up the dialog with one hand and look at the photographs. Ask them to imagine where the conversation takes place and what the people are saying to one another. Finally, have students look through the dialog quickly to find cognates.

Diálogo II
¿Te gusta la sopa?

JULIO: Mamá, pásame esa cucharita, por favor.
MAMÁ: ¿Cuál? ¿Ésta?
JULIO: Sí, ésa mamá.

PAPÁ: Sara, ¿cómo está la sopa?
SARA: Me gusta, pero necesita un poco más de sal.
JULIO: Mira, aquí está la sal.

MAMÁ: ¿Y tú, amor? ¿Te gusta la sopa?
PAPÁ: No sé. No tengo cuchara.
MAMÁ: Lo siento. Aquí está.
PAPÁ: Esta arepa está buena.

19 ¿Qué recuerdas?

1. ¿Qué quiere Julio?
2. ¿Le gusta a Sara la sopa?
3. ¿Qué necesita un poco más de sal?
4. ¿Qué no tiene el papá?
5. ¿Qué le gusta al papá?

20 Algo personal

1. ¿Tiene comedor tu casa?
2. ¿Cómo es la mesa del comedor de tu casa?
3. ¿Qué sopa te gusta? Explica.

21 Yo necesito. . .

 Selecciona la letra de la frase que completa lógicamente cada oración que oyes. *(Select the letter of the phrase that logically completes each sentence you hear.)*

A. de agua mineral
B. sal
C. tenedor
D. el lavaplatos

E. arepas
F. sobre el pan caliente
G. una cuchara y un plato
H. mantel

¿Te gustan estos platos?

Mi casa tiene un comedor elegante.

 **Notes** Point out to students the lack of article in Spanish when using negative phrases: *No tengo cuchara.; No quiero postre.; Nunca como pan.*

Provide some of the following expressions as students discuss quantities at the table: *más* (more), *menos* (less), *mucho* (a lot), *poco* (a little), *un poco de sal* (a little salt), *un poquito* (very little), *un poco más/menos* (a little more/less).

Whereas *uno*, *mucho* and *poco* have masculine, feminine, singular and plural forms, *más*, *menos*, *un poco (de)* and *(ni) un poquito* require no additional changes in their forms.

Las arepas venezolanas

Arepas are perhaps the most common food in Venezuela. Originally they were made from corn that was ground to make corn meal. As with many everyday foods in the United States, however, *arepas* today are usually prepared using packaged, precooked white corn flour, salt and water. The resulting easy-to-make buns can be eaten alone or as a kind of bread to accompany a meal. *Arepas* can also be stuffed with meat, cheese, scrambled eggs or other fillings, much like *tortillas* or *empanadas*. Another very popular Venezuelan dish is *hallaca*, which is served in nearly every Venezuelan home at Christmas. This typical food consists of a corn-flour pie filled with pork, chicken, vegetables and spices. It is cooked in plantain leaves from a variety of bananas called *plátano*.

Las arepas son populares en Venezuela.

Preparando arepas.

De la cocina de _____

Las arepas
2 tazas de harina de maíz
2 cucharitas de sal
2 tazas de agua caliente

Preparación
Para empezar, poner la harina de maíz[1] en una taza grande y poco a poco poner el agua con sal. Luego, mezclar[2] el agua con la harina hasta que se convierta en masa. Después, dejar[3] la masa en reposo[4] por cinco minutos. Hacer con la masa unos rollos[5] de tres pulgadas[6] de diámetro y de una pulgada a dos pulgadas de ancho[7]. En una sartén[8] con un poco de aceite, freír[9] las arepas hasta ver los rollos dorados[10]. Después, poner las arepas en el horno a 350 grados para cocinar por aproximadamente treinta minutos, hasta tener arepas crujientes[11].

[1]corn flour [2]mix [3]leave [4]rest [5]rolls [6]inches [7]thick [8]frying pan [9]fry [10]golden [11]crunchy

22 Conexión con otras disciplinas: habilidades para la vida diaria

You can easily prepare the recipe at home for a taste of this typical Venezuelan bread. Look at the recipe for *arepas* and answer these questions.

1. ¿Cuáles son los ingredientes para hacer arepas?
2. ¿Qué debes hacer para empezar?
3. ¿Qué diámetro deben tener los rollos?
4. Después de hacer rollos con la masa, ¿qué debes hacer?
5. ¿A qué temperatura tiene que estar el horno?
6. ¿Cuánto tiempo deben estar las arepas en el horno?

Capítulo 6

trece 13

Teacher Resources

 Las arepas venezolanas
Activity 22

Activity 5

Answers

22 1. Los ingredientes son sal, harina de maíz y agua.
2. Para empezar, debo poner la harina de maíz en una taza grande y poco a poco poner el agua con sal.
3. Los rollos deben tener tres pulgadas de diámetro.
4. Debo poner un poco de aceite en una sartén para cocinar las arepas hasta ver los rollos dorados.
5. El horno tiene que estar a 350 grados.
6. Deben estar en el horno aproximadamente treinta minutos.

Activities

Multiple Intelligences (bodily-kinesthetic)
Have students prepare *arepas* using the recipe found in *Cultura viva*. Then they may share the *arepas* with the rest of the class.

Spanish for Spanish Speakers
Ask students to explain to the class (in Spanish) how to prepare their favorite dish. Make sure they give a detailed explanation.

 Notes The special flour made from ground corn is not cornmeal and is not available everywhere. Suggest students look for ground corn in a specialty foods store or a store that specializes in Hispanic foods.

Tell students the meaning of *habilidades para la vida diaria* (life skills).

Before students attempt to make *arepas* at home, point out that the shapes should not look like pancakes. The *arepas* should look more like small hamburger buns.

Activity 22 is a cross-curricular activity that addresses Spanish as well as cooking.

Activities

Critical Thinking

You can practice both demonstrative and possessive adjectives by providing several models and then cuing students with words to which they may respond: *Este libro es mi libro. Ese libro es tu libro. Aquel libro es su libro* (pointing to another student). Cue students with a variety of nouns that are masculine, feminine, singular and plural.

Idioma

Estructura

Pointing out someone or something: demonstrative adjectives

Use a demonstrative adjective *(adjetivo demostrativo)* before a noun to point out or draw attention to where someone or something is located in relation to yourself ("this house," "that car," etc.).

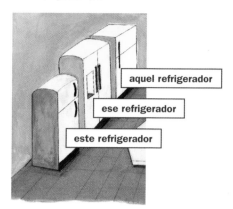

aquel refrigerador

ese refrigerador

este refrigerador

Los adjetivos demostrativos

singular		plural	
masculino	**femenino**	**masculino**	**femenino**
este vaso *(this glass)*	esta taza *(this cup)*	estos vasos *(these glasses)*	estas tazas *(these cups)*
ese vaso *(that glass)*	esa taza *(that cup)*	esos vasos *(those glasses)*	esas tazas *(those cups)*
aquel vaso *(that glass over there)*	aquella taza *(that cup over there)*	aquellos vasos *(those glasses over there)*	aquellas tazas *(those cups over there)*

When pointing out people or objects that are nearby, use *este, esta, estos* or *estas* (this/these). Use *ese, esa, esos* or *esas* (that/those) to draw attention to people or objects that are farther away. Call attention to people or objects that are even farther away ("over there") by using *aquel, aquella, aquellos* or *aquellas* (that/those over there).

near speaker *(aquí)*	Me gusta **este** *refrigerador.*	I like **this** refrigerator.
away from speaker *(allí)*	¿Te gustan **esos** *refrigeradores?*	Do you like **those** refrigerators?
far away from speaker *(allá)*	Prefiero **aquel** *refrigerador.*	I prefer **that** refrigerator **(over there).**

Notes Emphasize that *este, esta, estas* and *estos* in English mean **this/these**. *Ese, esa, esos* and *esas* mean **that/those** and *aquel, aquella, aquellos* and *aquellas* mean **that/those over there.**

The demonstrative pronouns will be taught in the *Navegando 2* textbook.

Tell students that demonstrative adjectives always precede the noun they modify.

 **Práctica**

23 ¡Otra cocina!

Completa las oraciones con la forma apropiada de *este*.

Quiero otra cocina para mi casa porque (1) cocina es muy fea. (2) paredes tienen un color muy triste. La puerta de (3) horno microondas no cierra. (4) fregadero es muy pequeño, necesito un fregadero doble. (5) refrigerador está muy viejo y (6) lavaplatos es muy malo. (7) luces no encienden y (8) lámpara es muy fea. No me gusta (9) mesa y (10) sillas son horribles.

24 ¿Qué vamos a poner en la mesa?

With a classmate, pretend you are discussing whether or not you need the following items as you are preparing the table for dinner. Answer each question negatively as shown in the model.

MODELO las servilletas verdes
A: ¿Quieres estas servilletas verdes?
B: No, no quiero esas servilletas verdes.

1. los cubiertos	4. el aceite	7. el cuchillo
2. el mantel	5. los platos de sopa	8. los vasos nuevos
3. la mantequilla	6. las tazas	9. la silla

25 ¿Qué prefieres?

Imagine you are in a department store buying kitchenware for your new house. Use the appropriate form of *este, ese* or *aquel* to say what items you prefer, based upon the cues shown in the illustration.

MODELO ¿Qué platos prefieres?
Prefiero esos platos.

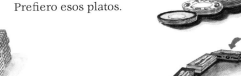

1. ¿Qué mantel prefieres? 2. ¿Qué cubiertos prefieres? 3. ¿Qué servilletas prefieres?

4. ¿Qué lámpara prefieres? 5. ¿Qué taza prefieres? 6. ¿Qué vasos prefieres?

Capítulo 6

quince 15

Teacher Resources

 Activity 24

Answers

23 1. esta; 2. Estas; 3. este;
4. Este; 5. Este; 6. este; 7. Estas;
8. esta; 9. esta; 10. estas

24 1. ¿Quieres estos cubiertos?/No, no quiero esos cubiertos.
2. ¿Quieres este mantel?/No, no quiero ese mantel.
3. ¿Quieres esta mantequilla?/No, no quiero esa mantequilla.
4. ¿Quieres este aceite?/No, no quiero ese aceite.
5. ¿Quieres estos platos de sopa?/No, no quiero esos platos de sopa.
6. ¿Quieres estas tazas?/No, no quiero esas tazas.
7. ¿Quieres este cuchillo?/No, no quiero ese cuchillo.
8. ¿Quieres estos vasos nuevos?/No, no quiero esos vasos nuevos.
9. ¿Quieres esta silla?/No, no quiero esa silla.

25 1. Prefiero este mantel.
2. Prefiero aquellos cubiertos.
3. Prefiero esas servilletas.
4. Prefiero aquella lámpara.
5. Prefiero esta taza.
6. Prefiero esos vasos.

Activities

Language through Action
Assemble several common kitchen items. Have students work in small groups to act out activity 24.

Notes Point out that the distinction among the demonstratives that many Spanish speakers make is to use forms of *este* for items near the speaker, forms of *ese* for items near the person spoken to and forms of *aquel* for items that are far from both.

15

Activities

Multiple Intelligences (spatial)
Locate and bring to class a map of
your state. Then ask students to
imagine that they are in an
airplane flying over the state as
they look at the map. Working in
pairs, have students identify
geographical sites (rivers, cities,
etc.) they might see from the air
and, then, say where they intend
to go *(pensar ir)* at some point in
their future.

❖ Comunicación

 26 Para la nueva casa de mi familia

Imagine you are with a friend in the store shown in the illustration. With a
classmate, discuss which items you are thinking about buying. Express your
preferences, ask each other's opinion and try to decide which things you
want to, have to or ought to buy.

MODELO **A:** ¿Qué piensas de estos cubiertos?
B: Prefiero aquellos cubiertos porque son más bonitos.

 27 En un restaurante en Caracas

During lunch with a friend in Caracas, you discuss your plans for the week.
Talk about some things you want to do, ought to do, have to do or prefer to do
each day this week. Make the conversation realistic by politely interrupting
one another, asking for things to be passed to you and commenting on things
and people you see.

MODELO **A:** El lunes tengo que ir con mi mamá a la tienda a mirar unas estufas
nuevas.
B: ¿Unas estufas?... ¡Ay, qué aburrido! Por favor, pásame esa cucharita.
A: Sí, cómo no.

Notes For simple activities, have
students write out the answers before
assigning students to work with a partner;
for more difficult activities, pair students
requiring additional help with stronger
students. Follow up some oral activities
(e.g., activity 27) by assigning a variation
of the exercise as written homework.

Comparisons. You may wish to explain to
students that demonstrative adjectives are
also used to indicate time in relation to
the present moment: *esta tarde* (**this**
afternoon); *esa tarde* (**that** afternoon);
aquella tarde (**that** afternoon **farther off
in the past**).

28 En el comedor

 Working in small groups, pretend you are having dinner together in your dining room in Venezuela. Each member of the group should make at least four questions or statements including some of the following: requests for items at the table, questions about what your friends think and need, comments about the food, questions about what your friends are going to do during the week, and so on. Be polite (use *por favor* and *gracias*).

MODELO
A: Pásame ese cuchillo y la mantequilla, por favor.
B: Aquí tienes. ¿Qué piensan de las arepas?
C: Están muy buenas, pero la ensalada necesita un poco de aceite.

¡Extra!

Más comida

el flan	caramel custard
el panecillo	bread roll
la papa	potato
el pastel (la torta)	cake
las verduras	vegetables

La comida está muy buena.

El plato.

El aceite.

Answers

28 Creative self-expression.

Activities

Cooperative Learning
Ask small groups of students to prepare a dinner menu featuring items from several Spanish-speaking countries. Possible sources of information include *Navegando 1B,* personal experiences, ethnic cookbooks and foreign exchange students in your school. Each group should share its menu with the class. As a follow-up activity, you may wish to identify a day or event when the students prepare and then bring sample menu items for tasting.

Notes Ask for volunteers or select several groups to present their dining-room conversations for the entire class. Consider bringing utensils and table items to class that students can use for role-playing.

If you or your students prepared *arepas* using the recipe in the *Cultura viva* on page 13, this would be a good time to share the recipe with the class.

Lectura cultural

Una deliciosa tradición

Es diciembre y, por toda Venezuela, muchas familias hacen las tradicionales hallacas. Es una vieja tradición y es el plato representativo de la Navidad venezolana. El origen de las hallacas viene de un plato de los indígenas llamado[1] Hayaco Iritari. La hallaca es similar a un tamal grande envuelto[2] en una hoja de plátano[3].

La mayoría de las familias hacen una fiesta de la preparación de las hallacas. En las cocinas, se reúnen[4] parientes y amigos para participar en este animado proceso. Mientras que[5] escuchan la gaita — ritmo típico venezolano — todos en la cocina ayudan en la labor, desde lavar[6] las hojas donde se pone la masa[7] hasta amarrar[8] las hallacas.

El proceso es laborioso[9] porque la preparación es elaborada y porque se preparan muchas para almacenar[10] en el refrigerador y comer durante todo el mes de diciembre.

Cuando los venezolanos piensan en la Navidad, piensan en hallacas.

Cuando comes hallaca, tienes que abrir la hoja de plátano. Comes la masa con un tenedor. No debes comer la hoja. Muchas personas prefieren comer las hallacas con pan.

[1]called [2]wrapped [3]plantain/banana leaf [4]get together [5]While [6]from washing
[7]dough [8]tie [9]tedious [10]to store

29 ¿Qué recuerdas?

Completa las siguientes oraciones.

1. En Venezuela, el plato típico de la Navidad es...
2. El nombre *hallaca* viene de...
3. La hallaca es como un...
4. La preparación de hallacas es...
5. . . . se reúnen en la cocina para ayudar a hacer hallacas.

• How do Venezuelans make the preparation of *hallacas* fun? Describe something your family or your acquaintances do that is also hard work yet fun.

30 Algo personal

1. ¿Cuál es un plato representativo de la Navidad en los Estados Unidos? Compara ese plato con las hallacas de Venezuela.
2. ¿Se reúnen tu familia o tus amigos en la cocina? ¿Qué hacen?
3. ¿Preparan en tu casa un plato que tiene un proceso laborioso? ¿Cómo dividen la labor?

18 *dieciocho*

Lección A

Notes Encourage students to find out more about Venezuela by going to the following Web sites:

The Venezuela Online Tour
http://www.ve.net/travel/
Electronic Embassy
http://www.embassy.org

Organization of American States
http://www.oas.org
general travel information
http://www.expedia.com

¿Qué aprendí?

Autoevaluación
As a review and self-check, respond to the following:

Visit the web-based activities at www.emcp.com

1. Name three items you might see on the table while having dinner with a Venezuelan family in Caracas.

2. You are in charge of preparing dinner. Tell the people helping you three things they have to do or should do to help you.

3. What might you say to ask a friend what he or she is thinking about?

4. Ask two friends what they are thinking about doing this Saturday.

5. Say that you like *arepas* but that you prefer bread with butter.

6. Imagine you are seated at the dining-room table and the glass and silverware you need are far away from you, near your friend. How can you ask your friend politely to pass you that glass and that silverware?

7. Name two typical Venezuelan dishes.

Palabras y expresiones

En la cocina
el aceite
el azúcar
la cocina
los cubiertos
la cuchara
la cucharita
el cuchillo
la estufa
el fregadero
el horno microondas
el lavaplatos
la luz
el mantel
la mantequilla
la mesa
el pan

la pimienta
el plato
el postre
el refrigerador
la sal
la servilleta
la sopa
la taza
el tenedor
el vaso

Otras expresiones
allá
aquel, aquella
   (aquellos, aquellas)
el comedor
la cosa

de todos los días
después
entonces
ese, esa (esos, esas)
especial
este, esta (estos, estas)
la lámpara
otra vez
pensar de/en/que
un poco de
poner la mesa
ya

Verbos
ayudar
cerrar (ie)
deber
empezar (ie)
encender (ie)
pásame
pensar (ie)
poner
preferir (ie)
querer (ie)
sentir (ie)
tener que
viajar

Una taza.

Los cubiertos.

Teacher Resources

- Activity 16

- Information Gap Activities
  Postcard Activities
  Funciones de Comunicación

Answers

Autoevaluación
Possible answers:
1. Hay un mantel, unas servilletas y unos vasos.
2. Deben encender las luces. Tienen que poner la mesa. Tienen que ayudar con la comida.
3. ¿En qué piensas?
4. ¿Qué piensan hacer este sábado?
5. Me gustan las arepas, pero prefiero el pan con mantequilla.
6. Pásame ese vaso y esos cubiertos, por favor.
7. arepas, hallacas, ropa vieja, cachapas

Activities

Communities
Ask small groups of students to identify interesting professions involving Spanish. In turn, they should discuss the requirements and obligations of this job by using the expressions *tener que* (+ infinitive) and *deber* (+ infinitive). Have students share their conclusions with the class.

Notes Talk with the class about Venezuela's national hero, Simón Bolívar (1783–1830). This diplomat and military leader was born in Caracas. He was a Pan-American and helped liberate Bolivia, Ecuador, Colombia, Peru and Venezuela from Spain. Bolivia was named after him.

The monetary unit of Venezuela, *el bolívar,* is named after the national hero Simón Bolívar.

Teacher Resources

 La casa de Julián

 Activity 1

 Activities 44–45

 Activities 1–3

 Activity 1

 Activities 1–4

> **Content reviewed in *Lección B***
> • noun/adjective agreement
> • present tense of regular verbs
> • the verbs *deber* and *querer*
> • family

Activities

Critical Listening
Play the audio CD of the letter. Tell students to listen for the main ideas the speaker is addressing. Finally, have several individuals state what they believe is the main theme of the reading.

Expansion
You may want to ask some of the following questions about the letter: *¿Cuál es la fecha de la carta?; ¿Dónde está Cartagena?; ¿De dónde son Daniela y Santiago?; ¿Qué no le gusta a Daniela?; ¿Adónde van a viajar Daniela y Santiago con su tío?; ¿Cuándo va a llamar Daniela a sus padres?; ¿Qué escribe Jorge para terminar la carta?*

Lección B
Colombia

Vocabulario I
La casa de Julián

Cartagena, 15 de agosto

Hola papás,
¿Qué tal? Escribo desde Cartagena. Cartagena es una ciudad muy bonita e interesante. Cada día le gusta más a Daniela la idea de vivir aquí, pero también le gustaría vivir con Uds. en Caracas.
La casa del primo Julián es muy cómoda. Aquí va el dibujo de la casa donde vive él. Entramos en la casa por una puerta en el patio. El cuarto de Daniela está al lado de la cocina. Tiene unas ventanas pequeñas. Yo estoy en el cuarto de Julián. Cuando yo estoy aburrido, voy a la sala a ver televisión. Por las noches siempre comemos en el patio.
Mi tío dice que en dos semanas vamos a ir a Barranquilla. Vamos a pasar siete u ocho días allí en la casa de su tía Isabel. Allá vamos a montar a caballo. Tenemos muchas ganas de ir.
A Daniela no le gusta escribir cartas. Entonces, ella los va a llamar por teléfono en estos días.

un abrazo,

Santiago

el primer piso

la planta baja

la escalera

pequeña

grande

Santiago escribe una carta.

el cuarto de Daniela

las plantas

el garaje

el baño

la cocina

el patio

el cuarto de Julián

el cuarto de los padres

la sala

el comedor

la piscina

Notes Remind students that when two verbs are combined in one sentence, the first verb is conjugated and the second verb is usually an infinitive.

Cultures. Note that Daniela and Santiago are visiting a cousin in Colombia. In the Spanish-speaking world it is common to spend vacation time with extended family members.

Point out several characteristics of informal letter writing in Spanish. The month is not capitalized; the most popular salutation is *Querido(s)* or *Querida(s)* plus one or more names; common farewells include *un abrazo; un fuerte abrazo; besos.*

1 Dictado

 Escucha la información y escribe lo que oyes.

2 ¿Dónde están?

Look at these illustrations and tell what Santiago and Daniela's relatives are doing somewhere in their house in Cartagena.

MODELO   su abuela
Su abuela come en el patio.

1. su prima pequeña
2. su abuelo
3. su primo Julián
4. su tío
5. su tía

3 ¿Adónde deben ir?

Read the statements and say where the people should go.

MODELO   Quiero un vaso de agua.
Debes ir a la cocina.

1. Mi hermana quiere buscar una naranja y un refresco.
2. Mis padres necesitan usar el carro.
3. Yo tengo ganas de ver televisión.
4. Mis abuelos están aquí para comer con la familia.
5. Mi hermana viene de jugar al fútbol.
6. Voy a leer y escuchar CDs.

4 Conexión con otras disciplinas: dibujo

Create a blueprint (or make a pop-up) of the floor plan of your home and label the rooms in Spanish. Make up the information if you wish. Then write at least five sentences in Spanish that describe your blueprint. For example, state if the blueprint is of a house *(casa)* or an apartment *(apartamento)*, how large it is, the number and type of rooms, etc.

Capítulo 6

veintiuno 21

Teacher Resources

 Activities 1 and 3

Answers

1 Play a portion of the recorded letter and have students write what they hear. As an alternative, you may choose to read the selection yourself. Check the accuracy of student spelling.

2 Possible answers:
1. Su prima pequeña juega en el garaje.
2. Su abuelo lee el periódico en el comedor.
3. Su primo Julián juega en el cuarto con la computadora.
4. Su tío lee un libro en la sala.
5. Su tía ve televisión en la cocina.

3 Possible answers:
1. Debe ir a la cocina.
2. Deben ir al garaje.
3. Debes ir a la sala.
4. Deben ir al comedor.
5. Debe ir al baño.
6. Debes ir al patio/a tu cuarto.

4 Creative writing practice.

Activities

Critical Thinking
Ask students to think of typical activities in different parts of a house. Mention various rooms/areas and ask the students to explain what they do there.

Notes **Comparisons.** Note that the concept of *casa* may vary among cultures and even among Spanish speakers. For example, a home for a family in an urban area may be an apartment or a condominium in a multiresidence building. In other cases, a home may be a freestanding structure with a yard and a garage.

Additional words students might want to use when talking about their home: *el ático/el desván* (attic), *el apartamento* (apartment), *el jardín* (garden, yard), *el sótano* (basement), *el techo* (ceiling), *el tejado* (roof).

21

La casa de Elisa
Activities 5–7

Answers

5 1. Juan dice que la casa de
       Elisa es grande.
   2. Rosa tiene ganas de ir a la
      casa de Elisa.
   3. A Javier le gustaría mucho
      verla.
   4. La casa de Elisa es grande e
      interesante.
   5. Tiene tres pisos.
   6. Tiene siete u ocho cuartos.

6 Answers will vary.

7 1. Está en la casa.
   2. Está en el colegio.
   3. Está en la casa.
   4. Está en el parque.
   5. Está en la casa.
   6. Está en la casa.
   7. Está en el colegio.
   8. Está en la casa.

Activities

Critical Listening
Play the audio CD version of the
dialog. Tell students to listen for
the main ideas. They should then
summarize them for the class.

Multiple Intelligences
(spatial/linguistic)
Have students draw a plan of
their dream house and label all
the rooms and items in it.

Diálogo I

La casa de Elisa

JAVIER: Juan dice que la casa de
Elisa es muy grande.
ROSA: Sí, yo tengo ganas de ir a
su casa.
JAVIER: A mí también me
gustaría mucho verla.
ROSA: ¡Vamos mañana!

JAVIER: Mira, allí está Juan.
ROSA: Oye, Juan, ¿cómo es la
casa de Elisa?
JUAN: Es una casa grande e
interesante. Tiene tres pisos.

ROSA: ¡Qué grande!
JUAN: Sí, tiene siete u ocho
cuartos, dos salas y una piscina.
JAVIER: ¡Es la casa ideal!
ROSA: ¿Ideal? No pienso eso,
prefiero casas pequeñas.

5 ¿Qué recuerdas?

1. ¿Quién dice que la casa de Elisa es grande?
2. ¿Quién tiene ganas de ir a la casa de Elisa?
3. ¿A quién le gustaría mucho ver la casa de Elisa?
4. ¿Cómo es la casa de Elisa?
5. ¿Cuántos pisos tiene la casa de Elisa?
6. ¿Y cuántos cuartos tiene?

6 Algo personal

1. ¿Cómo es tu casa ideal?
2. ¿Te gustan las casas grandes o pequeñas? Explica.

> **¡Extra!**
>
> **Las palabras *e* y *u***
>
> Before words that begin with *i* or *hi*, the word *y*
> becomes *e*. Similarly, the word *o* changes to *u*
> before words that begin with *o* or *ho*.
>
> *Marcos **e** Inés viven en Cartagena.*
> *Dicen que van a montar a caballo mañana **u** otro*
> *día.*

7 ¿Está en la casa, en el colegio o en el parque?

 Di dónde están las siguientes personas según lo que oyes.

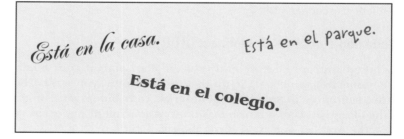

Está en la casa.   *Está en el parque.*

Está en el colegio.

Notes Point out that *gustaría* is the
conditional tense of the verb *gustar*. (The
conditional tense will not be taught until
level 2.) Tell students they can use this
form of the verb with the indirect object
pronouns *(me, te, le, nos, les)* to say what
people would or would not like, as Javier
does in the dialog.

Students have already learned to use the
indirect object pronouns with *gusta* and
gustan. Give them examples of indirect
object pronouns used with *gustaría*: *¿Te
gustaría ir a Venezuela?; A mi hermana le
gustaría hacer un viaje.*

Cultura viva

Colombia

Bogotá, Colombia.

The Spaniards founded *Cartagena de Indias* on the northwest coast of Colombia in 1533. Pirates frequently attacked the port seeking gold and other valuables, so a wall was constructed around the city as a means of defense. The wall *(la muralla)* remains today, one of the symbols of colonial times in Colombia. The capital, *Bogotá*, was founded in 1538. The city is vibrant and modern today, but you can catch a glimpse of the country's extensive history if you visit the exceptional *Museo del Oro* (Gold Museum), which holds over 30,000 pieces of pre-Columbian gold.

Colombia has a varied terrain, consisting of mountains, tropical jungles, plains, lowlands and a lengthy coastline that touches on two oceans. The country's climate does not change with the seasons but rather is determined by Colombia's elevations. Whereas the

Cartagena, Colombia.

Máscara de oro en el Museo del Oro, Bogotá.

lowlands and the coastal areas offer a tropical climate, such as you might experience when visiting the beautiful city of *Cartagena,* the temperature in the capital ranges between fifty and seventy degrees all year long.

Most people know that Colombia is famous for producing large quantities of excellent coffee, but not everyone knows it is a major exporter of emeralds. The country is also famous for its music, including the distinctive dance rhythms of *la cumbia, el porro, el merecumbé* and the accordion accompaniment of songs known as *vallenatos.* Visit Colombia sometime and experience this South American jewel!

8 ¿Qué sabes de Colombia?

Tell whether the statements are *cierto* or *falso*.

1. Colombia está en América Central.
2. Cartagena es una ciudad muy nueva.
3. El clima en Colombia es determinado por la elevación.
4. Cartagena es un símbolo del período colonial.
5. Cali es la capital del país.
6. Colombia es famosa por el café, las esmeraldas y la música.

9 Conexiones con otras disciplinas: geografía

Create a map of Colombia that shows major cities and rivers, mountains and surrounding countries.

Capítulo 6

veintitrés 23

Notes Explain that in Colombia, coffee is the primary agricultural export product. Point out that many people are employed in this important industry. Also note that Colombian exports include many other important products such as coal, minerals, flowers and 95 percent of the world's emeralds.

The majority of the people in Colombia live in large cities, such as *Santa Fe de Bogotá, Medellín, Cali, Barranquilla, Cartagena* and *Bucaramanga*. Other towns with interesting names are *Anapoima, Facatativá, Tocaima, Cúcuta, Armenia* and *Popayán*.

23

Idioma

Estructura

Telling what someone says: *decir*

The present tense of *decir* (to say, to tell) has an irregular *yo* form and requires a stem change for all forms except *nosotros/as* and *vosotros/as*. Use *decir* to tell what someone says.

decir	
digo	decimos
dices	decís
dice	dicen

When you are summarizing what someone says, use *que* between *decir* and the expression or phrase that follows:

¿Qué dice Javier?
*Dice **que** la casa de Elisa es muy grande.*

What does Javier say?
He says (**that**) Elisa's house is very big.

Práctica

10 ¿Qué dicen?

What might the response be to what the following people say?

MODELO ¿Cómo te llamas? (Ramiro)
Ramiro dice "Me llamo Ramiro".

1. Estoy enfermo. (yo)
2. Hoy es mi cumpleaños. (nosotros)
3. No hay luz en mi casa. (Uds.)
4. ¿Te gustan mis plantas? (tú)
5. Voy a comprar una casa con una piscina muy grande. (ellas)
6. ¡Aló¡ ¿Puedo hablar con Daniela? (Daniela)

Me llamo Ramiro.

11 Una encuesta

Results of a poll show who would like to spend the summer in Colombia as part of an exchange program with a high school in Cartagena. Summarize whether the indicated people say they would like to participate or not.

MODELO Julia
Julia dice que no.

1. Ud.
2. Raúl y la señorita García
3. el señor Gaviria y César
4. Sara
5. la señora Sosa y Eva
6. Ernesto y yo

Viaje de Intercambio		
Sí	No	
☑	☐	Sara
☑	☐	yo
☑	☐	Ernesto
☑	☐	la señorita García
☑	☐	Raúl
☐	☑	Julia
☑	☐	Enrique
☐	☑	Eva
☐	☑	Ud.
☐	☑	el señor Gaviria
☐	☑	la señora Sosa
☐	☑	César

⬥ Comunicación

12 En tu casa

In groups, discuss your homes *(casa or apartamento)* and weekly activities. What is similar and what is different about the homes, your routines and your lives in general? You may wish to include some of the following activities in your discussion: *comer, escribir cartas, leer* and *ver televisión*. Make up any information you would like. Take notes as you talk and report what you discuss to the class.

MODELO
A: ¿Dónde come tu familia?
B: Comemos en la cocina. ¿Y Uds.?
A: Nosotros comemos mucho en restaurantes. En casa comemos en la sala y vemos televisión.
C: En mi casa comemos en la sala, pero no los domingos. Los domingos comemos en el comedor.
A: B dice que su familia come en la cocina. C dice que en su casa comen en la sala, pero no los domingos. Mi familia come mucho en restaurantes, pero en casa comemos en la sala y vemos televisión.

Nosotros comemos en el comedor.

Estructura

Expressing wishes with *querer* or *gustaría*

You have learned to express someone's wishes by using a form of *querer* and an infinitive. You can also express wishes by combining *me, te, le, nos, os* or *les* with the more polite but less emphatic *gustaría* and an infinitive.

Quiero viajar a Colombia.	**I want to travel** to Colombia.
Me gustaría viajar a Colombia.	**I would like to travel** to Colombia.
Quieren comprar una estufa nueva.	They **want to buy** a new stove.
Les gustaría comprar una estufa nueva.	They **would like to buy** a new stove.

 **Práctica**

13 Una casa nueva

Choose a word or expression from each column and create complete sentences telling what members of the Martínez family want when they buy a new house.

MODELO Nosotros queremos comprar una casa grande.

A	B
yo	quieren tener cuartos en el primer piso
a ti	te gustaría tener un cuarto en la planta baja
mi hermano	les gustaría tener un garaje para dos carros
a mis padres	queremos comprar una casa grande ✔
a nosotros	me gustaría tener plantas en el patio
a mí	quiero tener una piscina
mis hermanas	nos gustaría tener un comedor cómodo
nosotros ✔	quiere una cocina con un lavaplatos

14 ¿Qué te gustaría?

Completa las oraciones de una manera original.

MODELO Me gustaría tener...
Me gustaría tener una casa grande.

1. No me gustaría vivir....
2. Me gustaría viajar....
3. No me gustaría ir....
4. Me gustaría vivir....
5. Me gustaría comprar....
6. Me gustaría ir....

Me gustaría tener una casa grande.

Notes Remind students that they may need to add *a* (plus a person's name or a pronoun) or *a mí, a ti, a él, a ella, a Ud., a nosotros, a nosotras, a vosotros, a vosotras, a ellos, a ellas, a Uds.* to clarify the meaning of *gustaría: A mis padres les gustaría comprar un refrigerador nuevo.*

Encourage students to make up funny or out-of-the-ordinary sentences for activity 14.

15 Comparaciones

 Write a paragraph of four or five sentences describing the wishes, intentions and obligations of people you know well, using *gustaría*, *pensar*, *preferir* and *querer*. Then exchange your paper with a partner and take turns asking and answering questions about what each of you wrote.

MODELO **A:** ¿Adónde les gustaría ir a tus padres?
B: A mis padres les gustaría ir a Bogotá para ver a mis abuelos.

> Mis padres quieren viajar a Colombia en julio. Les gustaría ver a mis abuelos en Bogotá. Un día pienso vivir en Bogotá, pero tengo que terminar las clases en el colegio.

 Comunicación

16 Encuesta

 Complete a survey about what rooms and furnishings your classmates would like to have in their ideal house (*casa ideal*). Talk with at least two other people and, then, compare the information you obtained with a partner. Finally, one of you should report your survey results to the class.

MODELO **A:** ¿Cómo es tu casa ideal?
B: Me gustaría tener una casa grande de dos pisos.
C: Yo prefiero una casa cómoda de un piso y también quiero tener una piscina.
A: **B** dice que le gustaría tener una casa grande con dos pisos, pero **C** dice que prefiere una casa cómoda de un piso y tener una piscina.

17 ¿Cómo es tu casa?

 In Spanish, write several statements describing your home, what you or someone in your family would like to buy for the house and where you would like to live in the future (*el futuro*). Then, based on what you have written in small groups, talk about the homes. Try to use some of the alternative words suggested in the *Estrategia* during the discussion. You might talk about such things as the number of rooms, what you like or do not like, where the home is located and whether or not there is something you would like to buy for the house. Add details making up any of the information you wish.

MODELO **A:** ¿Cómo es tu casa?
B: Es muy grande. Tiene cinco piezas y cada pieza tiene un cuarto de baño. También tiene dos salas y un comedor grande. A mis padres les gustaría comprar una mesa grande para el comedor.
C: Pues, mi casa es pequeña. Tiene seis cuartos: dos alcobas, un baño, una sala, un comedor y una cocina.

Estrategia

Recognizing words in context
Words and expressions you read and hear in Spanish vary from speaker to speaker and from one country to another. You may hear *cuarto, habitación* and *pieza* are all used to refer to a **room.** For the word **bedroom** you may see the words *alcoba, dormitorio, habitación, pieza, recámara* and *cuarto de dormir* (literally, a **room for sleeping**), which is sometimes shortened to *cuarto.* However, you should not confuse this shortened form of *cuarto* for the expression *cuarto de baño* (bathroom), which is usually shortened to *baño.* Knowing that these differences exist will help you in your goal of becoming fluent in Spanish. Always keep in mind that your goal is communication.

Capítulo 6

veintisiete **27**

Notes Note that activity 15 has two parts. First students must write sentences that use *gustaría* or a form of *pensar*, *preferir* or *querer*; then they must have a conversation with a classmate about what they wrote.

Read and discuss the *Estrategia* with students before assigning activities 16 and 17. Encourage students to use context to determine meaning as they converse.

Un día en casa

 Activity 5

 Activity 46

 Activity 8

 Activity 4

 Activities 7–8

Activities

Prereading Strategy

Have students look at the illustration and determine what the people are doing. Inform them that what the people are saying matches their actions. Next, ask students to look at each speech bubble and look for cognates and other words they recognize. Finally, ask students to guess what each person is saying.

TPR

Write the expressions from the illustration *Un día en casa* on separate pieces of paper. Have students select one of the pieces of paper at random. Call on several students to act out the expressions while classmates guess what the expressions are.

28 *veintiocho*   **Lección B**

Notes Review the forms of the verb *tener* prior to introducing the *tener* expressions.

Comparisons. Compare the expressions using *tener* (+ noun) and meaning **to be** (+ adjective) with English equivalents. Examples: *tengo hambre* = **I am hungry;** *tengo miedo* = **I am afraid.** Then remind students that in Spanish, some expressions use *estar* (+ adjective) whereas others may use *tener* (+ noun).

Use support materials indicated under Teacher Resources at the top of the page to introduce and practice words and expressions in *Vocabulario II*.

Tengo dieciséis años.

Eso es mentira.
Debes pedir perdón.

Yo tengo
quince años.

Sí, lo siento.
Es una mentira.
Tengo treinta años.

Clara dice la verdad.

Guillermo quiere decir
que prefiere ser joven.

Lo siento. Eres
muy pequeño.

"Lo siento. Eres
muy pequeño."

El chico pide prestado
el carro de su hermano.

La chica repite lo que
dice su hermano.

18 ¿Cierto o falso?

 Di si lo que oyes es cierto o falso, según la información en el Vocabulario II.
Si es falso, di lo que es cierto.

19 Un día en casa

With a classmate, take turns asking and answering the following questions,
according to the illustration.

MODELO **A:** ¿Qué tiene Cristina?
         B: Cristina tiene prisa.

1. ¿Qué tiene Nicolás?
2. ¿Qué tiene Rogelio?
3. ¿Quién tiene mucha sed?
4. ¿Quién tiene frío?

5. ¿Qué tiene Mateo?
6. ¿Quién tiene mucha hambre?
7. ¿Quiénes tienen mucho calor?
8. ¿Qué tienes tú?

Marisela tiene hambre.

Notes Play the audio CD version of
activity 18 for listening comprehension
practice or read the activity using
the transcript that appears in the
ATE introduction.

Teacher Resources

 Activities 18–19

 Activities 9–10

Answers

18 Possible answers:
1. Falso. Nicolás tiene sueño.
2. Cierto.
3. Falso. El abuelo dice que
   tiene frío.
4. Falso. Los tíos tienen calor.
5. Cierto.
6. Cierto.

19 1. Nicolás tiene sueño.
2. Rogelio tiene poca hambre.
3. La abuela tiene mucha sed.
4. El abuelo tiene frío.
5. Mateo tiene ganas de
   correr.
6. Verónica tiene mucha
   hambre.
7. Los tíos tienen mucho
   calor.
8. Tengo....

Activities

Critical Thinking
See if students can use an
appropriate *tener* expression to
make a statement about the
following situations: *1) Carlitos
tiene nueve años. Está en casa solo
y son las 11:00 de la noche. 2) Son
las 2:30 de la mañana pero Juan no
va a su cuarto. Tiene mucho trabajo
y está cansado. 3) Don Pedro está
en el desierto del Sahara y es el
mediodía. 4) El señor Vega está en
Alaska en febrero. 5) Marisol busca
algo de comer pero no hay nada en
la casa.*

Activities

Critical Listening
Play the audio CD recording of the dialog. Instruct students to cover the words as they listen to the conversation to develop good listening skills before concentrating on reading Spanish. Have students look at the photographs and imagine what the people are doing. Ask several individuals to state what they believe is the main theme of the conversation. Finally, ask if students know where the conversation takes place.

Diálogo II
Tengo mucho calor

JAVIER: Tengo mucho calor.
ROSA: Ya estamos cerca de la casa de Elisa.
JAVIER: También tengo mucha sed.
ROSA: ¡Allí está la casa de Elisa!

ROSA: ¡Qué grande y bonita es tu casa!
ELISA: Muchas gracias. Es tu casa también.
JAVIER: A Rosa no le gusta tu casa.
ROSA: Mentira, Elisa. No es verdad.

JAVIER: Pero dices que te gustan las casas pequeñas.
ROSA: Lo que digo es que prefiero una casa pequeña.
ELISA: Está bien. Yo comprendo. ¡Vamos a la playa!
JAVIER: Buena idea. Tengo mucho calor.

20 ¿Qué recuerdas?

1. ¿Quién tiene mucho calor?
2. ¿Quién tiene mucha sed?
3. ¿De quién es la casa grande y bonita?
4. ¿Es verdad que a Rosa no le gusta la casa de Elisa?
5. ¿Adónde quiere ir Elisa?

21 Algo personal

1. ¿Tienes calor? ¿Y sed?
2. ¿Dices mentiras? Explica.
3. ¿Adónde vas cuando hace mucho calor?

22 ¿Qué tienen?

 Selecciona la ilustración apropiada que corresponda con lo que oyes.

A   **B**   **C**   **D**   **E**   **F**

Notes Explain that Elisa's statement *Es tu casa también* is an expression of courtesy to make Rosa feel at home.

The activities that follow the dialog are recorded and can be found in the Audio CD Program. Student answer sheets for activity 22 are located in the back of the Audio CD Program Manual.

Cultura viva

¡Hogar, dulce hogar!

Homes in Spanish-speaking parts of the world are like castles in sentiment, if not in actual size. They offer a private refuge from the outside world and vary in their styles to reflect individual tastes, customs and availability of construction materials. Homes in rural areas are often small and simple, whereas homes in large cities and suburbs can be large and impressive. Interestingly, many Hispanic families in metropolitan areas live in

Una casa grande en Cartagena.

Esta casa tiene un patio bonito.

front yard. These homes traditionally have a patio at the back or the center of the residence that offers privacy and a place to relax among plants, birds and, sometimes, even small trees and beautiful fountains. In addition, older homes often have a flat roof *(la azotea)*, which may be accessible by stairs, usually from the patio or a room near the back of the home. The *azotea* is sometimes used for hanging the laundry to dry or growing flowers and herbs, and even some vegetables, in pots. Today, *chalets* (e.g., houses with yards that resemble homes in the United States) are becoming popular, especially on the outskirts of some cities in part because city apartments and condos are becoming prohibitively expensive for most middle class families.

apartment buildings or condos, which they may own instead of renting. These homes can have as many as four or five bedrooms, a balcony, two bathrooms, a kitchen and a living room. In some older Hispanic neighborhoods, homes often adjoin the sidewalk, leaving little or no room for a

Una casa en México.

2\3 ¡Hogar, dulce hogar!

Write five sentences stating what you know about homes in the Spanish-speaking world.

24 Nuestras casas

Compare housing in the United States with what you know about homes in the Spanish-speaking world.

Capítulo 6   *treinta y uno* **31**

Teacher Resources

 Activity 5

Answers

2\3 Possible answers:
1. Home is a private place reserved for family and close friends.
2. Rural homes are often smaller and simpler than city homes.
3. Many Hispanic families in metropolitan areas live in apartment buildings or condos.
4. A patio offers a private place where families can relax amongst plants, birds and fountains.
5. Houses on the outskirts of town are becoming popular in part due to their lower cost.

24 Answers will vary.

Activities

Cooperative Learning
Working in pairs, have students take turns naming the rooms of a house as the partner makes a sketch of what he or she hears. Students may choose to describe the house more fully if they wish.

31

Answers

25 1. vivimos; 2. tenemos;
3. tiene; 4. prefiero;
5. quiere; 6. gustan;
7. estudio; 8. dice;
9. tenemos; 10. escribe;
11. escriben; 12. pienso;
13. Quiero

Activities

Cooperative Learning

Have students work in pairs to practice asking and answering questions using the *tú* and *yo* forms of several verbs (make sure they use the rising intonation of questions). Student A could ask *¿Comes ...?; ¿Corres ...?; ¿Comprendes ...?;* etc. Student B would then respond affirmatively to each question *(Sí, como ...)*. After all verbs have been covered, Student A again asks the questions and Student B responds negatively *(No, no corro ...)*. Then have students change roles.

Critical Thinking

For additional practice with *-ar*, *-er* and *-ir* verbs, have students prepare a list of seven or eight things they do during the week. They may use the following verbs and any other verbs they have learned: *caminar, cantar, comer, correr, estudiar, hablar, hacer, ir, leer, nadar* and *ver*. Then, working in pairs, have students talk about their lists of activities and take turns asking and answering when they do each activity listed.

Idioma

Repaso rápido: regular present-tense verbs

You are already familiar with how to conjugate regular verbs:

hablar		comer		vivir	
hablo	hablamos	como	comemos	vivo	vivimos
hablas	habláis	comes	coméis	vives	vivís
habla	hablan	come	comen	vive	viven

25 La familia de Elisa

Completa el siguiente párrafo con las formas apropiadas de los verbos entre paréntesis.

Me llamo Elisa y soy la amiga de Javier y Rosa. Mis padres y yo 1. *(vivir)* en Cartagena, Colombia. Nosotros 2. *(tener)* una casa muy grande. La casa 3. *(tener)* cinco cuartos y cuatro baños. Yo 4. *(preferir)* tener una casa más pequeña. Mi madre también 5. *(querer)* una casa un poco más pequeña. Mi padre es de San José, California, y le 6. *(gustar)* las casas grandes y cómodas. Ahora yo 7. *(estudiar)* inglés en el colegio. Mi padre 8. *(decir)* que yo hablo muy bien el inglés. Mis hermanos y yo 9. *(tener)* ganas de ir a Estados Unidos. Mi papá tiene mucha familia en California—sus padres, seis hermanos, tres tíos y quince primos. Él les 10. *(escribir)* muchos mensajes por correo electrónico a ellos, pero ellos 11. *(escribir)* muy poco. Yo 12. *(pensar)* que para Navidad vamos a California. 13. *(Querer)* conocer a la familia de mi padre.

¿Tienes ganas de ir a Cartagena, Colombia?

Notes Skip the *Repaso rápido* and activity 25 if you feel students have a good grasp of the present tense.

Estructura

Stem-changing verbs: e → i

You have already learned to use verbs like *pensar (ie)* that require the spelling change *e* → *ie: yo pienso, nosotros pensamos.* The verb *pedir (i, i)* requires the spelling change *e* → *i* in all forms of their present-tense stem except for *nosotros* and *vosotros.*

pedir	
pido	pedimos
pides	pedís
pide	piden

Pedir is the English equivalent of "to ask for, to request, to order (in a restaurant)". Take care to avoid using *pedir* instead of *preguntar* or *hacer una pregunta,* which are both used for "to ask a question." Other expressions with *pedir:*

- **Pedir permiso (para)** is "to ask for permission (to do something)."
- **Pedir perdón** can be used to excuse yourself and to ask for forgiveness for having done something wrong.
- **Pedir prestado/a** is "to ask for a loan" or "to borrow something."

> **¡Extra!**
>
> **Con permiso y Perdón**
>
> Although they may be used with the verb *pedir, Con permiso* and *Perdón* can also be used alone for "Excuse me" or "Pardon me."

The verbs *repetir* and *decir* follow the same pattern as *pedir,* with the exception of the irregular *yo* form or *decir: digo.*

 Práctica

26 Mi amigo Javier

Completa este párrafo con la forma apropiada del verbo *pedir* o *repetir.*

Hola, soy Juan. Javier y yo somos amigos. Javier siempre (1) prestado muchas cosas. Un día (2) prestado unos cubiertos; otro día (3) azúcar. A veces tiene que (4) prestado dinero para comer más porque siempre tiene hambre. Cuando va a un restaurante, él y su hermana (5) muchas bebidas porque siempre tienen sed, y cuando están en el colegio siempre (6) ropa prestada a sus amigos porque siempre tienen frío. Yo nunca (7) prestado nada, y lo (8), nada. A mí no me gusta cuando los estudiantes (9) cosas prestadas. ¡Es muy malo! Yo siempre le debo (10) a Javier una y otra vez, "No debes pedir más cosas prestadas" pero él dice que yo soy egoísta. Mmm, ¿qué opinas si nosotros le (11) prestadas cosas a Javier todos los días? ¿Qué va a pensar?

Teacher Resources

 Activities 6–7

 Activities 11–14

 Activity 6

 Activities 10–12

Answers

26
1. pide
2. pide
3. pide
4. pedir
5. piden
6. piden
7. pido
8. repito
9. piden
10. repetir
11. pedimos

Activities

Expansion
Have a class discussion about how to use the expressions *pedir permiso (para), perdir perdón* and *pedir prestado/prestada.* Then call on students to use the *pedir* expressions in sentences as a volunteer writes each on the board.

Students with Special Needs
Review the *e* → *ie* stem-changing verbs before introducing the change *e* → *i.*

Notes Explain that while the *e* → *ie* spelling change can occur in *-ar, -er* or *-ir* verbs, only *-ir* verbs make the *e* → *i* stem change. This change is indicated in *Navegando 1B* by the first *i* shown in parentheses after listed infinitives.

You may wish to let students know that the second *i* in parentheses after the verbs *pedir (i, i)* and *repetir (i, i)* will be explained in *Capítulo 7.*

The *vosotros/vosotras* verb endings are included for passive recognition. If you have decided to make these forms active, adapt the provided activities as needed.

33

Activities

Critical Thinking

Check your students' ability to write what they hear, using the following dictation: *Julio pide la cucharita a su mamá. Sara piensa que la sopa necesita sal. Julio le pasa la sal a Sara. Papá necesita una cuchara también. Al papá de Julio y Sara le gustan las arepas. La mamá de Julio y Sara cocina todos los días. Todos pedimos permiso para salir.*

27 ¿Pedir o preguntar?

Completa las siguientes oraciones con la forma apropiada de *pedir* o *preguntar*.

1. ¿__ Ud. ayuda con su tarea a sus amigos?
2. Mi hermana y yo nos __ ¿cuándo vamos a vivir en una casa nueva?
3. A veces Rocío tiene que __ blusas prestadas a su mamá.
4. Javier siempre __ perdón cuando no comprende lo que dice la profesora.
5. Claudia siempre __ mucho en la clase de historia.
6. ¿__ siempre tú permiso para hablar por teléfono en tu casa?
7. Mis padres siempre me __ adónde voy.
8. Mi abuela siempre __ ayuda para subir la escalera.

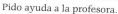
Pido ayuda a la profesora.

28 ¿Qué haces o dices?

Match the circumstances in the column on the left with the most appropriate response in the column on the right.

1. Tienes que poner una mesa para diez amigos.
2. Necesitas con qué escribir.
3. Dices lo que no debes decir a tu madre.
4. Quieres salir del comedor.
5. No comprendes nada en clase de matemáticas.
6. Caminas en la calle y tienes prisa.
7. Dices una mentira a tu padre y él lo sabe.

A. Pido prestado un lápiz.
B. Digo "con permiso".
C. Hago preguntas al profesor.
D. Pido perdón.
E. Pido ayuda.

29 En familia

¿Qué dices o haces en estas situaciones? Sigue el modelo.

MODELO Situación: Tu madre te pide hacer muchos quehaceres antes de poder ver la televisión.
Pido ayuda a mis hermanos menores.

1. **Situación:** Estás en el comedor y tu madre dice que debes hablar poco y comer más.
2. **Situación:** Eres el primero/la primera en terminar de comer y quieres ir a tu cuarto porque tienes mucho sueño.
3. **Situación:** Quieres ir con tus amigos a una fiesta por la noche.
4. **Situación:** Tú dices que tienes mucha sed y tu madre te pasa un refresco.
5. **Situación:** Vas a salir para ir al colegio y ves que no tienes una camisa limpia.

Nuestra madre nos pide hacer muchos quehaceres.

Notes Note that *pedir* doesn't require the preposition **for** because it is already included in the verb.

30 ¿Cuándo pides perdón?

In large groups, choose one person to be the moderator. Then conduct a discussion about circumstances in which you must ask someone to forgive you for what you have done. Make up any of the information you wish.

MODELO A: Margarita, ¿cuándo pides perdón?
B: Pido perdón cuando digo lo que no debo decir.

31 Para su cumpleaños

In groups or three talk first about a relative, and then say what he or she always asks for his/her birthday but never gets.

MODELO A: Tienes un hermano, ¿verdad?
B: Sí. Se llama Miguel. Tiene dieciocho años.
C: ¿Qué pide siempre tu hermano para su cumpleaños?
B: Mi hermano siempre pide un carro nuevo.

Mi hermano pide un carro nuevo para su cumpleaños.

32 ¿Qué piden prestado?

Working in pairs, each of you must create two columns on a piece of paper. In the first column, list five or six family members or friends you know very well. Leave the other column blank for your partner to fill in as you talk. Exchange lists and discuss what the people listed always ask to borrow (e.g., *un bolígrafo, dinero*). As your partner talks, list next to the person's name in the second column what your partner says each person borrows. See if the people on the lists seem to borrow some objects more than others.

MODELO A: ¿Qué pide siempre prestado tu prima?
B: Siempre pide prestado dinero.

mi prima	dinero
mi hermano	———
mi amigo Julio	———
Ana y Diego	———
yo	

Capítulo 6

treinta y cinco **35**

Answers

33 Possible answers:
1. Están en Pereira, en la región cafetera de Colombia.
2. Practican agroturismo.
3. Villa María es una finca cafetera. La casa tiene cinco cuartos, cuatro baños, una cocina y una sala.
4. Hay una piscina para nadar, caballos y senderos donde caminar.
5. Tiene ganas de continuar los conciertos.

34 Answers will vary.

Activities

Connections

As a connection to language arts, have students create the following scenario. They should imagine they are travel writers for a local newspaper. Have them write a one-page article about the Colombian city of their choice. They should include what to see and do, where to stay and where to find good, inexpensive restaurants.

Technology

Have students search the Internet for Web pages advertising trips to Colombia. They should skim the contents for phrases they recognize and then share the information with the class.

Lectura personal

Cantantes y grupos musicales

Dirección http://www.emcp.com/músico/ola/e.diario-5.htm ▲ Archivo Edición Ver Favoritos Herramientas Ayuda

página principal   miembros   e-diario

Grupo musical La Ola

Nombre: **Chantal Morales Rivera**
Edad: **16 años**
País natal: **República Dominicana**
Actividad favorita: **correr por la playa**

Una plantación de café en Colombia.

¡Otro gran concierto en Cali, Colombia! Ya son diez conciertos y la verdad es que estamos un poco cansados. Por eso[1] desde el viernes estamos en la región cafetera[2] de Colombia, disfrutando[3] de una forma de turismo relativamente nueva: el agroturismo. En los años noventa, los caficultores[4] decidieron que sus plantaciones de café no solamente servían[5] para exportar *"the richest coffee in the world"* sino también para importar turistas y generar ingresos[6] complementarios. Así fue como[7] cientos de fincas[8] han sido[9] adaptadas para invitar al turista. La finca en que estamos se llama Villa María y está a veinte minutos de Pereira. La casa tiene cinco cuartos, cuatro baños, una cocina y una sala. También hay piscina, caballos y muchos senderos[10]. De aquí me gustan mucho el olor[11] del café, el silencio del campo[12] y los diferentes verdes de las montañas. Ya comprendo por qué miles de personas se dedican al agroturismo en la tierra[13] del café. Ahora estoy descansada[14] y tengo ganas de continuar los conciertos. ¡Gracias, Colombia!

[1]That is why [2]coffee growing [3]enjoying [4]coffee growers [5]served [6]income [7]That is how [8]plantations [9]have been [10]pathways [11]smell [12]countryside [13]land [14]rested

33 **¿Qué recuerdas?**

1. ¿Dónde están los miembros del grupo musical La Ola?
2. ¿Qué tipo de turismo practican?
3. ¿Qué es Villa María? ¿Cómo es la casa?
4. ¿Qué hay para hacer en Villa María?
5. Al final, ¿qué tiene ganas de hacer Chantal?

34 **Algo personal**

1. ¿Adónde te gusta ir de vacaciones? ¿Qué haces allí?
2. Describe tu hotel ideal.
3. ¿Te gustaría hacer agroturismo? ¿Por qué sí o por qué no?

- Make several comparisons between the coffee-growing region of Colombia and the region in the United States in which you live. Which one emphasizes rural life more?

Notes Students may write to the Colombian embassy or the Organization of American States (OAS) in Washington, D.C., for information regarding tourism in Cali and other Colombian cities. They also may search the Internet, where they will find a number of different sites with information about travel in Colombia. (Give students the addresses listed in the ATE margin on page 37 or refer to the *Navegando 1B* ATE Introduction for help with using the Internet.)

¿Qué aprendí?

Visit the web-based activities at www.emcp.com

Autoevaluación

As a review and self-check, respond to the following:

1. Describe your house.

2. Tell a friend what two different people say, including yourself.

3. Say where you would like to live.

4. Tell how you feel in these situations: it is hot and your mouth is dry, it is noon and you have not eaten, you stayed up too late and it is the next morning.

5. Imagine a classmate needs to borrow a pen and paper. How can you tell the person he or she should borrow the items from someone else because you do not have them?

6. What two things have you learned about Colombia?

Palabras y expresiones

La casa
el baño
el cuarto
la escalera
el garaje
el patio
la piscina
el piso
la planta
la planta baja
el primer piso
la sala

Para describir
al lado de
cómodo,-a
cuando

desde
donde
el lado
pequeño,-a
poco, -a
por
por la noche
primer

¿Cómo estás?
el calor
el frío
la gana
el hambre *(f.)*
el miedo
la prisa
¿Qué (+ tener)?

la sed
el sueño
tener (calor, frío, ganas de, hambre, miedo de, prisa, sed, sueño)

Otras expresiones
el abrazo
la carta
el dibujo
lo que
me/te/le/nos/les gustaría
la mentira
pedir (perdón, permiso, prestado,-a)

por teléfono
querer decir
querido,-a
la verdad

Verbos
aprender a
correr
decir (+ que)
escribir
gustaría
pedir (i, i)
repetir (i, i)

Nuestra casa tiene una piscina.

¿Te gusta mi cuarto?

Capítulo 6

treinta y siete **37**

Notes Encourage students to find out more about Colombia by going to the following Web sites:

Lonely Planet World Guide
http://www.lonelyplanet.com/destinations/south_america/colombia/
Electronic Embassy
http://www.embassy.org

Organization of American States
http://www.oas.org
general travel information
http://www.expedia.com

Teacher Resources

Activity 15

Information Gap Activities
Postcard Activities
Funciones de Comunicación

Answers

Autoevaluación
Possible answers:
1. Mi casa es azul. Tiene dos pisos. Mi cuarto está al lado del baño en el primer piso.
2. Mi mamá dice que debo estudiar más. Yo digo que Colombia es un país interesante.
3. Me gustaría vivir en Cartagena.
4. Tengo sed. Tengo hambre. Tengo sueño.
5. Debes pedir prestados un bolígrafo y papel de otro/otra estudiante porque yo no los tengo.
6. Answers will vary.

Activities

Spanish for Spanish Speakers
Have students write a short composition in Spanish summarizing what they know about Colombia. Expand the activity by having students seek additional information about Colombia at the library or via the Internet.

37

La casa de mis sueños

Tú lees

Answers

Preparación
1. El dibujo es de una casa.
2. Hay tres cuartos.
3. Hay un piano.
4. Answers will vary.

Activities

Pronunciation *(las letras* g y j*)*
Review the sound of *g* with students by explaining that when *g* is followed by *a, o* or *u* or by a consonant, the sound is similar to the sound of *g* in the English word **goat**: *ganas, tengo, gustar.* In addition, be sure to point out that students should pronounce both vowels in the letter combinations *ua* and *uo (ambiguo, guapo),* whereas the letter combinations *ue* and *ui* should be pronounced as one sound *(Miguel, guitarra).* The letters *j* and *g* sound similar when the *g* is followed by *e* or *i.* The sound is similar to the sound of *wh* in the English word **who** *(baja, relojes, jirafa, dibujo, jueves, Cartagena, página).* **Note:** It may be necessary to explain the meaning of the two example words *ambiguo* (ambiguous) and *jirafa* (giraffe).

Estrategia

Using graphics to understand a reading
Look at graphics, artwork, photographs and so forth that accompany what you are reading. The visual support will help you predict what the reading is about.

Preparación
Mira el dibujo para contestar las siguientes preguntas como preparación para la lectura.

1. ¿De qué es el dibujo?
2. ¿Cuántos cuartos hay en el dibujo?
3. ¿Qué hay en la sala?
4. ¿Qué piensas que vas a leer?

La casa de mis sueños

Me llamo Santiago y soy de Caracas. Aquí hay un dibujo de la casa de mis sueños[1]. Claro que[2] el dibujo no es perfecto. En la casa de mis sueños hay tres cuartos y todos son grandes. En la sala hay un piano para tocar música clásica y una biblioteca con todos los libros que me gustan. Al lado de la sala hay un cuarto para ver la televisión y películas en DVD. También hay una computadora con quemador de CDs y muchos videojuegos. Mi cuarto es grande, con una cama también grande, muchos pósters en la pared y un equipo de sonido. El cuarto de mis padres tiene una puerta que abre al patio y al jardín. El patio y el jardín son bonitos, con muchas flores. La flor favorita de mi mamá es el jazmín. Nuestro jardín está rodeado[3] de jazmines. En el jardín hay también una piscina olímpica con un trampolín donde puedo nadar todos los días.

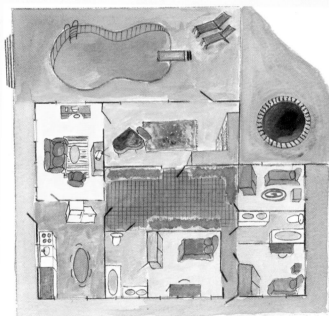

Notes Complete the *Preparación* with the class. Ask what students think the reading is about.

The reading *La casa de mis sueños* is recorded and available in the Audio CD Program. You may wish to play the CD to allow students to hear Santiago's description of his dream home.

En la casa de mis sueños, el lugar favorito de mis papás es la cocina. En la cocina papá y mamá preparan comidas exquisitas para cenar. Mi comida favorita es el ajiaco, ¡esa sopa de Colombia tan rica de papas, pollo, maíz, aguacate y crema de leche[4]! Como la cocina es tan grande[5], ellos siempre tienen muchos invitados[6]. La casa tiene muchas ventanas y mucha luz. ¡Quiero algún día construir[7] la casa de mis sueños!

[1]dreams [2]Of course [3]surrounded by [4]potatoes, chicken, corn, avocado and whipping cream [5]so big
[6]guests [7]some day build

A ¿Qué recuerdas?

1. ¿De quién es el dibujo de la casa?
2. ¿Cómo son los cuartos de la casa?
3. ¿Qué hay en la biblioteca?
4. ¿Dónde están la computadora y los videojuegos?
5. ¿Qué hay en el cuarto de Santiago?
6. ¿Cuál es el lugar favorito de los padres de Santiago?
7. ¿Qué hacen los padres en la cocina?
8. ¿Qué flores hay en el jardín?
9. ¿Qué es el ajiaco y de dónde es?

B Algo personal

1. ¿Cómo es la casa de tus sueños?
2. ¿En qué son diferentes la casa de los sueños de Santiago y tu casa de los sueños? ¿En qué son similares?
3. ¿Cómo es tu cuarto en la casa de tus sueños? ¿Qué hay en él?
4. ¿Cuál es tu lugar favorito en la casa de tus sueños?

¿Cómo es la casa de tus sueños?

Capítulo 6   *treinta y nueve* **39**

Notes Whereas in Spanish-speaking countries a patio is an outdoor area that may have plants and a place where people might sit and chat, when talking about homes in the United States, the word *patio* in Spanish can mean **yard.**

Tú escribes

Estrategia

Connecting phrases
Your writing style may seem choppy in Spanish unless you connect your thoughts using transition words like *a causa de* (because of), *como* (since, like, as), *después* (later), *entonces* (then), *pero* (but), *por eso* (therefore), *sin embargo* (however), *también* (also), *y* (and). These words can act like adhesive to bind together the ideas in a paragraph as a connected unit.

First, write several sentences that describe your *casa de tus sueños*. Include information such as what the house looks like, where it is located, what rooms it has, how many windows and doors it has, where rooms are located and any other details you wish to include. Then add transition words to make your sentences flow more smoothly and put the sentences together, one after another in paragraph form, to create a composition. Finally, create a colorful drawing of the house, including details that match your description.

MODELO   La casa de mis sueños está en una playa en América del Sur. Es muy grande. Tiene muchos cuartos y jardines....

La casa de mis sueños está en la playa.

Notes   Review the contents of the *Estrategia* with the class. Then give several examples of sentences that contain connecting words before assigning the writing.

Consider having students pair up to review one another's sentences before having them finalize their compositions.

Ask individuals if it is all right to display their composition for others in the class to read.

Proyectos adicionales

A Conexión cultural

Imagine you are traveling with your family to Venezuela and Colombia on vacation and your parents have asked you to make suggestions about what to see and do. Use the library or the Internet to investigate cities you might visit. Then create a travel itinerary offering suggestions for the trip to both countries. Consider including the following in your list of recommendations: cities to visit, tourist attractions, your recommendation for the best time to visit South America and any other information you can find that may be of use during the trip.

B Conexión con la tecnología

Write a short e-mail in Spanish to someone you know about your home and family. Use Santiago's letter (see p. 244) as a model, if necessary.

Castillo de San Felipe, Cartagena.

C Comparando

Working in pairs, talk about what you know about housing and home life in the United States and in Spanish-speaking parts of the world such as Venezuela, Colombia, Puerto Rico and the Dominican Republic. Then make a side-by-side comparison listing at least five similarities or differences.

D ¡A escribir!

Help Santiago's parents write back to him (see p. 244). Include the following information: They are happy to hear from their dear son; they know that he is far from home in Caracas, but not far from his family; they want to see the photos of the trip to Cartagena. Include any other details you wish. Remember to include the city and the date and use appropriate greetings and farewells.

Teacher Resources

 Situation Cards

 Capítulo 6

Answers

A Creative problem solving.
B Creative self-expression.
C Creative self-expression.
D Creative self-expression.

Activities

Critical Thinking
One of the many fascinating results of European exploration was the food exchange that brought new foods and animals to the Americas and took others to Europe. For example, the Spaniards brought cattle and spices to the Americas and returned with many foods new to Europe, such as tomatoes and potatoes. Ask students to research this food exchange and consider its impact on the diets of people around the world.

Multiple Intelligences (spatial)
Invite students to make a collage in which they profile a Spanish-speaking country of special interest. Good sources of information include sites on the Internet and materials provided by national tourism offices.

Notes **Cultures.** Note for students that in Latin America, many middle- and upper-class families traditionally employ a maid to assist with household chores.

Two well-known literary figures from Venezuela are Rómulo Gallegos, author of *Doña Bárbara* and former president of Venezuela, and Arturo Uslar Pietri, critic, short-story writer and novelist. Pietri's best-known work is *Las lanzas coloradas*. In 1990 he received the *Príncipe de Asturias* prize, one of the most important literary prizes in the Hispanic world.

One of Colombia's most famous citizens is Gabriel García Márquez, winner of the Nobel Prize in literature.

Teacher Resources

 Trabalenguas

Activities

Connections
In groups of four, have students research the life of Simón Bolívar. Then have them write a simple dialog, design a piece of art or prepare some other artistic reflection of an important period of his life and present it to the class.

Language through Action
Bring in table place settings and food items (or magazine pictures of these items). Then use the *tú* and *Uds.* commands of *pasar*, *comer*, *tomar* and other verbs, along with the food and table vocabulary from this lesson. Students should show comprehension by actually handing the items to the appropriate person: *pásame la sal, pásale el pan a* (name of student).

Spanish for Spanish Speakers
Have students research and write about Rómulo Gallegos, Arturo Uslar Pietri or Gabriel García Márquez.

Repaso

Now that I have completed this chapter, I can...

	Go to these pages for help:
identify items in the kitchen and at the dinner table.	2, 3
express obligations, wishes and preferences.	2
talk about everyday activities.	2
state an opinion.	7
discuss food and table items.	7
point out people and things.	14
describe a household.	20
tell what someone says.	28
say how someone is doing.	28

I can also...

talk about products and foods from Venezuela and Colombia.	5, 23
discuss home life in Venezuela and Colombia.	13, 31
describe my home.	20
recognize words in context.	27
recognize when to use *pedir* or *preguntar*.	33
plan a trip to Venezuela or Colombia.	41

Trabalenguas

La casa está en la plaza, en la casa hay un cuarto, dentro del cuarto hay un piso, encima del piso hay una mesa, encima de la mesa hay una jaula, dentro de la jaula hay un loro que canta y dice: de loro en jaula, jaula en mesa, mesa en piso, piso en cuarto, cuarto en casa, casa en la plaza.

¡Viento en popa!

Notes Loose translation of the *Trabalenguas:* The house is on the square, in the house there is a room, in the room there is a floor, on the floor there is a table, on the table there is a bird cage, in the bird cage there is a parrot who sings and says: from parrot to bird cage, bird cage to table, table to floor, floor to room, room to house, house to the square.

Although large earthquakes *(terremotos)* are not common in Colombia, they do sometimes occur. In January of 1999, an earthquake that measured 6.0 on the Richter scale destroyed the cities of Pereira and Armenia and several villages in the coffee-producing region of Colombia. The earthquake killed nearly 1,000 people.

Vocabulario

el **abrazo** hug *6B*
el **aceite** oil *6A*
al lado de next to, beside *6B*
allá over there *6A*
aprender a *6B*
aquel, aquella (aquellos, aquellas) that, (those) *far away 6A*
ayudar to help *6A*
el **azúcar** sugar *6A*
el **baño** bathroom *6B*
el **calor** heat *6B*
la **carta** letter *6B*
cerrar (ie) to close *6A*
la **cocina** kitchen *6A*
el **comedor** dining room *6A*
cómodo,-a comfortable *6B*
correr to run *6B*
la **cosa** thing *6A*
cuando when *6B*
el **cuarto** room, bedroom *6B*
los **cubiertos** silverware *6A*
la **cuchara** spoon *6A*
la **cucharita** teaspoon *6A*
el **cuchillo** knife *6A*
de todos los días everyday *6A*
deber should, to have to, must, ought *6A*
decir *(+ que)* to tell, to say *6B*
desde since, from *6B*
después afterwards, later, then *6A*
el **dibujo** drawing, sketch *6B*
dónde where *6B*
e and *(used before a word beginning with i or hi) 6B*
empezar *(ie)* to begin, to start *6A*
encender *(ie)* to light, to turn on *(a light) 6A*
entonces then *6A*
la **escalera** stairway, stairs *6B*
escribir to write *6B*
ese, esa (esos, esas) that (those) *6A*

especial special *6A*
este, esta (estos, estas) this (these) *6A*
la **estufa** stove *6A*
el **fregadero** sink *6A*
el **frío** cold *6B*
la **gana** desire *6B*
el **garaje** garage *6B*
gustaría would like *6B*
el **hambre** *(f.)* hunger *6B*
el **horno microondas** microwave oven *6A*
el **lado** side *6B*
la **lámpara** lamp *6A*
el **lavaplatos** dishwasher *6A*
lo que what, that which *6B*
la **luz** light *6A*
el **mantel** tablecloth *6A*
la **mantequilla** butter *6A*
me/te/le/nos/les gustaría I/you/he/she/it/we/they would like *6B*
la **mentira** lie *6B*
la **mesa** table *6A*
el **miedo** fear *6B*
otra vez again, another time *6A*
el **pan** bread *6A*
pásame pass me *6A*
el **patio** courtyard, patio, yard *6B*
pedir (i, i) to ask for, to order, to request; *pedir perdón* to say you are sorry; *pedir permiso (para)* to ask for permission (to do something); *pedir prestado,-a* to borrow *6B*
pensar (ie) to think, to intend, to plan *6A*
pensar de/en/que to think about *6A*
pequeño,-a small *6B*
el **permiso** permission, permit *6B*
la **pimienta** pepper *(seasoning) 6A*
la **piscina** swimming pool *6B*
el **piso** floor *6B*
la **planta** plant *6B*
la **planta baja** ground floor *6B*

el **plato** dish, plate *6A*
el **plato de sopa** soup bowl *6A*
poco, -a not very, little *6B*
poner to put, to place *6A*
poner la mesa to set the table *6A*
por through, by *6B*
por la noche at night *6B*
por teléfono by phone *6B*
el **postre** dessert *6A*
preferir (ie) to prefer *6A*
primer first *6B*
el **primer piso** first floor *6B*
la **prisa** rush, hurry, haste *6B*
¿Qué *(+ tener)?* What is wrong *(with someone) 6B*
querer (ie) to love, to want, to like *6A*
querer decir to mean *6B*
querido,-a dear *6B*
el **refrigerador** refrigerator *6A*
repetir (i, i) to repeat *6B*
la **sal** salt *6A*
la **sala** living room *6B*
la **sed** thirst *6B*
sentir (ie) to be sorry, to feel sorry, to regret *6A*
la **servilleta** napkin *6A*
la **sopa** soup *6A*
el **sueño** sleep *6B*
la **taza** cup *6A*
el **tenedor** fork *6A*
tener (calor, frío, hambre, miedo de, prisa, sed, sueño) to be (hot, cold, hungry, afraid, in a hurry, thirsty, sleepy) *6B*
tener ganas de to feel like *6B*
tener que to have to *6A*
u or *(used before a word that starts with o or ho) 6B*
un poco (de) a little (bit) *6A*
el **vaso** glass *6A*
la **verdad** truth *6B*
viajar to travel *6A*
ya already *6A*

Module 2

Episode 6

Testing/Assessment

Test Booklet
Portfolio Assessment

Activities

Critical Listening
Pronounce the following carefully, having students say the sentence several times before writing what they hear: *Zoraida, Susana y yo vamos a hacer un mapa de Venezuela con la tiza en la pizarra.* Ask students if they understand the meaning of the sentence.

Pronunciation *(las letras c, s y z)*
Review the pronunciation of the letters *c, s* and *z* with students by explaining that the letter *c* (followed by *e* or *i*), the letter *s* and the letter *z* are pronounced like the *s* in the English word **Sally,** except in most of Spain, where *c* and *z* followed by *e* or *i* are pronounced like *th* in the English word **thin.** Your students may find it interesting to hear you model this difference in pronunciation.

Notes Other ways to say *la estufa* include *la hornilla* and *el fogón.* In some countries people refer to the **stove** as *la cocina.*

El refrigerador is also called *el frigorífico,* although some people prefer to use the term *la nevera,* which is equivalent to **icebox.**

Activities

Critical Thinking

The poster and large photograph that appear on pages 44–45 depict the chapter functions, cultural setting and themes for *Capítulo 7*. The visual support is intended to help further student awareness of and connections to how Spanish is used outside the controlled environment of the classroom as well as to help prepare them for learning about *el tiempo libre.* Ask students what conclusions they can draw from the two images. Ask if students can guess in what two countries or part of the world this chapter takes place.

Capítulo **7**

El tiempo libre

Objetivos

- ❖ **talk about leisure time activities**
- ❖ **discuss sports**
- ❖ **say what someone can do**
- ❖ **discuss length of time**
- ❖ **describe what is happening**
- ❖ **talk about the seasons and weather**
- ❖ **indicate order**

Visit the web-based activities at www.emcp.com

44 *cuarenta y cuatro*

Notes Discuss the contents of pages 44–45. Explain that the small photo is a poster of Carlos Gardel, who is considered to be the father of the tango. The *Cultura viva* on page 55 discusses the tango in greater detail. The large photograph depicts two skiers in Portillo, Chile. Chile is discussed in greater detail on page 69.

Communicative objectives are provided here to prepare students for the chapter they are about to begin. Discuss the objectives for *Capítulo 7* with students. A checkoff list of functions appears on page 90, along with additional objectives, so students can do a self-check to evaluate their progress.

Contexto cultural

Argentina
Nombre oficial: **República Argentina**
Población: **37.488.000**
Capital: **Buenos Aires**
Ciudades importantes: **Córdoba, Mendoza, San Juan**
Unidad monetaria: **el peso**
Fiesta nacional: **9 de julio, Proclamación de la Independencia**
Gente famosa: **Jorge Luis Borges (escritor); Evita Perón (líder popular)**

Chile
Nombre oficial: **República de Chile**
Población: **15.403.000**
Capital: **Santiago de Chile**
Ciudades importantes: **Valparaíso, Viña del Mar**
Unidad monetaria: **el peso**
Fiesta nacional: **18 de septiembre, Día de la Independencia**
Gente famosa: **Pablo Neruda, Isabel Allende, Gabriela Mistral (escritores)**

Activities

Expansion
Ask students what they know about Argentina and Chile. Ask for two volunteers to go to the board. One student should list what students know about Argentina and the other student should write down what classmates say about Chile. After five or six points are listed for each country, have students decide how the countries are similar and how they are different. (Start the list by stating that both are countries in South America.)

cuarenta y cinco **45**

Notes The cultural focus of this chapter is on the South American countries of Argentina and Chile. Students will be learning to discuss what people do in their free time, in particular what people in Argentina and Chile do during their free time.

Los pasatiempos

 Activity 1

> **Content reviewed in *Lección A***
> • telling time
> • days of the week
> • direct object pronouns
> • the verb *estar*

Activities

Critical Thinking

Before playing the audio CD for *Vocabulario I,* ask students if they can guess who the people are. Then ask what they think the boy wants to watch and what the girl wants to watch. Finally, ask students if they have ever been in a similar situation.

Lección A
Argentina

Vocabulario I
Los pasatiempos

Toda Una Vida

¿Cuándo vas a hacer las tareas?

¿No recuerdas que quiero ver mi programa favorito? Vuelvo en cinco minutos.

Todavía no. Esta noche, después del partido.

Sí, sí, está bien.

el televisor

El Equipo de Argentina

A Graciela le gusta ver la telenovela *Toda Una Vida* y ahora no puede. A Graciela le gustaría tener un televisor en su cuarto pero cuestan mucho. El papá de Graciela le va a dar un televisor para su cumpleaños.

Notes The word *dar* is presented in *Lección A* in its infinitive form only. The present tense of *dar* is taught in *Lección B.*

Explain to the class that the word *televisor* refers specifically to the television set. Thus, native Spanish speakers say *poner el televisor* but *ver televisión.*

Point out that students may hear *encender* or *prender* used as they travel in some countries instead of *poner* to mean **to turn on** a light or appliance.

Telenovelas are very popular in Hispanic countries.

jugar a los videojuegos

jugar al fútbol americano

jugar al básquetbol

jugar al voleibol

jugar a las damas

jugar al ajedrez

hacer aeróbicos

jugar a las cartas

dibujar

1 ¿Qué actividad es?

Identifica la actividad que oyes.

A

B

C

D

E

F

2 ¡Yo sé lo que vas a hacer!

Create a list of at least ten leisure activities. Then, working in small groups, take turns playing charades to act out activities on your list. The winner is the person who first says *¡Yo sé lo que vas a hacer!*

Notes Point out for students that the word **volleyball** has several variations in Spanish, the most common being *voleibol* and *volíbol*.

Ask your students if they have ever seen a soap opera in Spanish. Spanish-language television channels in the United States present soap operas primarily from Mexico and Venezuela.

Teacher Resources

 Activity 1

 Activity 1

 Activities 47–48

 Activities 1–2

 Activity 1

 Activities 2–3

Answers

1 1. C
2. A
3. B
4. D
5. E
6. F

2 Creative self-expression.

Activities

TPR
In advance, write on separate pieces of paper the Spanish terms for the pastimes shown on page 47. Then have students select one of the pieces of paper at random. Call on several students to act out the expressions while classmates guess what the expressions are in Spanish.

Answers

3 1. Ella quiere jugar al ajedrez.
  2. Ve su telenovela favorita.
  3. Va a jugar el equipo de Argentina.
  4. Va a ver fútbol.
  5. Su vida ahora es ver televisión y jugar al fútbol.
4 Answers will vary.
5 1. Falso.; 2. Cierto.; 3. Cierto.;
  4. Falso.; 5. Falso.

Activities

Expansion
Additional questions *(Algo personal):* *¿Hay telenovelas en español en tu ciudad? ¿Cómo se llaman?; ¿Cómo se llama tu programa favorito? ¿A qué hora es el programa?; ¿Te gusta ver deportes en la televisión?*

Prereading Strategy
Prepare students for the reading by having them cover up the dialog with one hand and look at the photographs. Then ask them to imagine where the conversation takes place and what the people are saying to one another. Finally, have students scan the dialog to find cognates and other words they recognize.

48

Diálogo I
¿No quieres jugar al ajedrez?

LUZ: ¿No quieres jugar al ajedrez?
HUGO: Sí, pero después de este programa.
LUZ: ¿Qué programa es?
HUGO: Es mi telenovela favorita.

LUZ: ¿Ahora sí?
HUGO: ¿Por qué no vienes en dos horas?
LUZ: ¿Cómo? ¿No vamos a jugar al ajedrez?
HUGO: Es que el equipo de Argentina va a jugar ahora.

LUZ: ¡Veo que ya no sabes jugar al ajedrez!
HUGO: Sí, ya no recuerdo cómo jugar.
LUZ: ¡Claro! Tu vida ahora es ver televisión.
HUGO: No. ¡Mi vida ahora es ver televisión y jugar al fútbol!

3 ¿Qué recuerdas?

1. ¿A qué quiere jugar Luz?
2. ¿Qué programa ve Hugo?
3. ¿Qué equipo va a jugar?
4. ¿Qué va a ver Hugo?
5. ¿Cómo es ahora la vida de Hugo?

¡Extra!

La fiebre del gol

It is easy to understand why Hugo is distracted as he talks with Luz. For many people, soccer *(el fútbol)* is more than just a simple pastime in Argentina and throughout the Spanish-speaking world. During the World Cup *(la Copa Mundial)* fans of all ages follow the action and nearly everyone has *la fiebre del gol* (goal fever).

4 Algo personal

1. ¿Sabes jugar al fútbol?
2. ¿Te gusta jugar al ajedrez?
3. ¿Qué vas a hacer esta noche?
4. ¿Te gusta ver televisión?

5 ¿Qué comprendiste?

🔊 Di si los que oyes es cierto o falso, según el diálogo *¿No quieres jugar al ajedrez?*

¿Sabes jugar al ajedrez?

Lección A

Notes *La fiebre del gol* is at its peak during *la Copa Mundial de fútbol* (World Cup), which is held every four years. Ask if students are able to name recent World Cup winners or host countries.

The *Navegando 1* Video/DVD Program uses a soap opera format and was filmed on location by professional actors.

Episodes were written to reflect the content of corresponding chapters in the textbook. Students will enjoy meeting the characters and following them through the challenges they face in everyday life.

Cultura Viva

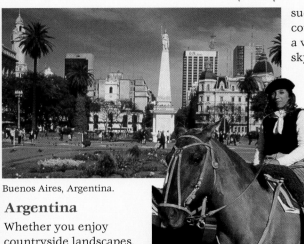
Buenos Aires, Argentina.

Argentina

Whether you enjoy countryside landscapes, soaring mountains, beautiful beaches or the hustle and bustle of modern city life, Argentina has it all. As the largest Spanish-speaking country in the world, the southernmost tip of Argentina begins near the frigid South Pole and extends north to the tropics of central South America. The plains of Patagonia in the south are the heart of the sheep-raising industry. In the central plains *(las pampas)*, cowboys known as *gauchos* tend herds of cattle on large ranches called *estancias*. (Argentina produces beef that is sold and shipped throughout the world.) In addition, world-class ski resorts,

Una gaucha.

Las cascadas de Iguazú.

such as Bariloche, draw visitors from many countries. Argentina's capital, Buenos Aires, is a vibrant, modern city that combines skyscrapers *(rascacielos)*, plazas and parks, outstanding food and interesting old buildings into what has been called the "Paris of the Spanish-speaking world."

While visiting Argentina, you may find yourself alone atop a mountain *(Aconcagua)* or in a crowded cafe. Argentina's population includes descendants from large numbers of people from Spain, Italy, Poland, Germany, Great Britain and Japan. Wondering what to do? Ski the famous slopes of the *Andes,* dance the tango in the colorful neighborhood called *La Boca,* participate in the national sport— *el fútbol* or sit back and gaze at the breathtaking *Iguazú* waterfalls. And before you leave, try grilled beef *(carne a la parrilla)* in one of the capital's many fine restaurants or have a seat and sip a wonderful tea-like hot drink called *mate.*

6 Argentina

¿Cierto o falso?

1. Hay playas bonitas en la Argentina.
2. El país más grande de habla hispana es Ecuador.
3. Los gauchos viven en grandes estancias de las pampas.
4. Bariloche es la capital de la Argentina.
5. Hay muchas personas en la Argentina de Italia y Polonia.
6. El baile más famoso de la Argentina es el tango.
7. *Mate* es una ciudad en la Argentina.
8. El deporte nacional de la Argentina es el fútbol.

Capítulo 7

Answers

6 1. Cierto.
2. Falso.
3. Cierto.
4. Falso.
5. Cierto.
6. Cierto.
7. Falso.
8. Cierto.

Activities

Critical Listening

Explain to the class that the term *rascacielos* (skyscraper) comes from a combination of the words *rascar* and *cielos.* Other such combinations exist in both Spanish and English. Ask students to listen to the following words and try to identify their English equivalents: *telenovela, aeropuerto, paraguas, parabrisas, quitasol, quitanieves.*

Notes The gauchos of Argentina have a rich and colorful history and can be compared in many ways to the cowboys of the United States. Their main tool is the *bola,* a type of sling consisting of heavy weights tied to the ends of a leather cord. It is thrown to entangle the legs of cattle or game.

Argentina produces a lot of beef, much of which is exported.

Aconcagua is the highest mountain peak in the Western Hemisphere.

The tango is discussed in greater detail later in this lesson.

Answers

7 1. Papá puede comprar....
2. Yo puedo buscar....
3. Mi mamá puede hacer....
4. Tú puedes poner....
5. Nosotros podemos preparar....
6. Mis hermanos pueden poner....

8 1. recuerdo; 2. juega; 3. puede; 4. podemos; 5. cuestan; 6. vuelve; 7. puede; 8. juego

Activities

Language through Action
Ask students to write out the conjugation of the present tense of either *poder* or *jugar*. Then have them draw a line around the forms that change and they will see the shape of a shoe. Remind the class that they learned other verbs that follow a similar shoe pattern in *Capítulo 6 (pensar, cerrar, empezar, preferir, querer, sentir).*

Students with Special Needs
Give a second model sentence for activity 7.

Idioma

Estructura

Stem-changing verbs: *o → ue* and *u → ue*

Some verbs require the change *o → ue (poder)* or *u → ue (jugar)* in all forms of their present-tense stem except for *nosotros* and *vosotros.* These stem changes do not interfere with regular verb endings.

poder		jugar	
pu**e**do	podemos	j**ue**go	jugamos
pu**e**des	podéis	j**ue**gas	jugáis
pu**e**de	pu**e**den	j**ue**ga	j**ue**gan

Other *o → ue* stem-changing verbs include *costar (ue), recordar (ue)* and *volver (ue).*

Práctica

7 Todos quieren ayudar

If everyone works together they will be free to do what they want later in the day. Say what these people can do to help with lunch, according to the cues.

MODELO Marta (buscar los platos)
Marta puede buscar los platos.

1. papá (comprar leche y pan)
2. yo (buscar los cubiertos)
3. mi mamá (hacer el almuerzo)
4. tú (poner la mesa)
5. nosotros (preparar un postre)
6. mis hermanos (poner los platos sucios en el lavaplatos)

¿Quién puede buscar los platos?

8 El televisor

Completa el siguiente párrafo con la forma apropiada de uno de los siguientes verbos: *poder, costar, volver, jugar, recordar.*

Yo siempre (1) cuando (2) el equipo de Argentina. Mi papá y yo vemos el partido por televisión. A mi hermana no le gusta el fútbol pero ella (3) leer o salir con sus amigos. No (4) tener otro televisor porque (5) mucho y nuestra casa no es grande. Mi hermana (6) a las cuatro, ella (7) ver su telenovela y entonces yo (8) al fútbol con mis amigos en el parque.

Notes The verbs *poder* and *recordar* can be followed by an infinitive in double-verb constructions: *puedo ir con ella a la tienda; recuerda comprar un vestido azul.*

The preposition *a* typically follows the verb *jugar* and precedes the name of a sport or game: *jugar al fútbol* and *jugar a las cartas.*

9 Una invitación

In pairs, take turns inviting one another to do the indicated activities. Answer by either refusing or accepting the invitation, giving an excuse if you refuse or changing the suggested time if you accept.

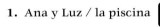 jugar al básquetbol

A: ¿Puedes jugar al básquetbol hoy?

B: Lo siento, pero no puedo. Es muy tarde.

1. jugar a los videojuegos esta tarde
2. ver mis fotos de Chile ahora
3. ir al cine pasado mañana
4. jugar al fútbol americano el sábado
5. jugar al voleibol a las 6:30
6. hacer aeróbicos mañana

10 ¿Cuándo vuelven?

In pairs, talk about when these people will be returning from the places mentioned.

 Eva / la casa de Gloria   **PM 7:00**

A: ¿A qué hora vuelve Eva de la casa de Gloria?

B: Eva vuelve de la casa de Gloria a las siete.

1. Ana y Luz / la piscina **PM 6:40**
3. tú / el cine **PM 1:50**
2. tú y yo / la tienda **PM 1:25**
4. Esteban / el partido **PM 9:30**

✦ Comunicación

11 ¿A qué juegan?

With a classmate, talk about what these people are doing.

 1  2  3  4

12 Los pasatiempos

In small groups, ask one another about your favorite pastimes *(pasatiempos)*. Start with the activities shown in *Vocabulario I*, taking notes as you talk. Then choose one member of the group to report the information to the class.

 **A:** ¿Juegas al fútbol?

B: Sí, (No, no) juego al fútbol. Es mi pasatiempo favorito. ¿Y tú?

Capítulo 7 *cincuenta y uno* **51**

Notes Tell students that many Spanish-speaking natives drop the *al, a la, a las* and *a los* after *jugar* when naming a sport or game they play: *juego fútbol*. This practice is becoming common in speech.

Jugar is the only verb in Spanish that changes *u* to *ue* as part of a regular pattern.

Inform students whether you will be selecting the person to present the information to the class for activity 12 or whether students may choose their own group representative.

El tiempo libre

 Activity 4

 Activity 49

 Activities 8–9

 Activity 3

 Activities 7–8

Activities

Critical Thinking

Before playing the audio CD for *Vocabulario II*, ask students questions about the scene: Who are the people? What do students think the boy is doing? What is the man saying? What are the girls doing? What do they want to do in the afternoon?

Vocabulario II
El tiempo libre

Es casi mediodía. ¿Cuánto tiempo hace que estás viendo televisión?

Bueno, parece casi un siglo. Debes apagar el televisor ahora.

Natalia tiene una lista de películas nuevas. Ella no quiere ver las mismas películas del mes pasado.

¿Cuándo vamos a alquilar la película?

Estupendo. ¿Cuándo jugamos a las damas?

Por la tarde.

Ahora mismo.

Hace una hora.

Sí, sí, en un segundo lo voy a apagar.

el control remoto

Pascual está durmiendo. Mario le permite a Pascual dormir a su lado.

Notes As you review *Vocabulario I*, explain that centuries are expressed with cardinal numbers in Spanish and that years cannot be abbreviated in spoken Spanish as they are in English. For example, **the 21st century** would be *el siglo veintiuno* and **2005** would be *dos mil cinco*.

Help students with the meaning of the sentences in the speech bubbles and in the boxes.

Note the pause word *Bueno* when the father talks. Ask students if they remember any other pause words he could have used.

13 El tiempo libre

🔊 Selecciona la ilustración que corresponde con lo que oyes.

A

B

C

D

E

F

14 ¿Cuánto tiempo hay en...?

Contesta las siguientes preguntas.

1. ¿Cuántas semanas hay en un año?
2. ¿Cuántos años hay en un siglo?
3. ¿Cuántas horas hay en un día?
4. ¿Cuántos cuartos de hora hay en una hora?
5. ¿Cuántos segundos hay en un minuto?
6. ¿Cuántos minutos hay en una hora?
7. ¿Cuántos segundos hay en una hora?
8. ¿Cuántas horas hay en una semana?

¿Cuántos minutos hay en una hora?

Capítulo 7

cincuenta y tres **53**

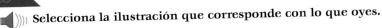

Activities 13–14

Answers

13
1. D
2. A
3. B
4. C
5. F
6. E

14
1. Hay cincuenta y dos semanas en un año.
2. Hay cien años en un siglo.
3. Hay veinticuatro horas en un día.
4. Hay cuatro cuartos de hora en una hora.
5. Hay sesenta segundos en un minuto.
6. Hay sesenta minutos en una hora.
7. Hay 3.600 segundos en una hora.
8. Hay ciento sesenta y ocho horas en una semana.

Activities

Critical Thinking
Additional questions: *¿Cuántos minutos hay en un cuarto de hora?; ¿Cuántos días hay en una semana? ¿en tres semanas?; ¿Cuántos minutos hay en cuatro horas y media?; ¿Cuántos segundos hay en cuarenta y siete minutos?; ¿Cuántos meses hay en siete años?; ¿Cuántos meses hay en dos siglos?; ¿Cuántos meses hay en siete siglos?*

Notes Activity 13 is intended for listening comprehension practice. Play the audio CD of the activity or use the transcript that appears in the ATE Introduction if you prefer to read the activity yourself.

Before assigning activity 13, point out the symbols AM and PM in the two clocks.

You may want to have students complete activity 14 working in pairs.

53

Answers

15 1. No, está viendo televisión.
2. Hugo quiere ir a alquilar una película.
3. Quiere ir ahora mismo. Antes de comer.
4. Hace mucho tiempo. Casi dos meses.

16 Answers will vary.

17 Play a portion of the recorded dialog as students write what they hear. As an alternative, you may choose to read the selection yourself. Check the accuracy of student dictations.

Activities

Critical Listening
Use a newspaper published in Spanish or Internet resources to obtain the Spanish titles of popular films made in the United States. Read the titles to the class and ask them to identify the name of each film in English.

Expansion
Additional questions (*Algo personal*): *¿Te gusta ver películas por la tarde o por la noche en casa?*; *¿Vas al cine también? ¿Cuándo vas?*; *¿Te gusta más ver una película en el cine o alquilar una y verla en la televisión?*; *¿Te gustan más las películas nuevas o las películas viejas?*

Diálogo II
Quiero alquilar una película

HUGO: ¿Estás durmiendo?
LUZ: No. Estoy viendo televisión. ¿Por qué?
HUGO: Porque quiero ir a alquilar una película.

LUZ: ¿Ahora mismo?
HUGO: Sí, quiero ir antes de comer. ¿Quieres ir?
LUZ: Un segundo.... Ya voy.

LUZ: No quiero ver las mismas películas otra vez.
HUGO: ¿Cuánto tiempo hace que no ves una película?
LUZ: ¡Uy! Hace mucho tiempo. Casi dos meses.
HUGO: ¡Entonces no vas a ver las mismas películas!

15 ¿Qué recuerdas?

1. ¿Está Luz durmiendo?
2. ¿Qué quiere hacer Hugo?
3. ¿Cuándo quiere ir Hugo?
4. ¿Cuánto tiempo hace que Luz no ve una película?

16 Algo personal

1. ¿Cuánto tiempo hace que no alquilas una película?
2. ¿Haces una lista de películas antes de ir a alquilar una?
3. ¿Cuánto tiempo hace que no ves una película?
4. ¿Por cuánto tiempo ves televisión en una semana?
5. ¿Cuánto tiempo libre tienes en una semana? ¿Qué haces?

17 Dictado

 Escucha la información y escribe lo que oyes.

¿Cuánto tiempo hace que no alquilas una película?

Notes Vary how you assign the *¿Qué recuerdas?* and *Algo personal* activities. For example, you may wish to have students listen to the audio CD of the activity and answer orally; you may decide to have students listen to the audio CD and then write their answers; or you may choose to have students write their answers and then do the activities in class orally.

Connections. Activity 18 makes the cross-curricular connection to the arts.

Cultura viva

Che, bailá conmigo...

In the world of dance and music, *tango* is synonymous with Argentina, and especially Buenos Aires. This well-known song was born a century ago near the docks of the capital in the neighborhood known as *La Boca*. While there, if you look carefully, you will see a street sign with the name *Caminito* that denotes the short dead-end street (*callejuela*). This street's name has its origins in one of Carlos Gardel's most famous tangos. Carlos Gardel is considered the father of the tango and he is revered in Argentina still today, decades after his death. From the docks in *La Boca,* the *tango* spread throughout the Americas to Europe and,

Bailamos el tango.

El Caminito, una callejuela en La Boca, Buenos Aires.

El tango es de la Argentina.

today, is popular in ballrooms throughout the world.

18 Conexiones con otras disciplinas: baile y música

Prepare a project on the tango, choosing from one of the following options or making up your own:

* Search the word *tango* on the Internet or by looking up the words *Argentina* and *tango* in an encyclopedia at the library and write a summary of your findings.
* Locate someone who teaches the tango and invite the person to speak or demonstrate the tango for the class.
* Attend tango classes at a local community center or at a local dance studio and demonstrate the dance for the class.
* Play a tango for the class, comparing it to another musical style.

Capítulo 7   *cincuenta y cinco* **55**

Teacher Resources

 Activity 19

 Activity 5

 Activities 10–11

 Activity 5

 Activities 9–10

Answers

19 1. Hace más de un siglo que juegan al béisbol en los Estados Unidos.
2. Hace un año que jugamos al voleibol.
3. Hace quince años que vivo aquí.
4. Hace veinte minutos que Uds. juegan a los videojuegos.
5. Hace un cuarto de hora que mi sobrina dibuja una casa.
6. Hace treinta segundos que jugamos al ajedrez.

Activities

Students with Special Needs
Give a second model sentence for activity 19.

 # Idioma

Estructura

Expressions with *hace*

You can describe an action that began in the past and has continued into the present using **hace** + **a time expression** + **que** + **the present tense of a verb.**

Hace diez minutos que veo televisión.   I have been watching television for ten minutes. (Ten minutes ago I started watching television.)

Reverse the order of *hace* and the time expression if a form of *¿cuánto?* introduces the question.

¿Cuánto tiempo hace que ves televisión?   How long have you been watching television?

 Práctica

19 **¿Cuánto tiempo hace?**

Say how long the following activities have been taking place.

MODELO   haces aeróbicos / una hora
         Hace una hora que haces aeróbicos.

1. juegan al béisbol en los Estados Unidos / más de un siglo
2. jugamos al voleibol / un año
3. vivo aquí / quince años
4. Uds. juegan a los videojuegos / veinte minutos
5. mi sobrina dibuja una casa / un cuarto de hora
6. jugamos al ajedrez / treinta segundos

Hace una hora que hacen aeróbicos.

Notes   Note for your students the difference between the use of *hace* as a form of the verb *hacer* and *hace* as it is used here to indicate an amount of time that has elapsed.

Point out to students the possible confusion between *¿Cuánto tiempo hace que...?* and *¿Qué tiempo hace?*

20 ¿Qué haces?

In pairs, take turns asking and answering the following questions. Then summarize your partner's answers for each question.

MODELO
A: ¿Juegas a los videojuegos?
B: Sí, juego a los videojuegos.
A: *(Write:* B juega a los videojuegos.*)*

1. ¿Cuánto tiempo hace que no juegas al ajedrez? ¿Y a las damas?
2. ¿Sabes jugar al ajedrez o a las damas?
3. ¿Cuánto tiempo hace que no lees una revista?
4. ¿Qué revistas lees?
5. ¿Cuánto tiempo hace que dibujas?
6. ¿Sabes dibujar?
7. ¿Cuánto tiempo hace que no ves una telenovela?
8. ¿Te gusta ver televisión? ¿Te gustan las telenovelas?
9. ¿Cuánto tiempo hace que estudias español?
10. ¿Cuánto tiempo hace que no escribes una carta?

Juego a los videojuegos.

◈ Comunicación

21 Mis pasatiempos

Prepare a list of your pastimes. Include at least six or seven activities. Then, with a partner, ask and answer questions about your favorite pastimes.

¡Extra!

¿Damas en los baños?

The games *ajedrez* (chess) and *damas* (checkers) are two of the world's oldest pastimes. However, if you see the word *Damas* (Ladies) on the door of a public restroom not very far from another door labeled *Caballeros* (Gentlemen), do not assume you are going in to play checkers. Remember what you have learned: The meaning of any word may vary according to the context in which the word is used.

Nuestro pasatiempo favorito es el ajedrez.

¿Te gusta dibujar?

Capítulo 7

cincuenta y siete **57**

Activities

Multiple Intelligences (interpersonal)
First, have students make a list in Spanish consisting of their relatives' and friends' favorite pastimes. For each person or activity identified, they should write a logical statement with *hace* (+ time + *que* + the present tense of a verb). For example, *Hace cinco años que mi amigo Marco juega al golf.* Then have students talk about their sentences with a partner or with the class.

Spanish for Spanish Speakers
Have students write a composition of at least 100 words describing their favorite *pasatiempos.*

Notes Vary the way you assign oral activities. For example, pair students requiring additional help with stronger students for activity 21. You might even consider asking several volunteers to share with the class some of the pastimes from their discussions in pairs.

In addition to *Damas* and *Caballeros,* students may see *Señoras* and *Señores* or *Mujeres* and *Hombres* to indicate women's and men's bathrooms.

Teacher Resources

 Activity 22

 Activities 6–7

 Activity 12

 Activity 6

 Activities 11–13

Answers

22 1. Mi padre y mi madre están saliendo....
2. Mi hermano está buscando....
3. Esteban está alquilando....
4. Tú estás pensando....
5. Uds. están apagando....
6. María está poniendo....

Activities

Critical Thinking
As follow-up to activity 22, ask students to name several well-known people in your state, and then explain what they think each person is doing right now.

Students with Special Needs
With their books closed, give students several verbs that have irregular present participles and have them form the present progressive tense.

Estructura

Saying what is happening: present progressive

You can say what is happening right now using the *presente progresivo*, which consists of the present tense of *estar* plus a present participle (*gerundio*).

*¿Qué **están haciendo** Uds.?*
*Marta **está dibujando**, Enrique **está comiendo** y yo **estoy saliendo**.*

What **are** (all of) you **doing**?
Marta **is drawing**, Enrique **is eating** and I **am leaving**.

Form the present participle of most verbs by changing the infinitive endings (*-ar, -er, -ir*) to *-ando* for *-ar* verbs or to *-iendo* for *-er* and *-ir* verbs.

-ar	-er	-ir
alquil**ar** → alquil**ando**	hac**er** → hac**iendo**	permit**ir** → permit**iendo**

Some *-ir* verbs with a stem change in the present tense require a different stem change in the present participle. This second change is shown in parentheses after infinitives in this book. Three verbs that follow this pattern are *dormir (ue, **u**), preferir (ie, **i**)* and *sentir (ie, **i**).*

verbo	presente	gerundio
dormir **(ue, u)**	d**ue**rmo	d**u**rmiendo
preferir **(ie, i)**	pref**ie**ren	pref**i**riendo
sentir **(ie, i)**	s**ie**nto	s**i**ntiendo

Some verbs have minor irregularities in their present participles. For example, the *i* in *-iendo* changes to *y* after most verb stems that end in a vowel and for the verb *ir: leer* (stem: *le*) → le**y**endo; *oír* (stem: *o*) → o**y**endo; *ir* → **y**endo. The present participle for the irregular verb *venir* requires a change in the stem from *e* to *i*: venir → v**i**niendo. Finally, the present participle for *poder* involves a stem change from *o* to *u*: p**u**diendo.

❖ Práctica

 22 Todos están haciendo algo

Using the *presente progresivo* and the provided cues, say what these people are doing right now.

MODELO nosotros / leer el periódico
Nosotros estamos leyendo el periódico.

1. mi padre y mi madre / salir de casa
2. mi hermano / buscar el control remoto
3. Esteban / alquilar una película estupenda
4. tú / pensar en tus pasatiempos
5. Uds. / apagar la luz de la cocina
6. María / poner la mesa

Ellas están leyendo el periódico.

Notes **Comparisons.** It may help some students to know that the present participle (*gerundio*) is equivalent to **-ing** in English.

Review the forms of the verb *estar* with students.

23 ¿Qué estás haciendo?

In pairs, take turns asking and answering what you are doing right now, according to the illustrations.

MODELO   A: ¿Qué estás haciendo?
         B: Estoy alquilando una película.

1   **2**   **3**   **4**   **5**

24 Tomando un mate

Pretend you are sitting in an outdoor café in Buenos Aires. Using the *presente progresivo,* describe what you see from your table.

MODELO   una chica / escribir una carta
         Una chica está escribiendo una carta.

1. otra chica / dibujar
2. el mesero / poner una mesa
3. un muchacho / hablar por el celular
4. el niño / mirar a sus padres
5. un padre y una madre / comer con sus hijos
6. unos señores / jugar al ajedrez
7. tú / salir

Notes **Comparisons.** Explain to students that in Spanish the present progressive is not used as frequently as it is in English. Rather, the present tense is normally used. The present progressive is reserved for stating more emphatically that the action is currently going on.

Comparisons. You may wish to note for students that in Spanish, present participles cannot be used as nouns as they are in English (Learning is fun). In Spanish, the noun form of the verb is the infinitive. This point will be explained later in the lesson.

Comunicación

25 Estoy...

Working in pairs, imagine you are in the following places: *una cafetería, Buenos Aires, una tienda de videos, una fiesta para tu cumpleaños, una clase de español, la sala de la casa, el museo, la calle, el parque.* Pretend you are talking on the phone with a friend and discuss what you are doing right now. Add to the conversation by asking such things as who you are with, where each place is located, etc.

MODELO **A:** ¿Qué estás haciendo?
      B: Estoy tomando café en una cafetería.
      A: ¿Dónde está la cafetería?
      B: Está en La Boca.

26 Están ocupados

With a classmate, pretend you are calling one another trying to reach various people on the phone. The person answering must apologize and say the person you are trying to reach is not home and, then, say what the person is doing. Be creative!

MODELO **A:** Hola. ¿Puedo hablar con Eduardo por favor?
      B: Lo siento. Eduardo está paseando por la calle ahora mismo.

Estrategia

Clarifying meaning by asking questions
If you hear a new word in a conversation but do not understand what it means, do not be afraid to ask someone to fill you in. Many words in Spanish have different uses depending on the region or country where they are used. So the next time you hear a word or expression you are unsure of, do not be embarrassed; ask someone to explain it to you.

Repaso rápido: direct object pronouns

You have already learned to use direct objects to show the person or thing in a sentence that receives the action of the verb. Do you remember the direct object pronouns?

los pronombres de complemento directo

me	*me*	**nos**	*us*
te	*you* (**tú**)	**os**	*you (vosotros,-as)*
lo	*him, it, you* (**Ud.**)	**los**	*them, you (Uds.)*
la	*her, it, you* (**Ud.**)	**las**	*them, you (Uds.)*

*No **la** veo.*
  I do not see **her.**
  I do not see **it.** (*la lista de las películas nuevas*)

*Nunca **lo** veo.*
  I never see **him.**
  I never see **it.** (*el programa*)

60 *sesenta*

Lección A

Estructura

Using the present progressive with direct object pronouns

You have already seen that direct object pronouns usually precede conjugated verbs. However, direct object pronouns may be attached to an infinitive.

> **Lo** *voy a alquilar.*
> *Voy a alquilar***lo.**   I am going to rent **it.** *(el DVD)*

Similarly, you may choose to attach an object pronoun to the end of a present participle. When doing so, however, you must add an accent mark to the present participle in order to maintain the original pronunciation of the present participle without the pronoun.

> **La** *estamos leyendo.*
> *Estamos leyéndo***la.**   We are reading **it.** *(la revista)*

 **Práctica**

27 Lo estamos haciendo

Tell what the following people are doing right now, using direct object pronouns.

1. la señora Herrera / empezar / un viaje a Venezuela
2. Uds. / escribir / la lista de películas nuevas
3. nosotros / leer / un libro sobre Buenos Aires ahora
4. yo / escuchar / la radio ahora
5. Pilar / buscar / el control remoto

Estamos tomando mate.

28 Haciéndolo

Imagine you and your friend are watching television and commenting on various characters and programs. Working in pairs, take turns asking and answering questions using the provided cues. Follow the model, attaching direct object pronouns to the verbs in each sentence.

> **MODELO** los hermanos / leer el diario de la hermana
> **A:** ¿Están leyendo los hermanos el diario de la hermana?
> **B:** Sí, están leyéndolo.

1. tú / buscar el programa
2. el cantante / cantar una canción de amor
3. Julia / escuchar la radio
4. nosotros / ver esta telenovela
5. Mónica / dibujar un mapa en la servilleta
6. mi equipo favorito / jugar un partido importante

Capítulo 7   *sesenta y uno* **61**

Teacher Resources

 Activities 27–28

 Activity 13

 Activity 7

 Activity 14

Answers

27 1. La señora Herrera lo está empezando.
2. Uds. la están escribiendo.
3. Nosotros lo estamos leyendo.
4. Yo la estoy escuchando.
5. Pilar lo está buscando.

28 1. ¿Estás buscando...?/...estoy buscándolo.
2. ¿Está cantando...?/...está cantándola.
3. ¿Está escuchando...?/...está escuchándola.
4. ¿Estamos viendo...?/...estamos viéndola.
5. ¿Está dibujando...?/...está dibujándolo.
6. ¿Está jugando...?/...está jugándolo.

Activities

Expansion
The present progressive tense can be made negative by placing a negative expression such as *no* before the conjugated form of *estar: estoy dibujando (no estoy dibujando)*. Practice this point by having students make these sentences negative: *(No) Estoy jugando al ajedrez.; ¿(No) Estás viendo televisión?*

Notes Write on the board several sentences that demonstrate the use of the present progressive tense with direct object pronouns. Remind students that the direct object answers the question (subject + verb +) **who?** or **what?**

Mate (shown in the photograph) is a hot beverage similar to tea. It is very popular in Argentina. It is customarily served in a wooden cup called a *mate* and sipped through a metal straw (the best of which are silver) called a *bombilla*.

Refer to the list of Teacher Resources at the top of the page to find ancillaries for practicing the present progressive with direct object pronouns.

29 Otra vez

Redo activity 27 by attaching the direct object pronouns to the end of the present participle. Make any other appropriate changes.

30 Conexión con otras disciplinas: estadística

Prepare a list of at least eight pastimes in Spanish *(ir al cine, jugar al voleibol)*. Then ask five people to rank the pastimes, with *1* being their favorite and *8* being their least favorite activity. Prepare a written summary of your findings in Spanish. Follow the model.

MODELO ¿Qué pasatiempos de mi lista son tus favoritos, en una escala del uno al ocho?

¡Extra!

Comparando inglés y español

You have learned to combine the present tense of *estar* with a present participle *(gerundio)* of a verb in Spanish to describe what is going on right now. This verb form is comparable to the *-ing* form of a verb in English. Notice, however, that words ending in *-ing* in English may require an infinitive in Spanish if the English word functions as a noun instead of a verb. Compare the following:

Me gusta **jugar** al voleibol.	I like **playing** volleyball. *(noun)*
Nadar es divertido.	**Swimming** is fun. *(noun)*

but:

Estoy **jugando** al voleibol.	I am **playing** volleyball. *(verb)*
¿Estás **nadando**?	Are you **swimming**? *(verb)*

¿Qué pasatiempos de mi lista son tus favoritos, en una escala del uno a ocho?

1. Me gusta leer revistas. 1 2 3 4 5 6 7 8
2. Me gusta escuchar la radio. 1 2 3 4 5 6 7 8

31 Mirando y haciendo

Mira a cuatro o cinco personas desde donde tú estás ahora. ¿Qué están haciendo?

MODELO El profesor está ayudando a un estudiante.

Notes Activity 30 offers a cross-curricular connection to mathematics (specifically, statistics).

Have students share the results of their surveys with the class. Ask a volunteer to write each new activity on the board.

Follow up activity 31 with a class discussion reviewing everyone's activities in the classroom.

 **Comunicación**

 32 Los pasatiempos

Write the names in Spanish of at least five or six of your favorite pastimes. Next to the list, add columns telling where you participate in the activity, how long you have done the activity and with whom you do the activity. Then, working with a partner, take turns asking and answering questions about each other's pastimes.

Juego al voleibol en la playa.

MODELO   **A:** ¿Cuál es tu pasatiempo favorito?
B: Mi pasatiempo favorito es jugar al voleibol.
A: ¿Dónde juegas al voleibol?
B: Juego en la playa.
A: ¿Cuánto tiempo hace que tienes este pasatiempo?
B: Hace dos años que tengo este pasatiempo.

 33 El tiempo libre

In small groups, talk about the activities and pastimes you enjoy during school breaks and vacation. Make sure each of you describes at least two activities/pastimes. Have a group member make a list of all the activities and pastimes you talk about and share the information with the class.

¡Nuestro pasatiempo favorito es el fútbol!

Answers

32 Creative self-expression.
33 Answers will vary.

Activities

Expansion
Ask students to find magazines containing pictures of different places where students would like to go. Working in pairs or small groups, each student should teach classmates any new vocabulary required for describing the pictures or naming the locations shown. Then have students try the following. Student A shows a picture and Student B asks: *¿Dónde estás?*. Student A responds as if he or she were at the place shown: *Estoy en un playa en Argentina*. After the response, Student B asks: *¿Qué estás haciendo?*. Student A responds with what he or she is doing, according to the picture: *Estoy nadando*.

Capítulo 7   *sesenta y tres* **63**

Answers

34 1. El fútbol es el deporte más popular de Argentina./El juego del pato es el deporte nacional de Argentina.
2. Hace más de 400 años que se originó el juego del pato.
3. Originalmente, los gauchos jugaban al pato con un pato vivo.
4. En 1822 fue prohibido el juego del pato.
5. Hoy, el juego del pato se juega entre ocho jinetes.

35 Answers will vary.

Activities

Multiple Intelligences (linguistic)

Ask individuals to research Argentina and then report their findings to the class. Possible topics: compare and contrast the Argentine *gaucho* with the American cowboy; discuss the Argentinean economy; compare what Evita Perón was really like to the image presented in the movie *Evita*.

Spanish for Spanish Speakers

Students write a short composition in Spanish in which they discuss something they know about Argentina. Expand the activity by having students seek out additional information about Argentina at the library or on the Internet.

Lectura cultural

El juego del pato

*E*n Argentina, el deporte más popular es el fútbol, pero el deporte nacional es el juego del pato[1]. Este es un deporte hípico[2] similar al polo que se originó hace más de 4 siglos entre los gauchos[3] de Argentina.

Originalmente, jugaba con un hacia arriba[5] y atropellaban[7] unos a otros. trágicos que

el juego del pato se pato vivo[4] que se arrojaba dos grupos de jinetes[6] se para capturarlo y pasarlo Había tantos resultados fue prohibido en 1822.

Pasando la pelota por el aro.

En 1937, el juego del pato volvió, reglamentado[8] y modernizado. Ya no se juega con un pato sino con una pelota blanca con seis asas[9]. Dos equipos de cuatro jugadores cada uno juegan en un campo de 220 metros por 90 metros. El objetivo del juego es pasar la pelota—a la que se llama pato—por un aro[10] que tiene un metro de diámetro. Los jugadores, a caballo, deben recoger[11] el pato y lanzarlo con la mano derecha. Es un deporte de fuerza[12] y habilidad, y aunque no es muy popular, es el deporte más tradicional de Argentina.

El juego del pato, el deporte nacional de la Argentina.

[1]the duck game [2]equine [3]Argentinian cowboys [4]live duck [5]thrown into the air [6]horsemen
[7]would trample each other [8]regulated [9]handles [10]hoop [11]pick up [12]strength

34 ¿Qué recuerdas?

Correct these false statements.

1. El juego del pato es el deporte más popular de Argentina.
2. Hace más de 40 años que se originó el juego del pato.
3. Originalmente, los gauchos jugaban al pato con una pelota blanca.
4. En 1953 fue prohibido el juego del pato.
5. Hoy, el juego del pato se juega entre dos jinetes.

> • Why do you think *el juego del pato* is not very popular today among Argentines? Do you think it could become popular in the United States if it were introduced here? Explain.

35 Algo personal

1. ¿Cuál crees que es el deporte nacional de Estados Unidos?
2. ¿Qué deporte practican los *cowboys* de Estados Unidos?
3. ¿A qué deporte es el juego del pato similar? Explica.
4. ¿Te gustaría aprender a jugar al pato? ¿Por qué sí o por qué no?

64 *sesenta y cuatro*   **Lección A**

Notes The *Lectura cultural* has been recorded and is available in the Audio CD Program along with activities 34 and 35. You may wish to help students with the reading and then assign the reading and the questions as homework. After reviewing the contents of the *Lectura cultural*, play the recording and allow students to read along silently. Then play the audio CD of the activities, pausing after each question and calling on students to provide an answer.

¿Qué aprendí?

Autoevaluación

As a review and self-check, respond to the following:

1. What are your favorite leisure activities?
2. Name a sport that is very popular in Argentina.
3. Ask in Spanish if a friend can play volleyball tomorrow.
4. How long have you been studying Spanish?
5. Say four things people around you are doing right now.
6. A friend asks if you have your Spanish book. Answer by saying that you are looking for it.
7. What do you know about Argentina?

Visit the web-based activities at www.emcp.com

Palabras y expresiones

Pasatiempos
los aeróbicos
el ajedrez
el básquetbol
las cartas
las damas
el equipo
el fútbol americano
hacer aeróbicos
el pasatiempo
el programa
la telenovela
el videojuego
el voleibol

Otras expresiones
ahora mismo
antes de
¿Cuánto (+ time expression) hace que (+ present tense of verb). . . ?
después de
esta noche
hace (+ time expression) que
el minuto
mismo
(number +) vez/veces al/a la (time expression)
por la (mañana, tarde, noche)
el segundo
el siglo
todavía

Verbos
alquilar
apagar
costar (ue)
dar
dibujar
dormir (ue, u)
jugar (ue)
permitir
poder (ue, u)
recordar (ue, u)
volver (ue, u)

Expresiones y otras palabras
americano,-a
casi
el control remoto
estupendo,-a
la lista
mismo,-a
remoto,-a
el televisor
la vida

Estoy buscando un programa.

Capítulo 7

El control remoto.

sesenta y cinco **65**

Teacher Resources

Activity 14

Information Gap Activities
Postcard Activities
Funciones de Comunicación

Answers

Autoevaluación
Possible answers:
1. Answers will vary.
2. El fútbol es muy popular en (la) Argentina.
3. ¿Puedes jugar al voleibol mañana?
4. Hace un año que estudio español.
5. Mi amigo está escribiendo ahora…
6. Estoy buscándolo.
7. Large cattle ranches there are called *estancias*.

Activities

Multiple Intelligences (bodily-kinesthetic/linguistic)
Assign students to read *The House of the Spirits* by Isabel Allende. Then have them write their own copy for a book jacket. They should include pictures, line drawings, type design, a blurb about the book and a sketch of the author.

Technology
Check with your media center or ask your students if they have access to a Spanish-speaking station on their cable network or from a satellite dish. Have them tape a segment of a Sunday afternoon soccer match and bring it in to share with the rest of the class.

Notes **Comparisons.** Remind students that in Spanish, present participles cannot be used as gerunds as they are in English (Learning is fun). In Spanish the noun form of the verb is the infinitive: *Me gusta cantar* (I like singing); *Bailar es divertido* (Dancing is fun).

65

Las estaciones en Chile

 Activity 1

 Activity 50

 Activities 1–3

 Activity 1

 Activities 1–2

Content reviewed in *Lección B*

- **months and seasons of the year**
- **expressing likes and dislikes**
- **present progressive tense**
- **sports**

Activities

Prereading Strategy
Conduct a discussion about the activities students enjoy during each of the four seasons. Then have students look through the scenes quickly to find cognates and words they recognize.

Spanish for Spanish Speakers
Call on students to state in Spanish activities people like to do during different seasons in their country of origin.

Lección B

Chile

Vocabulario I
Las estaciones en Chile

¡Este lugar es excelente!

Hace frío.

esquiar

patinar sobre hielo

No hace mucho calor.

montar en patineta

el otoño

el invierno

el verano

la primavera

hace sol

llover

dar un paseo por la playa

la flor

Hay flores por todos lados.

66 *sesenta y seis*

Lección B

Notes When speaking informally, native Spanish speakers occasionally abbreviate words. For example, *la bicicleta* may be referred to as *la bici* and *la televisión* may be called *la tele*. Ask students to think of similar abbreviations in English or Spanish.

Remind students that an infinitive can act as a noun in Spanish: *Esquiar es mi deporte favorito.*

No me gusta esquiar, pero en cambio me gusta ver televisión.

Sí, pero ya estoy lista.

¿Todavía continúas en la computadora?

La chica envía un correo electrónico a Juan. Ella copia la dirección de Juan en su cuaderno. Ella pone los papeles en su lugar.

Answers

1 1. el invierno; 2. la primavera; 3. el verano; 4. el otoño

2 1. Pueden patinar sobre hielo en Chile en el invierno.
  2. Hay muchas flores en los meses de septiembre, octubre y noviembre.
  3. Están esquiando en junio, julio y agosto.
  4. Es otoño.
  5. Es verano.
  6. Es invierno.

1 Las estaciones

Escoge la estación correcta, según lo que oyes.

la primavera

el otoño

el verano

el invierno

2 Las estaciones en Chile

Contesta las siguientes preguntas.

1. ¿En qué estación pueden patinar sobre hielo en Chile?
2. ¿En qué meses hay flores en Chile?
3. ¿En qué meses están esquiando en Chile?
4. ¿Qué estación es en abril y mayo en Chile?
5. ¿Qué estación es en enero y febrero en Chile?
6. ¿Qué estación es en junio y julio en Chile?

¡Extra!

¿Cuándo es verano?

In the Southern Hemisphere, the seasons are the reverse of the seasons in the Northern Hemisphere. For this reason, people ski in Chile from June to August because it is winter there. Similarly, the summer months in Chile are December, January and February.

Activities

Pronunciation (las letras m, n, ñ)
Review the sound of m *(mucho, tiempo, minutos, menos, primavera, mes)*, n *(cuestan, cuánto, verano, nuevas, tengo, poner)* and ñ *(año, cumpleaños, mañana, niño, otoño, cariñosa)*. Then pronounce the following carefully, having students say the sentence several times before writing what they hear: *Mañana es el primer día del invierno, que nos gusta mucho en Chile, pero que al señor Núñez no le gusta.* Ask students if they understand the meaning of the sentence.

TPR
Using TPR, introduce or review expressions that name various pastimes: *dar un paseo, montar en bicicleta, nadar, ver televisión, jugar al fútbol, jugar al tenis, esquiar, patinar.*

Capítulo 7

sesenta y siete **67**

Notes Tell students that although the infinitives *poner* and *dar* were introduced earlier, the present-tense forms of these verbs are taught in *Capítulo 7, Lección B.*

Your students may find it interesting that the school year in many South American countries begins in February or March.

Activity 1 is intended for listening comprehension practice. Play the audio CD of the activity that is part of the Audio CD Program or use the transcript that appears in the ATE Introduction if you prefer to read the activity yourself.

Teacher Resources

 ¡Vamos a esquiar!
Activities 3–5

Answers

3 1. Diego quiere dar un paseo por la playa.
2. Porque hace mucho calor.
3. Prefiere montar en patineta.
4. Quiere ir a esquiar.
5. Quiere ir a Colorado.
6. Pablo es tonto.
7. A Pablo le gusta el invierno.
8. Van a ir a tomar un refresco.

4 Answers will vary.

5 All answers begin with *Puedo* and end with an appropriate activity for the indicated season.

Activities

Critical Listening

Play the audio CD recording of the dialog as students cover the words and listen to the conversation. Then ask several individuals to state what they believe the conversation is about.

Expansion

Additional questions *(Algo personal)*: *¿Qué tiempo hace en tu ciudad en primavera/verano/otoño/ invierno?; ¿Qué te gusta hacer en la primavera/el verano/el otoño/el invierno?; ¿Vas a la playa en el verano? ¿A qué playa?; ¿Qué otros pasatiempos te gustan?*

Prereading Strategy

Instruct students to cover up the dialog with one hand and look at the photographs. Ask them to look through the dialog quickly to find cognates and words they recognize.

Diálogo 1

¡Vamos a esquiar!

DIEGO: ¿Vamos a dar un paseo por la playa?
PABLO: No, gracias. Hace mucho calor.
ELENA: Yo prefiero montar en patineta.

PABLO: ¡Vamos a esquiar!
ELENA: ¡En enero no podemos esquiar en Chile!
PABLO: No, aquí, no. ¡Vamos a Colorado!

ELENA: ¡Qué tonto eres!
PABLO: Me gusta el invierno.
ELENA: ¡Ya está bien! Vamos a tomar un refresco.

3 ¿Qué recuerdas?

1. ¿Quién quiere dar un paseo por la playa?
2. ¿Por qué no quiere Pablo ir a la playa?
3. ¿Qué prefiere hacer Elena?
4. ¿Qué quiere hacer Pablo?
5. ¿Adónde quiere ir Pablo a esquiar?
6. ¿Quién es tonto?
7. ¿A quién le gusta el invierno?
8. ¿Qué van a ir a tomar?

4 Algo personal

1. ¿Cuál es tu estación favorita? Explica.
2. ¿Qué te gusta hacer en tu estación favorita?
3. ¿Qué deportes practicas donde tú vives en la primavera? ¿Y en el verano? ¿Y en el otoño? ¿Y en el invierno?

5 ¿Qué actividades puedes hacer?

 Escucha la información y di qué actividad o actividades puedes hacer.

MODELO Puedo montar en patineta en el parque.

Montamos en patineta.

Notes Explain that the articles *el* and *la* may be omitted after *en* and after forms of the verb *ser: hace sol en (el) verano; mi estación favorita es (la) primavera.*

This dialog and activities 3, 4 and 5 have been recorded by native speakers and are included in the *Navegando* Audio CD Program. Have students cover up the dialog on page 68 and look at the photographs as you play the dialog. Then discuss the contents of the dialog to evaluate what students have understood.

Cultura viva

La Isla de Pascua.

La región de los lagos (southern lakes region), Chile.

Chile

Mainland Chile is located along the western coast of South America between the Andes Mountains and the Pacific Ocean. The country also has many interesting islands, including the *Juan Fernández Islands,* where Robinson Crusoe lived for four years, and Easter Island *(Isla de Pascua),* an island with a mysterious past which is inhabited by people of Polynesian ancestry. Most Chileans live in urban areas, like the capital, Santiago. The

Los rascacielos de Santiago.

population is well educated and the country has a strong literary tradition: Chileans are very proud of their two Nobel Prize-winning poets, Gabriela Mistral and Pablo Neruda. Since much of Chile's population has European origins, it is not uncommon to encounter people of Italian, English, German, Irish or Polish ancestry, or to see street signs with names that are obviously not of Spanish origin. Indeed, the southern city of Puerto Montt was for many years a German colony and the liberator and first ruler of Chile was Bernardo O'Higgins.

When you visit, you will discover that Chile is a country of magnificent contrasts offering everything, from large cosmopolitan cities with the latest in modern-day conveniences and skyscrapers *(rascacielos)* that reach to the sky to the beautiful rustic countryside of the southern lakes region. Just a short distance away from cosmopolitan Santiago, ski resorts like Portillo or Farellones in the Andes Mountains and resort beaches near Viña del Mar offer an escape from the pressures of modern life.

6 Chile

Contesta las siguientes preguntas sobre Chile.

1. ¿Está Chile en América del Sur o en América del Norte?
2. ¿Qué montañas están en Chile?
3. ¿Qué océano está al oeste de Chile?
4. ¿En qué isla vive gente de ancestro polinesio?
5. ¿Cuál es la capital del país?
6. ¿Quién es una persona famosa de Chile?
7. ¿Adónde puede uno ir a esquiar? ¿Y a nadar en la playa?

7 Conexiones con otras disciplinas: geografía

Use an encyclopedia or search the Internet for information about Chile. Then list four or five interesting details about places mentioned in the *Cultura viva* (e.g., Juan Fernández Islands, Isla de Pascua, Viña del Mar, etc.).

Capítulo 7

sesenta y nueve **69**

Teacher Resources

 Activity 6

 Activity 2

Activity 4

Answers

6 1. Está en América del Sur.
2. Los Andes están en Chile.
3. El océano Pacífico está al oeste de Chile.
4. En la Isla de Pascua vive gente de ancestro polinesio.
5. Santiago es la capital del país.
6. Gabriela Mistral (Pablo Neruda, Bernardo O'Higgins) es una persona famosa de Chile.
7. Uno puede ir a esquiar a Portillo o a Farillones. Uno puede nadar en la playa de Viña del Mar.

7 Answers will vary.

Activities

Connections
Ask students to find Chile on a world map. Then locate some of the sites mentioned in *Cultura viva.*

Spanish for Spanish Speakers
Suggest that students read several poems by Gabriela Mistral or Pablo Neruda and summarize the themes presented (either orally or in writing).

Notes Your students will find it interesting that a person with an Irish name, Bernardo O'Higgins, is the national hero of Chile.

Easter Island lies in absolute isolation about 2,300 miles west of the Chilean coast in the Pacific Ocean. Its nearest neighbor, Pitcairn Island, is 1,200 miles away. The

first Polynesian settlement took place around A.D. 400.

Before beginning activity 7, point out on a Chilean map where the sites named in the *Cultura viva* are located.

69

Answers

8 1. esquían
2. copia
3. continúas
4. envían
5. esquiamos
6. continúo
7. ve
8. patina
9. envía

Activities

Students with Special Needs
Model a second sentence for activity 8.

Idioma

Estructura

Verbs that require special accentuation

Sometimes verbs that end in *-uar* or *-iar* (*esquiar, enviar* and *continuar,* for example) require a written accent mark to indicate that a vowel should be stressed for all present-tense forms except for *nosotros*. You will have to learn which verbs follow this pattern since some verbs that end in *-uar* or *-iar* may not follow this pattern (such as the verb *copiar*).

esquiar: esquío, esquías, esquía, esquiamos, esquiáis, esquían
enviar: envío, envías, envía, enviamos, enviáis, envían
continuar: continúo, continúas, continúa, continuamos, continuáis, continúan

but:

copiar: copio, copias, copia, copiamos, copiáis, copian

 **Práctica**

8 Todos hacen algo

Indica qué hacen estas personas cuando tienen tiempo libre.

MODELO Yo (esquiar) con mis padres.
Yo esquío con mis padres.

1. Eva y Luis (esquiar) en Portillo.
2. Claudia (copiar) canciones de la internet.
3. Tú (continuar) dando paseos por el parque.
4. Sara y Paz (enviar) correos electrónicos a sus amigos.
5. Nosotros (esquiar) en Farillones.
6. Yo (continuar) montando en patineta, mi actividad favorita.
7. Alberto (ver) DVDs.
8. Victoria (patinar) sobre hielo.
9. Mamá (enviar) cartas a mis abuelos.

Yo esquío con mis padres.

Notes You may wish to mention that *mandar* is a synonym for *enviar*.

Syllabification and accentuation are explained in the Appendices.

Some other verbs that require an accent when conjugated are *criar* (to raise, breed); *fiar* (to confide); *guiar* (to lead); *telegrafiar* (to telegraph); *desafiar* (to challenge); *extraviar* (to lose).

9 ¿Qué pasa?

Read the following statements and indicate where there are missing accent marks. Then identify the letter of the illustration that best matches each statement.

1. Hace calor y juegan al básquetbol.
2. Esquiamos todos los días.
3. Ellos continuan patinando sobre hielo.
4. Ella copia el número de teléfono.
5. Continua haciendo sol.
6. Él envia una carta.
7. Está nublado.
8. Ellos esquian ahora mismo.

A

B

✿ Comunicación

10 Un correo electrónico

Imagine you have a key pal in Chile. Write an e-mail telling him or her about your home and school life. You may want to say, for example, that you like to ski during the winter, that you and your family ski once a month, that you would like to go to Portillo, that you continue studying Spanish at school and that you are sending pictures of you and your family with the e-mail. Add any other details you would like.

Yo envío un correo electrónico a Chile.

Answers

9 1. B
   2. A
   3. A/Ellos continúan patinando sobre hielo.
   4. B
   5. A/Continúa haciendo sol.
   6. B/Él envía una carta.
   7. B
   8. A/Ellos esquían ahora mismo.
10 Creative self-expression.

Activities

Multiple Intelligences (interpersonal/linguistic)
There are companies that can arrange pen-pal contacts if your students are interested. A friendship with a teacher or student abroad is another good way to initiate an e-mail exchange between students.

Students with Special Needs
Have students do activity 10 in pairs or in small groups.

Notes Inform students that a key pal (or pen pal) in Spanish is *amigo/amiga por correspondencia*.

Have students apply strategies they have already learned in previous chapters as they complete activity 10.

Answers

11 Answers may vary for the means of transportation; verb forms are as follows:
1. ...doy....
2. ...das....
3. ...damos....
4. ...dan....
5. ...da....
6. ...dan....

12 1. pone
2. pongo
3. ponen
4. pone
5. pones
6. ponemos

Activities

Expansion
Ask students to create sentences using the verbs *dar, hacer, poner, saber, salir* and *ver*, being sure that they use the first-person singular forms.

Estructura

Present tense of *dar* and *poner*

The verbs *dar* and *poner* have irregular present-tense *yo* forms. In addition, the verb *dar* has an irregular *vosotros,-as* form. Other verbs that are regular in the present tense except for the *yo* form of the verbs: *hacer (yo hago), saber (yo sé), ver (yo veo), salir (yo salgo).*

dar	
doy	damos
das	**dais**
da	dan

poner	
pongo	ponemos
pones	ponéis
pone	ponen

Práctica

11 ¿Dan un paseo a pie o en carro?

Create logical sentences using the expression *dar un paseo* and either *a pie* or *en carro*, according to what makes the most sense.

MODELO Enrique / por el parque
Enrique da un paseo por el parque a pie.

1. yo / por la playa
2. tú / por la ciudad
3. nosotros / por el centro
4. Marta y Esperanza / por la calle
5. mi amigo / por la Avenida de la Independencia
6. mis padres / por la plaza

Ellas dan un paseo a pie. (Bariloche, Argentina.)

12 ¡Ponen todo en su lugar!

Completa las oraciones con la forma apropiada del verbo *poner*.

MODELO Elena <u>pone</u> la patineta en su cuarto.

1. Paz __ las flores en la mesa del comedor.
2. Yo __ los papeles en el escritorio.
3. Carlos y Paula __ sus bicicletas en el garaje.
4. Mi padre __ el televisor en la sala.
5. Tú __ la leche en el refrigerador.
6. Todos nosotros __ los cubiertos sucios en el lavaplatos.

Notes The verb *poner* is sometimes used in place of *encender* when you are talking about turning on an appliance: *Voy a encender (poner) el televisor.*

Review the various uses of *poner: poner* (to put), *poner el televisor* (to turn on), *poner la mesa* (to set the table).

13 ¡Me gusta la primavera!

Completa el siguiente párrafo con la forma apropiada de *comer, poner, dar, salir* y *ver* para saber por qué Sara dice que le gusta la primavera.

En la primavera yo siempre (1) con mi madre los domingos por la mañana a buscar flores. Yo (2) flores por toda la casa. Casi todas las mañanas yo (3) paseos por el parque con mi hermana y por la tarde alquilamos películas en una tienda cerca de la casa para verlas por la noche. Mi padre siempre me (4) dinero para alquilarlas. Claro, a veces, nosotros no las (5) porque (6) a dar un paseo por la noche y entonces no hay tiempo para verlas. Ahora mis hermanos y yo (7) la mesa para la comida. Hoy vamos a (8) en el patio porque no hace calor y no llueve. ¡Me gusta la primavera!

Pongo flores por toda la casa.

◈ Comunicación

14 Preguntas personales

En parejas, alternen en hacer y contestar las siguientes preguntas en español.

1. ¿Qué haces cuando tienes tiempo libre?
2. ¿Te gusta dar paseos? ¿Dónde?
3. ¿Dan tu familia y tú paseos en carro los fines de semana? ¿Adónde van?
4. ¿Cómo das paseos en el verano? ¿En carro? ¿A pie? ¿En bicicleta?
5. ¿Dan tus amigos y tú paseos en el verano? ¿Adónde?
6. ¿En qué estación del año te gusta más dar paseos? ¿Por qué?
7. ¿Adónde vas de viaje con tu familia en el verano? ¿En la primavera? ¿En el otoño? ¿En el invierno?
8. ¿Quién pone las maletas en el carro cuando vas de viaje con tu familia?
9. ¿Pones flores en tu casa en la primavera? ¿Quién las pone?
10. ¿Dónde pones tu mochila en las vacaciones, cuando no hay clases?

15 ¿Qué actividades haces?

Working in small groups, talk about the activities you enjoy during different times of the year according to the season. Include activities such as going for a walk, taking rides, skiing, ice-skating, watching television or any other favorite pastimes. Include details such as when and with whom you do an activity, what the weather is like at that time of year and why you like or dislike the activity.

MODELO A: ¿Qué actividades haces en el verano?
B: En el verano doy paseos por las playas de Viña del Mar todos los fines de semana. Siempre voy con mi padre y caminamos por una hora.

Capítulo 7

setenta y tres **73**

Teacher Resources

  Activity 14

Answers

13 1. salgo
2. pongo
3. doy
4. da
5. vemos
6. salimos
7. ponemos
8. comer
14 Answers will vary.
15 Creative self-expression.

Activities

Expansion
After completing activity 15, have a member of each group summarize what members of their group discussed.

Students with Special Needs
Provide a model for activities 13 and 14.

Notes Complete one or two answers as a class before assigning activity 13.

You may wish to have students write out the answers for activity 14 before pairing up with a classmate. As an alternative, after doing the activity orally in pairs, have students write their answers to be sure they understand and can retain what they practiced.

El tiempo

 Activity 4

 Activity 51

 Activities 9–11

 Activity 4

 Activities 6–9

Activities

Critical Thinking
Play the audio CD of *Vocabulario II* as students observe and consider the following: what is happening in each scene; where and when each scene takes place; what the people are saying. Finally, have students guess what they believe is the main theme of each scene.

Language through Action
Using overhead transparency 51, have students come to the front of the class and point to the different scenes as you describe them randomly in Spanish.

Notes Encourage students to obtain current weather information in Spanish via the Internet:

The Weather Channel
http://espanol.weather.com/

It may help some students to know that it is also possible to ask for the temperature using the expressions *¿Cuál es la temperatura?* or *¿A cuánto está la temperatura?*. The answers could be *Es de* (number) *grados* or *Está a* (number) *grados*.

74

el corredor

		Corredor Nº
primero	1º	208
segundo	2º	103
tercero	3º	501
cuarto	4º	931
quinto	5º	002
sexto	6º	321
séptimo	7º	711
octavo	8º	600
noveno	9º	820
décimo	10º	030

Answers

16 1. C
  2. E or F
  3. A
  4. D
  5. B
  6. E

17 Possible answers:
  1. Hace frío en el invierno.
  2. Llueve mucho en la primavera.
  3. Hace mucho calor en el verano.
  4. Está nublado.
  5. Answers will vary.

18 Creative self-expression.

Activities

Expansion
Have students answer the following questions in relation to the weather where they live: *¿Qué tiempo hace en el invierno?*; *¿Cuándo hace mucho frío y nieva?*; *¿Cuándo hace mucho calor?*; *¿Cuándo hace un poco de frío y viento?*; *¿Cuándo hay muchas flores?*; *¿Nieva en tu ciudad? ¿Hay mucha nieve o poca?*; *¿Cuándo hay mucha nieve?*; *Cuando hace sol, ¿qué te gusta hacer?*; *¿Cómo sabes cuando va a llover?*; *¿Te gusta caminar o correr en la lluvia?*; *¿Qué haces cuando llueve?*

 16 **¿Quién es?**

 Selecciona la foto de la persona apropiada.

A   **B**   **C**   **D**   **E**   **F**

 17 **El tiempo**

Contesta las siguientes preguntas en español.

1. ¿En qué estación hace mucho frío?
2. ¿En qué mes llueve mucho?
3. ¿Cuándo hace mucho calor?
4. Cuando va a llover, ¿cómo está el día?
5. ¿Qué tiempo hace en primavera? ¿Y en verano? ¿Y en otoño? ¿Y en invierno?

18 **¿Qué tiempo hace?**

In small groups, take turns describing the weather during one of the seasons without naming the season. Others then try to guess which season you are describing.

Notes Using overhead transparencies 51 and 52, present and practice the vocabulary on pages 74 and 75.

Expand the presentation of weather-related vocabulary by providing the class with the following words and phrases: *huracán, ciclón, relámpago, trueno; hace fresco; hay neblina.*

Expand activity 18 by extending the discussion to the entire class.

Answers

19 1. Dice que hace calor. Hace treinta y cinco grados.
2. Quiere jugar al básquetbol.
3. Pablo es un buen esquiador.
4. Pueden ir a Portillo.
5. Pablo va a ser el primero en terminar el refresco.

20 Answers will vary.

21 1. F; 2. C; 3. D; 4. A; 5. B; 6. E

Activities

Critical Thinking

Remind students that in the Southern Hemisphere the seasons are the reverse of the seasons in the Northern Hemisphere. Check student understanding of weather expressions by asking several questions. For example, ask questions about the weather north and south of the equator: *En los Estados Unidos es invierno, ¿qué tiempo hace en Chicago? ¿Qué tiempo hace en Santiago? ¿Hace mucho frío en el sur de Chile?; En los Estados Unidos es primavera, ¿qué tiempo hace en Virginia? ¿Qué tiempo hace en Buenos Aires? ¿Hace mucho viento en Chile?; En los Estados Unidos es verano, ¿qué tiempo hace en Missouri? ¿Está nevando en el sur de Chile? ¿Hace calor en Buenos Aires?; En los Estados Unidos es otoño, ¿está lloviendo en Michigan? ¿Está nublado en Chile? ¿Está soleado en Argentina?*

Diálogo II
¿Qué temperatura hace?

DIEGO: ¡Qué buen refresco!
PABLO: ¿Qué temperatura hace?
ELENA: Hace calor. Hace treinta y cinco grados.

DIEGO: ¡Vamos a jugar al básquetbol!
PABLO: Soy mal jugador de básquetbol.
ELENA: Eres un buen basquetbolista.
PABLO: No, soy un buen esquiador.

ELENA: En julio podemos ir a esquiar a Portillo.
DIEGO: ¿Quién va a ser el primero en terminar el refresco?
PABLO: ¡Yo! Y el segundo vas a ser tú.

19 ¿Qué recuerdas?

1. ¿Dice Elena que hace calor o hace frío?
2. ¿A qué quiere jugar Diego?
3. ¿Quién es un buen esquiador?
4. ¿Adónde pueden ir a esquiar en julio?
5. ¿Quién va a ser el primero en terminar el refresco?

20 Algo personal

1. ¿Qué temperatura hace ahora?
2. ¿Qué tiempo hace?
3. ¿Te gusta cuando hace mucho calor? ¿Y cuando hace frío?

21 ¿Qué tiempo hace?

 Selecciona la ilustración que corresponde con lo que oyes.

A **B** **C**

D **E** **F**

76 *setenta y seis*

Lección B

Notes Using the recorded version of the dialog, ask students to cover the words and try to figure out what Diego, Pablo and Elena are saying to one another.

You may choose whether to have students do activities 19 and 20 orally or in writing since they are recorded and included in the *Navegando* Audio CD Program.

Activity 21 has been provided for listening comprehension practice. A recorded version of the activity is included in the Audio CD Program. A reproducible answer sheet for the activity has been provided at the end of the Audio CD Program Manual should you wish to have students use it.

Cultura Viva

¿Fahrenheit o centígrados?

Whereas in the United States most people generally refer to the temperature in degrees Fahrenheit (*grados Fahrenheit*), throughout most of the world the temperature is given in degrees centigrade, also referred to as degrees Celsius (*grados centígrados o grados Celsius*). To ask for and understand the temperature in Spanish, you must know more than just the words that tell the temperature. You must be able to use degrees centigrade. For example, the temperature at which water freezes is

Hace mucho calor.

Hace -5 grados centígrados.

0 in degrees centigrade and 32° in degrees Fahrenheit. You can make conversions using the following formula:

$$\frac{°C}{5} \times 9 + 32 = °F$$

2.2 Conexión con otras disciplinas: matemáticas

Cambia las temperaturas de grados centígrados a grados Fahrenheit para las siguientes ciudades en Chile.

MODELO La Serena 12°C
Hace 53.6°F.

1. Iquique   28°C
2. Arica   25°C
3. Concepción   20°C
4. Santiago   35°C
5. Balmaceda   30°C
6. Puerto Montt   18°C
7. Temuco   15°C
8. Punta Arenas   9°C

¿Qué temperatura hace en Santiago?

2.3 Pronóstico del tiempo

Present a weather forecast to your class in Spanish using any props, charts and maps you wish or ones that you create. Make believe you are an actual meteorologist reporting for the ten o'clock news.

Teacher Resources

 Activity 5

Answers

2.2
1. Hace 82.4 grados.
2. Hace 77 grados.
3. Hace 68 grados.
4. Hace 95 grados.
5. Hace 86 grados.
6. Hace 64.4 grados.
7. Hace 59 grados.
8. Hace 48.2 grados.

2.3 Creative self-expression.

Activities

Cooperative Learning
Divide the class into small groups and ask each group to choose one of the countries featured in *Navegando 1B*. The groups should each prepare a country-specific weather report to share with the class.

Technology
Have students do an Internet search for the five-day forecast for Santiago, Chile. They should then print out a copy of the report to share with the class.

Notes When converting Fahrenheit to centigrade, you may wish to use the following formula:

$$\frac{5(°F - 32)}{9} = °C$$

Note that metric measurements are commonly used in the Spanish-speaking world. For example, distances are measured in *kilómetros* and weight is given in *kilogramos* or simply *kilos*.

Select several students each day to present weather forecasts.

Teacher Resources

 Activity 24

 Activity 5

 Activity 12

 Activity 6

 Activity 10

Answers

24 1. Es futbolista.
2. Es patinadora.
3. Somos deportistas.
4. Es tenista.
5. Son esquiadores.
6. Soy basquetbolista.
7. Eres beisbolista.
8. Soy corredor(a).

Activities

Communities
Have students name several well-known athletes (past or present) from your state. They should then call on a classmate who must describe the person as a *corredor, corredora*, etc.

Students with Special Needs
Model a second sentence for activity 24.

Idioma

Estructura

Describing people using *-dor* and *-ista*

You can identify someone who participates in a particular sport or activity by changing the ending on the sport to *-dor (-dora)* in some cases or *-ista* in others (which remains the same for males or females).

patinar	– el patina**dor** /la patina**dora**		el tenis	– el/la ten**ista**
esquiar	– el esquia**dor**/la esquia**dora**		el básquetbol	– el/la basquetbol**ista**
correr	– el corre**dor**/la corre**dora**		el fútbol	– el/la futbol**ista**
jugar	– el juga**dor**/ la juga**dora**			

Note: The accent mark is not used on the newly formed word when these endings are added.

Práctica

24 ¿Qué son?

Describe a estas personas usando las siguientes palabras: *basquetbolista, beisbolista, corredor(a), deportista, esquiador(a), futbolista, nadador(a), patinador(a), tenista.*

MODELO Mis primas nadan en la piscina.
Son nadadoras.

1. Juan está jugando al fútbol.
2. Beatriz está patinando sobre hielo.
3. Nosotros tenemos práctica de deportes.
4. Marta está jugando al tenis.
5. Jorge e Iván esquían muy bien.
6. Estoy jugando al básquetbol.
7. Tú estás listo para jugar al béisbol.
8. Estoy corriendo en el parque.

Juan está jugando al fútbol.

Notes Take a few minutes to review the meaning of the new terms created by adding the endings *-dor* and *-ista*. Ask students, for example, if they can figure out the meaning of *patinador/patinadora, esquiador/esquiadora, corredor/corredora, tenista, basquetbolista* and *futbolista.* Finally, ask if students can guess what a *deportista* is.

25 ¿Qué deportes practican?

Di qué deportes practican las personas de las fotografías.

MODELO  Es beisbolista.

1 **2** **3**

4 **5** **6**

☙ Comunicación

26 Mis deportistas favoritos

In small groups, talk about your favorite athletes. Try to include the names of one or two Spanish-speaking athletes, if possible. Say the person's name, sport and where the person is from (if you know). If the person plays with a team, name the team. Be as specific and detailed as you can, and add any information you can to your classmates' descriptions.

MODELO **A:** Mi deportista favorito es Sammy Sosa. Es beisbolista y es de la República Dominicana.

B: Juega con Chicago, ¿verdad?

A: Sí. Juega con Chicago.

C: Pues, mi deportista favorito es un basquetbolista. Se llama Pau Gasol.

¡Oportunidades!

El español y los deportes
You probably are familiar with a number of Spanish-speaking sports figures who learned English either before becoming famous or while traveling internationally as they participated in their sport. Knowing another language has helped them communicate with people they have met in their travels. What opportunities do you think might occur for you if you participate in sports and become really good? How might knowing Spanish help you if you are an athlete? Can you think of ways Spanish might help if you were a member of a sports team that competes internationally?

Capítulo 7 *setenta y nueve* **79**

Teacher Resources

 Activity 27

 Activity 6

 Activities 13–15

 Activity 7

 Activities 11–12

Answers

27 1. sexto
2. séptima
3. noveno
4. octava
5. tercer
6. primera
7. segundo
8. cuarta
9. quinto
10. décima

Activities

Language through Action
Make several correct and incorrect statements about the order of finish shown in the *Competencia Anual* that accompanies activity 27. Students should raise their hands if what you say matches the information shown.

80

Estructura

Using ordinal numbers

You use ordinal numbers to place things in order (first, second, third, etc.). In Spanish, only the first ten ordinal numbers are used often. They generally follow definite articles and precede nouns. Like other adjectives in Spanish, the ordinal numbers agree in gender (masculine/feminine) and number (singular/plural) with the noun they modify.

> *¿Cuáles son los **primeros** corredores en terminar?*

When *primero* and *tercero* appear before a masculine singular noun, they are shortened to *primer* and *tercer*.

> *Francisco es el **primer** corredor en terminar.*
> *Lorenzo es el **tercer** corredor en terminar.*

You can abbreviate ordinal numbers ending in *-o, -a, -os, -as* or *-er* by placing those letters at the upper right-hand side of the number: *primero → 1º, primera → 1ª, primeros → 1ᵒˢ, primeras → 1ᵃˢ, primer → 1ᵉʳ, tercer → 3ᵉʳ.*

Práctica

27 La competencia anual del colegio

El Colegio San Ignacio de Santiago tiene una competencia de esquí en Portillo todos los años. Completa los resultados de la competencia de este año con el número ordinal apropiado.

MODELO Ingrid fue la <u>décima</u> esquiadora en terminar.

Competencia Anual			
1ª	Olga	6º	Javier
2º	Edgar	7ª	Paula
3º	Hugo	8ª	Paz
4ª	Natalia	9º	Alfonso
5º	Enrique	10ª	Ingrid

1. Javier fue el __ esquiador en terminar.
2. Paula fue la __ esquiadora en terminar.
3. Alfonso fue el __ esquiador en terminar.
4. Paz fue la __ esquiadora en terminar.
5. Hugo fue el __ esquiador en terminar.
6. Olga fue la __ esquiadora en terminar.
7. Edgar fue el __ esquiador en terminar.
8. Natalia fue la __ esquiadora en terminar.
9. Enrique fue el __ esquiador en terminar.
10. Ingrid fue la __ esquiadora en terminar.

Ingrid fue la décima esquiadora en terminar.

Notes Inform students that ordinal numbers are usually placed before a noun.

Point out the similarity in the spelling of the words *cuatro* (number four) and *cuarto* (fourth, room).

Note for students that the noun sometimes is omitted when using ordinal numbers:

Nosotros somos los primeros (corredores) en terminar.

Tell students that it is common to use the abbreviated forms of the ordinal numbers. For example, such abbreviations are very common in addresses (street and avenue names, floor numbers, etc.).

28 ¡El pasatiempo nacional!

Irene loves soccer and would like to find out the standings for her favorite Chilean teams. Use the information provided in the chart to update her.

Tabla de posiciones

Equipos	PJ	PG	PE	PP	Pts.
1. Palestino	38	32	2	4	66
2. Everton	38	30	4	4	64
3. Colo Colo	38	27	5	3	59
4. Cobresal	38	24	3	11	51
5. Concepción	38	23	2	13	48
6. La Española	38	20	5	13	45
7. O'Higgins	38	18	6	14	42
8. La Católica	38	15	10	13	40
9. Cobreloa	38	12	5	21	29
10. La Serena	38	9	7	22	25

PJ: Partidos jugados; PG: Partidos ganados; PE: Partidos empatados; PP: Partidos perdidos; Pts.: Puntos

1. El Cobresal es el __ equipo.
2. El O'Higgins es el __ equipo.
3. El Colo Colo todavía es el __ equipo.
4. El Concepción es el __ equipo.
5. La Serena es el __ equipo.
6. La Católica es el __ equipo.
7. El Everton es el __ equipo.
8. El Palestino es el __ equipo.
9. El Cobreloa es el __ equipo.
10. La Española es el __ equipo.

 Comunicación

 ## 29 ¿Quién fue el primero en terminar la carrera?

Working in pairs, talk about the final results of the girls' and boys' cross-country race.

MODELO A: ¿Quién fue el octavo en terminar?
B: Gerardo fue el octavo en terminar.

¿Quién va a ser el primero en terminar?

muchachos		muchachas	
1º	Jorge	1ª	Ana
2º	Pedro	2ª	Marta
3º	Carlos	3ª	Susana
4º	Ramiro	4ª	Paula
5º	Juan	5ª	Julia
6º	Javier	6ª	Luisa
7º	Alejandro	7ª	Yolanda
8º	Gerardo	8ª	Raquel
9º	Rogelio	9ª	Carlota
10º	Víctor	10ª	Paz

Capítulo 7

ochenta y uno **81**

Notes Before beginning activity 29, check to be sure that students know the meaning of the preterite-tense form *fue*, which they learned in *Capítulo 5*.

Point out that in everyday language only cardinal numbers are used after *décimo*. Therefore, Alfonso the Thirteenth is *Alfonso XIII (trece)*.

Follow up activity 29 by asking students to write out their answers.

Expansion

Ask questions pertaining to students' class schedules: *¿Cuál es tu primera clase del día?; ¿Cuál es tu segunda clase del día?; ¿Cuál es tu tercera clase del día?;* etc.

30 Los deportes en familia

David and Teresa are fraternal twins, so they have a lot in common. However, they like to participate in totally different sports. Working in pairs, talk about the information provided here depicting their activities during various times during the year. You may want to talk about what each person is doing, what the season is, what the weather is like or anything else you can say in Spanish. Correct any information your partner says that you think is wrong.

1   **2**

3

> **MODELO**   **A:** En el primer dibujo es otoño.
>   **B:** No, no es otoño, es primavera. Hace viento. El chico está jugando al básquetbol.
>   **A:** Sí, y la chica está jugando al tenis.

Notes Chile offers many impressive ski resorts in addition to Portillo and Farellones (see page 69). Valle Nevado near Santiago is the largest ski resort in South America. It has 50 ski lifts and 22,000 acres of Andean ski slopes. Some runs are 10 miles long and 17,908 feet high.

31 En el verano

In groups of three, each of you should list five summer activities in order from most to least favorite, using ordinal numbers. Then discuss your preferences.

> 1º ir a la playa
> 2º dar paseos por el parque
> 3º jugar al fútbol

MODELO
A: Primero, me gusta ir a la playa en el verano. Hace sol y es muy divertido. Segundo, me gusta dar paseos por el parque.
B: Bueno, primero me gusta dormir.
C: A mí, primero, me gusta montar en patineta.

Una playa en Chile.

Answers

31 Creative self-expression.

Activities

Multiple Intelligences (bodily-kinesthetic)
Borrow a soccer ball from the physical education department. Call out one of the ordinal numbers and throw the ball to a student, who must call out the next ordinal number in the sequence before catching the ball. You may vary the drill by having the students say the previous ordinal number to the one you call out before catching the ball.

Notes Spanish-speaking countries have won medals in several popular sports in the Olympics, including boxing *(boxeo)*, swimming and diving *(natación y clavado)*, weight lifting *(levantamiento de pesas)* and equestrian sports *(equitación)*.

Your students may find it interesting to learn that Chile was the first Spanish-speaking country to participate in the Olympics in 1896.

Just as *Estados Unidos* is abbreviated EE.UU., the abbreviation for *Juegos Olímpicos* is JJ.OO.

Answers

32 1. Carlos es de Chile. Él practica el andinismo.
2. Desde Santiago de Chile se puede ver la Cordillera Sur de los Andes.
3. El Monumento Natural de El Morado es una montaña en un parque a hora y media de Santiago. Está cerrado en el invierno porque hay mucha nieve.
4. El primer día, Carlos va a dar un paseo por la laguna El Morado.
5. El segundo día, va a hacer mucho frío.

33 Answers will vary.

Activities

Spanish for Spanish Speakers
Have students write a short composition in Spanish, summarizing what they know about Chile. Expand the activity by having students seek additional information about Chile in the library or via the Internet.

Lectura personal

Cantantes y grupos musicales

Dirección http://www.emcp.com/músico/ola/e.diario-6.htm ▲ Archivo Edición Ver Favoritos Herramientas Ayuda

página principal   miembros   e-diario

Grupo musical La OLA

Nombre: Carlos Cubillas Lorca
Edad: 19 años
País natal: Chile
Su estación favorita: verano

Un glaciar.

¡Otro excelente concierto en Santiago de Chile! Saben amigos, estoy muy contento de estar en mi país después de tantos meses. Eché de menos[1] mis montañas. Chile tiene 4200 kilómetros (2260 millas) de cordillera[2]. Desde casi cualquier[3] lugar de la capital se puede ver la majestuosa Cordillera Sur de los Andes. Cuando no toco la guitarra con el grupo La Ola, practico el andinismo: deporte de escalar[4] montañas, específicamente los Andes. ¡Me gusta mucho el andinismo! Después de enviar este mensaje, voy a ir al Monumento Natural de El Morado con un buen amigo (y excelente esquiador).

El Morado está a sólo hora y media de Santiago. El parque está cerrado entre[5] los meses de mayo y septiembre porque hay mucha nieve, pero estamos en otoño, entonces está bien. El primer día vamos a dar un paseo por la laguna[6] El Morado. Probablemente va a hacer fresco. El segundo día, en cambio, va a hacer mucho frío. Ese día pensamos escalar en hielo por el glaciar de San Francisco. A pesar de las bajas temperaturas, la falta[7] de oxígeno y el viento, vale la pena[8] visitar este lugar para poder presenciar[9] la magia de las montañas, mis montañas chilenas.

[1] I missed [2] mountain chain [3] any [4] climb [5] between [6] lagoon [7] lack [8] it is worthwhile [9] to witness

32 ¿Qué recuerdas?

1. ¿De dónde es Carlos? ¿Qué deporte practica?
2. ¿Qué se puede ver desde Santiago de Chile?
3. ¿Qué es el Monumento Natural de El Morado? ¿En qué estación está cerrado? ¿Por qué?
4. ¿Adónde va a dar un paseo Carlos el primer día?
5. ¿Qué tiempo va a hacer el segundo día?

- From what you can infer from the reading, what is Chile's geography and climate like? Compare it with the geography and climate of the state in which you live.

33 Algo personal

1. ¿Hay montañas donde vives? ¿Cómo se llaman?
2. ¿Te gustaría escalar El Morado? ¿Por qué sí o por qué no?
3. ¿Qué estación es buena para practicar el andinismo?

84   *ochenta y cuatro*

Lección B

Notes Encourage students to find out more about Chile by going to the following Web sites:

Chile http://www.chile.com/
LanChile http://www.lanchile.com
general travel information
http://www.expedia.com

¿Qué aprendí?

Autoevaluación
As a review and self-check, respond to the following:

Visit the web-based activities at www.emcp.com

1. Name a favorite activity during each of the seasons.

2. What is the weather like where you live in the spring? Summer? Fall? Winter?

3. How would you ask what the temperature is today in Santiago, Chile?

4. Ask a friend how to send an e-mail letter and where you should put the address.

5. Imagine you are recording finishing times at a school track meet and it is your job to rank the runners as they finish. Using the ordinal numbers, count the first ten runners to cross the line in order to tell each runner where they are ranked.

6. What do you know about Chile?

Palabras y expresiones

El tiempo
el cambio
está nublado,-a /soleado,-a
la estación
el fresco
el grado
hace (+ weather expression)
hay neblina/sol
el hielo
el invierno
la lluvia
máximo,-a
mínimo,-a
la neblina
la nieve
nublado,-a
el otoño
la primavera
¿Qué tiempo/ temperatura hace?

el sol
soleado,-a
la temperatura
el tiempo
el viento
Para describir
buen
cuarto,-a
décimo,-a
excelente
listo,-a
mal
noveno,-a
octavo,-a
quinto,-a
segundo,-a
séptimo,-a
sexto,-a
tercero (tercer),-a
todavía

Deportistas
el basquetbolista, la basquetbolista
el corredor, la corredora
el deportista, la deportista
el esquiador, la esquiadora
el futbolista, la futbolista
el jugador, la jugadora
el patinador, la patinadora
el tenista, la tenista

Verbos
continuar
copiar
enviar
esquiar
llover (ue)
montar en patineta
nevar (ie)
patinar sobre hielo
Expresiones y otras palabras
dar un paseo
en cambio
la flor
el lugar
el paseo
por
por todos lados

Teacher Resources

Activity 16

Information Gap Activities
Postcard Activities
Funciones de Comunicación

Answers

Autoevaluación
Possible answers:
1. Me gusta montar en patineta en la primavera....
2. En la primavera hace viento....
3. ¿Qué temperatura hace hoy en Santiago de Chile?
4. ¿Cómo envío mi carta por correo electrónico y dónde pongo la dirección?
5. Primero, segundo, tercero, cuarto, etc.
6. Two writers from Chile, Gabriela Mistral and Pablo Neruda, have won Nobel Prizes.

Activities

Multiple Intelligences (logical-mathematical)
Ask students to give the Fahrenheit equivalent of several temperatures: 39°C (102.2°F), 100°C (212°F) and so on.

Spanish for Spanish Speakers
As an alternative to one of the *Autoevaluación* activities, ask students to read one or two poems by Pablo Neruda and summarize the themes presented (either orally or in writing).

Notes The name Chile comes from the indigenous word *Tchili* meaning **the deepest point of the earth.**

In 1980, Chile initiated an intensive literacy campaign. The rate of adult literacy rose from 89 percent in 1980 to 93.4 percent in 1990.

Chile is a country of young people, with over half of the population under the age of twenty. The country has one of the lowest rates of population growth in South America, roughly 1.5 percent a year.

Teacher Resources

El mundo de los deportes

Answers

Preparación

1. El tema principal de esta lectura es los deportes en el mundo hispano.
2. El deporte más popular del mundo hispano es el fútbol.
3. Answers will vary.

Activities

Expansion

Talk with students about the Olympics (see the Notes below and on page 83). Then ask students to search the following key words for information on the Olympics: *deportes, deportes olímpicos, Comité Olímpico Internacional.* Have students list five facts they learned during their search and share the information with the class.

Tú lees

Estrategia

Previewing

Before starting to read, try various activities that will help you preview what the reading is about. For example, you will understand more and enjoy what you are about to read on this page if you quickly skim the first and last paragraph of the following reading.

Preparación

Contesta las siguientes preguntas como preparación para la lectura.

1. ¿Cuál es el tema principal de esta lectura?
2. ¿Cuál es el deporte más popular del mundo hispano?
3. Identifica cinco cognados en la lectura *El mundo de los deportes*.

Previewing Activities

Read the title.
Look for cognates.
Skim the first paragraph.
Skim the last paragraph.
Look at information in accompanying charts.
Ask yourself what the main points are.

El mundo de los deportes

Los deportes son populares e importantes en el mundo hispano, y el fútbol es sin duda alguna[1] el deporte favorito de todos. Miles de personas ven los partidos de fútbol todas las semanas y la Copa Mundial[2] de fútbol es el evento más importante del mundo deportivo. Millones de personas en todo el mundo miran los partidos de la Copa Mundial y se contagian de la fiebre del "¡Gol!"[3]. La Copa Mundial sólo se juega una vez cada cuatro años y países de todo el mundo participan en este gran espectáculo del deporte.

El béisbol es otro deporte muy popular en el Caribe, especialmente en Cuba, la República Dominicana y Puerto Rico. También es muy popular en algunas regiones de México y en

Futbolistas de Inglaterra y Argentina en la Copa Mundial.

Notes The first Hispanic Olympic medal winner was Ramón Fonst, from Cuba, in 1900. The first Olympic Games to be held in a Spanish-speaking country took place in Mexico in 1968. The most recent Spanish-speaking nation to host the Olympics was Spain (Barcelona, 1992). The Spanish-speaking country with most gold medal winners for one sport is Uruguay, which has eight athletes with two medals each in soccer. Cuba is the country that has won the most gold medals.

Many of most famous soccer players in the world have come from Argentina and Uruguay.

Estos chicos juegan al jai alai.

Venezuela. Muchos jugadores de estos países juegan en las grandes ligas de los Estados Unidos. Algunos[4] de los jugadores más famosos de todos los tiempos son hispanos, como Pedro Martínez y Sammy Sosa (de la República Dominicana) y Roberto Clemente (de Puerto Rico).

El boxeo (también llamado[5] el deporte de las narices chatas[6]) el frontón[7], el jai alai y el ciclismo son también deportes populares en los países hispanos. Estos dos últimos también son muy populares en España, junto con[8] el básquetbol (también llamado baloncesto).

En el mundo hispano se practican muchos otros deportes y desde hace décadas los hispanos, al igual que[9] el resto del mundo, practican deportes no sólo como pasatiempo, sino también para mantener buena salud[10] y una vida activa.

[1]Without a doubt [2]World Cup [3]they all catch "goal" fever [4]Some [5]called [6]flat noses [7]a sport similar to squash or handball [8]along with [9]just as [10]good health

El ciclismo es popular en los países hispanos.

A ¿Qué recuerdas?

1. ¿Cómo son los deportes en el mundo hispano?
2. ¿Qué ven miles de personas cada semana?
3. ¿Cuál es el evento más importante en el fútbol?
4. ¿Qué deporte es muy popular en la región del Caribe?
5. ¿Qué otros deportes son populares en el mundo hispano?

B Algo personal

1. ¿Haces alguno de estos deportes? ¿Cuál? ¿Dónde? ¿Con quién?
2. ¿Cuál es tu deporte favorito?
3. ¿Cuánto tiempo hace que haces ese deporte?
4. ¿Sabes algo de los deportes en el mundo hispano? ¿Qué sabes?
5. ¿Ves muchos deportes en la televisión? ¿Cuáles?

Nuestro deporte favorito es el béisbol.

 Activities A–B

Answers

A 1. Los deportes en el mundo hispano son populares e importantes.
2. Ven los partidos de fútbol.
3. El evento más importante es la Copa Mundial de fútbol.
4. El béisbol es muy popular en la región del Caribe.
5. Otros deportes populares son el boxeo, el frontón, el ciclismo, el básquetbol, el jai alai.

B Answers will vary.

Activities

Critical Listening
Describe a celebrity without stating his/her name and ask the students to identify the person described. As a follow-up activity, have students work in pairs to prepare and present similar descriptions.

Notes Discuss with the class what students know about some of the people mentioned in the reading. Pedro Martínez is one of the best pitchers in baseball. Sammy Sosa received international attention in 1998 during his race with Mark McGwire to break the single season home-run record. Roberto Clemente was a batting champion four times during his career playing right field for the Pittsburgh Pirates. His career ended with his untimely death in a plane crash on his way from Puerto Rico to Managua, Nicaragua, to help victims of a devastating earthquake on Christmas Eve of 1972.

87

Tú escribes

Estrategia

Questioning

The steps you are learning to take to improve a composition are sometimes referred to as the writing process. For example, after selecting a topic, coming up with ideas to include in the composition can be challenging. However, you have learned one technique to overcome this difficulty: brainstorming for ideas. Another way to get started involves answering questions that will guide you in considering your theme from different points of view.

Answer the questions that follow in order to generate ideas for writing on the theme *Mi tiempo libre*. Then select some of the ideas that you like and write a paragraph about your free time. Remember to incorporate some transition words *(en cambio, entonces, pero)* to tie your ideas together and make your composition flow smoothly.

1. ¿Cuáles de estas actividades te gustan?

montar en patineta	practicar deportes
ver la tele	escuchar música
leer revistas	esquiar
ir a un concierto	ir a partidos de béisbol, fútbol, etc.
hacer ejercicios	montar a caballo
montar en bicicleta	hacer un picnic
ir al cine	trabajar con la computadora
ir de compras	tocar un instrumento musical
patinar sobre hielo	ir a fiestas con amigos
dar un paseo	hablar por teléfono

2. ¿Qué otras actividades te gusta hacer?
3. Completa estas frases pensando en lo que te gusta hacer.
   A. En el verano, me gusta....
   B. En el invierno, me gusta....
   C. Cuando hace mal tiempo, yo....
   D. Cuando estoy enfermo/a, prefiero....
   E. Si estoy aburrido/a, yo....
   F. Cuando estoy solo/a, me gusta....
   G. Cuando estoy con mi familia, prefiero....
   H. Cuando estoy con mis amigos....
   I. Si tengo dinero, me gusta....
   J. Cuando no tengo dinero, prefiero....

Notes **Review.** The use of transition words was taught in the *Tú escribes* section of *Capítulo 6*.

Tú escribes provides a formal opportunity for students to improve their ability to write in Spanish. The *Estrategia* provides helpful tips that students must practice in the activities provided.

Proyectos adicionales

A Comunidades

Using the Internet, the newspaper, information from family and friends, etc., find out what you can about five well-known athletes in your local community or state (try to find at least one person who speaks Spanish). Try to find out where they are from, where they live, whether they speak Spanish, what they do when they have free time or anything else that interests you. Then write two or three statements describing each person.

B Comparisons

Compare sports where you live with what you know about sports in Spanish-speaking countries. Are the same sports popular? Does the weather have an effect on the sports being practiced? Are the sports played at the same time of the year? During the same season?

C Conexión con la tecnología

Using the Internet, visit a Web site that gives weather information for different cities around the world. Find the current weather conditions for several Spanish-speaking countries. Then write several paragraphs in Spanish to summarize what you find. Be sure to include the following information: identify the different symbols used to represent weather conditions, describe today's weather in several cities, give the current temperature, tell what season it is and predict what people are doing now due to the weather.

Santiago 22.7 ºC (73 ºF)
Valparaíso 17.6 ºC (64 ºF)

Santiago 9 ºC (48 ºF)
Valparaíso 11.4 ºC (53 ºF)

ANNUAL AVERAGE
Santiago 384 mm (15.1 inches)
Valparaíso 462.6 mm (18.2 inches)

Answers

A Creative-thinking skill development.
B Answers will vary.
C Creative self-expression.

Activities

Language through Action
Prepare cards with a variety of statements in the *presente progresivo,* such as *él/ella está bailando.* Pass the cards to different students and ask them to dramatize the actions. As a student performs an action, the class must say what he/she is doing.

Multiple Intelligences (linguistic)
Have students research and then summarize some similarities and differences in the lives of Bernardo O'Higgins and George Washington.

Technology
Have students search the Internet for ecotours to view Iguazú Falls or vacation packages to ski on the slopes in Argentina. They should print out some of the Web pages advertising these trips and report their findings to the class.

Notes Encourage students to find out more about Argentina by going to the following Web sites:

Lonely Planet World Guide
http://www.lonelyplanet.com/destinations/south_america/argentina/
La Nación http://www.lanacion.com.ar

Electronic Embassy
http://www.embassy.org
Organization of American States
http://www.oas.org
general travel information
http://www.expedia.com

Teacher Resources

Trabalenguas

Activities

Connections

Have students draw a map of Argentina that shows major cities, rivers, mountains and surrounding countries. They may add any other geographical features they wish.

Spanish for Spanish Speakers

Assign the book *El jardín de senderos que se bifurcan* by Jorge Luis Borges. Next, students must write a 50–100-word summary of the contents printed on colored paper. Then have students design a poster to promote the story by combining the summary with illustrations and appropriate lettering to create a visually attractive poster.

Repaso

Now that I have completed this chapter, I can...	Go to these pages for help:
talk about leisure time activities	46
discuss sports	47
say what someone can do	50
discuss length of time	56
describe what is happening	58
talk about the seasons and weather	66, 74
indicate order	80

I can also...	
talk about life in Argentina and Chile.	49, 69
talk about television and renting movies.	52
convert temperatures from centigrade to Fahrenheit.	77
understand a weather forecast in Spanish.	89

Trabalenguas

Es primavera: ¡Cuántas flores florean en el florido campo!

Notes Chile is the only Spanish-speaking Latin American country with two Nobel Prize winners in literature. Gabriela Mistral received the prize in 1945 and Pablo Neruda in 1971.

Argentina has long been noted for the high quality of its intellectual life and for its many artistic influences. Among its modern literary figures of international reputation are Jorge Luis Borges, Julio Cortázar, Ernesto Sábato and Manuel Puig.

Loose translation of the *Trabalenguas:* It is spring. How many flowers blooming in the flowery field!

Vocabulario

los **aeróbicos** aerobics 7A
ahora mismo right now 7A
el **ajedrez** chess 7A
alquilar to rent 7A
americano,-a American 7A
antes de before 7A
apagar to turn off 7A
el **básquetbol** basketball 7A
el **basquetbolista,** la **basquetbolista** basketball player 7B
buen good 7B
el **cambio** change 7B
las **cartas** playing cards 7A
casi almost 7A
continuar to continue 7B
el **control remoto** remote control 7A
copiar to copy 7B
el **corredor,** la **corredora** runner 7B
costar (ue) to cost 7A
¿**Cuánto** (+ *time expression*) **hace que** (+ *present tense of verb*) ... ? How long ... ? 7A
cuarto,-a fourth 7B
las **damas** checkers 7A
dar un paseo to go for a walk, to go for a ride 7B
dar to give 7A
décimo,-a tenth 7B
el **deportista,** la **deportista** athlete 7B
después de after 7A
dibujar to draw, to sketch 7A
dormir (ue, u) to sleep 7A
en cambio on the other hand 7B
enviar to send 7B
el **equipo** team 7A
el **esquiador,** la **esquiadora** skier 7B
esquiar to ski 7B
esta noche tonight 7A
está nublado,-a/soleado,-a it's cloudy, it's sunny 7B
la **estación** season 7B

estupendo,-a wonderful, marvelous 7A
excelente excellent 7B
la **flor** flower 7B
el **fresco** cool 7B
el **fútbol americano** football 7A
el **futbolista,** la **futbolista** soccer player 7B
el **grado** degree 7B
hace (+ *time expression*) **que** (*time expression* +) ago 7A
hace (+ *weather expression*) it is (+*weather expression*) 7B
hacer aeróbicos to do aerobics 7A
hay neblina/sol it is misting/it is sunny 7B
el **hielo** ice 7B
el **invierno** winter 7B
el **jugador,** la **jugadora** player 7B
jugar (ue) to play 7A
la **lista** list 7A
listo,-a ready 7B
llover (ue) to rain 7B
la **lluvia** rain 7B
el **lugar** place 7B
mal bad 7B
la **maquinita** little machine, video game 7A
máximo,-a maximum 7B
mínimo,-a minimum 7B
el **minuto** minute 7A
mismo,-a same 7A
montar en patineta to skateboard 7B
la **neblina** mist 7B
nevar (ie) to snow 7B
la **nieve** snow 7B
noveno,-a ninth 7B
nublado,-a cloudy 7B
octavo,-a eighth 7B
el **otoño** autumn 7B
el **pasatiempo** pastime, leisure activity 7A
el **paseo** walk, ride, trip 7B
el **patinador,** la **patinadora** skater 7B

patinar sobre hielo to ice-skate 7B
permitir to permit 7A
poder (ue, u) to be able to 7A
por la mañana in the morning 7A
por la noche at night 7A
por la tarde in the afternoon 7A
por todos lados everywhere 7B
por by 7B
la **primavera** spring 7B
el **programa** program 7A
¿**Qué temperatura hace?** What is the temperature? 7B
¿**Qué tiempo hace?** How is the weather? 7B
quinto,-a fifth 7B
recordar (ue, u) to remember 7A
remoto,-a remote 7A
el **segundo** second 7A
segundo,-a second 7B
séptimo,-a seventh 7B
sexto,-a sixth 7B
el **siglo** century 7A
el **sol** sun 7B
soleado,-a sunny 7B
la **telenovela** soap opera 7A
el **televisor** television 7A
la **temperatura** temperature 7B
el **tenista,** la **tenista** tennis player 7B
tercero (tercer),-a third 7B
el **tiempo** weather 7B
todavía yet 7A
todavía still 7B
(*number* +) **vez/veces al/a la** (*time expression*) (*number* +) time (s) per (+ *time expression*) 7A
la **vida** life 7A
el **viento** wind 7B
el **voleibol** volleyball 7A
volver (ue, u) to return, to go back, to come back 7A

CD-ROM **Module 3**

Episode 7

Testing/ Assessment
Test Booklet
Portfolio Assessment

Activities

Critical Thinking

See if students can guess the meaning of the words *bilingüe* (bilingual), *antigüedad* (antiquity) and *pingüino* (penguin). For practice, have students say some sentences that combine words that focus on the pronunciation of *u* in Spanish: *Querido Miguel: ¿Por qué no quieres ir a aquel parque en Mayagüez para ver los pingüinos?; ¿Qué película quieres alquilar?* Be sure to model the sentence several times before asking them to write what they hear. Finally, ask students if they understand the meaning of the sentences.

Pronunciation (*la letra* u)

Review the sound of *u*, pointing out that the sound is similar to the *u* sound in the English word **shoot**, but the sound is shorter: *octubre, gusta, mucho, muy, nunca, lugar.* Then note that the letter *u* is silent in the syllables *gue, gui, que* and *qui*: *Guillermo, guitarra, aquel, equipo.* Exceptions to this rule are indicated with two dots (*diéresis*) over the *u*: *bilingüe, antigüedad, pingüino.*

Notes Remind students that the *ue* or *u* shown in parentheses after infinitives listed in *Navegando 1B* help students remember how these verbs are formed, for example, *costar (ue)* and *jugar (ue)*.

Spanish is the official language of Argentina. However, it is a distinctly Argentine Spanish, characterized by special words, expressions and pronunciation. A dialect called Spanish *Lunfardo,* which developed in Buenos Aires before 1900, with many borrowed words from Italian and Portuguese, has had a significant impact on the Spanish that is spoken in the capital.

91

Teacher Resources

TPRS   *Capítulo 8*

   Capítulo 8

Connections with Parents

Try to encourage parents and guardians to have a larger role in their child's classroom education. In *Capítulo 8*, students will be learning vocabulary associated with chores and helping around the house. As you begin the new chapter, encourage students to talk with their parents or guardians about what they are learning in class. Consider having students ask if they may prepare a dish at home using a recipe from a Spanish-speaking country. A recipe for *paella* appears on page 117. Students might also find a recipe on the Internet, or you may prefer to provide a different favorite one of your own.

Capítulo **8**

Mis quehaceres

Objetivos

* ❖ talk about household chores
* ❖ say what just happened
* ❖ ask for and offer help
* ❖ talk about the past
* ❖ identify and describe foods
* ❖ discuss food preparation
* ❖ make comparisons

Visit the web-based activities at www.emcp.com

Notes   Communicative objectives are provided on page 92 to prepare students for the chapter they are about to begin. A checkoff list of the functions appears on page 136, along with additional objectives, that students use as a self-check to evaluate their own progress.

España
Nombre oficial: Reino de España
Población: 39.193.000
Capital: Madrid
**Ciudades importantes: Barcelona,
Valencia, Sevilla**
Unidad monetaria: el euro
**Fiesta nacional: 12 de octubre,
Día de la Hispanidad**
**Gente famosa: Antonio Banderas
(actor), Pablo Picasso (pintor),
Enrique Iglesias (cantante),
Penélope Cruz (actriz)**

Activities

Critical Thinking
Have students look at the photos
at the start of the chapter. Ask if
students can guess which country
they will be studying in this
chapter. Then call on several
students to say what they think
they will be learning about in
this chapter.

noventa y tres **93**

Notes The cultural focus of this chapter
is Spain.

Take some time reviewing the contents of
these two pages. First, point out and call
on students to read the objectives shown
on page 92. Then ask questions about what
students see in the photographs. For
example, ask if students can figure out
where the people are in the large
photograph. Ask what students think the
people in the small photograph are doing
(washing dishes).

Spain is the only Spanish-speaking
country with a monarchy. *Juan Carlos de
Borbón* has been king and his wife, *Sofía,*
queen since 1975.

93

Los quehaceres

 Activity 1

 Activities 53–54

 Activity 1

 Activity 1

 Activities 1–2

> **Content reviewed in *Lección A***
> • rooms in a house
> • family
> • direct object pronouns
> • present progressive
> • objects in a kitchen

Activities

Prereading Strategy
Ask students to identify cognates and any known vocabulary in *Vocabulario I.*

Lección A
España

Vocabulario I
Los quehaceres

colgar la ropa

doblar la ropa

hacer la cama

Quizás debo sólo adornar esta pared.

cocinar/preparar la comida

limpiar

felicidodes

adornar

el abrigo

Ramón sube algo al primer piso.
Él le sube una camisa a su hermano.

En la familia García hay mucha gente.
Ellos son nueve personas.
Juntos hacen los quehaceres de la casa.

El abuelo acaba de llegar y deja su abrigo en la sala.

94 *noventa y cuatro*

Lección A

Notes Use a variety of *Navegando 1B* support materials to teach and reinforce the vocabulary presented on pages 94–95. For example, support for the content of these pages is available in the Audio CD Program, the Listening Activities Manual, Overhead Transparencies, Workbook, Grammar and Vocabulary Exercises Manual and Quizzes.

Tell students that another common way of saying **to cook** is *hacer la comida.*

trabajar en el jardín

1 ¿Qué tienen que hacer?

 Write the names Julia and Enrique. Next, listen and list under each of their names what chores (*quehaceres*) each of them has to do. Then circle any items on the lists that they both have to do. The first one has been done for you.

MODELO

Julia	Enrique
adornar la sala	

2 La familia García

Contesta las siguientes preguntas según la información en el Vocabulario I.

1. ¿Quién acaba de llegar?
2. ¿Dónde deja el abrigo el abuelo?
3. ¿Qué le sube Ramón a su hermano?
4. ¿Hay mucha gente en la familia García? ¿Cuántas personas son?
5. ¿Hacen juntos los quehaceres?

3 Tu familia

Haz una lista de los quehaceres que hacen en tu casa según lo que aprendiste en el Vocabulario I. Luego, di quién hace cada uno de esos quehaceres en tu familia.

hacer las camas	mi hermana
limpiar la sala	yo
limpiar la cocina	mi padre y mi madre

Estrategia

Increasing your vocabulary

When reading or learning new vocabulary in Spanish, you can figure out the meaning of a new word by relating it to your knowledge of other words that are spelled similarly. Such groups of similar words are called "word families." All the "members" of a word family share a common, easily recognizable root. Can you see how the verb *cocinar* (to cook) and the noun *cocina* (kitchen) are related in this way since people cook in a kitchen? Recognizing word families can help you expand your Spanish vocabulary and can make learning new words easier.

Answers

1 Julia
1. adornar la sala
2. cocinar el pollo
3. trabajar en el jardín
4. hacer la cama
5. limpiar la cocina

Enrique
6. adornar la sala
7. preparar la ensalada
8. doblar la ropa
9. hacer la cama
10. limpiar la cocina

2 Possible answers:
1. El abuelo acaba de llegar.
2. Deja el abrigo en la sala.
3. Ramón le sube un abrigo a su hermano.
4. Sí, hay mucha gente en la familia García. Son nueve personas.
5. Sí, hacen juntos los quehaceres.

3 Answers will vary.

Activities

Prereading Strategy
Ask students to discuss the chores they are expected to do at home. Then instruct students to cover up the words in *Vocabulario I* with their hands and look only at the illustrations. Ask them to imagine what is taking place. Finally, have students look through the text bubbles and boxes quickly to find cognates and words they recognize.

Notes Remind students they have already learned that cognates (*cognados*) are words that are similar in English and Spanish. Words that appear the same but that are not cognates are considered false cognates (*cognados falsos*) because their meaning or usage is different in the two languages. Have students give the meaning for the cognate that appears on page 94, *preparar*, and the false cognates *sacar*, *ropa* and *aprender*, all of which students have already seen in previous chapters.

Answers

4 1. Hace unos quehaceres.
2. Ella quiere ir al cine.
3. Tiene que terminar de limpiar la casa.
4. Limpia la cocina.
5. Dice, ¡Qué casa tan limpia!
5 Answers will vary.
6 1. ...la tercera foto.
2. ...la primera foto.
3. ...la segunda foto.
4. ...la tercera foto.
5. ...la segunda foto.

Activities

Critical Listening

Play the audio CD recording of the dialog. Instruct students to cover up the words as they listen to the conversation. Have students look at the photographs and imagine what the people are saying to one another.

Expansion

Additional questions (*¿Qué recuerdas?*): *¿Qué deben limpiar?*; *¿Van a trabajar juntos en los quehaceres?*; *¿Es más divertido trabajar juntos?*

Prereading Strategy

Ask students to discuss the chores they are expected to do at home. Then instruct students to look through the dialog quickly to find cognates and words they recognize.

Diálogo I

¿Me ayudas?

INÉS: Víctor, ¿qué haces?
VÍCTOR: Hago unos quehaceres.

INÉS: ¡Qué aburrido! ¿Por qué no vamos al cine?
VÍCTOR: Tengo que terminar de limpiar la casa. ¿Me ayudas?
INÉS: Sí, dejo mi abrigo aquí y te voy a limpiar la cocina.

INÉS: Bueno, la cocina ya está limpia. Hola, señora Zea.
SRA. ZEA: Hola, Inés. Hola, Víctor. ¡Qué casa tan limpia!
VÍCTOR: Gracias, mamá. Ahora voy al cine con Inés.

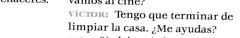

4 ¿Qué recuerdas?

1. ¿Qué hace Víctor?
2. ¿Adónde quiere ir Inés?
3. ¿Qué tiene que terminar Víctor primero?
4. ¿Qué limpia Inés?
5. ¿Qué dice la Sra. Zea?

5 Algo personal

1. ¿Cómo ayudas con los quehaceres en casa?
2. ¿Piensas que hacer los quehaceres es aburrido? Explica.
3. ¿Te gusta ir al cine?

6 ¿Me ayudas?

 Mira las tres fotos que van con el diálogo y di si lo que oyes va con la primera, la segunda o la tercera foto.

 Va con la tercera foto.

Todos ayudan en la cocina.

Lección A

Notes This dialog and activities 4, 5 and 6 have been recorded by native speakers and are included in the *Navegando* Audio CD Program. Have students cover up the words of the dialog and look at the photographs as you play the audio CD.

A reproducible student answer sheet for activity 6 has been provided for your convenience.

Cultura Viva

España: país multicultural

Spain's culture and diverse population today reflect the influence of people from many different ethnic groups and races over thousands of years. For example, cave paintings indicate people lived in an area (*Altamira*) of northern Spain between 25,000 and 10,000 B.C. Over 4,000 years ago the Iberians (*íberos*) invaded the area

Granada, España.

that would later be named the Iberian Peninsula (*Península Ibérica*) and that is shared today by Spain and Portugal. In 1100 B.C., the Phoenicians (*fenicios*) from present day Lebanon founded cities where *Cádiz* and *Málaga* are located. Blue-eyed, blond Celts (*celtas*) traveled from northern Europe south to Spain between 800 and 700 B.C., which explains why many Spaniards have those features today. The Greeks (*griegos*), who arrived between 800 and 700 B.C., along with the Phoenicians, brought with them olive trees and grapevines. As a result, both olives (*aceitunas*) and grapes (*uvas*) are important products in Spain's economy today. Many other people

Córdoba es una ciudad bonita.

arrived later: the Carthaginians (*cartagineses*) from the area known today as Tunisia; the Romans (*romanos*), who introduced Latin, which evolved into Spanish; the Visigoths (*visigodos*) from Germany; and the Arabs from northern Africa, also called Moors (*moros*), who introduced the cultivation of rice (*arroz*) and oranges (*naranjas*) and turned *Córdoba* and *Granada* into important and prestigious cities. By the time the Moors were defeated in Granada and removed from power in 1492 by the Catholic monarchs Ferdinand (*Fernando*) and Isabella (*Isabel*), many elements in contemporary Spain had taken root and are still evident today.

Los Reyes Católicos, Isabel y Fernando.

---

7 Conexiones con otras disciplinas: historia y ciencias sociales

Conecta la información de las dos columnas de una manera lógica.

1. los griegos y los fenicios
2. los moros
3. los celtas
4. los romanos
5. los fenicios
6. 25,000–10,000 B.C.

A. el latín
B. Altamira
C. el arroz y las naranjas
D. Cádiz y Málaga
E. las aceitunas y las uvas
F. rubios

Capítulo 8

noventa y siete **97**

Teacher Resources

 Activity 2

 Activity 2

Answers

7 1. E
2. C
3. F
4. A
5. D
6. B

Activities

Connections
Have students research one of the groups that inhabited Spain. Then have them list any influences or products they brought with them to Spain.

Expansion
Using transparencies 1, 2, 7 and 8, or the maps at the front of the book, show students where Spain is located and identify some of the country's larger cities.

Multiple Intelligences (linguistic/spatial)
Ask students to draw a time line indicating some of the various cultures that have existed in Spain. Then have students divide into small groups and use the media center and the Internet to research contributions these cultures made to the development of contemporary Spain. Include the contributions of the various cultures on the time line.

Notes As another indication of Moorish influence in Spain, inform students that approximately 25 percent of Spanish words come from Arabic. Examples include *alcalde*, *alfombra* and *ojalá*.

Encourage students to find out more about Spain by going to the following Web sites:

All about Spain
http://www.red2000.com/spain/1index.html
Traveling to Spain
http://www.sispain.org/english/travelli/

Teacher Resources

 Activity 8

 Activity 3

 Activity 3

Answers

8 1. Alfredo las está buscando./Alfredo está buscándolas.
2. María y Fernando la están preparando./Están preparándola.
3. Lo estamos adornando./Estamos adornándolo.
4. Carlos la está limpiando./Está limpiándola.
5. Mis hermanos las están haciendo./Mis hermanos están haciéndolas.
6. Yo los estoy colgando./Yo estoy colgándolos.
7. Los estamos haciendo juntos./Estamos haciéndolos juntos.

Activities

Multiple Intelligences (linguistic/spatial)
Divide students into groups of three or four and assign one-third of the groups to make a visual image of the direct object pronoun located to the left of the conjugated verb. Another third of the groups must make a visual image of the direct object pronoun attached to the infinitive. The final third must make a visual image of the direct object pronoun attached to the present participle.

Idioma

Repaso rápido: direct object pronouns

You have already learned that direct object pronouns can precede conjugated verbs, attach to the end of an infinitive or attach to the end of a present participle.

me	nos
te	os
lo/la	los/las

Remember to add an accent mark to the present participle in order to maintain the original pronunciation of the present participle without the pronoun.

Marta está limpiando la cocina.
*Marta **está limpiándola.*** *Marta **la está limpiando.***

8 Todos están haciendo quehaceres

Sigue el modelo para decir la misma oración de forma diferente, usando un pronombre de complemento directo.

MODELO Yo estoy doblando *la ropa.*
Yo la estoy doblando./Yo estoy doblándola.

1. Alfredo está buscando *las tazas.*
2. María y Fernando están preparando *la comida.*
3. Estamos adornando *el cuarto.*
4. Carlos está limpiando *la cocina.*
5. Mis hermanos están haciendo *las camas.*
6. Yo estoy colgando *los abrigos.*
7. Estamos haciendo juntos *los trabajos de la casa.*

¡Extra!

El verbo *colgar*
The present tense of *colgar* (to hang) follows the pattern of other verbs that require the change *o → ue: cuelgo, cuelgas, cuelga, colgamos, colgáis, cuelgan.*

Está haciendo la cama.

Lección A

Notes Remind students that they can find the direct object in a sentence by answering the question (subject + verb +) **who?** or **what?**
Use the following examples as you review direct object pronouns: ***La voy a terminar*** (before a conjugated verb); *Voy a terminarla* (attached to the end of an infinitive); *Estoy terminándola* (attached to the end of a present participle).

See if students can remember any other verbs with the *o → ue* change: *poder, dormir,* etc.

Indirect object pronouns

An indirect object indicates **to whom** or **for whom** something is said or done. An indirect object pronoun (*pronombre de complemento indirecto*) may replace an indirect object. You have already learned to use indirect object pronouns with the verb *gustar*. They look the same as direct object pronouns except for *le* and *les*.

los pronombres de complemento indirecto			
me	*to me, for me*	**nos**	*to us, for us*
te	*to you, for you (tú)*	**os**	*to you, for you (vosotros,-as)*
le	*to you, for you (Ud.)* *to him, for him* *to her, for her*	**les**	*to you, for you (Uds.)* *to them, for them*

Indirect object pronouns follow the same rules for placement in a sentence that you learned for the direct object pronouns:

- They usually precede the conjugated form of the verb, but they also may follow and attach to an infinitive or a present participle. (Add an accent mark to the present participle in order to maintain the original pronunciation of the present participle.)

*Pilar **me** va a preparar una ensalada.*
*Pilar va a preparar**me** una ensalada.*   Pilar is going make a salad **for me.**

***Te** estoy escuchando.*
*Estoy escuchándo**te**.*   I am listening **to you.**

- Place negative expressions (e.g., *nunca*) before the indirect object pronouns.

***Nunca nos** hacen la cama.*   They **never** make the bed **for us.**

Add the word *a* plus a pronoun or noun to a sentence in order to clarify the meaning of *le* and *les*, or in order to add emphasis.

Le escribo
a ella.
a María.
a mi hermana.

Les escribo
a ellas.
a María y a Mario.
a mis primos.

Le escribo a María.

Notes Show the class they can locate the indirect object in a sentence by asking themselves the following question: (subject + verb +) **to whom** or **for whom?**

Point out that in English sentences using an indirect object or indirect object pronoun, the word **to** is commonly understood: I'm writing **(to)** him.

 Activities 3–4

 Activities 4–6

 Activity 2

 Activities 4–7

Activities

Expansion
Ask the class for sample sentences using direct object pronouns.

Language through Action
Expand the discussion of the indirect object pronouns using gestures as you walk around the room and give objects to students. Tell students what you are giving them as you hand the object to a person: *Te estoy dando un libro; Le doy un lápiz a Jorge.* You can vary the verb forms, but use indirect object pronouns in your sentences. As a second step in this activity, have students repeat your sentences after you. Finally, call on a few volunteers to demonstrate the transfer of knowledge, asking several students to make a statement using an indirect object pronoun while performing an action.

Multiple Intelligences (musical)
Play music from Spain as you explain to your students the use of *vosotros/vosotras* to give students an auditory connection to help them remember that this subject pronoun is used in Spain.

Activities

Critical Thinking
Ask students for an alternative way of saying the sentences for activity 9, placing the object pronouns after the infinitives.

Students with Special Needs
Provide a second model for activity 11.

 Práctica

9 Antes de ir de vacaciones

Pablo y su familia van de vacaciones y unos amigos van a ayudar a la familia a prepararse para el viaje. Completa tus oraciones con *me, te, le, nos* o *les*, diciendo qué van a hacer.

MODELO Marta <u>nos</u> va a limpiar las ventanas (a nosotros).

1. Raúl __ va a buscar las maletas (a mí).
2. Marta __ va a doblar la ropa (a mi madre).
3. La Sra. Martínez __ va a preparar la comida (a mis padres).
4. El Sr. Martínez __ va a colgar los abrigos (a mi padre).
5. Raúl y Marta __ van a hacer las camas (a nosotros).

10 De otra manera

Estás hablando de los quehaceres de la casa con unos amigos. ¿Cómo puedes decir la misma oración de otra manera *(another way)*?

MODELO ¿*Me* estás colgando la ropa?
¿Estás colgándo*me* la ropa?

1. Él nunca *le* puede limpiar la casa.
2. Quizás Carlos *te* puede poner la mesa.
3. ¿No *me* quieres preparar la comida?
4. Quizás *te* debo escribir una lista de quehaceres.
5. *Les* estamos colgando la ropa.
6. ¿No *nos* está Ud. adornando el cuarto?

11 ¿Me ayudas?

 In pairs, take turns asking one another for help with the indicated tasks. The person responding may agree or refuse to help.

MODELO colgar los abrigos
A: ¿Me cuelgas los abrigos?
B: Sí, (No, no) te cuelgo los abrigos.

1. limpiar el patio
2. doblar las servilletas
3. limpiar la mesa del comedor
4. buscar la sal
5. encender las luces del comedor
6. hacer las camas
7. poner la mesa
8. subir la ropa a mi cuarto

¿Me estás colgando la ropa?

Lección A

 ¡Extra!

El uso de *vosotros*

It is common to use the direct and indirect object pronoun *os* in Spain in the same circumstances in which you have learned to use *vosotros*: when talking informally with two or more people.

Notes You may wish to remind students that in the fifth sentence of activity 11, the verb *encender* requires the stem change *e → ie*.

If you are teaching *vosotros/vosotras*, give students several sentences that practice the direct and indirect object pronoun *os*. You can easily accomplish this by modifying one or two of the sentences for each activity.

12 Ayudando en casa

Las personas de la ilustración están ayudándote en las tareas de la casa. Describe lo que hace cada una de las personas.

MODELO Marta

Marta me está limpiando la mesa./Marta está limpiándome la mesa.

1. Antonio y Carlota   **2.** Ernesto   **3.** Cristóbal   **4.** Julia

Comunicación

13 ¿Qué haces?

Make a list of your household chores and another list of what you do to help specific members of your family. Then talk with a classmate about what you do to help around the house and who you help with the household duties.

MODELO A: ¿Qué haces para ayudar en tu casa?
       B: Doblo mi ropa y la subo a mi cuarto. ¿Y tú? ¿Ayudas a tus padres?
       A: Sí. Le pongo la mesa a mi madre.

14 ¿Me ayudas?

A group of exchange students from Spain will be staying with families in your community. With a classmate, take turns asking one another when each of you will be able to help with various chores to prepare for their visit. Answers should indicate if and when the person answering will be able to help with the indicated tasks.

MODELO A: ¿Cuándo me puedes limpiar la cocina?
       B: Quizás te puedo limpiar la cocina por la tarde./Quizás puedo limpiarte la cocina por la tarde.

Capítulo 8

ciento uno **101**

Answers

15 Creative self-expression.
16 1. Ana acaba de doblarlas.
2. Pedro y Pablo acaban de hacerlas ahora mismo.
3. Alejandro y yo acabamos de limpiarlo juntos.
4. Elena acaba de adornarla.
5. Yo acabo de colgarlos.
6. Ángel acaba de limpiarlas hace media hora.

Activities

Language through Action
Expand on this presentation of *acabar de* by walking around the room and performing tasks as you describe what you have just done: *Acabo de cerrar la puerta; Acabo de abrir el libro.* Vary the verb forms, but use *acabar de* plus an infinitive for each sentence. As a second step in this activity, have students repeat your sentences after you. Finally, call on volunteers to demonstrate the transfer of knowledge, asking them to make a statement using *acabar de* plus an infinitive after performing an action.

102

---

15 ¿Qué les gusta hacer?

In small groups, discuss your most favorite and least favorite household chores. Each person should make a list of at least three chores you all like to do and a second list of three chores that you do not like to do. Each member of your group should then talk with members of other groups to find out how your lists compare. Finally, one person from each group should summarize the findings for the class.

MODELO
A: ¿Les gusta cocinar la comida?
B: Sí, nos gusta cocinarla.
A: A nosotros también nos gusta.

Nos gusta	No nos gusta
cocinar	poner la mesa

Estructura

Saying what just happened with *acabar de*

You can say what has just happened using a form of the verb *acabar* (to finish, to complete, to terminate) followed by *de* and an infinitive.

$$acabar \; de \; + \; infinitive$$

Acabo de llegar.   I just arrived.
Mi padre acaba de poner la mesa.   My father just set the table.

 Práctica

16 ¡Gracias por la ayuda!

Francisco tiene muchos quehaceres y muchos buenos amigos. A sus amigos les gusta ayudar con sus quehaceres. Contesta las preguntas para decir quién acaba de hacer cada quehacer, usando las pistas entre paréntesis.

MODELO
¿Los platos? (Alicia / limpiar)
Alicia acaba de limpiarlos.

1. ¿Las camisas? (Ana / doblar)
2. ¿Las camas? (Pedro y Pablo / hacer / ahora mismo)
3. ¿El cuarto? (Alejandro y yo / limpiar / juntos)
4. ¿La sala? (Elena / adornar)
5. ¿Los abrigos? (yo / colgar)
6. ¿Las ventanas? (Ángel / limpiar / hace media hora)

Alicia acaba de limpiar los platos.

102 *ciento dos*

Lección A

Notes The verb *acabar* is always followed by the preposition *de* before an infinitive because it refers to actions that have already happened or that are coming to an end.

Other verbs like *acabar* are *alegrarse, arrepentirse, dejar* and *terminar.*

17 La fiesta de despedida

You and a friend are organizing the farewell party for the Spanish exchange students who just spent the last week with families in your community. Take turns asking and answering questions to find out what everyone has just done to help out.

MODELO Uds. / limpiar la cocina
> A: ¿Qué acaban de hacer Uds.?
> B: Acabamos de limpiar la cocina.

1. Ana / poner la mesa
2. Andrés y Rosa / adornar las paredes
3. tú / limpiar las ventanas
4. Jaime y Cristina / preparar la comida
5. Mercedes / llegar con la comida
6. yo / leer la lista de quehaceres

Comunicación

18 ¿Qué acabas de hacer?

Imagine it is Saturday at noon and you are talking on the phone with a friend. Discuss some things each of you did just recently and what you are going to do later in the day. You may want to include in your conversation something interesting that someone in your family or a friend did recently, too.

MODELO A: ¿Qué haces?
> B: Bueno, yo acabo de poner la mesa. ¿Y tú?
> A: Pues, yo acabo de terminar mi tarea. Mis padres dicen que puedo salir. ¿Quieres hacer algo?

Acabo de poner la mesa.

¡Oportunidades!

Estudiante de intercambio
It is becoming more and more popular for language students to spend time overseas as exchange students. After you have studied Spanish for a couple of years, it would be a great opportunity for you to become an exchange student in Spain or in another Spanish-speaking country. What you learn at school will be very valuable to you. Living within the culture in a different country, practicing the language you have learned with native speakers, developing life long friendships, and gathering first hand experience will be very rewarding and exciting.

Teacher Resources

Activity 17

Answers

17 1. ¿...acaba de...?/Acaba de....
2. ¿...acaban de...?/Acaban de....
3. ¿...acabas de...?/Acabo de....
4. ¿...acaban de...?/Acaban de....
5. ¿...acaba de...?/Acaba de....
6. ¿...acabo de...?Acabas de....

18 Creative self-expression.

Activities

Critical Listening
Tell students that they will hear several statements that give impressions of recent travels in the Spanish-speaking world. They should listen to each statement and use *acabar de* to say where the speaker has recently traveled or visited. Possible statements include: *Madrid es una ciudad muy bonita; Me gusta mucho el Parque de Chapultepec; Caracas es grande y moderna; En San Juan y toda la isla el béisbol es muy popular; Me encantan las playas de Viña del Mar pero también me gusta esquiar en las montañas.* As closure, review what students have learned about different countries in *Navegando 1B*.

Teacher Resources

 Más quehaceres

 Activity 6

 Activities 55–56

 Activity 8

 Activity 4

GV Activities 9–10

Activities

Language through Action
In advance, write the expressions from *Vocabulario II* and other household chores students have learned on separate pieces of paper. Have individuals each select one of the pieces of paper at random. Then call on them to act out the expressions while classmates guess what the expressions are in Spanish.

Vocabulario II
Más quehaceres

La familia Gutiérrez arregla la casa hoy. Trabajaron mucho ayer también.

Notes Other *Navegando 1B* components that practice and reinforce the vocabulary presented on pages 104 and 105 include the Audio CD Program, the Listening Activities Manual, Overhead Transparencies, Workbook, Grammar and Vocabulary Exercises Manual and Quizzes. The Teacher Resources listed at the top of the page indicate the specific numbered activities coordinated to the content of these pages for your convenience. Use any of the other ancillaries you feel will help you to tailor the content to your teaching style.

Yo traigo el pan y la leche.

sacar la basura

Él va a buscar leche y pan a la tienda.

19 Los quehaceres

 Selecciona la foto de la persona que corresponda con lo que oyes.

   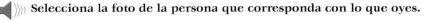

A   **B**   **C**   **D**

20 ¡Más quehaceres!

Di qué quehaceres debes hacer, según las ilustraciones.

MODELO  Debo poner la mesa.

1

2

3

4

5

6

Teacher Resources

Activity 19

Answers

19 1. C
2. A
3. D
4. B

20 1. ...pasar la aspiradora.
2. ...lavar las ollas.
3. ...dar de comer al perro.
4. ...sacar la basura.
5. ...lavar la ropa.
6. ...preparar la comida.

Activities

Cooperative Learning

Have students bring in pictures from magazines or newspapers of people performing household chores that were taught in the lesson. They should also bring in a picture of a household chore not taught in this lesson, learn the term and teach it to a classmate. Then have students work in pairs or small groups, pretending they are doing the chore shown in each picture. Use Spanish sentences as models, if necessary: *¿Arreglas el cuarto?/Sí (No, no) arreglo el cuarto.* You can extend the activity by having students review the present progressive with the same pictures: *¿Qué estás haciendo ahora?/Estoy arreglando el cuarto.*

Notes Play the audio CD of *Vocabulario I* to provide students with pronunciation practice before they try to figure out the meaning of the new words and expressions on pages 104 and 105.

Activity 19 is intended for listening comprehension practice. Play the audio CD of the activity or use the transcript that appears in the ATE Introduction if you prefer to read the activity yourself.

Hay mucho por hacer
Activities 21–23

Activities

Expansion

Additional questions *(Algo
personal)*: *¿Prefieres recoger la
mesa o lavar las ollas?; ¿Quién
pone la mesa en tu casa?; ¿Quién
recoge la mesa en tu casa?;
¿Siempre ayudas a limpiar la casa?*

Pronunciation *(la letra g)*

Demonstrate how the consonant
g changes its pronunciation with
all five vowels. Write *ga, ge, gi, go,
gu* on the board and practice the
sounds. Explain that the *g* has the
harder consonant sound with the
vowels that open the mouth *(a, o,
u)* and the softer *h* sound with the
vowels that close the mouth *(e, i).*

Diálogo II
Hay mucho por hacer

SRA. ZEA: Ayer trabajasteis
mucho, pero hoy hay quehaceres
también.
VÍCTOR: Pues, yo voy a recoger la
mesa y lavar las ollas.
SRA. ZEA: Entonces, David
puede pasar la aspiradora.

SRA. ZEA: ¿Quién va a la tienda a
buscar leche?
DAVID: ¿Qué?
SRA. ZEA: ¿No me oyes? ¡Qué
listo!

SRA. ZEA: ¿Puedes ir a buscar
leche a la tienda?
DAVID: ¿Y por qué yo? ¿Por qué
no va Víctor?
SRA. ZEA: Porque él va a lavar las
ollas. ¿Quieres hacer eso?

 21 ¿Qué recuerdas?

1. ¿Quiénes trabajaron mucho ayer?
2. ¿Qué va a hacer Víctor?
3. ¿Quién pasa la aspiradora?
4. ¿Quién es listo?
5. ¿Qué no quiere hacer David?

¡Extra!

El cambio de *g → j*

You have learned to use several verbs that are
regular in the present tense except for a minor
stem change *(poder, jugar)* or a spelling change.
These changes do not affect the verb's
present-tense endings. For verbs that end in *-ger*
(such as *recoger*) the letter *g* changes to *j* before
the letters *a* and *o* to maintain pronunciation:
Yo recojo la mesa muchas veces.

 22 Algo personal

1. ¿Qué quehaceres haces en casa?
2. ¿Eres listo/a?
3. ¿Te gusta ir a la tienda a buscar leche o pan? Explica.
4. ¿Quién saca la basura en tu casa? ¿Quién pasa la aspiradora?

 23 ¿Vais a hacer un quehacer o a hacer un deporte?

Las siguientes personas van a hablar de sus actividades de hoy. Di si lo que
oyes es *un quehacer* o *un deporte*.

Notes Ask students if they recognize
the verb form *trabajasteis,* which appears
in the dialog. Then ask what the infinitive
form of the verb is *(trabajar).* This would
be a good time to review this cultural and
linguistic point with students. Remind
them that many Spaniards (especially in
the south) use this plural informal form of
the verb. Note that the verb form may be

accompanied by the subject pronouns
vosotros or *vosotras* when the subject is not
clear. Finally, practice conjugating several
verbs using *vosotros* and *vosotras.*

Tell the class that they will remember the
spelling change for *-ger* and *-gir* verbs
if they think of them as the *yo-jo*
verbs *(recojo).*

Cultura viva

Los quehaceres en una casa española

Do you like doing chores? Helping with the household chores is a long-standing tradition in many homes throughout the world. In Spain, young people generally help with chores starting at an early age, and everyone helps out with the

Limpiando un suelo.

cleaning *(la limpieza)* and upkeep of the home. Spanish houses do not, as a general rule, have wall-to-wall carpeting *(alfombra, moqueta)*. Instead, floors often consist of uncovered tile *(losa)*, marble *(mármol)* or wood *(madera)* and they are usually washed every day. If there are teenagers in the house, they usually are the ones chosen to perform this chore. The laundry is another household task that must

Ropa en el tendedero (Almeria, España).

be performed nearly every day. Dryers *(secadoras de ropa)* are not common in Spanish homes because of the high cost of energy, so laundry *(lavado de ropa* or *colada)* in many instances must be washed daily or every other day, and clothes are left to hang from lines to dry *(tender la ropa en el tendedero)*. Both girls and boys often have to hang the laundry, take it down and fold it. In addition, boys are often required to run errands *(hacer recados)* for their parents, while girls, traditionally, help with cooking.

How do you help with the cleaning and maintenance of your home? Regardless of your answer, one thing you have in common with young people in Spain and throughout the world: Although you may accept that they are an integral part of living together as a family, nobody seems to like doing chores!

---

24 Los quehaceres en una casa española

¿Es cierto o falso? Si es falso, di lo que es cierto.

1. Es tradicional empezar a ayudar con los quehaceres de casa cuando uno es joven en España.
2. Sólo los padres hacen la limpieza en las casas españolas.
3. Muchas casas tienen alfombra o moqueta en los pisos.
4. Hay muchas secadoras porque la energía no cuesta mucho en España.
5. Las muchachas y los muchachos cuelgan la ropa y la doblan.

25 Comparando

Make two lists of chores, one with what you and your friends do and another one with the chores you know young people in Spain do. Do you see any differences? Are there similarities? In what other ways do you think young people in Spain help around the home?

Capítulo 8

ciento siete **107**

Teacher Resources

 Activity 7

 Activities 9–10

 Activity 6

 Activities 11–12

Answers

26 1. oyen
2. oye
3. oye
4. oyen
5. oímos
6. oigo
7. oyendo
8. oyes

Activities

Critical Thinking
Inquire whether students remember other verbs that have *-go* in the *yo* form (*vengo, tengo, pongo, salgo, hago*).

Expansion
Practice these two new irregular verbs by asking the following questions: *¿Qué traes a la escuela en un día típico?*; *¿Qué traes a la clase de español?*; *¿Qué trae el maestro/la maestra a la clase?*; *¿Oyen Uds. anuncios en la escuela? ¿Cuándo?*

Idioma

Estructura

Present tense of *oír* and *traer*

The verbs *oír* (to hear, to listen) and *traer* (to bring) are irregular.

oír	
oigo	oímos
oyes	oís
oye	oyen
gerundio: oyendo	

traer	
traigo	traemos
traes	traéis
trae	traen
gerundio: trayendo	

Práctica

26 A todos nos gusta oír la radio

Completa el siguiente párrafo con las formas correctas del verbo *oír*.

A toda mi familia le gusta oír la radio. Mis primos (1) las noticias todas las noches. Son muy listos. Mi tía (2) un programa de música española por las tardes. Mi hermano (3) los deportes, cuando no puede verlos en la televisión. Si mi abuelo y mi padre están trabajando en el garaje, (4) música popular y cantan. Mamá y yo siempre (5) el pronóstico del tiempo para saber si va a llover. Yo (6) la radio cuando escribo e-mails y también siempre estoy (7) música cuando hago la tarea. Y tú, ¿cuándo (8) la radio?

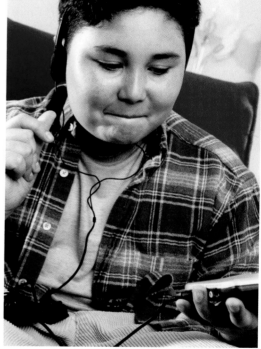

A mi hermano le gusta oír la radio.

108 *ciento ocho*   **Lección A**

Notes Note the use of *vosotros/vosotras* in the verb paradigm on page 108. Remind students that *vosotros/vosotras* is used in Spain, the country featured in *Capítulo 8*. If you are requiring students to learn the *vosotros/vosotras* form of verbs, be sure to practice the verbs *oír* and *traer* in sentences that contain either *vosotros* or *vosotras*.

108

27 ¿Qué trae cada uno?

Unos amigos vienen a una fiesta en tu casa y cada persona tiene que traer algo diferente. Trabajando en parejas, alterna con tu compañero/a preguntando y contestando qué trae cada persona.

MODELO

el Sr. y la Sra. Lorenzo
A: ¿Qué traen el Sr. y la Sra. Lorenzo?
B: El Sr. y la Sra. Lorenzo traen el pollo.

1. Paloma   **2. Enrique y Tomás**   **3. mi amiga y yo**

4. Alberto   **5. Blanca y Graciela**   **6. Pedro**

❖ Comunicación

28 En mi casa

Working in pairs, talk about how your families and friends balance fun and work, describing some of your families' and your friends' favorite pastimes and telling how everyone helps when organizing activities or when doing chores. Mention which of the activities people like a lot or do not like. You may wish to use some of these activities to get started.

oír la radio	cocinar	buscar la leche y el pan
mirar la televisión	lavar las ollas	limpiar la cocina
tener una fiesta	traer CDs	arreglar el cuarto

MODELO **A:** En mi familia nos gusta hacer quehaceres los sábados y, luego, algunas veces tenemos una fiesta con los amigos y la familia. Mis primos siempre traen la música para bailar.
B: Yo siempre oigo música y arreglo mi cuarto los fines de semana.

Activity 8

 Activity 11

 Activity 7

 Activity 13

Answers

29 1. llegaron
2. cociné
3. limpió
4. ayudó
5. pasó
6. sacaste
7. trabajaron
8. hablaron
9. lavó
10. bailamos

Activities

Students with Special Needs
Practice conjugating several verbs with students using *vosotros/vosotras*. First, try several verbs in the present tense. Then, after presenting the preterite tense of regular *-ar* verbs, practice conjugating some verbs in the preterite tense. Verb charts present forms throughout the book and the Appendices offer examples for reference.

TPR
The preterite can be introduced through TPR. Give students the commands: *Cierra la puerta* and *Abre la puerta*. Then have them restate the action: *Él/Ella cerró la puerta y luego la abrió.*

Estructura

Talking about the past: preterite tense of *-ar* verbs

Use the preterite tense when you are talking about actions or events that were completed in the past. Form the preterite tense of a regular *-ar* verb by removing the last two letters from the infinitive and attaching the endings shown.

lavar					
yo	lav**é**	I washed	nosotros nosotras	lav**amos**	we washed
tú	lav**aste**	you washed	vosotros vosotras	lav**asteis**	you washed
Ud. él ella	lav**ó**	you washed he washed she washed	Uds. ellos ellas	lav**aron**	you washed they washed they washed

Note: Regular verbs that end in *-car (buscar, explicar, sacar, tocar)*, *-gar (apagar, colgar, jugar, llegar)* and *-zar (empezar)* require a spelling change in the *yo* form of the preterite in order to maintain the original sound of the infinitive.

infinitivo				pretérito
bus**car**	*c*	→	*qu*	yo bus**qué**
apa**gar**	*g*	→	*gu*	yo apa**gué**
empe**zar**	*z*	→	*c*	yo empe**cé**

 ## Práctica

29 Ayer en la casa de Pilar

Completa las siguientes oraciones con la forma correcta del pretérito de los verbos entre paréntesis para decir lo que pasó ayer en la casa de Pilar.

1. Mis amigos *(llegar)* temprano.
2. Yo *(cocinar)* desde las nueve.
3. Daniel *(limpiar)* el piso del comedor.
4. Ángela me *(ayudar)* mucho también.
5. Ella *(pasar)* la aspiradora por la sala.
6. Tú *(sacar)* la basura antes de comer.
7. Uds. *(trabajar)* todo el día ayudándome.
8. Todos *(hablar)* bien de la comida.
9. Después de comer, Paco me *(lavar)* los platos.
10. Luego, nosotros *(bailar)* en la sala.

Notes Review some of the handy time expressions students can add to a sentence when they are talking about the past: *ayer, anoche, la semana pasada, el año pasado.* Ask students if they can add any other expressions to the list.

Do the first sentence of activity 29 as a class.

30 ¿Qué cocinaste?

Completa el siguiente párrafo con la forma apropiada del pretérito de los verbos entre paréntesis.

Yo (*1. cocinar*) una sopa ayer en mi casa para toda la familia. Mi hermana me (*2. ayudar*). Yo (*3. empezar*) a preparar todo muy temprano. Primero yo (*4. buscar*) los ingredientes. Luego (*5. lavar*) la olla grande y (*6. sacar*) los cubiertos. Después (*7. preparar*) unos refrescos. Al terminar de cocinar, (*8. apagar*) la estufa y (*9. arreglar*) los cubiertos en la mesa. Entonces, (*10. llamar*) a todos a comer.

31 ¿Qué hiciste?

In pairs, take turns asking whether your classmate has completed the indicated chores. Your partner should say that he or she did not do each task because someone else already did it.

MODELO comprar el pan / Roberto
A: ¿Compraste el pan?
B: No, yo no compré el pan porque Roberto ya lo compró.

1. buscar los platos / Ernesto
2. apagar la estufa / Miguel
3. sacar la basura / Pedro
4. colgar los abrigos / Alfonso y Ana
5. preparar la comida / Jorge y Luisa
6. lavar la olla grande / Isabel

◈ Comunicación

32 Mini-diálogos

Working in pairs, discuss some of the things that needed to be done around the home recently and whether or not either of you has done any of them. Some suggested chores and activities are provided to get you started.

MODELO A: ¿Preparaste la comida?
B: Sí, (No, no) la preparé.

preparar la comida   sacar la basura   arreglar el cuarto

pasar la aspiradora

colgar la ropa en tu cuarto   comprar la leche   lavar las ollas

33 Todos en mi familia ayudaron

Talk about what everyone in your family did last week to help around the house.

Capítulo 8

ciento once **111**

Teacher Resources

Activity 31

Answers

30 1. cociné; 2. ayudó;
3. empecé; 4. busqué; 5. lavé;
6. saqué; 7. preparé; 8. apagué;
9. arreglé; 10. llamé

31 1. ¿Buscaste...?/No, yo no busqué los platos porque Ernesto ya los buscó.
2. ¿Apagaste...?/No, yo no apagué la estufa porque Miguel ya la apagó.
3. ¿Sacaste...?/No, yo no saqué la basura porque Pedro ya la sacó.
4. ¿Colgaste...?/No, yo no colgué los abrigos porque Alfonso y Ana ya los colgaron.
5. ¿Preparaste...?/No, yo no preparé la comida porque Jorge y Luisa ya la prepararon.
6. ¿Lavaste...?/No, yo no lavé la olla grande porque Isabel ya la lavó.

32 Possible answers:
1. ¿Lavaste las ollas?/Sí, (No, no) las lavé.
2. ¿Pasaste la aspiradora?/Sí, (No, no) la pasé.
3. ¿Colgaste la ropa en tu cuarto?/Sí, (No, no) la colgué.
4. ¿Sacaste la basura?/Sí, (No, no) no la saqué.
5. ¿Compraste la leche?/Sí, (No, no) la compré.
6. ¿Arreglaste el cuarto?/Sí, (No, no) no lo arreglé.

33 Creative self-expression.

Notes Set a time limit for activities 31, 32 and 33.

To extend activities 32 and 33, have students write out a summary of what they discussed. As an alternative, have students make a list of the chores they will be discussing before assigning students to work with a partner.

Hold students accountable for their work and provide additional practice speaking by calling on several individuals to summarize the results of their discussions for activities 32 and 33.

Activities

Expansion

The *Lectura cultural* offers a good opportunity for you to conduct a class discussion or have a debate about who does what around the house. Be sure to review the conjugation of *deber* and *tener que* before starting the activity.

Lectura cultural

¿Quién lo hace?

En España, mientras la participación de las mujeres[1] en el mercado laboral incrementa cada día (40% de mujeres trabajan), la desigualdad[2] entre los sexos todavía existe en las tareas domésticas. Las mujeres dedican siete horas y veintidós minutos

cada día a los quehaceres. Los hombres, en cambio, dedican tres horas y diez minutos. Si nos referimos a quehaceres específicos de la casa (lavar, planchar, barrer, etc.), las mujeres dedican cinco veces más tiempo que los hombres.

Entre los jóvenes de 15–17 años, son las mujeres, otra vez, las que hacen más labores domésticas.

	Mujeres	Hombres
Total	7 h 22'	3 h 10'
Trabajo de la casa	3 h 58'	0 h 44'
Mantenimiento	0 h 27'	0 h 55'
Cuidado de la familia	1 h 51'	0 h 51'
Compras	0 h 53'	0 h 26'
Servicio	0 h 13'	0 h 14'

Fuente: Encuesta sobre "Usos del tiempo", Instituto de la Mujer, 2001.

Porcentaje de jóvenes que no hacen nunca o sólo en ocasiones los siguientes quehaceres

	Mujeres 15–17años	Hombres 15–17años
Cuidar a los niños	57,1%	65,7%
Limpiar la casa	50,6%	75,8%
Hacer la cama	32,2%	49,5%

Fuente: INJUVE, Informe Juventud en España, 2000.

En el año 2000, la Unión Europea recomendó a los estados miembros (España es uno) la inclusión en la escuela de una asignatura de trabajo doméstico. Quizás, esta nueva asignatura ayude a establecer la igualdad[3] en los quehaceres. Después de todo, la democracia empieza en casa.

[1]women   [2]inequality   [3]equality

34 ¿Qué recuerdas?

¿Sí o no?

1. 40% de las mujeres en España trabajan en casa.
2. Las mujeres españolas pasan siete horas y veintidós minutos todos los días en los quehaceres de la casa.
3. En España, 75,8% de los hombres entre quince y diecisiete años limpian la casa.
4. En España, 67,8% de las mujeres entre quince y diecisiete años hacen las camas.
5. La Unión Europea quiere que las escuelas enseñen trabajo doméstico.

35 Algo personal

1. ¿Qué tareas domésticas tienes que hacer en casa?
2. ¿Crees que las mujeres y los hombres deben compartir *(share)* todos los quehaceres? Explica.
3. ¿Piensas que todos los estudiantes deben tomar una asignatura de trabajo doméstico? ¿Por qué sí o por qué no?

- Complete a survey of your classmates like the one in the article. Find out the percentage of girls and boys that never or only occasionally take care of younger siblings, clean the house and make their beds. Compare yourselves with the fifteen- to seventeen-year-old Spaniards surveyed. In your group, is there more or less equality among who does the chores?

112 *ciento doce*

Lección A

Notes Remind students that when talking about numbers, a comma is used in Spanish where a period would be used in English (75,8%).

Help students with reading the tables that accompany the *Lectura cultural*.

¿Qué aprendí?

Autoevaluación

As a review and self-check, respond to the following:

1. What do you do to help around the house?

2. Name two things you have just done in the last week.

3. Your family is having a party at your house and you are in charge of getting the house ready for guests. Ask your sister or brother to do three or four things to help with preparations.

4. List three or four things you did to help your parents.

5. State something you learned in this lesson about Spain.

Visit the web-based activities at www.emcp.com

Palabras y expresiones

En casa
- el abrigo
- la aspiradora
- la basura
- la cama
- la gente
- el jardín
- la leche
- la olla
- pasar la aspiradora
- la persona
- el quehacer
- recoger la mesa

Verbos
- acabar
- adornar
- arreglar
- barrer
- cocinar
- colgar (ue)
- doblar
- dejar
- lavar
- limpiar
- llegar
- oír
- preparar
- recoger
- sacar
- subir
- trabajar
- traer

Expresiones y otras palabras
- acabar de (+ *infinitive*)
- algo
- dar de comer
- junto,-a
- listo,-a
- quizás
- sólo
- el trabajo

Él está sacando la basura.

Ella está limpiando la cocina.

Capítulo 8

ciento trece **113**

Teacher Resources

Activity 12

Information Gap Activities
Postcard Activities
Funciones de Comunicación

Answers

Autoevaluación
Possible answers:
1. Arreglo mi cuarto.
2. Acabo de preparar la comida y trabajar en el jardín.
3. ¿Me puedes colgar la ropa? ¿Puedes ayudarme a preparar la comida? ¿Puedes sacarme la basura?
4. Saqué la basura todos los días la semana pasada. Preparé la comida, barré, y colgé la ropa.
5. Spain's population is diverse and its history consists of a variety of ethnic groups and races, including the Iberians (*los íberos*), the Phoenicians (*los fenicios*) and the Moors (*los moros*).

Activities

Multiple Intelligences (interpersonal)
Ask students to work in small groups discussing how they feel about doing various household chores. They should use *gustar, molestar* and other verbs to discuss their likes and dislikes. Each group should then select one member to summarize the results of this informal discussion in front of the class.

Notes Tell the class that in Spain the Spanish language is commonly called *castellano* (the language of Castilla). Other regional languages include *gallego, catalán* and *vasco/euskera*.

Spain occupies most of the Iberian Peninsula, which is at the southwestern corner of the European continent.

Mainland Spain is divided into autonomous regions that make up 98 percent of the national territory. Other *autonomías* include the Balearic Islands, in the Mediterranean Sea, and the Canary Islands, 650 miles southwest of the mainland, off the coast of Africa.

Teacher Resources

 El supermercado

 Activity 1

 Activities 57–58

 Activities 1–2

 Activity 1

 Activities 1–5

> **Content reviewed in *Lección B***
> • jobs around the house
> • numbers
> • preterite tense of regular *-ar* verbs
> • celebrations

Activities

Critical Thinking
Before playing the audio CD for *Vocabulario I*, ask students if they can guess where the people are. Then ask what they are probably discussing.

Prereading Strategy
Have students find cognates and other words they know in *Vocabulario I*.

Lección **B**

España

Vocabulario I
El supermercado

¿Me prestas la receta de la paella?

Sí, claro.

De esta receta nos hace falta el ingrediente más importante, el arroz.

¡Ay, olvidamos añadirlo! La paella sin arroz no es paella.

Verduras

el guisante

la cebolla

el ajo

los peores tomates

el tomate

el pimiento

los mejores tomates

el aguacate

el arroz

la lata

la lechuga

No todos los tomates están frescos.
Algunos parecen muy maduros.
Los chicos van a escoger los mejores tomates.
A ellos les importa llevar tomates maduros.

114 *ciento catorce*

Lección B

Notes The word *receta* has two primary uses in Spanish: It may refer to a **recipe** for cooking or a **medical prescription** (*una receta médica*). Context will make the meaning clear.

Explain to students that the verb *escoger* is conjugated like the verb *recoger*, which students learned to use in *Lección A* of this chapter.

1 En el supermercado

 Selecciona la ilustración que corresponde con lo que oyes.

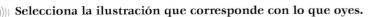

A   B   C   D   E   F

2 De compras en el supermercado

Di lo que *le(s) gusta, le(s) hace falta, le(s) parece* o *le(s) importa* a estas personas, usando las pistas y las ilustraciones y añadiendo los artículos indefinidos apropiados.

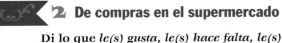

MODELO   a mí / parecer bien / llevar unos
A mí me parece bien llevar unos tomates.

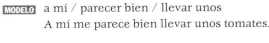

¡Extra!

Hacer falta, importar y parecer

The expressions *hacer falta* (to need), *importar* (to matter) and *parecer* (to seem) often require an indirect object pronoun and follow a pattern like the one you learned for the verb *gustar: Me gusta el ajo; Me hace falta un aguacate; No me importa si el tomate no es maduro; Me parece buena la receta.*

1. a Uds. / hacer falta / llevar una

2. a los chicos / hacer falta / llevar un

3. a la Sra. Herrera / gustar / los

4. a Pedro y a Julio / importar / comprar las mejores

5. a Rodrigo / hacer falta / comprar el

6. a Santiago / gustar / comprar mucho

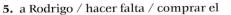

7. a mí / importar / llevar los mejores

8. a Elena / no importar / llevar una

Capítulo 8   *ciento quince*   **115**

Notes It is common for Spaniards to shop either at a supermarket *(supermercado)* or at small specialty shops, such as a *panadería.*

Shopping patterns vary from one country to another. Many Spaniards tend to shop for produce, meat and fish on a daily basis to have the freshest food possible for each meal.

Teacher Resources

Activity 1

Answers

1 1. E; 2. D; 3. A; 4. C; 5. F; 6. B

2 1. A Uds. les hace falta llevar una lata de guisantes.
2. A los chicos les hace falta llevar un pollo.
3. A la Sra. Herrera le gustan los aguacates.
4. A Pedro y a Julio les importa comprar las mejores cebollas.
5. A Rodrigo le hace falta comprar el arroz.
6. A Santiago le gusta comprar mucho pescado en lata.
7. A mí me importa llevar los mejores pimientos.
8. A Elena no le importa llevar una lechuga.

Activities

Cooperative Learning
Inform students that it is acceptable to use *no me importa* followed by a phrase, but that they usually should not use *no me importa* alone as a response to a choice. Responding to the question *¿Quieres estudiar o bailar?* with the phrase *no me importa* connotes **I don't give a darn!** and is even considered rude to some Spanish speakers. Suggest *me es igual* or *me da igual* (it's the same to me) as more polite ways of stating **it doesn't matter to me.** Have students practice mini-dialogs in which one person makes a statement and the other answers with one of these new expressions.

Answers

3 1. Víctor la tiene.
2. Les hace falta comprar
arroz, tomates y pimientos.
3. Ayer compraron el pollo.
4. No parecen frescos.
5. Víctor busca los pimientos.
6. Lo llaman el Sr. Pimiento.
4 Answers will vary.
5 1. D; 2. F; 3. B; 4. A, E; 5. C

Activities

Cooperative Learning
After discussing the content of
the dialog, have students practice
it in pairs. Circulate and assist
with pronunciation
and intonation.

Critical Listening
Play the audio CD recording of
the dialog as students cover the
words and listen. Ask several
individuals to state what they
believe the main theme of the
conversation is.

Expansion
Additional questions (¿Qué
recuerdas?): ¿Necesitan más pollo?;
¿Los tomates son para la paella?

Additional questions (Algo
personal): ¿Te gusta el pollo?; ¿Te
gusta el arroz?; ¿Te gustan
los tomates?

Diálogo I
¿Qué nos hace falta comprar?

INÉS: ¿Tienes la receta de la
paella?
VÍCTOR: Sí, aquí la tengo.
INÉS: ¿Qué nos hace falta
comprar?

VÍCTOR: Ayer compramos el
pollo. Todavía necesitamos
arroz, tomates y pimientos.
INÉS: Vamos primero a las
verduras.
VÍCTOR: ¡Ah, mira! ¿Qué te
parecen estos tomates?
INÉS: No parecen muy frescos.

VÍCTOR: ¿Y estos? ¿Qué te
parecen?
INÉS: Algunos parecen muy
maduros.
VÍCTOR: ¿Por qué no escoges los
tomates y yo escojo los
pimientos? Me llaman el Sr.
Pimiento.
INÉS: ¡Qué loco!

3 ¿Qué recuerdas?

1. ¿Quién tiene la receta de la paella?
2. ¿Qué les hace falta comprar?
3. ¿Cuándo compraron el pollo?
4. ¿Cómo parecen los tomates?
5. ¿Qué busca Víctor?
6. ¿Cómo llaman a Víctor?

4 Algo personal

1. ¿Te gusta ir de compras al supermercado? Explica.
2. ¿Qué verduras te gustan?
3. ¿Cuáles son los ingredientes de tu receta favorita?

5 ¿Qué les hace falta?

Di la letra de la ilustración que identifica lo que les hace falta comprar a las
siguientes personas, según lo que oyes.

A　　**B**　　**C**　　**D**　　**E**　　**F**

Notes The word *paella* is related to the
pan in which the food is prepared—a
paellera—which comes from the Latin
word for **pan**. The *paellera* is a round,
wide, shallow receptacle made of metal
with two or more handles and a depth
varying from 1 1/2 to 3 inches. This
utensil remains a legacy of the combined
influence of the Romans and the Moors.

The Romans introduced this type of pan,
and the Arabs are credited with first
having brought rice to Spain.

Activity 5 has been recorded as part of the
Audio CD Program.

Cultura viva

<u>La paella (ingredientes para seis personas)</u>

1 pollo en pedazos[1]	1 cebolla, troceada[6]	1 taza de
1/2 kg. de gambas[2]	2 dientes[7] de ajo, troceados	guisantes
1/2 kg. de langostinos[3]	2 zanahorias, limpias y cortadas[8]	5 hilos de azafrán[9]
1/4 kg. de mejillones[4]	2 tomates grandes	4 tazas de agua
1 lata de almejas[5] (200 gramos)	1 pimiento verde, troceado	5 cucharadas de aceite de oliva
2 tazas de arroz	1 lata de pimientos rojos, troceados	sal y pimienta

En una sartén[10] grande o paellera (sartén especial para la paella), poner el aceite y añadir el pollo, la cebolla troceada, el ajo y el pimiento verde; freír[11] hasta que se empiece a dorar—diez minutos. Luego, añadir el tomate, la zanahoria y media taza de guisantes. Cubrir[12] y dejar freír durante diez minutos. Después, añadir el arroz y el agua, los pimientos, el azafrán, sal y pimienta, y cocinar por otros quince minutos. Luego, añadir las gambas, los langostinos, los mejillones y las almejas y cocinar, con la sartén cubierta[13] otros diez minutos. Para terminar, adornar con la otra mitad de los guisantes, otra lata de pimientos (opcional) y un poco de perejil. Dejar que repose la paella durante quince minutos antes de servirla.

[1]pieces [2]shrimp [3]prawns [4]mussels [5]clams [6]diced [7]cloves [8]cut [9]saffron strings [10]frying pan [11]fry [12]cover [13]covered

6 La paella

Contesta las siguientes preguntas.

1. ¿Cuánto langostino tiene esta paella?
2. ¿Cuáles de los ingredientes en esta receta no son frescos?
3. ¿Qué verduras tiene la paella?
4. ¿Con qué puedes adornar la paella?
5. ¿Te gustaría preparar una paella? ¿Por qué?
6. ¿Hay un restaurante en tu ciudad con paella en el menú? ¿Cuál?

7 Conexión con otras disciplinas: matemáticas

Cambia los pesos (weights) a libras u onzas, según la pista entre paréntesis.

1. 2 kilos de aguacates (libras)
2. 200 gramos de pollo (onzas)
3. 1,5 kilos de tomates (libras)
4. 750 gramos de judías (libras)
5. 1/2 kilo de pimientos (onzas)
6. 1/4 kilo de arroz (onzas)

¡Extra!

¿Cuánto pesa?

1 kilogram, kg. (kilo, kg.)	=	2.2 pounds, lbs. (libras, lbs.)
1 kilogram	=	1000 grams, gr. (gramos, gr.)
1 ounce, oz. (onza, oz.)	=	28.35 grams

8 ¿Puedes preparar una paella?

Prepara una paella en tu casa y cuéntale la experiencia a la clase.

Capítulo 8

ciento diecisiete 117

Teacher Resources

La paella
Activity 6

Activity 2

Answers

6 1. Tiene medio kilo.
2. Los pimientos rojos, los guisantes, y las almejas no son frescos.
3. Tiene pimientos, cebolla, ajo, guisantes, zanahorias y tomates.
4. Puedo adornar la paella con guisantes, pimientos y perejil.
5. Answers will vary.
6. Answers will vary.

7 1. 4.4 lbs. de aguacates
2. 7.05 oz. de pollo
3. 3.3 lbs. de tomates
4. 1.65 lbs. de judías
5. 17.6 oz. de pimientos
6. 8.8 oz. de arroz

8 Creative self-expression.

Activities

Communities
Find a restaurant in your community that serves *paella*. Arrange a trip or have students meet there after school to taste this typical Spanish dish.

Multiple Intelligences (bodily-kinesthetic)
Have students find a simple recipe in a cookbook of Spanish cuisine, prepare it and share it with the class. Students should also explain the recipe and its history.

Notes The word for **shrimp** in Spain is *la gamba*.

As an alternative to or extension of activity 8, ask students to bring the ingredients from home and arrange with the Family and Consumer Science Department in your school to prepare and serve the dish in class.

Activity 7 offers a cross-curricular connection to mathematics in which students must perform calculations to convert the weights and measurements indicated to ounces or pounds. This is good preparation for actually having to perform the same conversions when traveling in Spain.

117

Activities

Expansion
Review the terms used to name classroom objects. Then have students compare the sizes of objects as you or other students hold up the items in the air: *El libro es más grande que el lápiz.*

Estructura

Making comparisons

You can use the following patterns when making comparisons in Spanish:

> **más/menos + noun/adjective/adverb + que**

*Hay **más/menos ajo que** sal.* — There is **more/less (fewer)** garlic **than salt.**

> **tanto, -a, -os, -as + noun + como**

*Hay **tanto** pescado **como** verduras en esa paella.* — There is **as much** fish **as** vegetables in that paella.

> **tan + adjective/adverb + como**

*Estos aguacates no están **tan maduros como** esos aguacates.* — These avocados are not **as ripe as** those avocados.

> **verb + tanto como**

*Pedro **cocina tanto como** Pilar.* — Pedro **cooks as much as** Pilar.

> **verb + más que/menos que**

*Pedro **cocina más que** Tomás.* — Pedro **cooks more than** Tomás.

You can also make comparisons by singling out a person, group, object or attribute as the best, most or least by using the following patterns:

> **definite article (+ noun) + más/menos + adjective**

*El ajo es **el ingrediente más importante.*** — Garlic is **the most important ingredient.**

> **verb + lo + más/menos + adverb + posible**

*Debes lavarla **lo más** pronto **posible.*** — You should wash it **as** early **as possible.**

Use *más de* or *menos de* and a number for stating there are "more than" or "fewer than" the number of items or people indicated.

*Veo **más de/menos de** cinco cebollas.* — I see **more than/fewer than** five onions.

Notes Point out that *mayor, menor, mejor* and *peor* are usually placed in front of the word they modify: *Es el/la mejor (peor) estudiante....*

Explain that the adjectives in comparisons must agree in gender and number with the items they describe: *El tomate es más fresco que la lechuga. La cebolla es más madura que el aguacate.*

The following adjectives and adverbs have irregular comparative forms:

better	–	*mejor*
worse	–	*peor*
older	–	*mayor*
younger	–	*menor*

Esos aguacates son **buenos,** *pero aquellos aguacates son* **mejores** *y estos aguacates son* **los mejores de todos.**

Those avocados are **good,** but those avocados over there are **better** and these avocados **are the best of all.**

Note: When referring to quantity, the comparative forms of *pequeño* and *grande* are *menor* (lesser, smaller, fewer) and *mayor* (greater, larger).

Hay un **menor (mayor)** *número de pimientos en lata que de pimientos frescos.*

There are **fewer** canned bell peppers than fresh bell peppers.

Práctica

9 En el supermercado

Estás haciendo compras en el supermercado. Completa estas comparaciones.

MODELO Estas cebollas son <u>más grandes</u> que esas cebollas. (grande)

1. Estos tomates están __ que esos tomates. (fresco)
2. Este pollo es __ que el otro. (pequeño)
3. Ese aguacate está __ que este aguacate. (maduro)
4. Estas lechugas son __ que esas lechugas. (pequeño)
5. Aquellos pimientos están __ que esos pimientos. (maduro)

¡Estos tomates son los mejores de todos!

Teacher Resources

Activities 10 and 12

10 Possible answers:
1. Javier (Clara) tiene tanto arroz como Clara (Javier).
2. Las lechugas del supermercado Día no son tan grandes como las lechugas del supermercado Hypercor.
3. Ana (Alberto) va al supermercado tanto como Alberto (Ana).
4. No hay tantos guisantes como pescado en una paella valenciana./Hay menos guisantes que pescado en una paella valenciana./Hay más pescado que guisantes en una paella valenciana.
5. Teresa y Armando compran tantas latas de tomates como de guisantes.
6. Alfonso no tiene tantas recetas como Belén.

11 1. tantas/como; 2. menos/que; 3. tantos/como; 4. más/que; 5. tantas/como

12 1. ...lo mejor posible.
2. ...lo más pronto posible.
3. ...lo más rápidamente posible.
4. ...lo mejor posible.
5. ...lo mejor posible.
6. ...lo más pronto posible.
7. ...lo más tarde posible.

10 Comparando

Use the information provided to make as many comparisons as you can.

MODELO **Información:** Ana puede ir de compras al supermercado en una hora pero yo necesito dos horas para ir de compras al supermercado.
Comparación 1: No puedo ir de compras al supermercado tan rápidamente como Ana.
Comparación 2: Ana puede ir de compras al supermercado más rápidamente que yo.
Comparación 3: Yo puedo ir de compras al supermercado menos rápidamente que Ana.

1. Javier tiene dos kilos de arroz y Clara tiene dos kilos de arroz.
2. Las lechugas del supermercado Día son pequeñas pero las lechugas del supermercado Hypercor son grandes.
3. Alberto va al supermercado tres veces al mes y Ana va al supermercado tres veces al mes.
4. Hay mucho pescado en una paella valenciana pero no hay muchos guisantes.
5. Teresa y Armando compran dos latas de tomates y dos latas de guisantes.
6. Belén tiene cincuenta recetas y Alfonso tiene sólo cinco recetas.

11 ¿Cuánto necesitas?

You are preparing a paella valenciana, using the recipe in the *Cultura viva*. Complete these sentences, saying what you will need and compare whether you will need more, less or the same amount of each of the listed ingredients.

MODELO Necesito <u>tanto</u> pimiento verde <u>como</u> cebolla.

1. Necesito __ latas de almejas __ latas de pimientos rojos.
2. Necesito __ mejillones __ gambas.
3. Necesito __ tomates __ zanahorias.
4. Necesito __ agua __ aceite de oliva.
5. Necesito __ gambas __ langostinos.

12 ¡Deben hacer lo siguiente!

If you were the owner of a restaurant, what instructions might you give your employees during the week?

¿Qué necesitas para hacer una paella?

MODELO abrir el restaurante / temprano
Debes abrir el restaurante lo más temprano posible.

1. preparar las recetas / bien
2. hacer las comidas / pronto
3. recoger las mesas / rápidamente
4. barrer el suelo / bien
5. limpiar la cocina / bien
6. sacar la basura / pronto
7. cerrar el restaurante / tarde

Notes Discuss activity 10 with the class to be sure students know what to do. Offer a second model if students have trouble.

Tell students they will need to look at the *Cultura viva* on page 117 for the recipe for paella to complete activity 11.

13 ¡Dos supermercados!

Compara lo que ves en las ilustraciones de estos dos supermercados, según las pistas.

MODELO   aguacates / ser grande

Los aguacates del supermercado Día son más grandes que los aguacates del supermercado Hypercor.

1. lechugas / ser pequeñas
2. tomates / ser mejores
3. los ajos / costar menos
4. las cebollas / ser grandes
5. los guisantes / costar más
6. los pimientos / ser peores
7. el señor / ser joven
8. la señora / ser vieja

13 Possible answers:
1. Las lechugas del supermercado Día son más pequeñas que las lechugas del supermercado Hypercor.
2. Los tomates del supermercado Día son mejores que los tomates del supermercado Hypercor.
3. Los ajos del supermercado Hypercor cuestan menos que los ajos del supermercado Día.
4. Las cebollas del supermercado Día son más grandes que las cebollas del supermercado Hypercor.
5. Los guisantes del supermercado Hypercor cuestan más que los guisantes del supermercado Día.
6. Los pimientos del supermercado Día son peores que los pimientos del supermercado Hypercor.
7. El señor del supermercado Día es más joven que el señor del supermercado Hypercor.
8. La señora del supermercado Día es más vieja que la señora del supermercado Hypercor.

Notes   This exercise uses metric measurements and the currency used by most European Union countries (the euro).

14 ¡Más comparaciones!

Mira las ilustraciones de la actividad 13 y completa estas comparaciones con la palabra apropiada.

MODELO Hay más <u>de</u> una persona en los dos supermercados.

1. El supermercado Hypercor tiene más tomates __ el supermercado Día.
2. Hay menos __ cinco lechugas en el supermercado Hypercor.
3. Hay menos cebollas en el supermercado Hypercor __ en el supermercado Día.
4. El supermercado Día tiene más __ tres pimientos.
5. Los aguacates en el supermercado Hypercor cuestan tanto __ los aguacates en el supermercado Día.

15 ¿Lo hacen tanto como tú?

Compare how much you help doing chores with how much your friends and family help around the house. You may make up any of the names you wish.

MODELO pasar la aspiradora
Mi hermano pasa la aspiradora tanto como yo.
Yo paso la aspiradora más que Julio.

1. cocinar
2. hacer las camas
3. trabajar en el jardín
4. limpiar la cocina
5. poner la mesa
6. ayudar en casa

16 En tu opinión

 Trabajando en parejas, alterna con tu compañero/a preguntando y contestando según las pistas.

¿Pasas la aspiradora tanto como yo?

MODELO el mejor supermercado de la ciudad donde vives
A: ¿Cuál es el mejor supermercado de la ciudad donde vives?
B: El mejor supermercado de la ciudad donde vivo es. . . .

1. el supermercado más grande de la ciudad donde vives
2. el supermercado más pequeño de la ciudad donde vives
3. el supermercado más nuevo de la ciudad donde vives
4. el supermercado más viejo de la ciudad donde vives
5. el ingrediente más importante de tu receta favorita
6. la mejor receta de tu mamá/papá

Notes When doing activity 15, point out that students should use the word *yo* when referring to themselves after *tanto como, más que* or *menos que*: *Ella cocina tanto como yo* (She cooks as much as I).

Comunicación

17 Me gusta la comida

Trabajando en parejas, hagan preguntas para comparar comidas diferentes y saber cuál les gusta más.

MODELO **A:** ¿Te gusta la lechuga tanto como el tomate?
B: Sí, (No, no) me gusta la lechuga tanto como el tomate.

18 Lo que más comes

Working in pairs, talk about what you eat and drink. Include in your conversation what you eat or drink, and tell which are your most and least favorite foods and beverages.

MODELO **A:** ¿Qué te gusta comer?
B: Como más pollo que pescado, pero la paella es la mejor comida.

19 En el supermercado

Imagine you are at a supermarket in Spain shopping for ingredients to make *paella*. Working with a partner, take turns playing the roles of two clients. Remember to make comparisons of quality, size and price for items in the store.

El señor compra ingredientes para hacer una paella.

Capítulo 8

ciento veintitrés **123**

After completing activity 18 orally in pairs, have students write out the list of foods and beverages that they included as their most and least favorite.

You may wish to have students make a list of their most and least favorite foods and beverages before asking them to work orally in pairs.

Hold students accountable for their work by calling on several pairs to present their dialogs in front of the class for activity 19.

123

El mercado

 Activity 6

 Activities 59–60

 Activities 7–8

 Activity 3

 Activities 11–13

Activities

Expansion
Model each word or expression and have students repeat. Then call on students to use the words or expressions in sentences.

Spanish for Spanish Speakers
Ask students to tell the class some foods that are common in their country of origin that cannot be found in the United States, and vice versa.

Notes Tell students that the words *papa* and *patata* both mean **potato.** In Spain, both terms are commonly heard; in other Spanish-speaking countries, the preferred word is *papa*.

el chorizo

el jamón

la carne

Answers

20 1. B
  2. C
  3. F
  4. A
  5. D
  6. E
21 1. chocolate
  2. jamón
  3. huevo
  4. café
  5. papa
  6. maíz
22 Answers will vary.

Activities

Cooperative Learning
Have students prepare a shopping list of six or seven foods they like and six or seven items they dislike. Then have them work in pairs or small groups to talk about their lists.

Expansion
Ask the following questions pertaining to the new vocabulary: *¿Prefieres tomar chocolate o café?; ¿Cuál es tu fruta favorita?; ¿Te gusta la carne?; ¿Prefieres comer carne, pollo o pescado?; ¿Comes muchos huevos?; ¿Te importa el colesterol?; ¿Te hacen falta vitaminas en tu dieta?*

20 En el mercado

)))) Selecciona la ilustración que corresponde con lo que oyes.

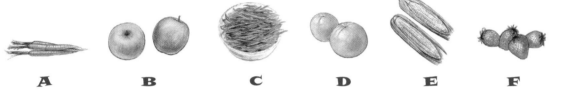

A **B** **C** **D** **E** **F**

21 Fuera de lugar

Say which food item does not belong in each of the following groups.

1. maíz   habichuela   zanahoria   chocolate
2. queso   mantequilla   jamón   leche
3. huevo   manzana   fresa   naranja
4. café   cebolla   pimiento   zanahoria
5. carne   pescado   pollo   papa
6. fresa   maíz   uva   plátano

22 Una dieta equilibrada

 Trabajando en parejas, escriban una dieta equilibrada *(balanced)* con todas las comidas básicas para cinco días de la semana. La dieta debe incluir el desayuno *(breakfast)*, el almuerzo y la cena *(dinner)*.

Notes Conduct a discussion about what items should be included in a healthy diet. If you are knowledgeable, talk with the class about good nutrition. As an alternative, you may want to ask the family and consumer science teacher in your building or district to spend a few minutes talking with the class about what items students should be eating.

Many fast-food restaurants have interesting and informative reading materials in Spanish that list the ingredients of the foods they serve. Some even offer tips about nutrition and a healthy diet.

Answers

23 1. Compró los ingredientes para hacer paella.
2. Quiere comprar chorizo.
3. Sí, es el mejor mercado de la ciudad.
4. El kilo de chorizo está a cuatro euros.
5. Sí, lo compra.

24 Answers will vary.

25 1. Cierto.
2. Falso. Compramos los ingredientes para hacer una paella.
3. Falso. Quiero comprar chorizo.
4. Cierto.
5. Falso. Este mercado es el mejor mercado de la ciudad.
6. Cierto.

Activities

Cooperative Learning
Have students work in pairs to practice the dialog while you circulate and help with pronunciation and intonation.

Expansion
Additional questions (*Algo personal*): *¿Te gustan los chorizos americanos?*; *¿Te gustan los chorizos italianos en las pizzas?*; *¿Quieres comer el chorizo español?*

Diálogo II

Comprando chorizo

INÉS: Ayer estuve con Víctor en el supermercado.
EVA: ¿Y qué compraste?
INÉS: Compramos los ingredientes para hacer paella.

EVA: Entonces, ¿qué venimos a hacer al mercado?
INÉS: Quiero comprar chorizo. El chorizo del supermercado no me gusta.
EVA: Bueno, este mercado es el mejor mercado de la ciudad.

INÉS: Señora, ¿a qué precio tiene el kilo de chorizo?
SEÑORA: El chorizo está a € 4,00 el kilo.
INÉS: De acuerdo, llevo un kilo por favor.

23 ¿Qué recuerdas?

1. ¿Qué compró Inés ayer en el supermercado?
2. ¿Qué quiere comprar Inés en el mercado?
3. ¿Es bueno el mercado donde están las chicas?
4. ¿A qué precio está el kilo de chorizo?
5. ¿Compra Inés el chorizo?

24 Algo personal

1. ¿Hay un mercado en tu ciudad? ¿Dónde está?
2. ¿Prefieres ir al mercado o al supermercado? Explica.
3. ¿Cuál es el mercado o supermercado más grande de tu ciudad?

25 ¿Qué comprendiste?

 Escucha lo que dicen las personas del diálogo *Comprando chorizo* y di si lo que oyes es cierto o falso. Corrige lo que no es cierto.

¡Extra!

El euro

The symbol for the European euro is €, which became the common currency of most European Union countries in 2002. Spain is a member of the European Union and adopted the euro as its currency, making the Spanish currency, *la peseta*, obsolete.

Notes Additional recipes may be obtained at the following Web sites:

La Paella
http://www.lapaella.net/paella.html
Las Recetas de Marita
http://www.acocinar.com/paella.htm

The value of the euro against the dollar fluctuates daily. Many newspapers provide a chart in their business section with the current value of a euro compared to other world currencies, including the dollar.

Cultura viva

¡Cómo se come en España!

Spain's cuisine is as diverse as its people are. Learning about the different regional cuisines will allow you to choose what you would like to try during a trip there. For example, *paella valenciana,* which you learned about earlier in the chapter, is a popular rice dish originally from the Mediterranean coast in the region of Valencia. It combines seafood, meat, chicken or pork. On the northern coast of Spain, in the region called Galicia, you might want to try *pulpo a la gallega,* a cooked and marinated octopus dish. In the north central and northeastern regions of Spain that border the Pyrenees, you might try the hearty Basque cuisine by ordering

Bacalao al pilpil.

cod prepared the "Basque way" *(bacalao al pilpil),* or Catalán cuisine, which is known for its delicious oxtail in *diabla* sauce and *butifarra con alubias* (beans with sausage).

Madrid, the capital, is famous for its *callos* (beef tripe). The area around

Madrid is also famous for its sheep and goat cheeses, like *manchego,* and its many and delicious varieties of pork or blood sausages called *chorizos* and *morcillas.*

The southern part of Spain is well known for its vegetables

Gazpacho.

and fish. Vegetables are used in the preparation of a cold soup called *gazpacho.* Gazpacho is popular in part because of its thirst-quenching qualities on hot summer days in sunny *Andalucía.* The region is also known for its ham *(jamón serrano)* and marvelous fresh sardines and smelt, fished right out of the Mediterranean Sea.

As you can see, Spaniards have plenty to choose from when it comes to meals!

Callos a la madrileña.

26 ¿Cómo se come en España?

Make a list of dishes mentioned in the *Cultura viva.* Then choose one that you would like to try, and find the recipe for it, using sources such as the Internet, cookbooks, etc.

Capítulo 8

ciento veintisiete **127**

Teacher Resources

 Activity 9

 Activity 4

Answers

26 Answers will vary.

Activities

Critical Thinking
Ask small groups of students to develop logical comparisons involving the following items: *la comida española/la comida mexicana; la comida italiana/ la comida china; los restaurantes/ las cafeterías; los supermercados/ los mercados.* Other possibilities not related to food include comparisons of classes, sports and music. The results should be shared with the class.

Expansion
As an additional activity, have students draw a map of Spain, separating the country into provinces and/or regions and placing the names of dishes given in the text in the corresponding regions.

Spanish for Spanish Speakers
Have students prepare a report in Spanish about the foods that the New World gave to Spain and how those were integrated into Spanish cuisine (e.g., the potato).

Notes Using a map, point out where the places mentioned in *Cultura viva* are located.

Tell the class that many people in the United States have a mistaken impression about what food is like in Spanish-speaking countries. For example, although some people may think of *tacos* and *tortillas* when they are talking about Spanish foods, *tacos* are considered Mexican fast food and *tortillas* are corn- or flour-based pancake-like shells that are filled with other ingredients or that serve as a substitute for bread in Mexico. Point out that if students ask for a *tortilla* in Spain, they will be served a Spanish omelet.

Teacher Resources

 Activity 27

 Activity 7

 Activities 10–12

 Activity 5

 Activities 14–15

Answers

27 1. ...compramos....
2. ...buscó....
3. ...busqué....
4. ...trabajó....

28 1. Daniel y Gloria estuvieron esta mañana.
2. Mi tía estuvo el mes pasado.
3. Los chicos estuvieron el fin de semana pasado.
4. Mis primas estuvieron anteayer.
5. Ud. estuvo el viernes.
6. Yo estuve el sábado pasado.
7. Uds. estuvieron ayer.
8. Tú estuviste el jueves.

Idioma

Repaso rápido: preterite tense of regular -*ar* verbs

Do you remember how to form the preterite tense of a regular -*ar* verb? Remove the last two letters from the infinitive and add the indicated endings.

hablar	
habl**é**	habl**amos**
habl**aste**	habl**asteis**
habl**ó**	habl**aron**

Note: Regular verbs that end in -*car* (*buscar, explicar, sacar, tocar*), -*gar* (*apagar, colgar, jugar, llegar, pagar*) and -*zar* (*empezar*) require a spelling change in the *yo* form of the preterite.

27 El diario de Marta

Marta siempre escribe en su diario por la noche. Haz oraciones completas con las pistas que se dan para saber lo que escribe esta noche.

1. nosotros / comprar zanahorias
2. mi madre / buscar el pollo
3. yo / buscar mi receta favorita
4. mi padre / trabajar todo el día

Estructura

Preterite tense of *dar* and *estar*

The verbs *dar* and *estar* are irregular in the preterite tense.

dar	
di	dimos
diste	disteis
dio	dieron

estar	
estuve	estuvimos
estuviste	estuvisteis
estuvo	estuvieron

28 Estuvieron en el mercado

Di cuándo las siguientes personas estuvieron en el mercado.

MODELO Enrique / el martes pasado
Enrique estuvo el martes pasado.

1. Daniel y Gloria / esta mañana
2. mi tía / el mes pasado
3. los chicos / el fin de semana pasado
4. mis primas / anteayer
5. Ud. / el viernes
6. yo / el sábado pasado
7. Uds. / ayer
8. tú / el jueves

Notes Review the spelling changes that are required in the first-person preterite tense for verbs that end in -*car* (change *c* to *qu*), -*gar* (change *g* to *gu*), -*zar* (change *z* to *c*). Then practice conjugating some of the verbs listed in the *Repaso rápido* before assigning activity 27.

❋ Práctica

29 Todos ayudaron

Last week your school held a food drive. In pairs, take turns reporting what food items people donated. Follow the model.

MODELO tú
  A: ¿Qué diste tú?
  B: Yo di unas frutas.

1. yo **2.** el Sr. y la Sra. García

3. tú y yo **4.** la profesora **5.** Pedro **6.** los hermanos Jiménez

30 Mi fiesta de cumpleaños

Completa el siguiente párrafo con la forma apropiada del pretérito de los verbos entre paréntesis.

El sábado pasado mi hermano mayor *(1. dar)* una fiesta para mi cumpleaños. Muchos de mis amigos *(2. estar)* allí. Mi amigo Pedro no *(3. estar)* y mis mejores amigas, Clara y Elvira, tampoco *(4. estar)*. Nosotros *(5. estar)* muy contentos. Mi hermano me *(6. dar)* un regalo que me *(7. gustar)* mucho. Luego, mis amigos Carlos y Gabriel *(8. dar)* un concierto muy bueno. Carlos *(9. cantar)* cinco canciones y Gabriel las *(10. tocar)* en su guitarra. Yo *(11. estar)* muy contento porque mis amigos *(12. estar)* muy contentos. Todos le *(13. dar)* las gracias a mi hermano por la fiesta tan buena.

❋ Comunicación

31 ¿Dónde estuvieron?

Working in pairs, discuss where you and people you know were last weekend, adding any details you wish.

MODELO **A:** ¿Dónde estuviste el fin de semana pasado?
  B: Estuve con mi madre en el mercado.

32 ¿Qué dieron?

In pairs, talk about your last birthday celebration. Discuss, among other things, when your birthday was, where it took place, what kind of food was served and the gifts that were given to you. Make up any information you want.

Capítulo 8 *ciento veintinueve* **129**

Notes After completing activities 31 and 32 orally in pairs, consider asking students to summarize their work for either one or both activities.

Answers

33 1. La Tomatina.
2. En Buñol, un pueblo de Valencia, el último miércoles de cada agosto.
3. Participan aproximadamente treinta mil personas y se tiran 68.000 kilos de tomates.
4. Se tiran tomates en las calles.
5. Todos paran de tirar tomates y los residentes limpian las calles.
6. El agua la traen de un acueducto romano que está cerca.
34 Answers will vary.

Activities

Spanish for Spanish Speakers
Have students prepare a report on the Tomatina.

Lectura personal

Cantantes y grupos musicales

Dirección http://www.emcp.com/músico/ola/e.diario-7.htm ▲ Archivo Edición Ver Favoritos Herramientas Ayuda

página principal   miembros   e-diario

Grupo musical La OLA

Nombre: **Yadira Torres Ortega**
Edad: **15 años**
País natal: **México**
Verdura favorita: **lechuga**
Postre favorito: **arroz con leche**

Ayer miércoles fue un día que nunca voy a olvidar. Acabábamos[1] de dar un concierto en Madrid, la capital de España, y estábamos[2] en ruta a Valencia para otro concierto. Al mediodía, paramos en un pueblo llamado Buñol. Al bajar del camión, miles de personas en las calles estaban tirándose[3] tomates maduros los unos a los otros. ¡Fue la pelea[4] de comida más grande del mundo! Parece que lo hacen todos los años. Se llama la Tomatina, un festival popular, divertido y—debo añadir—para personas a las que no les importa estar sucios[5]. El último miércoles de cada agosto, entre las 11:00 de la mañana y la 1:00 de la tarde, treinta mil personas se tiran[6] tomates: 68.000 kilos de tomates, para ser exacta. ¡Imaginen el desastre! Las calles parecen ríos de sopa de tomate. Cuando suena[7] una sirena, todos paran[8] y los residentes empiezan a barrer las calles y lavarlas con enormes mangueras[9]. (El agua la traen de un acueducto romano que está cerca.) En unas pocas horas, las calles de Buñol están limpias, sin evidencia de que hubo[10] más tomates que en ninguna otra parte del mundo.

[1]we just finished [2]we were [3]were throwing at each other [4]fight [5]dirty [6]they throw at each other [7]blows [8]stop [9]hoses [10]there were

33 ¿Qué recuerdas?

1. ¿Cuál es la pelea de comida *(food fight)* más grande del mundo?
2. ¿Dónde y cuándo es?
3. ¿Aproximadamente cuántas personas participan? ¿Cuántos tomates usan?
4. ¿Qué hacen los participantes entre las 11 A.M. y la 1 P.M.?
5. ¿Qué hacen los residentes cuando suena una sirena *(a siren blows)*?
6. ¿De dónde traen el agua?

• Although people know that the Tomatina began in the 1940s, nobody knows for sure how it started. How do you think it all started? Compare your theory with those of your classmates.

34 Algo personal

1. ¿Has participado alguna vez en una pelea de comida?
2. En lugar de tomates, ¿qué otra fruta crees que es buena para una pelea de comida?
3. Imagina que vas a ir a la Tomatina. ¿Qué ropa llevas? ¿Por qué?

130 *ciento treinta*

Lección B

Notes The *Lectura personal* and activities 33–34 are recorded and available on audio CD as part of the Audio CD Program.

Have students pair up and take turns asking the questions for activities 33–34. Then have students write the answers to the two activities to turn in for a grade.

¿Qué aprendí?

Autoevaluación
As a review and self-check, respond to the following:

1. Name some foods found in a supermarket. Which ones might you also find at an outdoor market (*mercado al aire libre*)?

2. Name some of the ingredients and how much of each is needed in a recipe to make *paella valenciana* for six people.

3. Compare several foods you like and dislike.

4. Name two or three things that are the most, the best or the worst possible.

5. Imagine you keep a journal and every day you write where you went, where you were and other interesting information about what you did during the day. Make a brief list of five things that you would write about today in your journal.

6. What are two things you have learned about Spain in this lesson?

Visit the web-based activities at www.emcp.com

Palabras y expresiones

En el mercado
- el aguacate
- el ajo
- el arroz
- el café
- la carne
- la cebolla
- el chocolate
- el chorizo
- la fresa
- la fruta
- el guisante
- la habichuela
- el helado
- el huevo
- el ingrediente
- el jamón
- el kilo

- la lata
- la lechuga
- el maíz
- la manzana
- el mercado
- la papa
- el pimiento
- el plátano
- el precio
- el queso
- el tomate
- la uva
- la verdura
- el vinagre
- la zanahoria

Para describir
- fresco,-a
- maduro,-a
- mayor
- mejor
- menor
- peor

Verbos
- añadir
- escoger
- importar
- olvidar
- parecer

Expresiones y otras palabras
- el/la/los/las (+ *noun*) más/menos (+ *adjective*)
- el/la/los/las mejor/mejores/peor /peores (+ *noun*)
- hacer falta
- lo más/menos (+ *adverb*) posible
- más/menos (+ *noun/adjective/ adverb*) que
- la paella
- sin
- tan (+ *adjective/adverb*) como
- tanto como
- tanto,-a (+ *noun*) como

Frutas y verduras (*fruits and vegetables*).

Capítulo 8

Notes Mention to students that the authentic *paella valenciana* was cooked outdoors over a wood fire. The classic way of eating *paella* is for everyone to sit in a circle and eat directly from the pan. Each person would have an intricately carved boxwood spoon for eating, and exact triangles would be marked out as portions for each person.

One interesting aspect of preparing *paella* is that in Valencia the dish has traditionally been prepared by males in the family. This may be due in part to the fact that making *paella* is a social event that takes place in the open air, away from the kitchen.

Teacher Resources

📄 **Activity 13**

💬 **Information Gap Activities**
Postcard Activities
Funciones de Comunicación

Answers

Autoevaluación
Possible answers:

1. En un supermercado puedo comprar una cebolla, unos tomates y una lata de guisantes. En un mercado al aire libre puedo comprar una cebolla y unos tomates.

2. un pollo, medio kilo de gambas, medio kilo de langostinos, una taza de guisantes, dos tazas de arroz

3. Me gustan los tomates más que los aguacates.

4. Aprender el español es lo más importante para mí.

5. Fui al colegio esta mañana. Estuve allí todo el día. Hablé con mis amigos para hacer planes para el sábado.

6. Answers will vary.

Activities

Cooperative Learning
Have students imagine they are at an outdoor market doing grocery shopping for different foods. Then, working in pairs, they should take turns playing the roles of the vendor and the client.

Preparación
1. D
2. A

Activities

Critical Thinking
The reading presents a very different meal schedule and work schedule from what is common in the United States. Ask students their opinion of the schedules in each country and to consider the advantages and disadvantages of each.

¡Viento en popa!

Tú lees

Estrategia

Gathering meaning from context
When reading in another language, you will often encounter words you do not know. Before looking in a dictionary, look for clues that tell you what a word means. For example, you have already learned to recognize some unknown words because they are cognates (e.g., *familia*) or because they are related to words you have already learned (e.g., *baile/bailar*). At other times it may be necessary to look at the words before and after an unknown word (the context) in order to guess its meaning. Looking for these contextual clues will help improve your reading skills and will also make reading more enjoyable because you will spend less time looking up words in a dictionary.

Preparación

¿Qué quieren decir las palabras *tertulia* y *tapas* en las siguientes oraciones?

1. Un pasatiempo español es la **tertulia** con amigos en un café o un restaurante.
   A. comer empanadas
   B. ir de compras
   C. tomar café
   D. reunirse y conversar con amigos
2. A los españoles les gusta comer **tapas** con sus amigos antes de ir a casa para comer.
   A. comida pequeña antes de una comida principal
   B. pan con mantequilla
   C. frutas y verduras
   D. comida grande con carne y pescado

Ir de tapas y a merendar

Hay un par de pasatiempos que son muy populares entre la gente en España: ir de tapas e ir a merendar.[1] Ir de tapas es reunirse[2] con amigos o parientes para conversar y tomar aperitivos[3] antes de ir a casa para comer con la familia. Durante la conversación (o tertulia) las personas hablan de todo y comen tapas muy diversas (aceitunas, jamón serrano, patatas bravas[4], diferentes quesos, empanadas[5], etc.). Hay restaurantes y bares que sólo tienen tapas. Los grupos de amigos o familia pueden ir a tres o cuatro lugares diferentes para comer las tapas típicas de ese lugar. Hay dos

Aquí sirven tapas.

¡Viento en popa!

Notes One style of *tapa* called *banderillas* (named after the colorful darts used in bullfights) consists of skewering various ingredients onto toothpicks. They should be eaten by putting the entire contents of each *banderilla* into the mouth at once so that the tastes of the various ingredients blend together.

razones para comer tapas en España: la primera es que los españoles toman el almuerzo muy tarde (a las 2:00 o a las 3:00 de la tarde) y también cenan[6] muy tarde (a las 9:00 o a las 10:00 de la noche), y la segunda, la verdadera[7] razón, es que a los españoles les gusta mucho hablar y pasar tiempo con sus amigos y familia.

Merendar es otra forma de pasar tiempo con amigos y familia en donde los españoles salen para hablar y comer. En España la gente puede merendar en cafeterías, en merenderos[8] o en casa. Merendar, o la merienda, consiste de café para los adultos y de leche o chocolate para los jóvenes, además de[9] pasteles[10] y dulces. La merienda se come entre las cinco y las seis de la tarde, tres o cuatro horas antes de la cena[11], o ¡una hora antes de las tapas!

Unas tapas ricas.

[1]to have an afternoon snack   [2]to get together   [3]appetizers   [4]spicy potatoes   [5]bread dough filled with meat or fish   [6]eat dinner   [7]real   [8]places to have *merienda*   [9]in addition to   [10]pastries and cakes   [11]supper

A ¿Qué recuerdas?

1. ¿Qué es ir de tapas?
2. ¿Qué es merendar?
3. ¿Qué tapas comen los españoles?
4. ¿Adónde puede ir la gente para merendar?
5. ¿Por qué salen los españoles de tapas y meriendas?

B Algo personal

1. ¿Te gustan los aperitivos? ¿Cuáles te gustan?
2. ¿Qué te gustaría más, ir de tapas o ir a merendar?
3. ¿Qué te gustaría comer de tapas?
4. ¿Qué te gustaría comer de merienda?

Ellas meriendan.

Capítulo 8 *ciento treinta y tres* **133**

Teacher Resources

Activities A–B

Answers

A 1. Ir de tapas es reunirse con amigos o parientes para conversar y tomar aperitivos antes de ir a casa para comer.
2. Merendar es salir con amigos y familia para hablar y comer.
3. Comen aceitunas, jamón serrano, patatas bravas, diferentes quesos y empanadas.
4. La gente puede ir para merendar en cafeterías, merenderos o en casa.
5. Salen de tapas y meriendas porque toman el almuerzo y cenan muy tarde y porque les gusta salir con amigos y familia.

B Answers will vary.

Activities

Language through Action
Have your students prepare some *tapas* from home to bring to school and share with the class. As an alternative, arrange with the consumer science department to prepare *banderillas* as a fun class project.

Notes How to prepare *banderillas:* Your students can prepare *banderillas* by skewering four or five of the following ingredients on a toothpick: pitted green Spanish olives, pitted ripe black olives, pearl onions, small marinated mushrooms, pieces of canned pimento, chunks of solid white tuna, boiled shrimp, hard-boiled egg, marinated artichoke heart and pieces of bell pepper.

Critical Thinking

Have students write a short composition of one or two paragraphs about chores in their home. Ask them to be as specific as they can, including who does the chores and when. Encourage students to try to use as much new vocabulary and grammar from this lesson as possible.

Tú escribes

Estrategia

Using graphic organizers
It is useful to brainstorm ideas about your topic before actually beginning to write. If the subjects you are going to write about are related in some way, a graphic organizer such as a Venn diagram will help you visualize different aspects of your theme.
A Venn diagram, consisting of two intersecting circles, is especially good when your writing includes a comparison of what two subjects (such as people, places or events) have in common.

A Imagine you are going to celebrate a special event by having a special dinner with friends. First, write the name of the event you are celebrating (e.g., *cumpleaños de mi amigo Julio, viaje de mi amiga Elena*), and the date and the time the dinner will begin. Next, draw two intersecting circles (a Venn diagram). In one circle, list in Spanish the things you plan to do. In the second circle, list the things your friends plan to do. In the shared space, list the activities that the two of you plan to do together. Place each activity you think of in the appropriate area of the graphic. Be sure to include the *quehaceres* that must be completed both before and after the dinner.

B Underneath the circles of the Venn diagram you prepared, write a paragraph in Spanish describing the dinner you are planning, who is invited and who is responsible for carrying out the preparations.

Notes Note for students that eating in Spain may be unlike anything they are accustomed to. Meals and snacks are planned throughout the day and offer coveted opportunities for socialization. With regard to the meal times mentioned in the reading *Ir de tapas y a merendar* (pages 132–133), note that typical business hours in Spain are 9:00–2:00 and 5:00–8:00.

Inform students whether you want them to work individually or in pairs to do activities A and B.

Proyectos adicionales

A Conexión con la tecnología

Search the Web for sites about Spanish cuisine using key words (cuisine, food, Spanish, paella, etc.). How many different recipes *(recetas)* can you find? For example, how many ways can *paella* be prepared? How are the recipes different? List the ingredients. Can you locate any restaurants that serve *paella*? How much does it cost? Share your findings with the class.

La comida española.

B Comparaciones

Working with three or four classmates, compare your food habits. For example, ask your classmates if they eat more often at home or in restaurants; talk about the location and names of restaurants where members of the group eat; find out what foods your classmates think are the best at home and in each of the restaurants they name; and find out what foods each person prepares at home (and ask whether it is better or worse than the same food at a restaurant or when someone else prepares it. Take notes and report your findings to the class.

MODELO A: ¿Comes más en restaurantes que en tu casa?
        B: No, como más en mi casa que en restaurantes.

C Conexión cultural

What comes to mind when you think about Spain? Prepare a list of at least ten Spanish words that convey what you associate with Spain. Try to include words that relate to Spain's history as well as to modern Spain. Then, based on the words in your list, create a poster using pictures, art and other graphics to depict the images you have of Spain. Finally, display the poster and tell the class about your project. Be creative!

La Feria de abril (Sevilla, España).

 Situation Cards

 Capítulo 8

Answers

A Creative self-expression.
B Creative self-expression.
C Creative self-expression.

Activities

Communities
Have students visit the school or city library and prepare a report on any Spaniards who explored your state. Students should report what influences those visits have had on life in your state today.

Critical Thinking
Discuss with students the images they associate with Spain. Then ask what images they think of in relation to the United States. Do any of the responses overlap?

Multiple Intelligences (musical)
Play flamenco music for students and have them compare it to the rhythms of rap.

Spanish for Spanish Speakers
Have students prepare a report on the origins of flamenco music and dancing.

Notes The Spaniards heard about Aztec chocolate and took it to Spain in 1520. They added sugar, an important contribution, and later, cinnamon and vanilla. Spain zealously guarded the secret of chocolate production as long as it could and maintained a monopoly on the supply of cocoa, which came from its American colonies. *Chocolate a la española* is the thickest hot chocolate possible.

Teacher Resources

 Trabalenguas

Activities

Connections

Give students a recipe for preparing *churros con chocolate a la española* in Spanish. Read it in class, and using TPR, have students demonstrate how to prepare these fun snacks. You may ask students to prepare them at home and then bring them to class to share.

Critical Thinking

Ask students to name ten foods and compare them: *Me gustan las zanahorias tanto como las manzanas; no me gusta el chorizo tanto como el pollo.*

Repaso

Now that I have completed this chapter, I can...	Go to these pages for help:
talk about household chores.	94
say what just happened.	94
ask for and offer help.	99
talk about the past.	110
identify and describe foods.	114
discuss food preparation.	114
make comparisons.	118

I can also...	
talk about Spain's past.	97
talk about life in Spain today.	107
use survival skills.	117
name foods from different regions of Spain.	127

Trabalenguas

Pepe Pecas pica papas con un pico, con un pico pica papas Pepe Pecas.

Notes A custom that coincides with the tradition of *tapas* is the *paseo*, an afternoon or evening stroll with family or friends. The *paseo* provides a bit of exercise but is primarily a social activity.

Through the *Repaso,* students can measure their own progress in learning the main elements of the chapter.

Loose translation of the *Trabalenguas:* Pepe Pecas chops potatoes with a pickax, with a pickax chops Pepe Pecas potatoes.

A popular breakfast in Spain is *churros con chocolate. Churros* consist of a fried batter of flour and water. It is also customary to end the evening by eating *churros con chocolate* at a *churrería.*

Vocabulario

el **abrigo** coat *8A*
  acabar to finish, *8A*
  acabar de (*+ infinitive*) to have just *8A*
  adornar to decorate *8A*
el **aguacate** avocado *8B*
el **ajo** garlic *8B*
  algo something, anything *8A*
  añadir to add *8B*
  arreglar to arrange, to straighten, to fix *8A*
el **arroz** rice *8B*
la **aspiradora** vacuum cleaner *8A*
  barrer to sweep *8A*
la **basura** garbage *8A*
el **café** coffee *8B*
la **cama** bed *8A*
la **carne** meat *8B*
la **cebolla** onion *8B*
el **chocolate** chocolate *8B*
el **chorizo** sausage (*seasoned with red peppers*) *8B*
  cocinar to cook *8A*
  colgar (ue) to hang *8A*
  dar de comer to feed *8A*
  dejar to leave *8A*
  doblar to fold *8A*
  escoger to choose *8B*
la **fresa** strawberry *8B*
  fresco,-a fresh, chilly *8B*
la **fruta** fruit *8B*
la **gente** people *8A*
el **guisante** pea *8B*
la **habichuela** green bean *8B*
  hacer falta to be necessary, to be lacking *8B*

el **helado** ice cream *8B*
el **huevo** egg *8B*
  importar to be important, to matter *8B*
el **ingrediente** ingredient *8B*
el **jamón** ham *8B*
el **jardín** garden *8A*
  junto,-a together *8A*
el **kilo (kg.)** kilogram *8B*
la **lata** can *8B*
  lavar to wash *8A*
la **leche** milk *8A*
la **lechuga** lettuce *8B*
  limpiar to clean *8A*
  listo,-a smart *8A*
  llegar to arrive *8A*
  llevar to take, to carry *5A*
  maduro,-a ripe *8B*
el **maíz** corn *8B*
la **manzana** apple *8B*
  más (*+ noun/adjective/adverb*)
    que more (*+noun/adjective/adverb*) *8B*
  mayor older, oldest *8B*
  mejor better, *8B*
  menor lesser, least *8B*
  menos (*+ noun/adjective/adverb*)
    que less (*+noun/adjective/adverb*) *8B*
el **mercado** market *8B*
la **olla** pot, saucepan *8A*
  olvidar to forget *8B*
  oír to hear, to listen *8A*
la **paella** paella (*traditional Spanish dish with rice*) *8B*
la **papa** potato *8B*
  parecer to seem *8B*
  pasar la aspiradora to vacuum *8A*
  peor worse *8B*
  peor/peores (*+ noun*) the worst (*+noun*) *8B*

la **persona** person *8A*
el **pimiento** bell pepper *8B*
el **plátano** banana *8B*
el **precio** price *8B*
  preparar to prepare *8A*
  prestar to lend *8B*
el **quehacer** chore *8A*
el **queso** cheese *8B*
  quizás perhaps *8A*
la **receta** recipe *8B*
  recoger to pick up *8A*
  recoger la mesa to clear the table *8A*
  sacar to take out *8A*
  sin without *8B*
  sólo only, just *8A*
  subir to climb, to go up, to go upstairs, to take up, to bring up, to carry up *8A*
el **supermercado** supermarket *8B*
  tan (*+ adjective/adverb*) **como** (*person/item*) as (*+person/item*) as *8B*
  tanto como as much as *8B*
  tanto,-a (*+ noun*) **como** (*person/item*) as many/much (*+noun*) as *8B*
el **tomate** tomato *8B*
  trabajar to work *8A*
el **trabajo** work *8A*
  traer to bring *8A*
la **uva** grape *8B*
la **verdura** greens, vegetables *8B*
el **vinagre** vinegar *8B*
la **zanahoria** carrot *8B*

El jamón.

¡Hay buen chorizo! ¿Cuántos kilos quiere?

Capítulo 8

ciento treinta y siete **137**

Teacher Resources

Módule 3

Episode 8

Testing/ Assessment

Test Booklet
Portfolio Assessment

Activities

Multiple Intelligences (spatial/linguistic)
Have students create a map of Spain, detailing the locations and names of important cities, rivers, mountains, regions, etc. As an alternative, have students write a short composition about an aspect of Spain that interests them.

Spanish for Spanish Speakers
Have students write a composition in Spanish summarizing what they know about Spain. Expand the activity by having students seek out additional information about Spain at the library or via the Internet.

Notes   Remind students that the words and expressions listed here are provided for easy reference and consist of all vocabulary they must know from *Capítulo 8*. Students should review and test themselves over the content of the *Vocabulario* in preparation for the chapter test and for future chapters in *Navagando 1B*.

137

Activities

Connections

Have students name some cities in Ecuador and Panama. Then ask if anyone in class has visited or knows someone who has visited either country. Ask what students know about these countries.

Critical Thinking

Use the visuals that appear at the start of the chapter to discuss the functions, cultural setting and themes of the chapter ahead. For example, ask students to answer the following: 1) Where are the people shown in these photographs?; 2) What are the people doing?; 3) What do students think they will be studying in the chapter?; 4) Can they guess which countries the chapter features?; 5) What similarities or differences do they note between shopping in the United States and shopping as it is depicted on these pages?

Capítulo 9

La ropa

Objetivos

❖ **describe clothing**

❖ **identify parts of the body**

❖ **express disagreement**

❖ **talk about the past**

❖ **discuss size and fit**

❖ **discuss price and payment**

Visit the web-based activities at www.emcp.com

138 *ciento treinta y ocho*

Notes The communicative objectives are provided here to help prepare students for what they will be learning in *Capítulo 9*. Spend a few moments discussing the objectives with the class.

A checkoff list of these functions, along with additional objectives, appears on page 184 so students can evaluate their own progress.

Panamá
Nombre oficial: **República de Panamá**
Población: **2.845.000**
Capital: **Ciudad de Panamá**
Ciudades importantes: **San Miguelito, Colón, David**
Unidad monetaria: **el balboa**
Fiesta nacional: **3 de noviembre, Separación de Panamá de Colombia**
Gente famosa: **Rubén Blades (cantante, actor), Ómar Torrijos (ex-presidente)**

Ecuador
Nombre oficial: **República del Ecuador**
Población: **13.183.000**
Capital: **Quito**
Ciudades importantes: **Guayaquil, Cuenca, Machala**
Unidad monetaria: **el sucre**
Fiesta nacional: **10 de agosto, Primer Grito de la Independencia de Quito**
Gente famosa: **Jorge Enrique Adum (escritor), Oswaldo Guayasamin (pintor)**

ciento treinta y nueve **139**

Notes Talk with the class about the contents of pages 138 and 139. The large photograph depicts shopping in Panama at a retail clothing store; the small photograph shows an open-air market in Quito, Ecuador.

In this chapter students will be learning how to use Spanish when shopping for clothing and gifts. They will also learn to evaluate their own shopping tastes. Finally, students will learn what it is like to go shopping in Panama and in Ecuador and what they might find in stores and markets if they travel to one of these Spanish-speaking countries in Central and South America.

139

En la tienda por departamentos

 Activity 1

 Activities 61–62

 Activities 1–3

 Activity 1

 Activities 1–4

Content reviewed in *Lección A*
- colors
- preterite tense of regular *-ar* verbs
- preterite tense of *ser*
- negation

Activities

Prereading Strategy
Using overhead transparencies 61 and 62, introduce the lesson vocabulary. Say the words and have students repeat after you to practice individual words and to begin to become familiar with the new words. Be sure to include both the articles of clothing and colors. Then follow up by practicing the vocabulary, asking students to identify and spell the words you indicate.

Lección A
Panamá

Vocabulario I
En la tienda por departamentos

Departamento de ropa para hombres

el pijama
la camisa de algodón
la ropa interior
el traje de baño
la corbata
el traje
Departamento de ropa para mujeres
la blusa de seda
morada
marrón
rosada
anaranjada
el vestido
el traje de baño
el pijama
la ropa interior
las medias
el cuerpo
la cabeza
el dedo
el brazo
la bota
la mano
el zapato bajo
el zapato de tacón
la pierna
el pie
el dedo

Notes Ask students what they know about Panama. Most students are familiar with the Panama Canal, which is discussed on page 143. Ask for student volunteers to create a bulletin board or travel brochure about this Spanish-speaking Central American country.

Have students find cognates and words they already know in *Vocabulario I*. Quickly check student comprehension of the descriptions that accompany the illustrations on these two pages.

¿Prefieres la camisa roja o la verde?

Prefiero la roja. Yo le pedí una roja a mis padres para mi cumpleaños, pero me dieron una azul.

1 Comprando ropa

Selecciona la ilustración que corresponde con lo que oyes.

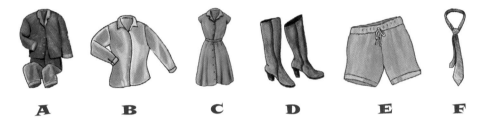

A   **B**   **C**   **D**   **E**   **F**

2 ¿De qué color son?

Describe la ropa de la actividad anterior, usando los colores.

1. el vestido
2. las botas
3. el pijama
4. la corbata
5. la blusa
6. el traje de baño

3 El cuerpo

Nombra (name) las partes del cuerpo.

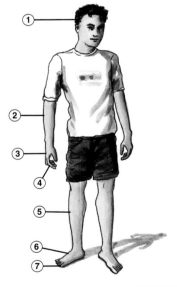

Activities

Critical Thinking
Ask individuals about the *Vocabulario I* illustration using simple questions with **yes** or **no** for answers: *¿Es roja la corbata?* Then gradually begin to ask questions that require more elaborate answers: *¿De qué color es el vestido?* Finally, personalize the questions: *¿De qué color son tus zapatos?*

Capítulo 9   *ciento cuarenta y uno*   **141**

Notes Activity 1 is intended for listening comprehension practice. Play the audio CD of the activity or use the transcript that appears in the ATE Introduction if you prefer to read the activity yourself. A reproducible answer sheet for the activity can be found at the end of the Audio CD Program Manual.

You may want to have students write answers for activities 2 and 3.

Use overhead transparencies 61 and 62 to present and practice the new words and expressions in *Vocabulario I*.

Answers

4 1. Busca un vestido de seda.
2. Prefiere el vestido rosado.
3. No, no cuesta mucho.
4. No le gusta ni un poquito.
5. Prefiere el vestido morado.
6. Lo puede llevar con unas medias verdes.

5 Answers will vary.

6 1. B
2. A
3. B
4. B
5. A
6. A
7. A
8. B

Activities

Multiple Intelligences (bodily-kinesthetic/spatial)
Review colors by playing the game Scattergories: Divide the class into teams of four or five students. Name a color; allow one to two minutes for the groups to find and name classroom objects they see that are that color. One student in each group (the recorder) should write down the list of descriptions (remind students the color adjectives must agree with the nouns they describe).

Diálogo 1
¿Cuál prefieres?

ROCÍO: ¿Dónde está el departamento de ropa para mujeres?
PEDRO: ¿Qué buscas?
ROCÍO: Busco un vestido de seda para la fiesta del sábado.

ROCÍO: Aquí hay unos vestidos. ¿Cuál prefieres?
PEDRO: Prefiero el vestido rosado. Y no cuesta mucho.
ROCÍO: ¿El rosado? No me gusta ni un poquito. Prefiero el morado.

PEDRO: Con el rosado puedes llevar unas medias verdes.
ROCÍO: ¿Una medias verdes? ¡Estás loco!
PEDRO: Sí, te vas a ver muy bonita, como una flor.

4 ¿Qué recuerdas?

1. ¿Qué busca Rocío?
2. ¿Qué vestido prefiere Pedro?
3. ¿Cuesta mucho el vestido rosado?
4. ¿Le gusta el vestido rosado a Rocío?
5. ¿Qué vestido prefiere Rocío?
6. Según Pedro, ¿con qué puede llevar Rocío el vestido rosado?

5 Algo personal

1. ¿Cuál es tu color favorito?
2. ¿Tienes un color favorito para la ropa?
3. ¿Qué ropa te gustaría comprar?
4. ¿Qué colores te gusta llevar juntos?
5. ¿Te gusta ayudar a tus amigos/as a comprar ropa? Explica.

¡Extra!

¿Recuerdas?

Do you remember learning the following colors?

amarillo	negro
azul	rojo
blanco	verde
gris	

6 ¿Cuál prefieres?

Selecciona la letra de la ilustración que corresponde con lo que las siguientes personas prefieren.

A **B**

Notes This dialog and activities 4, 5 and 6 have been recorded by native speakers and are included in the *Navegando* Audio CD Program.

Teenagers are often fairly fashion conscious, but they also recognize that how they dress represents only one aspect of who they are. With that in mind, your students may enjoy learning a proverb in Spanish that says it is not the clothes you wear that are important, but rather who you are: *Aunque la mona se vista de seda, mona se queda* (Even though it may be wearing silk, the monkey is still a monkey).

Cultura viva

La ciudad de Panamá.

Panamá, el cruce del mundo

Although small by comparison with many Spanish-speaking countries, Panama serves as an important crossroads for the world due to its geographic location and physical features. You are probably familiar with the canal (el Canal de Panamá) that divides the country in two. This valuable international travel route took years to build and many people died during its construction. Today the canal serves a critical function connecting the Atlantic and the Pacific oceans, shortening the time and energy required to transport goods from one part of the world to another.

Panama's people (los panameños) have a varied background. When Rodrigo de Bastidas, Juan de la Cosa and Vasco Nuñez de Balboa arrived in Panama in 1501, followed by Columbus in 1502, the land was inhabited primarily by natives of two indigenous groups, the kuna and the chocó. Panama's citizens today are descendants of these and other indigenous groups, Spanish conquistadors, African slaves and workers from China (who were involved in constructing the railroad in the mid-1800s), among others. Direct descendants of the kuna and chocó people still inhabit the San Blas archipelago.

Most Panamanians prefer to live in cities along the canal. For example, Panama City (la Ciudad de Panamá), the capital and largest city, is located along the canal. Panama City has become an important financial center, with more than ninety banks from throughout the world registered to do business.

El canal de Panamá.

7 Panamá, el cruce del mundo

Di si lo siguiente es *cierto* o *falso*.

1. Panamá es un país pequeño.
2. La capital de Panamá es San José.
3. El Canal de Panamá va del Océano Pacífico al Atlántico.
4. La capital es la ciudad más grande del país.
5. Bastidas, de la Cosa y Balboa llegaron a Panamá en 1905.
6. Descendientes de los kuna y los chocó viven en el archipiélago de San Blas.

8 Conexión con otras disciplinas: arquitectura e historia

Working in small groups, research the history of the Panama Canal. Try to find information regarding its construction, how long the project took, etc. Share your findings with the class.

Answers

7 1. Cierto.
2. Falso.
3. Cierto.
4. Cierto.
5. Falso.
6. Cierto.
8 Creative self-expression.

Activities

Connections (Social Studies)
Have students prepare a report about President Theodore Roosevelt's involvement in Panama's independence from Colombia.

Spanish for Spanish Speakers
Encourage interested students to study the development and operation of the Panama Canal, using the Internet and library resources. Then have students prepare a report about the canal and explain its construction to the class.

Notes The Kuna Indians who live on the San Blas archipelago are famous for their *molas*—colorful reverse appliqués— made of several layers of colorful cotton fabric.

Connections. Activity 8 makes the cross-curricular connection to architecture and history.

Activity 3

 Activity 5

 Activity 2

 Activity 5

Answers

9 Answers will vary.
10 1. el
    2. el
    3. —
    4. los
    5. —
    6. —
    7. la
    8. El

Activities

Students with Special Needs
Remind students that for agreement in gender and number, color words and other adjectives ending in -*o* have four forms; those ending in -*e* or a consonant have two forms. Practice the point by choosing a color such as *negro* or *rosado* and then say several nouns to which students may respond individually when you call on them or in chorus. Do the same with *verde* and then with an adjective ending in a consonant such as *gris* or *azul*.

Idioma

Estructura

Adjectives as nouns

Although a definite article is not usually needed when a color describes an object (because the color is an adjective), a definite article is required when naming colors in Spanish (because they are considered nouns).

> *Pedí un pantalón negro de cumpleaños.*   I asked for black pants for my birthday.

but:

> *Prefiero **el** (color) rojo.*   I prefer red.

In addition, sometimes a word being described may be omitted in order to avoid repeating a noun. In such cases the article remains and the adjective must agree with the noun that was omitted.

> *¿Te gusta el vestido azul o **el** (vestido) gris?*   Do you like the blue dress or **the grey one?**
> *Compré la camisa blanca, no **la verde**.*   I bought the white shirt, not **the green one.**

 Práctica

9 Los colores de mi ropa

Completa las oraciones con el adjetivo apropiado para describir algunos artículos de ropa en tu cuarto.

MODELO Tengo un pantalón <u>rojo</u>.

1. Tengo mucha ropa __.
2. Tengo unas botas __.
3. Tengo unos zapatos __.
4. Tengo un pijama __.
5. Tengo una camisa __.
6. Tengo un traje de baño __.

Tengo un pantalón rojo.

10 Los gustos personales

Completa las siguientes oraciones con un artículo definido si lo necesitan.

1. A Marta le gusta __ color verde.
2. El color favorito de Enrique es __ morado.
3. A mi prima le gustaría comprar un impermeable __ amarillo.
4. ¿Elena prefiere los calcetines verdes o __ rojos?
5. Mi madre tiene una blusa de seda __ rosada porque es su color favorito.
6. A Pedro le gustan sus botas __ negras.
7. Esperanza compró la ropa interior azul ayer, no __ blanca.
8. __ anaranjado es mi color favorito.

Notes You may want to share with students the following additional color names: *la violeta* (violet), *el azul marino* (navy blue), *el verde claro* (light green), *el rojo vivo* (bright red).

Practice using color names as nouns before assigning activity 10.

11 **¡Vamos de compras!**

Imagina que tienes $300.00. Haz una lista de la ropa que te gustaría comprar este sábado, añadiendo los colores y los materiales que te gustan.

 ## Comunicación

 12 **¿Cuánto cuesta?**

Trabajando en parejas, un estudiante hace de cliente *(customer)* y el otro de vendedor(a) *(salesperson)*. Alternen en regatear los precios de los artículos en las ilustraciones.

MODELO

A: ¿Cuánto cuestan las botas?
B: Las botas cuestan $80.
A: Le doy $70.
B: No puedo. Se las doy por $75.

Estrategia

Developing language survival skills: *regatear*

Most shops and stores in Spanish-speaking parts of the world have a fixed price *(precio fijo)*, and trying to negotiate a lower price would be inappropriate. However, in some instances negotiating *(regatear)* the price for an item is a common and accepted practice. For example, street vendors selling clothing, baskets, jewelry, etc. in Panama City would expect you to negotiate with them on prices.

How might knowing Spanish help you negotiate a price while visiting a Spanish-speaking country? Do you feel confident enough with your Spanish skills to be able to negotiate a price?

¡Oportunidades!

Regatear
Is there a flea market where you live? Go there and practice bargaining for items. Learning how to bargain will be beneficial if you travel to a Spanish-speaking country where you can combine your ability to bargain with your ability to speak Spanish.

1

2

3

4

5

6

Capítulo 9 — *ciento cuarenta y cinco* **145**

Notes For activity 11, ask students to assign a price (they may make up the price or check a newspaper advertisement) to each item on their list. Then follow up the activity by having students pair up and ask one another about their lists.

Follow up activity 12 by asking students to write down several lines as they role-play. Then select several pairs of students or ask for volunteers to present their dialog in front of the class.

Answers

11 Creative self-expression.
12 Creative self-expression.

Activities

Expansion
Ask additional personalized questions: *¿Te gusta usar corbata?*; *¿Prefieres la ropa formal o la ropa informal? ¿Qué ropa llevas a una fiesta formal? ¿Qué ropa llevas a la playa? ¿Qué ropa llevas en un día típico?*; *¿Prefieres las botas o los zapatos de tacón?*; *Para la piscina o la playa, ¿llevas bikini o traje de baño de una pieza?*

Multiple Intelligences (bodily-kinesthetic)
Have students divide into groups to write and perform a skit demonstrating how to barter as in activity 12. Have them bring in items for their vendor to sell and base the prices on the current value of the balboa. (Students can locate the current price of a balboa in the newspaper, on the Internet or by calling a local bank.)

Answers

13 Creative self-expression.
14 Answers will vary.

Activities

Expansion

Review the present-tense forms of these verbs with students before teaching the preterite tense. Then compare the present-tense stem changes with the preterite-tense stem changes.

---

 13 ¿Qué ropa ves?

 Trabajando en parejas, habla con tu compañero/a sobre la ropa de la tienda del Vocabulario I. Miren el dibujo y señalen *(point out)* con el dedo los artículos de ropa.

MODELO **A:** ¿Qué te gustaría comprar en la tienda?
B: Me gustaría comprar los zapatos negros, los marrones no me gustan.

 14 ¿Qué ropa llevan?

Discuss what clothing people around you are wearing. Begin by saying who is wearing the article of clothing. Your partner then must describe the material or color. Each student must name and describe at least five articles of clothing.

MODELO **A:** Estoy mirando el pantalón de Julia.
B: Su pantalón es azul y es de algodón.

Estructura

Talking about the past: preterite tense of *-er* and *-ir* verbs

Form the preterite tense of regular *-er* and *-ir* verbs by removing the last two letters from the infinitive and adding the same set of endings for either type of verb.

correr	
corrí	corr**imos**
corr**iste**	corr**isteis**
corr**ió**	corr**ieron**

escribir	
escribí	escrib**imos**
escrib**iste**	escrib**isteis**
escrib**ió**	escrib**ieron**

*¿Quién **corrió** a la tienda?*   Who **ran** to the store?
*¿Le **escribió** Julia una carta a su prima?*   **Did** Julia **write** a letter to her cousin?

Note: Stem changes that occur in the present tense for *-ar* and *-er* verbs do not occur in the preterite tense. However, *-ir* verbs that have a stem change in the present tense require a different stem change in the preterite tense for *Ud., él, ella, Uds., ellos* and *ellas*. This second change is shown in parentheses after infinitives in this book. Some verbs that follow this pattern include *dormir (ue, **u**), mentir (ie, **i**), pedir (i, **i**), preferir (ie, **i**), repetir (i, **i**)* and *sentir (ie, **i**)*. The stem changes do not interfere with the verb endings.

dormir	
dormí	dormimos
dormiste	dormisteis
d**u**rmió	d**u**rmieron

pedir	
pedí	pedimos
pediste	pedisteis
p**i**dió	p**i**dieron

preferir	
preferí	preferimos
preferiste	preferisteis
pref**i**rió	pref**i**rieron

Notes Review the preterite tense of *-ar* verbs before beginning the *Estructura* on *-er* and *-ir* verbs.

Be sure to practice conjugating several *-er* and *-ir* verbs so students are clear about what they need to do for the activities that follow.

 **Práctica**

15 ¿Lo hiciste ayer o no?

Use each of the verbs shown to state ten things you did or did not do yesterday.

abrir   aprender   **recoger**   comer
correr   escribir   dormir   barrer
mentir   **salir**   repetir

MODELO   recoger
Recogí unas fotos ayer.

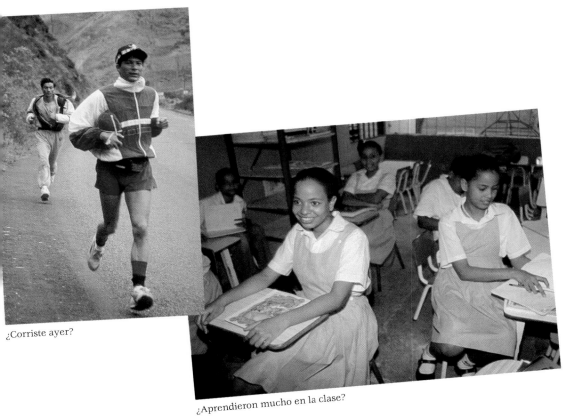

¿Corriste ayer?

¿Aprendieron mucho en la clase?

Answers

16 1. ¿Aprendiste...?/...los
         aprendí a arreglar
         (...aprendí a arreglarlos).
       2. ¿Barriste...?/...lo barrí....
       3. ¿Pediste...?/...las pedí.
       4. ¿Escogiste...?/...las escogí.
       5. ¿Subiste...?/...la subí.
17 Answers will vary.

Activities

Cooperative Learning
After completing activity 17,
students can work in pairs,
talking about what other people
did yesterday. Possible subjects
include classmates, friends and
family members.

---

16 En la tienda de ropa

Working in pairs, one person plays the part of the owner of a clothing store who has returned from vacation and one person plays the part of an employee who has been managing the store during the owner's absence. What might the conversation sound like, based upon the provided cues?

MODELO recoger las corbatas nuevas
            A: ¿Recogiste las corbatas nuevas?
            B: Sí, (No, no) las recogí.

1. aprender a arreglar los pantalones
2. barrer siempre el suelo de la tienda por la mañana
3. pedir las camisas
4. escoger las corbatas para los clientes
5. subir la ropa nueva a la oficina

17 ¿Qué hicieron ayer?

Usa elementos de cada columna para hacer siete oraciones completas y decir lo que pasó ayer.

MODELO Yo pedí tres corbatas.

I	II	III
tú y yo	pedir	al departamento de ropa para hombres
Uds.	estar	comprarte unas botas nuevas
la profesora	dormir	toda la tarde
Ud.	correr	ropa interior blanca
los chicos	preferir	en la tienda por departamentos
tú	repetir	tres corbatas
yo		los trajes de baño
		el precio dos veces

Estuvimos en el centro comercial ayer.

Notes Review direct object pronouns and their position in sentences before beginning activity 16.

Consider completing one or two of the sentences in activity 17 with students to be sure they understand what they are to do.

18 En la tienda por departamentos

En parejas, hablen Uds. de lo qué pasó en la tienda por departamentos ayer, según las pistas y las ilustraciones.

MODELO   Belén/pedir ver

A: ¿Qué pidió ver Belén?
B: Belén pidió ver unas botas marrones.

1. Jorge y Edgar/
   pedir ver

2. Manuel/escoger

3. Alfonso y su hermano/
   volver para comprar

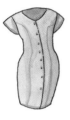

4. la amiga de Ernesto/
   correr a comprar

5. Carmen y su
   mamá/escoger

6. Pedro/preferir comprar

✦ Comunicación

19 La semana pasada

Make a list of some things you did in the past week. Then, in small groups, talk about the activities on everyone's list. One person starts by mentioning something he or she did. Then others in the group ask questions such as when and with whom you did each activity. You may wish to include some of the following activities: *escribir un correo electrónico, dormir tarde, comer en un restaurante, salir con amigos,* etc.

MODELO   **A:** Escribí un correo electrónico.
          B: ¿A quién lo escribiste?
          A: Lo escribí a un amigo en Panamá.
          C: ¿Cuándo escribiste el correo?
          A: Lo escribí anteayer.

Capítulo 9   *ciento cuarenta y nueve*   **149**

Answers

18 1. ¿...pidieron ver...?/
        ...pidieron ver unos trajes
        de baño.
     2. ¿...escogió...?/...escogió
        una corbata roja y una
        camisa azul.
     3. ¿...volvieron para
        comprar...?/...volvieron
        para comprar un pijama
        morado.
     4. ¿...corrió a comprar...?/
        ...corrió a comprar un
        vestido anaranjado.
     5. ¿...escogieron...?/
        ...escogieron unas blusas
        de seda.
     6. ¿...prefirió comprar...?/
        ...prefirió comprar unas
        camisetas.
19 Creative self-expression.

Activities

Pronunciation (*las letras* p y f)
The English sound of the letter *p* is "explosive": that is, if you hold your hand over your mouth when you pronounce it, you will feel a slight puff of air. In Spanish this does not happen. Try saying: *Pepe (pepepepepepe...)*. Have students practice the sound by saying the following words: *compra, impermeable, palabra, pantalón, pijama, pedir, Pilar, ropa, zapato.* Remember that the English combination *ph* does not exist in Spanish. That sound is usually represented by an *f*. Have students practice the sound by saying the following words: *café, diferente, difícil, falda, famoso, frío, fue, prefiero, Rafael.*

Notes Before beginning activity 18, call on students to identify the illustrated objects.

Follow up activity 18 by asking students to write out their answers for each question.

You may wish to assign one person in each group to take notes as people talk. Then have the person summarize the results of the group's discussion.

Teacher Resources

 Artículos para todos

 Activity 5

 Activity 63

 Activity 9

 Activity 4

 Activity 9

Activities

Critical Thinking

Students create a survey chart with items of clothing across the top *(camisas, pantalones, blusas, faldas, vestidos, etc.)* and colors listed down the side. They should then interview classmates asking *¿Qué ropa llevaste ayer?* and *¿de qué color?*. You may have interviewers report student names in relation to clothing and colors or the total number of students who wore each of the different items.

150 *ciento cincuenta*   **Lección A**

Notes Have students find cognates and words they already know in *Vocabulario II*. Quickly check student comprehension of the text boxes and bubbles that accompany the illustrations on these two pages.

An *abrigo* is called a *gabán* in Argentina and a *tapado* in Uruguay.

Use overhead transparency 63 to present and practice the new words and expressions in *Vocabulario II*.

¿Te gusta alguna chaqueta?

No, ninguna. ¿Hay alguien a quién preguntar si tienen más?

No, no veo a nadie.

la chaqueta

20 ¿Qué es?

 Activity 20

Escribe el artículo de ropa que oyes.

MODELO el <u>sombrero</u>

1. los __   2. un __   3. una __   4. un __   5. tu __   6. el __

21 ¿Qué llevo?

Escoge la palabra apropiada para completar lógicamente las siguientes oraciones.

MODELO Si hace frío llevo un (ropa interior, <u>abrigo</u>, blusa).

1. Ay, está nevando y no tengo (corbata, amarillo, botas).
2. Hace sol y calor. Debo llevar mi (suéter, traje de baño, falda) a la playa.
3. Me gusta caminar por la playa sin (zapatos, seda, gris).
4. No quiero llevar una (chaqueta, corbata, camisa) porque no hace frío.
5. Hace mucho viento y no debo llevar el (sombrero, camisa, suéter).
6. El pantalón del (rosado, traje, falda) está sucio.

22 La ropa que usas

Haz una lista de la ropa que necesitas para esquiar en la nieve y otra lista para pasar un día en la playa.

Answers

20 1. guantes
2. abrigo
3. chaqueta
4. impermeable
5. suéter
6. pantalón
21 1. botas
2. traje de baño
3. zapatos
4. chaqueta
5. sombrero
6. traje
22 Answers will vary.

Activities

Critical Listening
As an extension of activity 22, select and read aloud the names of articles of clothing from both lists, having students raise their left hand if the item is worn on the beach or their right hand if the item is used when snow skiing.

Expansion
As a follow-up to activity 22, ask students what items besides clothing they would take on a ski trip or to the beach.

Notes Activity 20 is intended for listening comprehension practice. Play the audio CD of the activity or use the transcript that appears in the ATE Introduction if you prefer to read the activity yourself. A reproducible answer sheet for the activity can be found at the end of the Audio CD Program Manual.

Consider allowing students to do activity 22 in pairs. For example, students might ask one another what they need to ski (*¿Qué necesitas par esquiar en la nieve?*) or what they need to spend a day at the beach (*¿Qué necesitas para pasar un día en la playa?*). Follow up by having students list on paper the clothing they need for each activity.

Diálogo II
Un vestido de seda

ROCÍO: ¿Hay alguien a quien preguntar por otros vestidos?
PEDRO: Sí, allí. Señora, ¿nos puede ayudar?
SEÑORA: Sí, cómo no.

ROCÍO: Busco un vestido de seda.
SEÑORA: ¿No le gusta ninguno de aquí?
ROCÍO: No, ninguno. Bueno, este azul, pero no me queda bien.

SEÑORA: Bueno, aquí hay otros pero son de lana.
ROCÍO: No, los vestidos de lana no me gustan nada.
SEÑORA: Le gustaría ver algo más, ¿guantes, abrigos, faldas?

23 ¿Qué recuerdas?

1. ¿Hay alguien a quien preguntar por otros vestidos?
2. ¿Le gustan los vestidos de seda a Rocío?
3. ¿Qué vestidos no le gustan a Rocío?
4. ¿Qué más puede ver Rocío?

24 Algo personal

1. ¿Prefieres los vestidos de lana o los de seda?
2. ¿Qué color de ropa te queda bien?
3. ¿Qué ropa compras cuando vas de vacaciones?

¿Qué vestido prefieres?

25 ¿Cuándo?

Listen carefully to statements made by several people. Indicate whether each sentence you hear is in the past *(pretérito)* or in the present *(presente)*.

Notes This dialog and activities 23, 24 and 25 have been recorded by native speakers and are included in the *Navegando* Audio CD Program.

You may choose to use the recorded version of activity 25 or you may wish to read the transcript of the activity, which can be found in the ATE Introduction. A reproducible answer sheet for activity 25 has been included at the end of the Audio CD Program Manual for your convenience.

Cultura viva

También se dice

As you have seen many times now, words that are used to name items in Spanish often vary a great deal as you travel from one country or region to the next. Even common articles of

clothing are referred to in many different ways. For example, the item you know as a *falda* may be called a *saya* in the Caribbean or a *pollera* in parts of South America. However, in Panama the term *pollera* refers to the national dress, which consists

Tiene ojos castaños.

of a brightly colored blouse that is connected to a full skirt. In the Caribbean, *zapatos de tacón* are sometimes called simply *tacones.* In addition, an *abrigo* may be called a *sobretodo* in Chile, and many people use *almacén* instead of *tienda de ropa* to refer to the place where they shop for clothing.

Words used to refer to some colors vary, too, as you travel from

Un tacón de color café.

one Spanish-speaking part of the world to another. For instance, there are many different words to refer to the color brown. In countries that have been influenced by the French many people favor the word *marrón* for **brown.** In the Caribbean, *carmelita* and the expressions *color café* or *color tabaco* are used. In some countries the word for brown varies according to what is being described. For example, the word *castaño* describes brown hair or brown eyes.

26 Juego: ¿Quién es?

In small groups, play this game: Take turns describing what someone in the class is wearing, one article of clothing at a time, without looking directly at the person; next, ask *¿Quién es?* and have one member of the group answer after the piece of clothing has been described. If the person does not guess correctly who the person is, describe another article of clothing and continue. The winner is the person that correctly identifies the classmate who is wearing the clothing being described.

MODELO   **A:** Lleva una camisa blanca. ¿Quién es?
　　　　B: Es Carlos.

Lleva un abrigo rosado. ¿Quién es?

Teacher Resources

📝 **Activity 5**

Answers

26 Creative self-expression.

Activities

Spanish for Spanish Speakers
Pair bilingual and nonbilingual students for activity 26.

Technology
Have students search the Internet using the word *pollera.* (See the ATE Introduction for suggestions on using the Internet for searches.) Students will find many different Web pages that discuss *polleras.* Ask students to find Web pages that discuss *polleras* in Panama. Follow up and ask students if they found any sites written in Spanish. Students should print pages from a Spanish-language site, skim it for phrases that they recognize and then share it with the class. You may also want students to summarize what they found on any English-language sites as additional support for a class discussion.

Activities

Multiple Intelligences (linguistic/spatial)
Have students think of a memory device and make a visual representation to depict the forms of *ser* and *ir* in the preterite. Share their ideas with the rest of the class and display the best ones on a bulletin board.

Idioma

Estructura

Preterite tense of *ir* and *ser*

You have already seen forms of the preterite tense of *ser*. The irregular preterite-tense forms of *ir* (to go) and *ser* (to be) are identical.

ir/ser	
fui	fuimos
fuiste	fuisteis
fue	fueron

*¿Quién **fue** al centro comercial ayer?*	Who **went** to the mall yesterday?
*¿**Fueron** ellos al centro comercial?*	**Did** they **go** to the mall?

but:

*¿Qué día **fue** ayer?*	What day **was** yesterday?
*Esos días **fueron** fantásticos.*	Those days **were** fantastic.

¿Fueron ellos al centro comercial?

Notes The preterite tense of *ser* was introduced briefly in *Capítulo 5* so students could talk about the days of the week.

Remember to select from the Teacher Resources indicated at the top of the page to find support materials for teaching from the pages of the textbook. For example, you will find activities that practice and reinforce the preterite tense of *ir* and *ser* in the Listening Activities Manual, Workbook and Grammar and Vocabulary Exercises Manual.

Práctica

27 ¿Adónde fueron ayer?

 Indica adónde fueron estas personas, según las ilustraciones.

MODELO

Ana y Pablo
Ana y Pablo fueron al cine ayer.

1. yo

2. tú

3. Julia

4. mis padres

5. mi amigo y yo

6. Raúl e Inés

28 Haciendo compras en la isla Contadora

Completa el siguiente párrafo con el pretérito de los verbos indicados para decir qué ropa compraron Juanita y sus dos hermanas en la isla Contadora.

Primero yo (*1. escoger*) un traje de baño porque el que tengo no me queda bien. Lo (*2. comprar*) por poco dinero. Mis hermanas también (*3. comprar*) en la misma tienda unos vestidos de algodón muy bonitos. Cuando nosotras (*4. volver*) al centro comercial, yo (*5. ir*) a buscar otro traje de baño para mí. Ese día en la tienda, los dependientes (*6. vender*) todos los trajes de baño rápidamente. Nosotras (*7. comprar*) el último. Me gustaría tener dos. Luego, mi tía Julia (*8. ir*) con nosotras de compras. Ella (*9. prometer*) comprarme ropa para mi cumpleaños y yo le (*10. pedir*) unos zapatos bajos, de color marrón. ¡Qué bonitos son! Nosotras (*11. estar*) comprando todo el día y (*12. llegar*) tarde al hotel, ¡cansadas pero contentas!

Capítulo 9

ciento cincuenta y cinco **155**

Notes Before assigning activity 27, have students identify the illustrated sites.

Note for students that Contadora Island (mentioned in activity 28) is part of Panama.

You can use the Appendices that begin on page 206 to offer a comprehensive overview of how to conjugate verbs in the tenses that are taught in *Navegando 1*.

Teacher Resources

 Activity 27

Answers

27 Possible answers:
1. Yo fui a la Ciudad de Panamá ayer.
2. Tú fuiste al parque ayer.
3. Julia fue al centro comercial ayer.
4. Mis padres fueron a la playa ayer.
5. Mi amigo y yo fuimos a un restaurante ayer.
6. Raúl e Inés fueron al concierto ayer.

28
1. escogí
2. compré
3. compraron
4. volvimos
5. fui
6. vendieron
7. compramos
8. fue
9. prometió
10. pedí
11. estuvimos
12. llegamos

Activities

Students with Special Needs
Before assigning activity 27, have students identify the sites in the illustrations.

29 Fueron y compraron lo siguiente

Imagina que tus amigos y tú fueron de compras al centro comercial el sábado pasado. Di lo que las siguientes personas fueron a comprar. Sigue el modelo.

MODELO

Andrés
Andrés fue a comprar un suéter verde.

1. Marta   2. Lola y Rita   3. tú   4. nosotros   5. yo

✤ Comunicación

30 Haciendo cosas

With a partner, talk about where family and friends went yesterday, last week, last month or last year. Include in your discussion how the people named went to each place, whom they went with and what they did. Take notes as you talk. Then share the most interesting bit of information you learned with the class.

MODELO
A: ¿Fueron tú y tu familia a un buen restaurante la semana pasada?
B: Sí. Fuimos a un restaurante nuevo en el centro comercial.
A: ¿Te gustó?
B: Sí, me gustó mucho.

31 Una encuesta

Haz una investigación sobre las actividades que hacen tus compañeros(as) de clase. Prepara una lista de actividades (quehaceres, deportes, pasatiempos, etc.) y trata de encontrar una persona que haya hecho *(has done)* cada actividad y pregúntale cuándo la hizo durante la semana pasada. Puedes usar las siguientes frases para completar la investigación: *dormir tarde, escribir un correo electrónico, ir al centro comercial, ir a un buen restaurante, ir al cine, ir a la playa, ir al parque.*

MODELO
A: ¿Dormiste tarde la semana pasada?
B: Sí, dormí tarde el jueves.

Actividad	Nombre	Día
dormir tarde		jueves
escribir un correo electrónico		

156 *ciento cincuenta y seis*

Lección A

Estructura

Affirmative and negative words

You have learned to make a sentence negative by placing *no* before a verb.

No *veo la chaqueta.*   I do **not** see the jacket.

Unlike English, in Spanish it is sometimes possible to use two negative expressions in the same sentence. The following chart contains a list of common negative expressions along with their affirmative counterparts.

Expresiones afirmativas	Expresiones negativas
sí *(yes)* **Sí,** ella habla español. Él dice que **sí.**	**no** *(no)* **No,** él **no** habla español. Ella dice que **no.**
algo *(something, anything)* ¿Quieres comprar **algo**? ¿Compraste **algo** ayer?	**nada** *(nothing, anything)* **No** quiero comprar **nada.** **Nada** me gustó.
alguien *(somebody, anybody)* ¿Lo sabe **alguien?** **Alguien** debe saberlo.	**nadie** *(nobody, anybody)* **No** lo sabe **nadie.** **Nadie** lo sabe.
algún, alguna, -os, -as **(some, any)** ¿Le gusta **algún** abrigo? ¿Le gusta **alguna** blusa? ¿Compras **algunos** calcetines? ¿Buscas **algunas** corbatas?	**ningún, ninguna, -os, -as** **(none, not any)** No, **ningún** abrigo me gusta. No, **ninguna** me gusta. No, **no** compro **ningunos** calcetines. No, **no** busco **ningunas** corbatas.
o...o *(either... or)* Puedes comprar **o** un abrigo **o** un sombrero.	**ni... ni** *(neither... nor)* **No** voy a comprar **ni** un abrigo **ni** un sombrero.
siempre *(always)* Él **siempre** lleva botas.	**nunca** *(never)* Ella **no** lleva botas **nunca.** Ella **nunca** lleva botas.
también *(also, too)* Ella viene hoy **también.** Ella **también** viene hoy.	**tampoco** *(neither, either)* Él **no** viene mañana **tampoco.** Él **tampoco** viene mañana.

Note: The words *alguno,-a* (some, any) and *ninguno,-a* (none, not any) sometimes are used as pronouns.

*¿Va **alguno** o **alguna** de Uds.*
 al centro comercial ahora?   *No, **ninguno** de nosotros va al*
 centro comercial ahora.

Activities

Expansion
Call on several students to give examples of sentences that use these affirmative and negative expressions.

Students with Special Needs
Return to previously studied dialogs and readings and ask students to find examples of affirmative and negative expressions.

Notes Tell the class that the plural negative words *ningunos* and *ningunas* are used very little. In most cases, the singular words *ningún* and *ninguna* are preferred.

Inform students that *algún* and *ningún* are shortened forms of *alguno* and *ninguno.*

157

When combining negative expressions in one sentence in Spanish, it is often possible to use one of the negative expressions before the verb and another negative expression (and sometimes even more than one) after the verb. However, *no, nada, nadie, nunca, tampoco* and forms of *ninguno* may be used alone, before the verb, without the word *no*.

No *voy* **nunca** *al centro.*	I **never** go downtown.
Nunca *voy al centro.*	
No *estoy comprando* **nada tampoco.**	I am **not** buying **anything either.**
Tampoco *estoy comprando* **nada.**	

When *nadie* or a form of *ninguno* are direct objects referring to people they require the personal *a*.

No *veo* **a nadie** *aquí.*	I don't see **anyone** here.
No *veo* **a ningún** *amigo aquí.*	I don't see **any** friends here.

 Práctica

32 A completar

Completa estos mini-diálogos lógicamente, usando una de las siguientes palabras: *algo, alguien, nada* o *nadie*.

1. __ debe ir con Uds.
   No queremos ir con __.
2. __ te llama por teléfono.
   Marta te quiere decir __.
3. ¿Va __ con Uds.?
   Sí, Isabel va con nosotras porque quiere comprar __.
4. ¿Ves a __ en esa tienda de ropa?
   No, no veo a __.
5. ¿Quieres comprar ___?
   No, no me gusta __.

33 ¡No!

Contesta las preguntas en forma negativa.

 ¿Qué quieres mirar?
No quiero mirar nada.

1. Yo no voy a la tienda de ropa. ¿Y tú?
2. ¿Con quién fueron Uds. de compras ayer?
3. ¿Prefieres las botas anaranjadas o las verdes?
4. ¿Viste alguna falda de algodón?
5. ¿Ves a algún amigo del colegio?
6. ¿Compraron Uds. el suéter rojo o el suéter azul?
7. ¿Sus padres siempre les dan dinero para ir de compras?
8. ¿Te gustaría vender ropa interior o carros?
9. ¿Siempre van Uds. de compras al centro?
10. ¿Quiénes de Uds. son de Panamá?

¿Compraron el suéter rojo?

Notes Model several sentences that use the negative expressions before assigning the activities on pages 158 and 159.

Ask students to pair up before starting activity 33. Follow up by having students write their answers.

34 ¡Estoy enfermo/a y no quiero hacer nada!

Estás de mal humor porque estás enfermo/a y tus padres te hacen muchas preguntas. Trabajando en parejas, alternen en hacer las siguientes preguntas y en dar respuestas negativas a cada una.

MODELO A: ¿Piensas ir de compras o vas a estudiar?
B: No, no pienso ni ir de compras ni estudiar.

1. ¿Qué vas a hacer hoy?
2. ¿Quién te va a visitar en casa?
3. ¿Siempre juegas con el perro cuando estás enfermo/a?
4. ¿Quieres comer algo?
5. ¿Vas a hablar con alguien por teléfono?
6. ¿Quieres ver alguna película en DVD?
7. ¿Te puedo comprar algo?

❖ Comunicación

35 No se hace

Trabajando en parejas, hablen Uds. de lo que nadie hace nunca y hagan una lista de siete u ocho cosas que nadie hace nunca. Luego, deben leer las mejores frases de la lista a la clase.

MODELO Nadie va al centro comercial sin zapatos.

36 ¿Qué llevas mucho?

Talk with a classmate about the clothing you like to wear and when. Include in your discussion how often you wear various articles of clothing, the colors you prefer, when and where you went shopping and whether or not you purchased something, which articles of clothing each of you purchased last week/month/year (naming a specific time) and anything else you wish.

MODELO A: ¿Qué ropa te gusta llevar mucho?
B: Me gusta llevar este suéter anaranjado casi todos los días.
A: ¿Dónde lo compraste?
B: No lo compré, me lo regaló mi hermano.

Me gusta llevar mi vestido rojo y azul.

Answers

34 Possible answers:
1. No voy a hacer nada hoy.
2. Nadie me va a visitar en casa.
3. No, nunca juego con el perro cuando estoy enfermo/a.
4. No, no quiero comer nada.
5. No, no voy a hablar con nadie por teléfono.
6. No, no quiero ver ninguna película en DVD.
7. No, no me puedes comprar nada.

35 Creative self-expression.
36 Creative self-expression.

Activities

Critical Listening
Tell students that they will hear a series of erroneous statements with affirmative or negative words. For each statement given, the students should state the opposite to provide the correct information. Possible statements: *La clase de español siempre empieza tarde; Tenemos clase el sábado y el domingo también; En esta clase no tenemos ningún examen; El profesor/la profesora no conoce a nadie en (país); Para mañana no tenemos que hacer nada.*

Notes Activities 34, 35 and 36 can be repeated. Have students work on each activity with one partner. Then have them switch partners and try the activity again.

Set time limits for the paired activities on page 159 and keep a brisk pace.

Remember to circulate around the room as students complete these activities to keep students on task and to offer help as needed.

Activity 36 serves as a good starting point for a composition on a favorite teen topic: clothing.

Answers

37 1. Los kunas viven en el archipiélago de San Blas a 200 millas de la costa de Panamá.
2. El traje tradicional de las mujeres kunas consiste en faldas coloridas, blusas decoradas con molas y anillos de oro en las narices.
3. Las molas se hacen con telas de diferentes colores.
4. Usan las molas para decorar las blusas.

38 Answers will vary.

Activities

Multiple Intelligences (spatial)
Have students make *molas* out of construction paper.

Lectura cultural

Las molas: símbolo de la cultura kuna

En el mar[1] Caribe, a 200 millas de la costa de Panamá, está el archipiélago de San Blas *(Kuna Yala)*. En estas islas tropicales viven los indios kuna. Uno de los elementos más conocidos de los indios kuna es su vestimenta tradicional[2] que es espectacular: las mujeres llevan anillos de oro[3] en la nariz, faldas coloridas y blusas decoradas con las famosas molas. Las molas son paneles de intricados diseños[4] cosidos a mano[5].

Las mujeres kuna observan, transforman y representan el mundo que ven y su medio ambiente y los convierten en estas obras de arte usando aguja, hilos y telas de colores vivos[6].

Los paneles adornan la parte delantera y trasera de las blusas y los diseños pueden ser muy antiguos, con piezas geométricas y animales sagrados, relativos a la vida diaria de las mujeres. Las molas son apreciadas piezas de arte indígena y pueden encontrarse en museos y colecciones privadas. Las molas pueden alcanzar un precio muy elevado, dependiendo del número de capas, los detalles y el mérito artístico del diseño.

[1]sea [2]traditional clothing [3]gold [4]designs [5]hand-sewn [6]threads and fabrics of bright coloring

37 ¿Qué recuerdas?

1. ¿Dónde viven los kunas?
2. ¿Cómo es el traje tradicional de las mujeres kunas?
3. ¿Cómo se hacen las molas?
4. ¿Para qué usan las molas?

38 Algo personal

1. En tu opinión, ¿son las molas ropa, arte o los dos? Explica.
2. Imagina que vas a crear una mola. Describe el diseño y los colores de tu mola.

- Compare and contrast the molas of the Kuna Indians with a traditional piece of clothing of another culture. Are they worn just by women? Are they sold as art pieces? Are they made of cotton? Do they have colorful designs?

160 *ciento sesenta*

Lección A

Notes The *mola* designs come from the body paintings of Kuna ancestors who didn't wear clothes until French Huguenot settlers introduced clothing in the mid-nineteenth century. The Kuna simply transposed the body paintings onto cotton fabrics.

Connections. This *Lectura cultural* makes the cross-curricular connections to art, history and geography.

¿Qué aprendí?

Autoevaluación
As a review and self-check, respond to the following:

1. Describe three of your favorite clothing items, saying what color they are and what they are made of.

2. Imagine you are deciding either to take a vacation to Panama to enjoy warm weather or go to Chile for a winter ski trip. List at least three articles of clothing you will need to take with you for each vacation choice.

3. State three things you did yesterday.

4. Name two places you went yesterday.

5. Make two affirmative and two negative statements about something that happened yesterday.

6. Name two things you have learned about Panama.

Visit the web-based activities at www.emcp.com

Palabras y expresiones

Para describir
algún, alguna
anaranjado,-a
marrón
morado,-a
ningún, ninguna
rosado,-a

Pronombres
algo
alguien
alguno,-a
nada
nadie
ninguno,-a

La ropa
la bota
la chaqueta
la corbata
el guante
el impermeable
las medias
el pijama
la ropa interior
el sombrero
el suéter
el traje (de baño)
el vestido
el zapato (bajo/de tacón)

Partes del cuerpo
el brazo
la cabeza
el cuerpo
el dedo
la mano
el pie
la pierna

Verbos
combinar
contar (ue)
prometer
quedar
vender

Expresiones y otras palabras
el algodón
el centro comercial
el departamento
el hombre
la lana
la mujer
ni... ni
o... o
quedarle bien a uno
la seda
las vacaciones

Unas botas marrones.

Un traje de baño rosado.

Un traje de baño azul.

Capítulo 9

ciento sesenta y uno **161**

Teacher Resources

Activity 14

Information Gap Activities
Postcard Activities
Funciones de Comunicación

Answers

Autoevaluación
Possible answers:
1. Answers will vary.
2. Necesito llevar una chaqueta y mis botas./Necesito traer el traje de baño y una camisa de algodón.
3. Compré unas botas nuevas....
4. Fui al centro comercial.
5. Escribí algunas cartas./ Nunca salí con mis amigos.
6. La capital es la Ciudad de Panamá....

Activities

Cooperative Learning
Have students work in pairs to play guessing games. Students take turns describing an object in the classroom (being certain to use the colors) while the partner guesses what the object is.

Notes **Communities.** Ask if students know who Rubén Blades is. Explain that he is from Panama and is a well-known actor and singer.

Students may find it interesting that although the monetary unit in Panama is the *balboa,* in larger cities the U.S. dollar is also widely used.

Tell students that the Panama Canal is not only important to Panama, it is also vital to international trade, because it allows ships to pass from one ocean to another in a matter of hours.

Panama wasn't established as a nation until November 3, 1903. Before that date, Panama was part of Colombia.

Regalos

 Activity 1

 Activities 64–65

 Activity 1

 Activity 1

 Activities 1–3

Content reviewed in *Lección B*

- clothing
- family
- adjective-noun agreement
- talking about the past
- prepositions
- places in a city

Activities

Prereading Strategy
Play the audio CD recording of the vocabulary and have students repeat the words while showing them overhead transparency 64.

Notes Have students find cognates and words they already know in *Vocabulario I*. Quickly check student comprehension of the descriptions that accompany the illustrations on these two pages.

Ask students what they know about Ecuador. Most students are probably familiar with the Galapagos Islands, which

are discussed on page 165. Ask for student volunteers to create a bulletin board or travel brochure about this Spanish-speaking South American country.

Inform students that they are about to study the country that was named for the equator: *Ecuador*.

la escalera mecánica

el ascensor

el regalo

el paraguas

1 ¿Qué les gustaría recibir de regalo?

 Selecciona la letra de la ilustración que corresponde con lo que oyes.

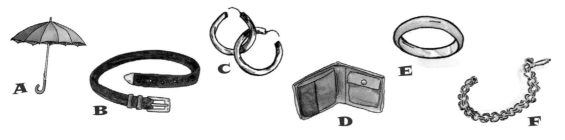

A B C D E F

2 Hablando de los artículos de la tienda

Contesta las siguientes preguntas en español.

1. ¿Qué puede ser de cuero?
2. ¿Qué puede ser de plata?
3. ¿Qué puede ser de perlas?
4. ¿Te gusta usar perfume? Explica.
5. ¿Cuándo llevas pañuelo?
6. ¿Cuándo llevas bufanda?
7. ¿De qué materiales puede ser un bolso?
8. ¿Qué joyas te gusta llevar?

3 Regalos para todos

Trabajando en parejas, preparen tres listas de regalos, una para hombres, otra para mujeres y otra para hombres y mujeres. Cada lista debe tener tres o cuatro regalos en cada columna.

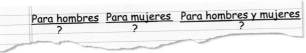

Para hombres	Para mujeres	Para hombres y mujeres
?	?	?

Capítulo 9

ciento sesenta y tres **163**

Notes Use overhead transparencies 64 and 65 to present and practice the new words and expressions in *Vocabulario I*.

Activity 1 is intended for listening comprehension practice. Play the audio CD of the activity that is included in the Audio CD Program or use the transcript that appears in the ATE introduction if you prefer to read the activity yourself. A reproducible answer sheet for the activity can be found at the end of the Audio CD Program Manual.

Teacher Resources

 Activity 1

Activities 2–3

Answers

1. 1. D; 2. F; 3. A; 4. C; 5. B; 6. E
2. Possible answers:
   1. Pueden ser de cuero un cinturón, un bolso o una billetera.
   2. Pueden ser de plata unos aretes, una pulsera, un collar o un anillo.
   3. Pueden ser de perlas un collar, una pulsera o unos aretes.
   4. Answers will vary.
   5. Answers will vary.
   6. Llevo bufanda cuando hace frío.
   7. Un bolso puede ser de material sintético o de cuero.
   8. Answers will vary.
3. Answers will vary.

Activities

Expansion

Use overhead transparencies 64 and 65 to introduce the new words and expressions in *Vocabulario I*. Begin by showing students transparency 64 and point to one of the items in the store and identify it in Spanish. Students should repeat after you. Continue with the next item and repeat the process. As a second step, show students transparency 65. Once again identify the objects in Spanish, allowing students to see how each word is spelled.

Busco un regalo
Activities 4–6

Answers

4 1. Busca un regalo.
2. Busca un regalo bueno, bonito y barato.
3. Busca algo para una mujer.
4. No.
5. Le parece perfecto el perfume.

5 Answers will vary.

6 1. A; 2. A; 3. B; 4. A; 5. B; 6. B

Activities

Critical Listening
Play the audio CD recording of the dialog. Instruct students to cover up the words as they listen to the conversation. Have students look at the photographs and ask several individuals to state what they believe is the main theme of the conversation.

Expansion
Additional questions *(Algo personal): ¿Te gusta comprar regalos?; ¿Prefieres comprar regalos en el centro comercial o en las tiendas?; ¿Para quién compras regalos más caros, para la familia o para los amigos?; Por lo general, ¿qué compras para regalos—ropa, artículos personales, aparatos eléctricos, discos compactos?*

Prereading Strategy
Instruct students to cover up the dialog with one hand and to look at the photographs. Ask them to imagine where the conversation takes place and what the people are saying to one another.

Diálogo I

Busco un regalo

DANIEL: Busco un regalo, bueno, bonito y barato.
SEÑORA: ¿Para hombre o para mujer?
DANIEL: Para mujer.

SEÑORA: ¿Qué le parece una pulsera de oro?
DANIEL: No. Ella dijo que joyas no.

SEÑORA: Entonces, ¿qué le parece este perfume?
DANIEL: El perfume es perfecto.

¡Extra!

En otras palabras

el anillo	*la argolla, la sortija*
los aretes	*los zarcillos, los aros, los pendientes*
el bolso	*la cartera, la bolsa, el monedero*
el material sintético	*el plástico, el acrílico*
el paraguas	*la sombrilla*
el pijama	*el payama/el piyama*
la pulsera	*el brazalete*

4 ¿Qué recuerdas?

1. ¿Qué busca Daniel?
2. ¿Qué tipo de regalo busca?
3. ¿Para quién busca algo Daniel?
4. ¿Va a comprar Daniel una pulsera de oro?
5. ¿Qué le parece perfecto?

5 Algo personal

1. Cuando buscas un regalo, ¿lo buscas bueno, bonito y barato? Explica.
2. ¿Piensas que es más fácil comprar un regalo para un hombre o una mujer?
3. En tu opinión, ¿qué regalos piensas son para hombres? ¿Y para mujeres?

6 Bueno, bonito y barato

 Selecciona la letra de la ilustración que corresponde con lo que buscan las siguientes personas.

A

B

Notes This dialog and activities 4, 5 and 6 have been recorded by native speakers and are included in the *Navegando* Audio CD Program. A reproducible student answer sheet for activity 6 is available at the end of the Audio CD Program Manual.

Cultura viva

Ecuador, país de maravillas naturales

Ecuador is located southwest of Colombia and north of Peru. The equator (*ecuador*), which is located high in the Andes Mountains, cuts through the country just a few miles north of the nation's capital, Quito. A monument here marks the dividing point between the Northern and the Southern Hemisphere.

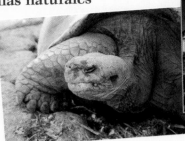
Soy de las Islas Galápagos.

Quito, Ecuador.

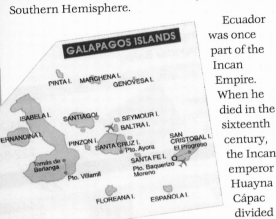
GALAPAGOS ISLANDS

PINTA I.   MARCHENA I.   GENOVESA I.
ISABELA I.   SANTIAGO I.   SEYMOUR I.   BALTRA I.
ERNANDINA I.   PINZON I.   SANTA CRUZ I.   Pto. Ayora   SAN CRISTOBAL I.   El Progreso
Tomás de Berlanga   SANTA FE I.   Pto. Baquerizo Moreno
Pto. Villamil
FLOREANA I.   ESPAÑOLA I.

Ecuador was once part of the Incan Empire. When he died in the sixteenth century, the Incan emperor Huayna Cápac divided the empire between two sons: Atahualpa ruled the portion that was based in Quito, and Huáscar ruled the portion that was based in Cuzco, Peru. Huayna Cápac did not know, however, that the division would weaken the empire and lead to its rapid conquest by the Spanish conquistadors. Ecuador remained Spanish until becoming the first South American nation to declare its independence in 1809.

Remains of Ecuador's colorful past are still evident throughout the nation today. Along with historical reminders of the past, Ecuador offers visitors compelling natural wonders, as well. One of these, the *Archipiélago de Colón,* also known as the Galapagos Islands (*Islas Galápagos*), is located off the coast of Ecuador in the Pacific Ocean. The islands were formed by volcanic eruptions. Today they have become a national park (*parque nacional*) consisting of more than 600 miles of coastline, where an interesting mix of tropical and cold-climate animals (*animales*) and plants (*plantas*) live that cannot be found in any other part of the world.

7 Conexión con otras disciplinas: geografía

Completa las frases de la izquierda con una de las frases de la derecha, según la información en la Cultura viva.

1. El ecuador divide...
2. La capital del Ecuador...
3. El Ecuador formó parte...
4. El Ecuador declaró su independencia...
5. Al Archipiélago de Colón se le llama también...
6. Las Islas Galápagos están...
7. En las Galápagos hay...

A. ...en el Océano Pacífico.
B. ...en 1809.
C. ...el mundo en norte y sur.
D. ...un parque nacional con plantas y animales.
E. ...es Quito.
F. ...las Islas Galápagos.
G. ...del imperio inca.

Teacher Resources

 Activity 2

 Activity 4

Answers

7 1. C
   2. E
   3. G
   4. B
   5. F
   6. A
   7. D

Activities

Connections
Show students where Ecuador is located, using the maps in the book or the transparencies that are part of this program.

Expansion
Have a class discussion about Ecuador. You may choose to ask the following questions to stimulate other student questions: *¿Cómo se llama el inca que dividió el imperio entre sus dos hijos?; ¿Cómo se llaman los dos hijos?; ¿Existen los incas hoy?; ¿Existe la cultura india en Ecuador hoy?*

Notes **Connections.** Activity 7 makes the cross-curricular connection to geography.

It is noteworthy that the word *galápagos* is a Spanish term that refers to the large tortoises that live on the islands.

Connections. The six Galapagos Islands are also called *Las Islas Encantadas.* Charles Darwin's observations of life on the islands led to his theory of evolution, which he explained in his book *On the Origin of Species.*

Answers

8 1. el bolsito
2. la billeterita
3. el cinturoncito
4. el pañuelito
5. la bufandita
6. el collarcito
7. las botitas
8. los guantecitos
9. el suétercito

9 1. la chaqueta
2. el zapato
3. las joyas
4. el traje
5. la puerta
6. el sombrero
7. la corbata
8. el jardín
9. el hijo

10 Creative self-expression.

Activities

Critical Thinking

Ask students to give the original form of several words: *chiquita (chica), Sarita (Sara), hermanito (hermano)*. Then see if students can give diminutive forms for several words: *casa (casita), regalo (regalito), muchacha (muchachita)*.

Idioma

Estructura

Diminutives

Indicate affection or convey the idea that something is small by replacing the final vowel of a noun with the endings *-ito, -ita, -itos* and *-itas: Ana (Anita)*. For nouns that end in a consonant, add the endings *-cito, -cita, -citos* or *-citas* to the complete word: *collar (collarcito)*. Additional diminutive endings you may encounter include *-illo, -illa, -uelo, -uela, -ico* and *-ica*. Other words may require a spelling change: *poquito (poco)*.

Although many exceptions exist for the diminutive forms, most are easily recognized: *hotelito (hotel), Daniel (Danielito)*. It is best to learn the variations as you encounter them since they can vary from country to country and even from one person to another within countries.

 ## Práctica

 ### 8 Todo es pequeñito

Cambia las siguientes palabras al diminutivo.

1. el bolso
2. la billetera
3. el cinturón
4. el pañuelo
5. la bufanda
6. el collar
7. las botas
8. los guantes
9. el suéter

 ### 9 ¿De dónde vienen?

Indica la palabra original.

MODELO el regalillo → el regalo

1. la chaquetilla
2. el zapatico
3. las joyitas
4. el trajecillo
5. la portezuela
6. el sombrerito
7. la corbatica
8. el jardincito
9. el hijuelo

Los guantes.

Comunicación

10 Comprando un regalo con mucho cariño

 Imagine you and a close friend are in a department store shopping for a birthday gift for someone you like a lot. Create a conversation using the diminutive to refer to the objects you are considering buying and to convey your affection for the person for whom you are shopping.

MODELO **A:** Mira estas joyitas tan lindas para tu mamita. Me gustan mucho.
B: No me gustan mucho. Me gusta más este bolsito.
A: El bolsito no está mal, pero prefiero aquel collarcito de perlitas.

Notes Explain that the diminutive of *poco* is *poquito*. This spelling change occurs to maintain the original sound of the *c* in *poco*. Ask if students recall any other words that change their spelling from *c* to *qu: buscar → busqué*.

Some adverbs that use the diminutive form include the following: *ahora (ahorita), despacio (despacito)*.

Estructura

Preterite tense of *leer, oír, ver, decir, hacer* and *tener*

The verbs *leer, oír, ver, decir, hacer* and *tener* all have irregularities in the preterite tense. For example, for *leer* and *oír*, an *i* between two vowels changes to a *y*. Both *leer* and *oír* require additional accent marks to separate vowel sounds and to indicate how these words are pronounced. The preterite tense of the verb *ver* uses the regular *-er* verb endings, but without any accent marks.

leer	
leí	leímos
leíste	leísteis
leyó	leyeron

oír	
oí	oímos
oíste	oísteis
oyó	oyeron

ver	
vi	vimos
viste	visteis
vio	vieron

Learning the irregular preterite-tense stem of *decir (dij), hacer (hic)* and *tener (tuv)* and the endings *-e, -iste, -o, -imos, -isteis* and *-ieron* will help you when you wish to use the preterite tense of these three irregular verbs.

Note: The *c* in the preterite-tense stem for *hacer* changes to *z* in *hizo*; *dijeron* is also an exception to the above because no *i* is required for the preterite ending.

decir	
dije	dijimos
dijiste	dijisteis
dijo	dijeron

hacer	
hice	hicimos
hiciste	hicisteis
hizo	hicieron

tener	
tuve	tuvimos
tuviste	tuvisteis
tuvo	tuvieron

Práctica

11 ¡No oí!

Imagina que estás en una tienda comprando ropa con tu familia y todos te dicen algo al mismo tiempo y no oyes algunos de los comentarios. ¿Qué debes decir?

MODELO mi mamá
¿Qué dijo mi madre? No la oí.

1. tú
2. la Sra. de la tienda
3. mis hermanos
4. mi padre
5. mis hermanas
6. mi prima y mi tío

¿Qué dijo mi madre?

Capítulo 9

ciento sesenta y siete 167

Notes Review the regular preterite tense forms for *-ar, -er* and *-ir* verbs and the preterite tense of *ir* and *ser*. Model and ask for students to give several examples of verbs they already know how to conjugate in the preterite tense before introducing the new irregular preterite tense verbs that appear here.

Review the use of the direct object pronouns before assigning activity 11.

Teacher Resources

 Activity 4

 Activities 6–10

 Activity 3

 Activities 5–8

Answers

11 1. ¿...dijiste...? ...te....
2. ¿...dijo...? ...la....
3. ¿...dijeron...? ...los....
4. ¿...dijo...? ...lo....
5. ¿...dijeron...? ...las....
6. ¿...dijeron...? ...los....

Activities

Cooperative Learning
Give each student an index card to use in a verb drill. Have them choose five different verbs that are irregular in the preterite tense. Include *ser* and *ir* if you want to recycle them as well. Vary the subjects for each verb and write the correct preterite form of each infinitive to agree with its subject: *leer (tú) = leíste* (you read), *hacer (nosotros) = hicimos* (we did; we made), etc. When finished, students may exchange cards to look for errors and make corrections. Then pair students to drill each other with their verb cards. Collect the cards, double-check for errors and save them to use another time for a quick review before a quiz or when there are a few minutes left in the class period.

Answers

12 1. (Yo) Dije que...guantes.
2. ...dijeron que...cuero.
3. ...dijo que...bolso.
4. ...dijo que...joyas.
5. ...dijo que...paraguas.
6. ...dijimos que...billeteras.
7. (Tú) Dijiste que...suéter.
8. ...dijeron que...zapatos.

13 1. Sí, (No, no) tuve que ir....
2. Sí (No, no) oí....
3. Sí (No, no) vi....
4. Sí (No, no) hice....
5. Sí (No, no) dije....
6. Sí (No, no) compré....
7. Sí, (No, no) tuve....
8. Sí, (No, no) leí....

14 1. ¿...hicieron Uds.?/Nosotros (Nosotras) tuvimos que comprar un regalo y lo hicimos por la internet.
2. ¿...hicieron tus amigos?/ Mis amigos hicieron la tarea y fueron a jugar al fútbol con sus amigos.
3. ¿...hizo tu hermana?/Mi hermana tuvo que comprar unos zapatos cómodos e hizo unos quehaceres.
4. ¿...hiciste tú?/Yo leí un libro muy interesante y vi una película divertida en DVD.
5. ¿...hizo tu madre?/Mi madre tuvo que ir a trabajar y, luego, volvió a casa a hacer la comida.
6. ¿...hicieron tus tías?/Mis tías hicieron un viaje a las Islas Galápagos pero olvidaron llevar sus trajes de baño.

12 ¿Qué le(s) gustaría recibir?

Di qué dijeron las siguientes personas que les gustaría recibir de regalo para su cumpleaños, según las ilustraciones.

MODELO   mi padre
Mi padre dijo que le gustaría recibir unos pañuelos.

1. yo   2. mis primos   3. mi tía   4. mi mamá

5. mi hermano   6. nosotros   7. tú   8. Uds.

13 ¿Qué hice?

Di cuáles de las siguientes cosas hiciste o no hiciste ayer.

MODELO leer un libro
Sí, leí un libro ayer./No, no leí un libro ayer.

1. tener que ir a la tienda para comprar pan y leche
2. oír un CD de mi cantante favorito
3. ver televisión
4. hacer la tarea de español
5. decir una mentira
6. comprar un regalo para alguien
7. tener un examen
8. leer una revista

14 Todos hicieron algo

 En parejas, hablen de lo que hicieron las siguientes personas, usando las pistas que se dan.

MODELO tu amigo: leer un libro / y / oír un disco compacto
A: ¿Qué hizo tu amigo?
B: Mi amigo leyó un libro y oyó un disco compacto.

1. Uds.: tener que comprar un regalo / y / hacerlo por la internet
2. tus amigos: hacer la tarea / y / ir a jugar al fútbol con sus amigos
3. tu hermana: tener que comprar unos zapatos cómodos / e / hacer unos quehaceres
4. tú: leer un libro muy interesante / y / ver una película divertida en DVD
5. tu madre: tener que ir a trabajar / y luego / volver a casa a hacer la comida
6. tus tías: hacer un viaje a las Islas Galápagos / pero / olvidar llevar sus trajes de baño

Notes Before doing activity 12, ask students to identify the articles that people would like to receive as gifts. Also, remind students how to use *gustaría:* they should not change the verb form, only the indirect object pronoun that precedes *gustaría.*

Follow up activity 13 with a class discussion of what members of the class did or did not do yesterday.

15 En la tienda por departamentos

Di lo que hicieron algunas personas el fin de semana en la tienda, según las ilustraciones y los verbos indicados.

MODELO comprar

Algunas personas compraron paraguas.

1. oír

2. hacer

3. tener

4. arreglar

5. ver

6. leer

 ## Comunicación

 ### 16 ¿Qué hicimos?

 Trabajando con un/a compañero/a de clase, hablen de lo que hicieron el fin de semana pasado.

MODELO
A: ¿Qué hiciste el sábado?
B: Leí un libro fascinante.

A: ¿Y qué más hiciste?
B: El sábado oí música por la mañana, luego tuve que .... Y tú, ¿qué hiciste?

 ### 17 ¿Qué tuviste que hacer?

Imagine you and a classmate work at a department store. Yesterday was a very busy day at the store and you each had to do too many things. Make up activities and talk with your classmate about all the things each of you had to do.

MODELO
A: Ayer tuve muchas cosas que hacer en la tienda.
B: ¿Qué tuviste que hacer?
A: Para empezar, tuve que llegar muy temprano. Luego, otra persona y yo tuvimos que arreglar las billeteras, los cinturones y las bufandas en la sección de regalos antes de abrir. Luego, tuve que....

Capítulo 9

ciento sesenta y nueve **169**

Teacher Resources

 En la caja

 Activities 5–6

 Activity 66

 Activities 11–12

 Activity 4

 Activities 9–10

Activities

Prereading Strategy
Have students look through *Vocabulario II* quickly to find cognates and other words they recognize.

TPR
Ask students to do things with clothing and colors. For example, say *Toca algo azul (rojo, verde, etc.)* and observe to see that students respond appropriately. You may choose to bring in a bag of old clothing, especially items that are out of style, awful colors or unusual sizes as a humorous way to allow students to find and point out colors and items of clothing that you name or describe. As an alternative, you may use paper doll clothing and have students merely touch the item to show comprehension. Use commands such as *toca, ponte, quítate, guarda*.

Vocabulario II
En la caja

170 *ciento setenta*

Lección B

Notes Quickly check student comprehension of the text bubbles and boxes that accompany the illustrations on these two pages.

Note the pronunciation of *ahorrar* in *Vocabulario II* by reminding students that the *h* is silent and the *rr* is trilled.

170

18 ¿Cuál es la respuesta correcta?

Escoge la letra de la respuesta correcta a lo que oyes.

A
Sí, es una seda
muy buena.

B
Necesita el recibo.

C
Pago con tarjeta
de crédito.

D
No, está en oferta.

E
Son tres dólares con
cincuenta.

F
Sí, voy contigo.

19 Lo opuesto

Completa las siguientes oraciones para decir lo opuesto de las palabras
indicadas.

MODELO No compré el anillo *caro*, preferí el anillo <u>barato</u>.

1. No compré ningún perfume *de mala calidad*, compré un perfume __.
2. No pagué *a crédito*, pagué __ en una de las cajas.
3. No me gustó el bolso *de tamaño pequeño*, me gustó el bolso __.
4. No vi los aretes *caros*, vi los aretes __.
5. No vi cinturones *cortos*, sólo vi cinturones demasiado __.
6. No le pagué *al dependiente*, le pagué __.
7. No me gusta ir de compras *contigo*, porque a ti no te gusta ir de compras __.

Capítulo 9

ciento setenta y uno **171**

Teacher Resources

Activity 18

Answers

18 1. C
2. F
3. B
4. E
5. A
6. D

19 1. de buena calidad
2. en efectivo
3. de tamaño grande
4. baratos
5. largos
6. a la dependienta
7. conmigo

Activities

Expansion
Use overhead transparency 66 to
introduce and practice the new
words and expressions in
Vocabulario II.

Prereading Strategy
Play the audio CD recording of
the vocabulary and have students
repeat the words while showing
them overhead transparency 66.

Spanish for Spanish Speakers
Ask students to write a dialog
between two friends who want to
go shopping in a mall. Make sure
they include a variety of stores
they want to go to and the things
they want to buy.

Students with Special Needs
Model a second sentence for
students in activity 19.

Notes Activity 18 is intended for
listening comprehension practice. Play
the audio CD of the activity that is
included in the Audio CD Program or use
the transcript that appears in the ATE
Introduction if you prefer to read the
activity yourself.

A reproducible answer sheet for the
activity can be found at the end of the
Audio CD Program Manual.

Activities

Cooperative Learning
Pair bilingual and nonbilingual students to invent a dialog in which they discuss things they would like to buy at the mall.

Expansion
Additional questions: *¿Qué está haciendo Daniel?*; *¿Con una oferta especial el precio es más barato o más caro que el precio normal?*; *¿Compras algo en oferta especial si no te gusta?*; *¿Te gusta ir de compras solo/sola o con los amigos o la familia?*; *¿Tienes una tarjeta de crédito?*

Diálogo II

¿Cómo va a pagar?

DANIEL: ¿Cuánto cuesta el perfume?
SEÑORA: Está en oferta. Cuesta treinta dólares.
DANIEL: Sí, no está caro. Lo llevo.

SEÑORA: ¿Cómo va a pagar? ¿En efectivo o a crédito?
DANIEL: Voy a pagar en efectivo.

SEÑORA: Aquí tiene diez dólares de cambio y su recibo.
DANIEL: Muchas gracias.

20 ¿Qué recuerdas?

1. ¿Qué está en oferta?
2. ¿Cuánto cuesta el perfume?
3. ¿Cómo va a pagar Daniel?
4. ¿Cuánto es el cambio?
5. ¿Qué más le da la señora a Daniel?

21 Algo personal

1. ¿Qué compras en oferta?
2. ¿Prefieres pagar a crédito o en efectivo? Explica.
3. ¿Te gusta dar regalos caros o baratos? Explica.
4. ¿Qué haces con el dinero que recibes de cambio?

22 ¿Sí o no?

 ¿Son lógicos los diálogos? Corrige lo que no es lógico.

¿Cuánto cuesta el perfume?

Compro camisetas en oferta.

Notes This dialog and activities 20, 21 and 22 have been recorded by native speakers and are included in the *Navegando* Audio CD Program. A reproducible answer sheet for activity 22 is available for your convenience at the end of the Audio CD Program Manual.

Tell students that the adjective *caro* normally is used with the verb *ser*. Here Daniel uses the verb *estar* to emphasize a special sale price.

Cultura viva

De compras en Guayaquil

Para hacer compras en Ecuador, debes ir a
Guayaquil. Para las compras modernas
está en Guayaquil el Mall del Sol, el centro
comercial más grande del Ecuador con
más de 187 tiendas, veinticinco
restaurantes de comida rápida, cinco
bancos, un supermercado grande
(Megamaxi), nueve cines, cibercafés,
discotecas, tiendas de souvenirs, parques
y estacionamiento (parking) para más de
2.000 carros. Es un centro comercial
supergigante y muy divertido.

Si te gustan las compras menos
modernas y más de artesanía, y no te
gustan los centros comerciales, puedes ir al
Mercado Artesano de Guayaquil. En el
Mercado Artesano hay 280 exhibiciones y puestos
de venta (sales stands) donde trabajan sólo

Unos chicos ecuatorianos
en el mall.

Una artesana vendiendo
su arte.

Unos chalecos (vests) en el Mercado Artesano.

artesanos (las personas que hacen artesanía)
creando y vendiendo su arte. Al dar un paseo por
las exhibiciones puedes escuchar música
ecuatoriana a la vez que admiras los diferentes
estilos de los artistas del país.

Como puedes ver, tanto si te gusta la compra
moderna y dinámica, como la más tranquila y
tradicional, Guayaquil te ofrece infinitas
posibilidades.

23 Comparando

Compara el
centro
comercial Mall
del Sol en
Guayaquil con
un centro
comercial de tu
ciudad.

Centro comercial Mall del Sol	Centro comercial de tu ciudad
1. 187 tiendas	1. 150 tiendas
2.	2.
3.	3.

Capítulo 9

ciento setenta y tres **173**

Teacher Resources

 De compras en Guayaquil

Activity 5

Answers

23 Answers will vary.

Activities

Expansion
As a follow-up to this reading and
to activity 23, tell students that
you recently bought a present for
a friend and their task is to find
out what it is. They may ask a
maximum of twelve yes/no
questions in trying to identify the
mystery gift. The first student to
correctly name the gift should
then think of another present
and the activity is repeated.

Notes You may wish to have students
create Venn diagrams for activity 23. See
the section *Tú escribes* (page 134) at the
end of *Capítulo 8*.

Note that this *Cultura viva* is written in
Spanish. Unknown words have been
translated and the content has been edited
to be interesting and of an appropriate

reading level so students will find it
enjoyable. All the *Cultura viva* readings in
Navegando 2 are in Spanish.

173

Answers

24 1. en, sobre
2. de
3. con
4. en
5. para
6. desde
7. sin
8. por

Activities

Critical Thinking
Review the prepositions by asking students to generate original sentences about their school and city (e.g., *Uds. estudian en la biblioteca con amigos; La biblioteca está cerca de/lejos de la cafetería*).

Multiple Intelligences (linguistic/spatial)
Have students think of a memory device and make a visual representation to depict the meanings of the prepositions. For example, a drawing of a male stick figure standing beside a house with the words "There is a lad beside the house" could represent *al lado de*. Ask students to share their ideas with the rest of the class and display the best representations on a bulletin board.

Idioma

Repaso rápido: prepositions

How many of the following prepositions (*preposiciones*) in Spanish do you remember?

preposiciones				
a	de	para	con	desde
por	en	sin	hasta	sobre

24 Unos aretes para mi mamá

Completa las siguientes oraciones, escogiendo una palabra apropiada de la lista.

con	de	desde	en
para	por	sin	sobre

1. ¿Cuánto cuestan los aretes que están (1) aquella mesa?
2. Los aretes son (2) plata y cuestan veinte dólares.
3. ¿Va a pagarlos (3) tarjeta de crédito?
4. No, voy a pagarlos (4) efectivo.
5. Los aretes son (5) mi mamá.
6. Mi madre usa aretes (6) pequeña.
7. Ella nunca sale a la calle (7) aretes.
8. Muchas gracias (8) su compra.

Estructura

Using prepositions

You have already learned to use prepositions with prepositional pronouns. For example, prepositional pronouns are sometimes used in combination with the preposition *a* to add emphasis or to clarify the meaning of a sentence: *A mí me gusta comprar todo lo que está en oferta.* The following prepositional pronouns also may be used with the other prepositions you have learned.

los pronombres después de las preposiciones			
sin mí	*without me*	sin nosotros,-as	*without us*
sin ti	*without you*	sin vosotros,-as	*without you*
sin Ud.	*without you*	sin Uds.	*without you*
sin él	*without him*	sin ellos	*without them*
sin ella	*without her*	sin ellas	*without them*

174 *ciento setenta y cuatro*

Lección B

Notes Remind students that prepositions connect verbs, nouns and adjectives with their complements. English, like Spanish, uses prepositions as linking words. However, the two languages do not always use the same preposition to convey the same meaning.

Explain that prepositional pronouns are the same as subject pronouns with the exception of *yo* and *tú*, which become *mí* and *ti* after most prepositions. Let students know that *mí* has an accent to distinguish it from the possessive *mi* (my). The pronoun *ti*, however, does not need a written accent.

Two exceptions are the words *conmigo* (with me), which is used instead of *con* followed by *mí,* and *contigo* (with you), which is used instead of *con* followed by *ti.*

¿Quieres ir de compras **conmigo**?   Do you want to go shopping **with me?**
Sí, me gusta ir de compras **contigo**.   Yes, I like to go shopping **with you.**

 Práctica

25 Un regalo para mi tío

Completa este correo electrónico con palabras de la lista. Puedes usar las palabras más de una vez.

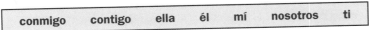

| conmigo | contigo | ella | él | mí | nosotros | ti |

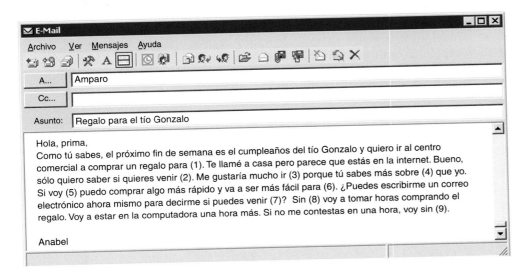

E-Mail

Archivo   Ver   Mensajes   Ayuda

A...   Amparo
Cc...
Asunto: Regalo para el tío Gonzalo

Hola, prima,
Como tú sabes, el próximo fin de semana es el cumpleaños del tío Gonzalo y quiero ir al centro comercial a comprar un regalo para (1). Te llamé a casa pero parece que estás en la internet. Bueno, sólo quiero saber si quieres venir (2). Me gustaría mucho ir (3) porque tú sabes más sobre (4) que yo. Si voy (5) puedo comprar algo más rápido y va a ser más fácil para (6). ¿Puedes escribirme un correo electrónico ahora mismo para decirme si puedes venir (7)? Sin (8) voy a tomar horas comprando el regalo. Voy a estar en la computadora una hora más. Si no me contestas en una hora, voy sin (9).

Anabel

26 ¿Puedes venir conmigo?

Trabajando con un(a) compañero/a de clase, alternen en hacer las invitaciones indicadas y en dar excusas para cada invitación.

MODELO   al cine
    A: ¿Puedes venir conmigo al cine?
    B: No, no puedo ir contigo porque no tengo dinero.

1. el banco
2. a comprar unos zapatos que están en oferta
3. la tienda de artículos electrónicos
4. la tienda por departamentos
5. el centro comercial
6. a cambiar un cinturón que compré y ahora no me gusta

Capítulo 9

ciento setenta y cinco 175

Notes   Ask students to guess what the terms at the top of the e-mail page mean: *archivo* (file), *ver* (view), *mensajes* (messages), *ayuda* (help), *a* (to), *cc* (copy), *asunto* (subject).

Use the e-mail message in activity 25 as an opportunity to reinforce reading skills in Spanish.

Teacher Resources

 Activity 26

Answers

25 1. él
    2. conmigo
    3. contigo
    4. él
    5. contigo
    6. mí
    7. conmigo
    8. ti
    9. ti

26 1. ¿...al banco?/No, no puedo ir contigo....
    2. ¿...a comprar unos zapatos que están en oferta?/No, no puedo ir contigo....
    3. ¿...a la tienda de artículos electrónicos?/No, no puedo ir contigo....
    4. ¿...a la tienda por departamentos?/No, no puedo ir contigo....
    5. ¿...al centro comercial?/No, no puedo ir contigo....
    6. ¿...a cambiar un cinturón que compré y ahora no me gusta?/No, no puedo ir contigo....

Activities

Students with Special Needs
As a class activity, return to previously studied dialogs and readings and ask students to find examples of prepositions. Then, for activity 25, complete the first blank space with the appropriate pronoun (*él*) as a model.

Answers

27 1. (Yo) vivo lejos de ti.
2. (Él) vive cerca de nosotros.
3. Uds. están al lado de nosotros.
4. (Él) compró un regalo para mí.
5. (Nosotras) vamos a recibir unos bolsos de ellos.

28 Answers will vary.

Activities

Multiple Intelligences (kinesthetic/visual)

Allow for creativity by letting students work in groups of four or five to present a fashion show to the class. Have each group select a narrator to read descriptions of the clothing while the other group members act as models.

27 En la tienda por departamentos

Da conclusiones apropiadas para las siguientes situaciones, usando las preposiciones y pronombres apropiados. Sigue las indicaciones entre paréntesis.

MODELO **Situación:** Yo llegué a la tienda a las cuatro de la tarde, tu amigo llegó a las cuatro menos diez y tú llegaste allí a las tres y media. (yo/después de)

Conclusión: (Yo) llegué después de Uds.

1. **Situación:** Tú llegaste primero porque vives más cerca de la tienda que yo. (yo/lejos de)
2. **Situación:** Tu amigo me dijo que vive en la Calle 128, N° 171, y mi familia y yo vivimos en la Calle 128, N° 173. (él/cerca de)
3. **Situación:** Son las cinco de la tarde y mi amigo y yo estamos mirando cinturones en el departamento para hombres y tú y tu amigo están mirando perfumes en el mismo departamento. (Uds./al lado de)
4. **Situación:** Mi amigo y yo nos compramos regalos el uno para el otro. Yo compré un regalo para mi amigo. (él/para)
5. **Situación:** Yo voy a recibir un bolso de mi amigo y tú también vas a recibir un bolso de tu amigo. (nosotras/de)

28 ¿Qué hiciste?

Trabajando con un(a) compañero/a de clase hagan mini-diálogos, tomando elementos de cada columna para hablar de lo que hiciste en días pasados.

MODELO **A:** ¿Adónde fuiste después de las clases?
B: Fui a la biblioteca.

A: ¿Quién fue contigo?
B: Mi hermano Pedro.

A	B	C
antes de venir aquí	la tienda por departamentos	mis padres
ayer por la noche	de compras	nadie
después de las clases	la tienda de artículos electrónicos	mi hermano/a
el domingo por la mañana	el cine	mi tío/a
el sábado por la noche	el centro comercial	mis abuelos
el viernes por la tarde	la biblioteca	mi primo/a
la semana pasada	el parque	mi amigo/a

¿Fuiste al cine?

176 *ciento setenta y seis*

Comunicación

29 Fuimos de compras

Trabajando con un(a) compañero/a de clase, hablen de la última vez que fueron de compras. Pueden hablar de lo que compraron, para quién lo compraron y con quién fueron.

MODELO
A: ¿Cuándo fue la última vez que fuiste de compras?
B: Fui el sábado pasado.

A: ¿Qué compraste y para quién?
B: Compré unos aretes para mi mamá.

A: ¿Con quién fuiste?
B: Fui contigo.

Fui de compras el sábado pasado.

30 De compras

Trabajando con un(a) compañero/a de clase, preparen un diálogo de cinco o seis oraciones sobre un día de compras. Uno de Uds. puede preguntar si la otra persona quiere ir contigo o no. Luego, pueden hablar de lo que van a comprar, el precio, la calidad, el tamaño y cómo van a pagar. Recuerden usar en forma apropiada las preposiciones.

MODELO
A: ¿Te gustaría ir de compras conmigo al centro comercial?
B: Sí, claro, voy contigo. ¿Vas con tu hermana?
A: No, voy sin ella.
B: ¡Qué lástima! ¿Qué vas a comprar?

31 Seguimos de compras

In groups of six to eight, form concentric circles so three or four students in an inside circle face the same number of students in an outside circle. Then the opposing pairs of students should take turns asking and answering what each of you bought the last time you went shopping and what each of you would like to buy when you return there. Take notes as your partner speaks. Then students in the outer circle move one to the right and begin a similar conversation with the new partner. Continue until you have spoken with everyone in the other circle. One person from each circle should report the findings to the class.

MODELO
A: ¿Qué compraste la última vez que fuiste de compras?
B: Compré un bolso de material sintético para mí.

Capítulo 9

ciento setenta y siete **177**

Notes Inform students that you will be asking several pairs of students to present their dialogs in front of the class.

Set time limits for the paired activities on page 177 and keep a brisk pace.

Remember to circulate around the room as students complete these activities to keep students on task and to offer help as needed.

The circle technique used for activity 31 works anytime you would like to have students pair up to ask the same question of several people, but you prefer that students not be up and moving around the room.

Answers

32
1. el sombrero "panamá"
2. el nombre verdadero del sombrero "panamá"
3. provincia de Ecuador en la costa y centro de producción de sombreros de jipijapa
4. pueblo colonial en Manabi donde se produce los mejores sombreros "panamá" llamados "superfinos"
5. la planta que se usa para tejer el sombrero "panamá"

33 Answers will vary.

Activities

Spanish for Spanish Speakers
Have students write a short composition in Spanish summarizing what they know about Ecuador. Expand the activity by having students seek out additional information about Ecuador at the library or on the Internet.

Lectura personal

Cantantes y grupos musicales

Dirección http://www.emcp.com/músico/ola/e.diario-2.htm ▲ Archivo   Edición   Ver   Favoritos   Herramientas   Ayuda

página principal   miembros   e-diario

Grupo musical La OLA

Nombre: **Xavier Rodríguez Guerra**
Edad: **18 años**
País natal: **Estados Unidos**
Artículo de ropa favorito: **sombreros**
Artículo de ropa que nunca usa: **pantalones de cuero**

Estamos en Ecuador, un país muy lindo. Después del concierto, el grupo se fue de compras a Quito. Yo también me fui de compras pero no a una tienda por departamentos con escaleras mecánicas y todo eso. Yo me fui en avión a la provincia de Manabi, que está en el centro de las costas ecuatorianas. Manabi tiene playas lindas, pero ésa no es la razón por la cual fui. Estuve en el pueblo[1] colonial de Montecristi, para comprar un sombrero "panamá" para mi nuevo *"look"*. Grandes personajes como Humphrey Bogart, Gary Cooper y Winston Churchill han usado sombreros "panamá". Creo

Hacen sombreros "panamá" en Ecuador.

que se ven muy elegantes. Saben, el sombrero "panamá" no es de Panamá; es un producto de Ecuador. Ecuador empezó a exportar estos sombreros en los años 1800s. En los años 40, era el producto de exportación número uno de Ecuador. Como se vendían[2] en los puertos[3] de Panamá, se les llamó sombreros "panamá", pero su verdadero[4] nombre es sombrero de jipijapa o sombrero de Montecristi. Montecristi produce los mejores sombreros "panamá" del mundo llamados "superfinos". Están hechos con la planta Carludovica palmata, que se hierve[5], se seca[6] y luego se teje[7]. Tardan tres meses en hacer un sólo sombrero. Son bastante caros, pero también son muy *"cool"*, ¿no creen?

[1]town   [2]were sold   [3]ports   [4]real   [5]boil   [6]dry   [7]weave

32 ¿Qué recuerdas?

Identifica cada uno.

1. el producto de exportación número uno de Ecuador en los cuarenta
2. sombrero de jipijapa   4. Montecristi
3. Manabi   5. Carludovica palmata

33 Algo personal

1. En tu opinión, ¿son los sombreros "panamá" elegantes? ¿Por qué sí o por qué no?
2. Donde tú vives, ¿hay un centro de producción de ropa? ¿Qué artículos de ropa hacen o venden?
3. Imagina que quieres tener un nuevo *"look"*. Describe tu nueva ropa.

- Panama hats are really from Ecuador. Can you think of other products (such as foods) that have a country in their names even though they did not originate from that country? How do you think this happens?

178 *ciento setenta y ocho*   **Lección B**

Notes The *Lectura personal* and activity 32 are recorded and available in the *Navegando 1* Audio CD Program.

Conduct a class discussion about clothing, using the questions in the *Algo personal* as your starting point.

¿Qué aprendí?

Autoevaluación
As a review and self-check, respond to the following:

Visit the web-based activities at www.emcp.com

① Name at least three items sold in a mall department store.

② Name something that can be made of gold, silver or pearl.

③ Imagine you are buying a gift for your best friend. Describe the item you purchased.

④ Say at least three things you read, heard or saw yesterday.

⑤ The last time you made a purchase, did you pay cash or did you use credit?

⑥ Imagine you are shopping in a Spanish-speaking country. How would you ask how much an item costs and if it is on sale?

⑦ Say two things you learned about Ecuador.

Palabras y expresiones

Para describir
barato,-a
bastante
caro,-a
corto,-a
demasiado
largo,-a
lindo,-a
perfecto,-a
sintético,-a

En la tienda
el anillo
el arete
el ascensor
la billetera

el bolso
la bufanda
la caja
la calidad
el cambio
el cinturón
el collar
el crédito
el cuero
el dependiente,
   la dependienta
el efectivo
la escalera mecánica
la joya
el material

mecánico,-a
la oferta
el oro
el pañuelo
el paraguas
el perfume
la perla
la plata
la pulsera
el recibo
el regalo
el tamaño
la tarjeta (de crédito)

Verbos
ahorrar
cambiar
pagar
recibir
usar

Expresiones y otras palabras
a crédito
conmigo
contigo
en efectivo

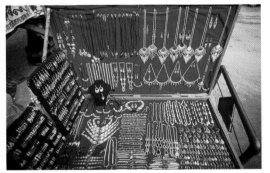

Venden aretes, collares y otras joyas.

Un paraguas negro.

Capítulo 9

ciento setenta y nueve **179**

Teacher Resources

📝 **Activity 14**

💬 **Information Gap Activities**
Postcard Activities
Funciones de Comunicación

Answers

Autoevaluación
Possible answers:
1. las bufandas, las billeteras, los paraguas
2. Un anillo puede ser de oro.
3. Le compré unos guantes de cuero.
4. Leí el periódico....
5. Pagué en efectivo por las cosas que compré.
6. ¿Cuánto cuesta? ¿Está en oferta especial?
7. La capital del Ecuador es Quito....

Activities

Pronunciation *(el sonido* ch*)*
In Spanish, *ch* sounds like the English *ch* in **church.** It never sounds like the combination *ch* in **machine** or in **chemistry.** Model these words with students: *archipiélago, chisme, chica, chorizo, Conchita, muchacho.*

Spanish for Spanish Speakers
Ecuador is one of the OPEC nations. Have students investigate and prepare a report on the impact that petroleum had on the Ecuadorean economy during the 1970s.

Notes Encourage students to find out more about Ecuador by going to the following Web sites:

Organization of American States
http://www.oas.org
Embassy of Ecuador
http://www.ecuador.org

general travel information
http://www.expedia.com
Virtual Countries, Inc.
http://www.ecuador.com/macie.html

Teacher Resources

Las rebajas de Danté

Answers

Preparación
1. A
2. C
3. B

Activities

Critical Thinking
To further reinforce the importance of visual organization to content, ask students to describe the typical format and related information for the following items: a job application, a recipe, a movie poster.

Multiple Intelligences (logical-mathematical)
Have students find out the value in dollars for the *balboa* (Panamanian currency) and for the *sucre* (currency of Ecuador). Sources for currency exchange rates include the business section of the local paper, the *Wall Street Journal*, other newspapers or the Internet. The school media specialist may be able to help students find other sources for exchange rates as well.

Tú lees

Estrategia

Using visual format to predict meaning
Visual details of printed information such as the style and format of printed media can tell you a lot about its probable content. For instance, the format of a letter will indicate whether it is for business or if it is personal. Similarly, cartoons are easily recognized by the style of the illustration and the way the contents appear on the page. Advertisements and brochures can differ greatly from one another depending on the intended population. Before starting to read, look at the layout, the artwork, the pictures, the titles and the format of the writing for hints about its content and meaning.

Preparación
Observa el título, el arte y la forma de esta lectura y contesta las siguientes preguntas.

1. ¿Qué tipo de lectura es ésta?
   A. Es un anuncio *(ad)*.
   B. Es un artículo *(article)* de periódico.
   C. Es una encuesta *(survey)*.
2. ¿Qué venden?
   A. Venden artículos electrónicos.
   B. Venden frutas y verduras.
   C. Venden ropa y servicios.
3. ¿Para quién es lo que venden?
   A. Para hombres.
   B. Para hombres, mujeres y jóvenes.
   C. Para mujeres.

Las rebajas de Danté

Las fabulosas rebajas de Danté te ofrecen grandes ahorros en ropa casual para todos. Tenemos grandes rebajas del 20%, 30%, 40% y hasta el 50%. Aquí puedes conseguir la ropa que necesitas para ir al cine, las fiestas y al colegio. Tenemos todos los estilos que te gustan en todas las marcas y colores.

Servicios generales

- ❖ Sastrería
- ❖ Pedidos especiales de vestidos
- ❖ Sorteos
- ❖ Danté Café
- ❖ Abrimos los domingos
- ❖ Tarjeta de crédito Danté

Notes *Almacenes Danté* is a large department store in Panama. You may wish to inform your students that they can visit the Web site for the store by searching the term *Almacenes Danté* in the search box of any browser. (See the *Navegando 1B* ATE Introduction for suggested browsers or use one of your choosing.)

¿Adónde vas de compras con más frecuencia?

Un centro comercial en Quito, Ecuador.

A ¿Qué recuerdas?

1. ¿En qué tipo de ropa puedes ahorrar dinero si la compras en esta tienda?
2. ¿De cuánto son las rebajas en esta tienda?
3. ¿Para ir a qué tipo de lugares puedes comprar ropa en Danté?
4. ¿Qué servicios tiene esta tienda?

B Algo personal

1. ¿Qué piensas del anuncio?
2. ¿Para qué tipo de personas piensas que es este anuncio?
3. ¿Buscas anuncios con rebajas antes de ir de compras? Explica.
4. ¿Qué tipo de anuncios te gustan?
5. ¿Adónde vas de compras con más frecuencia?

Notes Encourage students to find out more about Panama by going to the following Web sites:

Organization of American States
http://www.oas.org
Lonely Planet
http://www.lonelyplanet.com/destinations/central_america/panama/

Presidential Homepage
http://www.presidencia.gob.pa/
Panamainfo
http://www.panamainfo.com
general travel information
http://www.expedia.com

Answers

A 1. Puedo ahorrar dinero en ropa casual.
2. Las rebajas son del 20%, 30%, 40% y hasta el 50%.
3. Puedo comprar ropa para ir al cine, a las fiestas y al colegio.
4. Possible answers: sastrería, pedidos especiales de vestidos, sorteos, café, abren los domingos, tarjeta de crédito.

B Answers will vary.

Activities

Prereading Strategy
Note for students that it is not essential to understand every word to read in Spanish. Have students scan the advertisement to find cognates and other words they know. Be sure to cover the *Preparación* activity prior to beginning the reading.

Activities

Communities

In small groups, students prepare a survey *(encuesta)* about shopping. Have them send the survey via e-mail to a collaborating class and request a response. Share the results with the class. (Before assigning the activity, search the Internet for "Intercultural E-mail Connections" to find Spanish teachers in the United States or English teachers in other Spanish-speaking parts of the world.) As an alternative, you may prefer to have students survey just the class, your school or some segment of your community.

Critical Thinking

Ask students to identify appropriate gifts for each of the following people: *mi mejor amigo; mi mejor amiga; un abuelo o una abuela; una hermana de ocho años; un hermano de veinte años; el maestro/la maestra de español.* Then, in addition to naming the presents, students should justify the gift selection.

Tú escribes

Estrategia

Indicating sequence

You have already learned to use transition words to make your writing flow smoothly. When writing about past activities or events, transition words can indicate the sequence in which actions occurred. Some sequence words you may want to use in your writing include the following: *primero* (first), *luego* (later, then), *antes de* (before), *después de* (after), *finalmente* (finally).

Shopping centers and malls are more than just convenient places to shop. Going to a *centro comercial* often turns into a social event that offers shoppers an opportunity to spend time with friends and to meet new people. What does shopping at the mall mean to you? Write a short composition telling about your last visit to the mall *(Mi última visita al centro comercial)*. Include when you went, with whom you went, what places you visited, if you visited a *tienda por departamentos*, what you did, whom you met, what you bought and any other information you wish. Be sure to use connecting words for making smooth transitions and for telling the sequence of events.

Compré una bolsa de cuero en la tienda por departamentos.

Notes Explain that when shopping in most Hispanic countries, shoppers will notice that the clerk who waits on the customer does not usually collect the money for the purchase. Instead, the clerk gives a copy of the bill to the customer. Another copy of the bill, along with the item being purchased, is given by the clerk to the cashier. The customer then stands in line at the cashier's register to pay for and receive the item purchased. Students should be aware that shopping in a store in Ecuador and in other Spanish-speaking countries may take more time and require more waiting in line.

Proyectos adicionales

A Conexión con la tecnología

You learned how to create a dialog journal in the *Tú escribes* activity in the *¡Viento en popa!* section of *Capítulo 2*. Create an electronic dialog journal entry to send to your teacher. Write about your last trip to a *tienda por departamentos* to shop for something special (e. g., clothing for yourself, a gift). You may wish to tell about where and with whom you went shopping, what you purchased and how much you paid. Include any other information you would like and e-mail the journal entry to your teacher.

B Conexión con otras disciplinas: arte y diseño

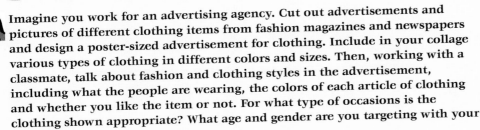

Imagine you work for an advertising agency. Cut out advertisements and pictures of different clothing items from fashion magazines and newspapers and design a poster-sized advertisement for clothing. Include in your collage various types of clothing in different colors and sizes. Then, working with a classmate, talk about fashion and clothing styles in the advertisement, including what the people are wearing, the colors of each article of clothing and whether you like the item or not. For what type of occasions is the clothing shown appropriate? What age and gender are you targeting with your advertisement?

C Comunidades

How do people in your community dress? Write a short composition describing how young people dress during a specific season of the year. What are the most popular colors and materials? What statement do you think they wish to convey by how they dress?

Unas mujeres en Otavalo, Ecuador.

Unos niños Amish en Ohio.

ciento ochenta y tres **183**

Capítulo 9

Teacher Resources

 Trabalenguas

Activities

Multiple Intelligences (spatial/linguistic)

Have students prepare a travel brochure about the Galapagos Islands. Brochures should include what visitors can see, how to get there, lodging, etc. Students can use their own drawings or cut pictures from magazines.

Spanish for Spanish Speakers

Ask students to write an essay describing their favorite gift and stating who gave it to them and on what occasion (e.g., their birthday) they received it.

Repaso

Now that I have completed this chapter, I can...	Go to these pages for help:
describe clothing.	140
identify parts of the body.	140
express disagreement.	150
talk about the past.	150
discuss size and fit.	162
discuss price and payment.	170

I can also...	
talk about life in Panama and Ecuador.	143, 165
ask questions when I do not understand something.	150
talk about personal taste in clothing.	150
use affirmative and negative expressions in conversations.	157
use diminutives to express affection or that something is small.	166

Trabalenguas

Venancio vendía bonitas boinas, bonitas, baratas, embalaba baberos, bolillos, botas bellas y boinas buenas.

¡Viento en popa!

Notes Review the functions and other objectives in the *Repaso* and assign the activities and answer questions so students can prepare for the Chapter Test. Follow up by reviewing the activities as a class.

Loose translation of the *Trabalenguas*:
Venancio sold pretty berets, pretty cheap; he packed bibs, bobbins, beautiful boots and good berets.

Vocabulario

ahorrar to save 9B
algo something, anything 9A
el algodón cotton 9A
alguien someone, anyone, somebody, anybody 9A
algún, alguna some, any 9A
alguno,-a some, any 9A
anaranjado,-a orange (color) 9A
el anillo ring 9B
el arete earring 9B
el ascensor elevator 9B
barato,-a cheap 9B
bastante rather, fairly, sufficiently, enough, sufficient 9B
la billetera wallet 9B
el bolso purse 9B
la bota boot 9A
el brazo arm 9A
la bufanda scarf 9B
la cabeza head
la caja cashier's desk 9B
la calidad quality 9B
cambiar to change, to exchange 9B
el cambio change 9B
caro,-a expensive 9B
el centro comercial shopping center, mall 9A
la chaqueta jacket 9A
el cinturón belt 9B
el collar necklace 9B
combinar to combine 9A
conmigo with me 9B
contar (ue) to tell (a story) 9A
contigo with you 9B
la corbata tie 9A

corto,-a short (not long) 9B
el crédito credit 9B
a crédito on credit 9B
el cuero leather 9B
el cuerpo body 9A
el dedo finger 9A
demasiado too (much) 9B
el departamento department 9A
el dependiente, la dependienta clerk 9B
el efectivo effective 9B
en efectivo in cash 9B
la escalera mecánica escalator 9B
estar en oferta to be on sale 9B
el guante glove 9A
la joya jewel 9B
el hombre man 9A
el impermeable raincoat 9A
la lana wool 9A
largo,-a long 9B
lindo,-a pretty 9B
la mano hand 9A
marrón brown 9A
el material material 9B
las medias pantyhose, nylons 9A
morado,-a purple 9A
la mujer woman 9A
nada nothing 9A
nadie nobody 9A
ni... ni neither... nor 9A
ningún, ninguna none, not any 9A
ninguno,-a none, not any 9A
o... o either... or 9A
la oferta offer 9B
el oro gold 9B

pagar pay 9B
el pañuelo handkerchief, hanky 9B
el paraguas umbrella 9B
perfecto,-a perfect 9B
el perfume perfume 9B
la perla pearl 9B
el pie foot 9A
la pierna leg 9A
el pijama pajamas 9A
la plata silver 9B
prometer promise 9A
la pulsera bracelet 9B
quedar to remain, to stay 9A
quedarle bien a uno to fit, to be becoming 9A
recibir to receive 9B
el recibo receipt 9B
el regalo gift 9B
la ropa interior underwear 9A
rosado,-a pink 9A
la seda silk 9A
sintético,-a synthetic 9B
el sombrero hat 9A
el suéter sweater 9A
el tamaño size 9B
la tarjeta (de crédito) credit card 9B
el traje (de baño) swimsuit 9A
usar to use 9B
las vacaciones vacation 9A
vender to sell 9A
el vestido dress 9A
el zapato bajo flat shoe 9A
el zapato de tacón high-heeled shoe 9A

Teacher Resources

Module 4

Episode 9

Testing/ Assessment

Test Booklet
Portfolio Assessment

Activities

TPR
Try using TPR to teach and reinforce the parts of the body. Teach the following commands, combining them with the appropriate parts of the body: *toca, mueve, rasca, tira, levanta, baja, abre, cierra*. Parts of the body you may wish to include are: *el brazo, la cabeza, el dedo, la mano, el pie, la pierna*, which have been introduced in the book. In addition, you may want to teach other parts of the body including the following: *la boca, la cara, el codo, el cuello, el diente, el estómago, la garganta, el hombro, la lengua, la muñeca, la nariz, el ojo, la oreja, el pecho, el pelo, la rodilla, el tobillo.*

Llevamos las corbatas a la escuela.

Venden ropa interior para mujeres.

Notes The Panama Canal has a fascinating history. After the canal was built by the United States, U.S. presence and control in the Panama Canal area became a source of increasing resentment in Panama. To ease the growing conflict, the United States and Panama signed the Panama Canal Neutrality Treaty in 1978 to increase Panamanian control gradually over the entire Canal Zone. The year 2000 marked the first year that Panama was in complete control of this important economic and political resource.

Remind students to return to either *Lección 9A* or *Lección 9B* (as indicated after each English equivalent) to review words and expressions they do not recognize.

Activities

Critical Thinking

The two photographs that appear on these pages depict the cultural setting for the chapter ahead and serve to help provide a cultural context as motivation for students as they begin *Capítulo 10*. Ask if students recognize anything in either picture or if they can guess where the large photograph was taken.

Technology

Visit the EMCParadigm Web site at www.emcp.com.

Capítulo **10**

Un año más

Objetivos

- ❖ discuss past actions and events
- ❖ talk about everyday activities
- ❖ express emotion
- ❖ indicate wishes and preferences
- ❖ write about past actions
- ❖ talk about the future
- ❖ make polite requests
- ❖ describe personal characteristics

Visit the web-based activities at www.emcp.com

186 *ciento ochenta y seis*

Notes *Capítulo 10* offers a broad review of the content of *Navegando 1*. This final chapter contains no new vocabulary or grammar. Therefore, select specific content you would like to review (e.g., the preterite tense, comparisons, expressions or vocabulary), complete the entire chapter or stop using the book after *Capítulo 9*. The authors have left the choice up to you to decide, according to time constraints and your own particular curricular needs.

The large photograph is of Machu Picchu in Peru. This interesting remain of a past civilization is discussed in greater detail on page 192. The smaller photograph shows the colonial architecture typical of Antigua, Guatemala.

Perú
Nombre oficial: **República del Perú**
Población: **27.483.000**
Capital: **Lima**
Ciudades importantes: **Arequipa, Trujillo**
Unidad monetaria: **el nuevo sol**
Fiesta nacional: **28 de julio, Día de la Independencia**
Gente famosa: **Mario Vargas Llosa, César Vallejo (escritores)**

Guatemala
Nombre oficial: **República de Guatemala**
Población: **12.974.000**
Capital: **Ciudad de Guatemala**
Ciudades importantes: **Antigua, Chichicastenango, Quetzaltenango**
Unidad monetaria: **el quetzal**
Fiesta nacional: **15 de septiembre, Día de la Independencia**
Gente famosa: **Rigoberta Menchú (líder popular)**

Activities

Connections
Using the maps at the front of the book, the *Navegando 1* transparencies or a wall map, conduct a class discussion about some of the geographical features of Peru and Guatemala.

ciento ochenta y siete **187**

Notes If you decide to use this chapter, you may skip activities or expand your review of a particular topic, according to the time you have available and according to student needs. *Capítulo 10* offers your students an opportunity to do interesting projects in which they talk about the past year (what they have learned, what they have done, what some of their favorite classes were). They also will have an opportunity to consider careers, future travel, relationships and other topics that are challenging and enjoyable.

Fue un año divertido
Activities 1–3

Activities 1–2

Activity 67

Activity 1

Activity 1

Activity 1

Content reviewed in *Lección A*

- **talking about the past**
- **school**
- **leisure activities**
- **talking about the future**
- ***gustar***

Answers

1
1. No hay más tareas.
2. Mario estudió mucho.
3. Le gustó más jugar al fútbol y las clases de historia.
4. Le gustó más la clase de biología.
5. No le gusta la biología.
6. Silvia tiene amigos en el equipo de voleibol.

2 Answers will vary.

3
1. Falso. ...divertido.
2. Cierto.
3. Falso. ...biología.
4. Cierto.

Lección A

Perú

Diálogo I

Fue un año divertido

MARIO: ¡Un año más! No hay más tareas por unos meses.
SILVIA: ¡Qué bueno! Fue un año divertido.
MARIO: Estudié mucho.

SILVIA: ¿Qué fue lo que más te gustó?
MARIO: ¡Jugar al fútbol y las clases de historia!
SILVIA: A mí me gustó más la clase de biología.

MARIO: A mí la biología no me gusta.
SILVIA: Sí, yo sé. Bueno, también hice nuevos amigos.
MARIO: ¿Tus amigos del equipo de voleibol?
SILVIA: Sí, y voy a verlos ahora. Adiós.

1 ¿Qué recuerdas?

1. ¿Qué no hay por unos meses?
2. ¿Quién estudió mucho?
3. ¿Qué fue lo que más le gustó a Mario?
4. ¿Qué le gustó más a Silvia?
5. ¿Qué no le gusta a Mario?
6. ¿Quién tiene amigos en el equipo de voleibol?

2 Algo personal

1. ¿Fue tu año divertido? Explica.
2. ¿Te gusta hacer tareas? ¿Por qué?
3. ¿Qué fue lo que más te gustó del colegio este año?
4. ¿Qué deporte jugaste más este año?

3 ¡Fue un año divertido!

 Di si lo que oyes es cierto o falso, según el Diálogo I. Si es falso, corrige la información.

Notes *Capítulo 10* offers you the choice of whether to teach the contents to the entire class or to individuals based upon their interests, abilities or needs. For example, graduating seniors may benefit from some of the topics covered as they prepare for college, work or travel. Gifted and highly motivated students may enjoy doing portions of the chapter independently. In addition, you may have one or two students in class who are planning a trip to Peru or Guatemala and would like to learn about those countries.

Cultura viva

El Perú, centro del imperio inca

Peru formed the center point of the Incan Empire (el imperio inca). Located on the Pacific Ocean along the western shores of South America, and situated between Ecuador and Chile, Peru, with its rich gold and silver deposits, quickly attracted many Spanish explorers in the sixteenth century. Although the Spaniards introduced their language and religion, the influence of the Inca civilization is evident throughout the modern-day culture of Peru. Descendants of the Incas still populate the Andean (Andes) highlands and

Descendientes de los incas viven en Perú.

Somos del Perú.

the eastern jungles (selvas del este). Many of them do not speak Spanish and they continue to live as their ancestors did centuries ago.

In direct contrast to Peru's indigenous past is the country's contemporary capital, Lima, where 30 percent of Peru's population lives and works. Lima is the most important area of development in the country. However, remnants of the past can be found even in this modern city. One example is the University of San Marcos, which is one of the oldest universities in the world.

La iglesia Santo Domingo en Cuzco, Perú.

4 El Perú

Contesta las siguientes preguntas sobre el Perú.

1. ¿De qué imperio fue Perú el centro?
2. ¿Por qué vinieron los exploradores españoles al Perú?
3. ¿En qué zona del Perú viven todavía los descendientes de los incas?
4. ¿Cómo se llama la capital del Perú?
5. ¿Cómo se llama una de las universidades más viejas del mundo?

5 ¡A viajar!

Imagina que te gustaría visitar Perú para practicar tu español. ¿Qué te gustaría ver o hacer allí? Busca información sobre Perú en la internet. Luego, haz un itinerario con fechas, hoteles, restaurantes, lugares interesantes para visitar, precios, etc. Prepara un póster de viaje sobre el lugar y presenta la información a la clase.

¡Oportunidades!

En otro país
Have you ever visited another country? What did you see? What did you do there? After studying Spanish for a year, you probably realize the many opportunities that are available to you to use your language skills. Have you ever considered attending school in a different country for a year? Studying and living in a Spanish-speaking country could increase the Spanish skills you acquired this year.

Notes Founded in 1551, the University of San Marcos is the oldest university in South America.

Peru's indigenous peoples comprise nearly half of the population. Peru has more indigenous people than any other country in South America. Most indigenous people live in Peru's *Altiplano*, all areas of the Andes above 6,500 feet.

Teacher Resources

 Activity 4

 Activity 3

 Activities 2–4

 Activity 2

Answers

4 1. Fue el centro del imperio inca.
2. Vinieron por el oro y la plata.
3. Viven todavía en las zonas de los Andes y las selvas del este del Perú.
4. Se llama Lima.
5. Se llama la universidad de San Marcos.

5 Creative self-expression.

Activities

Cooperative Learning
Have students work in pairs preparing a dialog in which two people are talking about a trip one of them has just taken to Peru.

Expansion
Ask the following questions for discussion: ¿Qué países conoces?; ¿Qué hiciste en ese país/esos países?; ¿Qué lugares visitaste?; ¿Qué país(es) te gustaría visitar? ¿Por qué?; ¿En qué país te gustaría estudiar? ¿Por qué?; ¿Por qué es importante el español?

Multiple Intelligences (musical)
Play Andean music to students and have them compare it to their favorite music.

Activity 4

 Activities 5–7

 Activities 3–4

 Activities 2–3

Answers

6 Creative self-expression.
7 Creative writing practice.
8 Answers will vary. You may also want to conduct the poll again with groups composed of all males and all females. Then compare the results to those of the mixed groups.

Activities

Cooperative Learning
After completing activity 8, have students conduct a similar survey on an issue of interest in your school.

Expansion
Select several students to summarize for the class what they learned about their partner in activity 6.

Spanish for Spanish Speakers
Pair bilingual and nonbilingual speakers for activity 6.

◈ Proyectos

 6 Una entrevista para el periódico del colegio

Prepara una entrevista para hacerla a un(a) compañero/a de clase para saber sobre sus experiencias y actividades durante este año. Pregúntale sobre las cosas más importantes que hizo, las más divertidas, las más aburridas, lo que más le gustó del año, lo que menos le gustó, algo interesante que le pasó y cualquier otra información de su vida en el colegio o en su casa. Luego, escribe un artículo en español de una página y preséntalo a la clase.

7 Tus experiencias

Escribe un ensayo *(essay)* en español de uno o dos párrafos sobre algo especial que te pasó durante tu vida escolar este año. En tu composición puedes hablar por ejemplo sobre alguien interesante que conociste, una actividad importante que hiciste, una clase que te gustó mucho, un deporte que hiciste o un evento al que fuiste. Añade detalles *(details)* importantes que rodearon *(surrounded)* el hecho *(event)*, como por ejemplo, la fecha en que pasó, el lugar, el tiempo que hizo, lo que pasó antes y lo que pasó después, etc.

Estrategia

The importance of reviewing
It is important to review what you have learned. No one remembers everything they have studied. You have made progress this year with Spanish, and reviewing will help keep everything fresh in your mind.

8 Encuesta estudiantil

 Haz la siguiente encuesta a diez compañeros(as) de clase para averiguar *(to find out)* cuáles fueron las clases favoritas de tus compañeros(as) este año. Primero, completa la encuesta en cualquier clase que no sea la de español y hazte la encuesta a ti mismo y luego a tus compañeros(as) de español del grupo, compartan los resultados. Finalmente, reporten los resultados del grupo a la clase.

Encuesta sobre las clases favoritas del año

Por cada una de las siguientes clases di el número que representa mejor tu opinión.

1. el arte	0	1	2	3	4
2. las ciencias (biología, química, etc.)	0	1	2	3	4
3. la computación	0	1	2	3	4
4. la educación física	0	1	2	3	4
5. el español	0	1	2	3	4
6. los estudios sociales	0	1	2	3	4
7. la historia	0	1	2	3	4
8. el inglés	0	1	2	3	4
9. las matemáticas (álgebra, geometría, etc.)	0	1	2	3	4
10. la música (banda, orquestra, coro, etc.)	0	1	2	3	4
11. (¿otras?) _____	0	1	2	3	4

0 = No sé. No tengo una opinión.
1 = Fue horrible. Me disgustó *(disliked)* mucho.
2 = Fue aburrida. No me gustó mucho.
3 = Fue buena. Me gustó.
4 = Fue excelente. Me gustó mucho.

Notes **Review.** Review the preterite tense with students before assigning activity 6.

Before assigning activity 7, review some of the writing strategies students have learned over the course of the year. Tell students they should apply as many of these strategies as possible when writing their essay.

Review classes and the use of *gustar* before assigning activity 8.

9 Encuesta electrónica

Prepara un e-mail o una página de la Web con una encuesta como la que hiciste en la actividad anterior sobre las clases favoritas. Envíala a otra clase (de tu colegio, de cualquier otro colegio del país o de un país de habla hispana), pidiendo a los estudiantes contestarla también por la internet. Comparte los resultados con la clase, comparando y contrastando los resultados de la encuesta.

10 Un país hispanohablante

Crea un collage que represente al país hispanohablante que encontraste *(found)* más interesante durante tu año de clases de español. Luego, muéstralo a la clase y da una corta explicación del collage.

Un collage de fotos de la Argentina.

11 Tu poesía

Escribe un poema o una canción en español sobre algún tema que aprendiste este año. Después, puedes leer tu poema o cantar tu canción a la clase.

Estoy escribiendo un poema.

Teacher Resources

 Activities 8–9

 Activities 4–6

Answers

9 Creative self-expression.
10 Creative self-expression.
11 Creative self-expression.

Activities

Cooperative Learning
Tell the class that it is time for a role-reversal: Instead of answering the teacher's questions or a partner's questions, it is their opportunity to ask questions of the teacher. The students should work in pairs to develop appropriate questions; the interview session follows.

Multiple Intelligences (musical)
Ask for volunteers to teach the class a song they know in Spanish. The song may be traditional or contemporary. As an alternative, ask if anyone in class would like to recite the poem or perform the song they wrote for activity 11.

Notes   Activity 10 is meant to provide an additional opportunity for visual and artistic learners to excel and show what they have learned during the year.

Ask permission of students to place some of the better collages and poems on the wall or in a public display in the school.

You may also wish to contact the editor and supervisor of the school newspaper to arrange to print one or two of the poems.

Machu Picchu
Activities 12–13

Activities

Expansion

Have students look in the media center for pictures of Machu Picchu and bring them in to share with the class.

Lectura cultural

Machu Picchu

Miles de turistas visitan este sitio arqueológico cerca de Cuzco, Perú. ¿Por qué?

Belleza[1]...

Los incas construyeron[2] Machu Picchu entre dos picos[3] altos. Las construcciones de piedra[4] parecen desplegarse[5] sobre la montaña. Abajo, el torrencial río[6] Urubamba corre por la selva amazónica. Es un lugar mágico.

Historia...

Machu Picchu fue construida[7] en el siglo XV cuando el imperio inca se extendía desde Ecuador a Argentina. Se la conoce como la Ciudad Perdida porque permaneció[8] escondida[9] hasta 1911 cuando Hiram Bingham la descubrió[10] intacta.

Misterio...

Machu Picchu, en quechua, quiere decir "Cima[11] Vieja" pero su verdadero nombre no se conoce. Tampoco se sabe la historia o la función de esta ciudad fortificada inca. Algunos creen que fue un monasterio pero como los incas no tenían escritura[12], este lugar estará siempre rodeado[13] de misterio.

Respeto...

La perfección de las paredes de Machu Picchu sorprende[14]. No usaron argamasa[15], y sin embargo[16], la unión entre las piedras es tan perfecta que no se puede introducir ni la hoja[17] de un cuchillo. La construcción de Machu Picchu—con sus paredes perfectas, acueductos, terrazas, observatorios, reloj solar—es evidencia de la sabiduría[18] de los incas.

[1]Beauty [2]built [3]peaks [4]stone [5]unfold [6]river [7]built [8]remained [9]hidden [10]discovered [11]Peak [12]writing [13]surrounded [14]amazes [15]mortar [16]however [17]blade [18]wisdom

12 ¿Qué recuerdas?

¿Sí o no?

1. Machu Picchu fue la capital secreta del imperio inca en el siglo XV.
2. Hiram Bingham descubrió las ruinas de Machu Picchu en 1911.
3. La geografía de Machu Picchu incluye montañas y selva.
4. La construcción de las paredes de Machu Picchu es perfecta.
5. Los incas sabían escribir y leer.

13 Algo personal

1. ¿Qué más sabes sobre Machu Picchu? Comparte algunos datos con la clase.
2. ¿Por qué crees que nadie, ni los conquistadores españoles, descubrieron Machu Picchu hasta 1911? ¿Cuál crees que fue la función de esa ciudad inca?

- Compare and contrast the architecture and landscape of Machu Picchu with that of the city in which you live.

Notes Before beginning the *Lectura cultural* have students identify cognates and known words.

The Incas were the rulers of the largest native empire of the Americas. At the time of their demise, the Incas consisted of and ruled an estimated twelve million people in much of what is now Peru and Ecuador, as well as in large parts of Chile, Bolivia and Argentina.

¿Qué aprendí?

Autoevaluación
As a review and self-check, respond to the following:

1. Use the preterite tense to state six things you did this year.
2. State four things you learned about Peru.
3. Name two opportunities you have because you know Spanish.
4. Why is it important to review what you have learned?
5. Summarize the results of the surveys you did about favorite classes for activities 8 and 9.
6. State two things you learned about Machu Picchu.

Visit the web-based activities at www.emcp.com

Lima, la capital de Perú.

Unas paredes en Machu Picchu.

¡Aprendimos mucho este año!

Capítulo 10

ciento noventa y tres **193**

Teacher Resources

- Activity 10
- Activity 5
- Information Gap Activities
  Postcard Activities
  Funciones de Comunicación

Answers

Autoevaluación
Answers will vary.

Activities

Pronunciation *(las letras l e y, y el sonido ll)*
The sound of *l* in Spanish is similar to the sound of *l* in English, but shorter. Model several words for students: *la, lavar, limpiar, lista, lugar, el, abril, telenovela.* In Spanish, *ll* has a sound that is similar to the English *y* as in **yet**. Have students practice the sound by having them pronounce the following words: *ella, paella, silla, olla, llueve, cuchillo, llegan, Guillermo, vainilla.* The letter *y* in Spanish is similar to the English *y* in **yet,** when preceding a vowel: *ayudar, ya, yo, mayo, playa, oyendo, leyendo.* When following a vowel, the Spanish *y* sounds like an *i.* This usually happens at the end of the word: *soy, estoy, hoy, hay, doy, voy, muy.*

Notes Students can find out more about Cuzco and Machu Picchu by visiting these Web sites:

Cuzco http://www.peru.com/cuzco/
Machu Picchu general information
http://www.machupicchu.org

Teacher Resources

 ¿Adónde van de vacaciones?
Activities 1–3

 Activities 1–3

 Activity 68

 Activities 1–2

 Activity 1

 Activities 1–2

Content reviewed in *Lección B*

- **talking about the past**
- ***tener que***
- **talking about the future**
- **adjective/noun agreement**
- **leisure activities**
- **careers that use Spanish**

Answers

1 1. Tuvo que ayudar a sus padres.
2. Va a ir a las ruinas de Tikal.
3. Fue a Tikal.
4. Le gustaría ir a California a la casa de su tía.

2 Answers will vary.

3 1. Luis; 2. Luis; 3. Inés; 4. Inés; 5. Luis

Lección B

Guatemala

Diálogo I

¿Adónde van de vacaciones?

LUIS: Hola, Inés.
INÉS: Hola, Luis. ¿Qué hiciste el sábado?
LUIS: Tuve que ayudar a mis padres.

INÉS: ¿Van a ir de vacaciones?
LUIS: Vamos a ir a las ruinas de Tikal.
INÉS: Fui a Tikal el año pasado. Me gustó mucho.

LUIS: Y tú, ¿qué vas a hacer en las vacaciones?
INÉS: No sé. Me gustaría ir a California a la casa de mi tía, o trabajar en la tienda de mi padre.
LUIS: Pienso que debes ir a California. Va a ser más divertido.

1 ¿Qué recuerdas?

1. ¿Qué hizo Luis el sábado pasado?
2. ¿Adónde va Luis de vacaciones?
3. ¿Adónde fue Inés el año pasado?
4. ¿Adónde le gustaría a Inés ir de vacaciones?

2 Algo personal

1. ¿Qué hiciste el sábado pasado?
2. ¿Qué vas a hacer en las vacaciones?
3. ¿Adónde te gustaría ir de vacaciones?
4. ¿Piensas que trabajar durante las vacaciones es una buena idea?

3 ¿Quién dijo qué?

 ¿Quién dijo lo siguiente, Inés o Luis?

¡Extra!

Me gustaría

Remember to use *gustaría* combined with *me, te, les, nos* and *les* in order to make a request, to politely express a wish or to ask about another person's wishes.

Me gustaría ir a California.
¿Te gustaría ir de vacaciones?

194 *ciento noventa y cuatro*

Lección B

Notes Before beginning the dialog, review the preterite tense, family vocabulary, the use of *tener que*, the *futuro próximo* and adjective-noun agreement.

194

Cultura viva

Guatemala, tierra maya

One aspect of Guatemala that fascinates anyone who visits the country is that Guatemala is the land of the Maya Indian civilization. Although the ancient Mayan civilization disappeared mysteriously, traces of the advanced Mayan culture remain today. The Mayans had an extensive knowledge of astronomy, mathematics and architecture. Tikal, one of the most well-known Mayan cities, was founded around 700 B.C. The Mayan languages (mainly *quiché*) and traditions are still very much alive among the Mayans in today's Guatemala. The colors and patterns of the traditional ceremonial costumes that many Mayan descendants wear are visible evidence of one tradition that has been passed on for many years from one generation to the next.

The cities of *Antigua, Chichicastenango, Huehuetenango* and *Quetzaltenango* still contain remnants of the Spanish colonial period, which started in 1524. The capital, Guatemala City *(Ciudad de Guatemala),* was founded in 1776, and in 1821 the region declared its independence from Spain.

Today Guatemala offers a mix of old and new, rustic and urban. The modern capital is the commercial, industrial, educational and governmental center of the country. However, Guatemala's rich farmland serves as the main source of income for the country's 14 million inhabitants, just as it has for centuries.

Tikal, Guatemala.

Los colores de Guatemala.

Unas chicas mayas.

4 Guatemala, tierra maya

Di si las siguientes oraciones sobre Guatemala son ciertas o falsas.

1. Guatemala es un centro de la civilización maya.
2. Los mayas estudiaron astronomía, matemáticas y biología.
3. La ciudad más famosa del imperio maya es Tikal.
4. La lengua maya es el español.
5. Antigua es una ciudad muy moderna.
6. La capital de Guatemala es la Ciudad de Guatemala.

Activity 3

 Activities 3–5

Answers

5 Answers will vary.
6 Creative writing practice.
7 Answers will vary.

Activities

Cooperative Learning
As follow-up to activity 6, ask students to make predictions about their lives in ten to fifteen years: *¿Qué carreras van a tener?; ¿Dónde van a vivir y trabajar?; ¿Van a usar el español en sus carreras?*

Multiple Intelligences (linguistic/spatial)
Have students do a variation on the theme for activity 6 by assigning a composition in the past tense to tell what they did last summer. Have them attach a picture or a visual to make their paragraph more interesting and display their work on a bulletin board.

 **Proyectos**

 5 Otra entrevista para el periódico del colegio

 Trabajando con un(a) compañero/a de clase, hazle las siguientes preguntas en combinación con cinco preguntas originales para saber sobre sus planes para el verano. Después de la entrevista, escribe un artículo de uno o dos párrafos sobre los planes de tu compañero/a y léelo a la clase.

1. ¿Cuál de los trabajos de la lista te gustaría hacer este verano?
2. ¿Qué otro trabajo de la lista te gustaría hacer?
3. ¿Tienes experiencia en alguno de estos trabajos? ¿En cuál? ¿Cuánta experiencia tienes?
4. ¿En cuáles de los trabajos de la lista no te gustaría trabajar? Explica.
5. ¿Vas a viajar durante tus vacaciones? ¿Adónde?
6. – 10. ¿...?

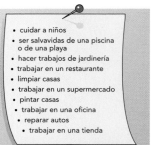

- cuidar a niños
- ser salvavidas de una piscina o de una playa
- hacer trabajos de jardinería
- trabajar en un restaurante
- limpiar casas
- trabajar en un supermercado
- pintar casas
- trabajar en una oficina
- reparar autos
- trabajar en una tienda

6 Tus vacaciones de verano

Escribe un ensayo en español de uno o dos párrafos sobre tus planes para las vacaciones. Di qué actividades piensas hacer, con quién las piensas hacer, cuál es la actividad que más te gusta hacer durante el verano, etc. Añade detalles relevantes asociados con cada actividad, como por ejemplo, cuándo piensas hacer la actividad, en dónde, por cuánto tiempo, etc.

7 Otra encuesta

Haz la siguiente encuesta a diez compañeros(as) de clase para averiguar cuáles son las actividades favoritas de tus compañeros(as) durante el verano. Hazte la encuesta a ti mismo y luego a tus compañeros(as). Añade otras actividades a la encuesta si es necesario. Después, en grupos de cuatro o cinco estudiantes compartan los resultados. Finalmente, reporten los resultados del grupo a la clase.

Encuesta sobre las actividades favoritas durante el verano

Por cada una de las siguientes actividades di el número que representa mejor tu opinión.

dormir	0	1	2	3	4
hacer deportes	0	1	2	3	4
hacer quehaceres	0	1	2	3	4
ir a la playa	0	1	2	3	4
ir al centro comercial	0	1	2	3	4
ir al cine	0	1	2	3	4
jugar a videojuegos	0	1	2	3	4
leer	0	1	2	3	4
nadar en una piscina	0	1	2	3	4
navegar en la internet	0	1	2	3	4
ver la televisión	0	1	2	3	4
viajar	0	1	2	3	4
(¿otras?) _____	0	1	2	3	4

0 = No sé. No tengo una opinión.
1 = Es horrible. Me disgusta mucho.
2 = Es aburrida. No me gusta mucho.
3 = Es buena. Me gusta.
4 = Es excelente. Me gusta mucho.

Notes **Communities.** Activities 5, 10 and 11 provide the basis for a class discussion about career options and work opportunities that students have available to them because of their Spanish skills.

8 Las próximas vacaciones

Trabajando en los mismos grupos de la actividad anterior, creen un collage que represente las actividades favoritas del grupo durante las vacaciones y luego, preséntenlo a la clase.

9 Un proyecto en la internet

Trabajando en grupos de tres a cinco estudiantes, busquen información en la internet sobre algún lugar en un país hispanohablante adonde les gustaría ir de vacaciones. Luego, preparen un póster sobre el lugar, indicando las principales actividades que se pueden hacer allí y creando un slogan para decir por qué creen Uds. que este lugar es el mejor para ir de vacaciones. Finalmente, presenten el póster a la clase.

10 ¿Qué te gustaría ser?

Numera del 1 al 12 las siguientes profesiones en el orden de tu preferencia, siendo la número 1 la que más te gusta y la número 12 la que menos te gusta. Luego, en grupos de tres, compara los resultados de cada persona. Explica por qué crees que ciertas carreras y profesiones son más populares que otras, considerando el salario, los beneficios, las condiciones de trabajo, el horario, etc. Reporta los resultados de tu grupo a la clase.

agricultor/a
arquitecto/a
artista
banquero/a
cocinero/a
enfermero/a

hombre/mujer
 de negocios
ingeniero/a
maestro/a
médico/a
programador/a
veterinario/a

¡Oportunidades!

Pensando en el futuro, las carreras y el español
You are already aware that knowing how to communicate in a foreign language can enhance your career *(carrera)* opportunities. The following are some interesting careers requiring foreign language expertise that you may want to consider investigating:

border patrol agent
court interpreter
customer service representative
foreign broadcaster
foreign diplomat
hotel sales manager
imported clothing merchandiser

journalist
language
  teacher
lawyer
travel
  agent

11 Tu futuro

Escribe uno o dos párrafos en español sobre la carrera que te gustaría estudiar. En tu composición, debes decir por qué te gustaría estudiar esa carrera y qué características piensas que tienes y son importantes para poder trabajar en esa profesión.

Notes Extend activities 8 and 9 by having students summarize their work in writing.

Communities. Try to locate someone in your community who uses Spanish in his or her job and ask the person to speak to the class. Be sure to have students prepare questions in advance to keep the discussion going.

Review some of the writing strategies students have learned over the course of the year. Encourage students to apply as many of these strategies as possible in the composition for activity 11.

Teacher Resources

 Activities 5–6

 Activities 4–5

 Activity 4

 Activities 6–7

Answers

8 Creative self-expression.
9 Creative self-expression.
10 Creative self-expression.
11 Creative writing practice.

Activities

Communities

Suggest to students that they talk with their parents about ways they may use Spanish and communication skills they have developed during the year to volunteer in the community. Over the summer, students may decide to volunteer at the local library, using Spanish with Spanish-speaking customers. Start a class discussion of other ways students may be able to participate in community service.

Multiple Intelligences (interpersonal/intrapersonal/ linguistic)

Begin a discussion about how students intend to use Spanish in the future. Ask questions and let them express thoughts about places they would like to visit, careers they are now considering and contributions they will be able to make to their community because they know Spanish.

Answers

12 1. En Guatemala viven 6 millones de mayas.
2. El libro sagrado de los mayas quichés se llama el Popol Vuh.
3. La blusa que usan las mujeres mayas se llama el huipil.
4. Los días de mercado en Chichicastenango son los jueves y los domingos.
5. El mercado de Chichicastenango es interesante porque se presencia la cultura maya: los trajes coloridos, las diferentes lenguas, los rituales.

13 Answers will vary.

Activities

Expansion
Ask students to summarize what they have learned to date about Guatemala. Then conduct a class discussion about places in Guatemala and elsewhere in the Spanish-speaking world that they would like to visit.

Lectura personal

Cantantes y grupos musicales

Dirección http://www.emcp.com/músico/ola/e.diario-4.htm ▲ Archivo Edición Ver Favoritos Herramientas Ayuda

página principal | miembros | e-diario

Grupo musical La OLA

Nombre: Ceci Eugenia Madrigal
Edad: 18 años
País natal: Uruguay
Pasatiempos: dormir, comer, escuchar música

Mercado de Chichicastenango.

Iglesia de San Tomás, Chichicastenango.

El domingo, tempranito por la mañana, tomamos un bus de la Ciudad de Guatemala a Chichicastenango. Nosotros hemos viajado[1] mucho este año y hemos visto[2] muchos mercados pero ninguno como el mercado de Chichicastenango. Es más que un mercado: es un impresionante espectáculo de colores, sonidos y aromas. Miles de indígenas de la región llegan al mercado cada jueves y domingo a vender, comprar, hablar, comer, reír, regatear. Chichicastenango se distingue por sus tejidos[3], particularmente el huipil, blusa femenina de los mayas. Yo me compré una muy colorida y después fui a la plaza. Allí está la iglesia[4] de San Tomás, construída[5] en 1540. Fue en esta iglesia donde un español vio por primera vez el Popul Vuh, el libro sagrado[6] de los mayas quichés. Aunque[7] es una iglesia católica, muchas de las ceremonias y los rituales son mayas. En las escaleras, vi a un hombre maya quemar[8] incienso[9]. En Guatemala viven 6 millones de mayas y hablan 20 lenguas mayas. Presenciar[10] la cultura maya fue una gran manera de concluir nuestra gira mundial.

[1]have traveled   [2]have seen   [3]weavings   [4]church   [5]built   [6]sacred   [7]Although   [8]burn   [9]incense   [10]To witness

12 ¿Qué recuerdas?

1. ¿Cuántos mayas viven en Guatemala?
2. ¿Cómo se llama el libro sagrado de los mayas quichés?
3. ¿Cómo se llama la blusa que usan la mujeres mayas?
4. ¿Cuáles son los días de mercado en Chichicastenango?
5. ¿Por qué es el mercado de Chichicastenango interesante?

• Compare the market in Chichicastenango with a place in your town where people go to buy, talk, eat, laugh. What are the similarities? What are the differences?

13 Algo personal

1. ¿Hay un mercado en tu comunidad? ¿Qué venden allí?
2. ¿Existe una cultura indígena en tu comunidad? ¿Cómo es su traje tradicional?
3. ¿Cuándo fue la última vez que oliste incienso? ¿Dónde fue?

198 *ciento noventa y ocho* **Lección B**

Notes **Connections.** This activity makes cross-curricular connections to geography and history.

The embroidered garments that are worn by the Maya today have a signature pattern that identifies them as members of a particular community. Each village has a characteristic woven or embroidered design. Often these ornate designs form a cross when the blouse or shirt is open and flat. The cross shape represents eternal life and the four cardinal points, the four winds and the four phases of the moon.

¿Qué aprendí?

Autoevaluación

As a review and self-check, respond to the following:

Visit the web-based activities at www.emcp.com

1. Where is Tikal?

2. State four things you learned about Guatemala.

3. Tell what you are going to do this summer. Say where you are going to go, whom you are going to be with and what you are going to do there.

4. Summarize the results of the survey you did about favorite summer activities for Activity 7.

5. Name a place in a Spanish-speaking country you would like to go for vacation. Why would you like to go there?

6. Name three careers that may be open to you because you know Spanish.

7. What do you know about Chichicastenango?

Tikal, Guatemala.

Venden artesanías en Guatemala.

Mercado de Chichicastenango, Guatemala.

Capítulo 10

ciento noventa y nueve **199**

Notes Rigoberta Menchú and Miguel Ángel Asturias are two well-known Guatemalans. Menchú is an advocate for the indigenous people of her country and the winner of the 1992 Nobel Peace Prize; Asturias received the Nobel Prize in literature in 1967.

The currency of Guatemala is the *quetzal*, which is also a typical bird of the region.

Teacher Resources

Activities 6–8

Activity 5

Information Gap Activities
Postcard Activities
Funciones de Comunicación

Answers

Autoevaluación
Possible answers:
1. Está en Guatemala.
2–7. Answers will vary.

Activities

Pronunciation (*las letras* d y t)
The letter *d* is similar in Spanish and in English, but in Spanish the tip of the tongue touches the inside of the upper front teeth, not the palate. Have students try these words: *damas, deber, décimo, deportista, desde, día, dibujar, donde.* After a vowel, *d* is pronounced much like the *th* in the English word **mother.** Have students practice the sound by saying these words: *nublado, poder, rápidamente, todavía, vida, usted.* The Spanish *t* is also formed by touching the tip of the tongue to the inside of the upper front teeth. The sound is much like the *t* in the English word **stop.** Students can practice the sound by saying the following words: *continuar, estación, carta, tener, tiempo, tonto.*

199

*Es sólo una cuestión
de actitud*

¡Viento en popa!

Tú lees

Conexión con otras disciplinas: música

Estrategia

Strategy summary
You have learned several ways of understanding different types of Spanish narratives. You know how to use cognates, you have learned to anticipate possible vocabulary and you have learned to gather information by skimming the content before starting to read. Use these techniques to read *Es sólo una cuestión de actitud* sung by La Ola.

Preparación
Contesta las siguientes preguntas como preparación para la lectura de la canción.

1. ¿Qué crees que quiere decir el título de la canción?
2. ¿Cuál es el tema principal de la canción?

Es sólo una cuestión[1] de actitud

Por Fito Páez

Es sólo una cuestión de actitud,
si lo cuentas no se cumple el deseo[2].
Es sólo una cuestión de actitud,
caballero, ¿me podría[3] dar fuego[4]?

Es sólo una cuestión de actitud
atreverse[5] a desplazarse[6] en el tiempo.
Es sólo una cuestión de actitud
entender[7] lo que está escrito en el viento.

Es sólo una cuestión de actitud
ir con taco aguja[8] en pista de hielo[9].
Es sólo una cuestión de actitud
recibir los golpes[10], no tener miedo.

Es sólo una cuestión de actitud
y no quejarse[11] más de todo, por cierto.
Es sólo una cuestión de actitud
atreverse a atravesar[12] el desierto[13].

Notes The song *Es sólo una cuestión de actitud* has been recorded and is included in the Audio CD Program. Consider playing the recording as students follow the words in the *Tú lees*.

Hay un pozo profundo[14] en la esquina[15] del sol, si caés[16], la vida te muele a palos[17].

Tengo rabia[18], que todo se pase y adiós mis peleas[19] por estar a tu lado.

Cuando vos decidís elegir[20] la razón yo prefiero siempre un poco de caos.

Soy tu rey[21], soy tu perro, soy tu esclavo[22] y soy tu amor,

soy tu espejo[23] mirando el otro lado.

Es sólo una cuestión de actitud reírse[24] del fracaso[25] y del oro.

Es sólo una cuestión de actitud no tener nada y tenerlo todo.

Es sólo una cuestión de actitud y nunca nadie sabe nunca nada, para colmo[26].

Es sólo una cuestión de actitud, espada[27], capa[28], torero[29] y toro[30].

[1]It's only a matter of   [2]the wish will not come true   [3]could   [4]light   [5]to dare   [6]to travel   [7]understand   [8]stiletto heels   [9]ice arena   [10]receive a beating   [11]not complain   [12]to cross   [13]the desert   [14]deep well   [15]corner   [16]if you fall   [17]life gives you a beating   [18]I am mad   [19]fights   [20]to choose   [21]king   [22]slave   [23]mirror   [24]to laugh   [25]failure   [26]to top it all off   [27]sword   [28]cape   [29]bullfighter   [30]bull

A ¿Qué recuerdas?

Completa las frases de la izquierda con una de las frases de la derecha, según la canción *Es sólo una cuestión de actitud*.

1. si lo cuentas...
2. caballero,...
3. atreverse a...
4. entender...
5. recibir los golpes,...
6. Tengo rabia,...
7. soy tu espejo...
8. reírse...

A. ...¿me podría dar fuego?
B. ...lo que está escrito en el viento
C. ...mirando el otro lado
D. ...que todo se pase y adiós
E. ...no se cumple el deseo
F. ...desplazarse en el tiempo
G. ...del fracaso y del oro
H. ...no tener miedo

B Algo personal

1. ¿Qué piensas de esta canción? ¿Te gusta? Explica.
2. ¿Piensas que en la vida todo es cuestión de actitud? Explica.
3. ¿Qué actitud puedes cambiar hoy para hacer tu vida mejor?
4. ¿Te gustan las canciones con mensajes para pensar? ¿Por qué sí? ¿Por qué no?

Teacher Resources

  Activity B

Answers

A 1. E; 2. A; 3. F; 4. B; 5. H; 6. D; 7. C; 8. G
B Answers will vary.

Activities

Pronunciation (*las letras* ca, co, cu, que *y* qui)
Practice the sound of the letter combinations *ca, co, cu, que* and *qui* by noting for students that the English sound of the consonant *k*, just like the sound of *p*, is explosive: that is, if you hold your hand over your mouth when you pronounce them, you will feel a slight puff of air. Note, however, that in Spanish this does not occur. Have students say and compare the English words **café, capital, card, kiss** and **quality** with the Spanish words *cada, cocina, cuarto, que* and *quince*, which begin with a similar sound, but without the puff of air that occurs in the English words. To help students who are experiencing difficulty avoiding the explosive burst of air, have them repeat *tatatata*, then *cocococo*, until they are able to say *taco* without the puff of air. Then have students practice the following sentences: *¿Quién está comiendo en el comedor?; No sé, pero Carlota está comiendo coco en la cocina.*

Notes Rodolfo "Fito" Páez (born in Rosario, Argentina) is the composer of this song. He is very famous throughout the Spanish-speaking world. Fito started his first rock band (Staff) during his teen years. His songs and lyrics have been popular for more than thirty years and both new and old Hispanic rock bands often borrow his materials.

Expansion

Give students this additional example of an acrostic poem and have them try to write their own poem following the model:

Moreno y muy romántico,
Artístico, mis amigos me describen.
Responsable y cooperativo con
mis maestros.
Impulsivo, cómico y popular con
mis compañeros.
Optimista de mi carrera de
artista gráfico.

Multiple Intelligences (linguistic/spatial)

Have artistic students create an interesting visual for the poem about Mario mentioned in the preceding ATE activity. They might rewrite the poem in the center of a collage of items, either cut from newspapers and magazines or hand drawn, that depict some aspect of the poem (for example, artist's supplies like paintbrushes, graphic pens).

Tú escribes

Estrategia

Defining your purpose for writing
Before you begin a writing assignment, it is a good idea to identify your purpose. Then keep your purpose in mind throughout the writing process as you brainstorm your topic, formulate your rough draft and edit your finished product.

The purpose of this writing assignment is to describe yourself, using the format of an acrostic poem. In an acrostic poem, certain letters of each line spell out the letters of a specific word the author has in mind.

Use the letters of your name or nickname, in their correct order, as your acrostic word. Design the pattern for placing a letter of your name in each line. For instance, you might choose to highlight the first letter of each line, the first letter of the last word in each line, etc.

Then, in the lines, include some personal information you have learned this year to describe your personality, your appearance and your preferences. Also, work in some information about what you are going to do in the future. Be sure to make the letters of your acrostic word stand out in the poem (as was done in the poem on this page). Finally, you may wish to accompany your poem with artwork or graphics to make it more visually appealing.

> Juego al fútbol, al básquetbol, y mucho más.
> Soy un jugador, fuerte y rápido.
> Quiero jugar al fútbol profesional algún día.
> Las matemáticas, no me gustan ni un poquito.

Notes Inform students how you will be grading their poems.

Allow some time for students to recite their poems in front of the class. You might ask students to vote for the best work as they would in a poetry slam or competition.

Proyectos adicionales

A Conexión con la tecnología

Prepare an electronic survey about favorite careers or jobs, using an e-mail or a Web page similar to the surveys you completed in this chapter. Ask another class (preferably in a different state or country) to complete the survey and send the results back to you via Internet. Share the information with your classmates, comparing and contrasting the results of your survey.

B Conexión con otras disciplinas: música

Working in pairs, find a song in any language you like. Using the music for the song, create lyrics in Spanish about some aspect of your life (school, vacations, family, etc.). Sing the song to the class.

C Conexión cultural

In groups of three to five students, research a group or culture that is native to your state or region. Find out the name of the group, where they lived, their social activities, number of inhabitants and where any ruins or remains may be found. Share the results with another group of students (a class in another region of the world, for example) and request the same information about civilizations that inhabited their region of the world.

Un indígena de North Dakota.

Ruinas de un pueblo de los Anasazi, indígenas de norteamérica.
(Mesa Verde National Park, Colorado, U.S.A.)

Answers

A Creative self-expression.
B Creative self-expression.
C Creative self-expression.

Activities

Critical Thinking
Have students complete a culture project in which they look back on the countries studied this year and make a collage that reflects what they have learned about one or more of the nations. A possible theme for the collage is *Mirando hacia el pasado.*

Multiple Intelligences (interpersonal/linguistic/ logical-mathematical/spatial)
In groups of four, students should decide what are the main contributions of the Mayas, Aztecs and Incas. Then have them create posters showing the contributions.

Notes Activities A, B and C provide opportunities in keeping with the philosophy and goals of *Navegando 1* for students as they become lifelong learners. These activities encourage students to learn about communities in the world where Spanish is spoken and to begin to make comparisons between the student's background knowledge and the reality of life in the Spanish-speaking world. In addition, students are invited to use what they have learned in Spanish class to establish connections with their neighborhood and with the larger world community.

203

Activities

Expansion

Review adjective-noun agreement by having students write a composition describing a favorite relative. The composition should address the person's personality, appearance and typical activities. Encourage students to include a photo or drawing of the relative as well.

Repaso

Now that I have completed this chapter, I can...

	Go to these pages for help:
discuss past actions and events.	188
talk about everyday activities.	188
express emotion.	194
indicate wishes and preferences.	194
write about past actions.	194
talk about the future.	197
make polite requests.	197
describe personal characteristics.	202

I can also...

talk about Peru and Guatemala.	189, 195
research a topic in the library and on the Internet.	189
name some personal benefits to learning Spanish.	189
recognize some benefits to reviewing what I have already learned.	190
recognize the importance of reviewing what I have learned.	190
talk about Machu Picchu and Chichicastenango.	192, 198
identify some careers that use Spanish.	197
express myself artistically about what I have learned.	202

Trabalenguas

Pedro Pérez pide permiso para partir para París, para ponerse peluca postiza porque parece puerco pelado.

Notes Students can find out more about Peru by visiting these Web sites:

Organization of American States
http://www.oas.org
Peru Gateway
http://www.peru-explorer.com
PromPerú   http://www.peru.org.pe

general information
http://www.expedia.com

Loose translation of the *Trabalenguas*:
Pedro Pérez asks for permission to leave for Paris, to get a wig since he looks like a hairless pig.

204

Café de Colombia.

¡Vamos a esquiar!

El Angelito, México, D.F.

Mi nombre es Panamá.

My name is Panama.

INSTITUTO PANAMEÑO DE TURISMO

El Morro, San Juan, Puerto Rico.

El viaje a Guatemala

Module 4

Episode 10

Testing/Assessment

Test Booklet
Portfolio Assessment

Activities

Communities
Ask students if they know people who use a foreign language in their professions. Encourage students to interview these individuals and share their findings with the class.

Expansion
Ask students personalized questions that require them to practice forms of *tener que* (they may make up any answers they wish): *¿Qué tienes que hacer hoy?*; *¿Qué tienes que hacer mañana?*; *¿Qué tienes que hacer este fin de semana?*

Spanish for Spanish Speakers
Have students write a short composition in Spanish summarizing what they know about Peru. Expand the activity by having students seek out additional information about the country on the Internet and at the library.

Notes Students can find out more about Guatemala by visiting these Web sites:

Organization of American States
http://www.oas.org
Visita Guatemala
http://www.terra.com.gt/turismogt/
general information
http://www.expedia.com/

Appendices

Appendix A

Grammar Review

Definite articles

	Singular	Plural
Masculine	el	los
Feminine	la	las

Indefinite articles

	Singular	Plural
Masculine	un	unos
Feminine	una	unas

Adjective/noun agreement

	Singular	Plural
Masculine	El chico es alto.	Los chicos son altos.
Feminine	La chica es alta.	Las chicas son altas.

Pronouns

Singular	Subject	Direct object	Indirect object	Object of preposition
1st person	yo	me	me	mí
2nd person	tú	te	te	ti
	Ud.	lo/la	le	Ud.
3rd person	él	lo	le	él
	ella	la	le	ella
Plural				
1st person	nosotros	nos	nos	nosotros
	nosotras	nos	nos	nosotras
2nd person	vosotros	os	os	vosotros
	vosotras	os	os	vosotras
3rd person	Uds.	los/las	les	Uds.
	ellos	los	les	ellos
	ellas	las	les	ellas

Interrogatives

qué	*what*
cómo	*how*
dónde	*where*
cuándo	*when*
cuánto, -a, -os, -as	*how much, how many*
cuál/cuáles	*which (one)*
quién/quiénes	*who, whom*
por qué	*why*
para qué	*why, what for*

Demonstrative adjectives

Singular		Plural	
Masculine	**Feminine**	**Masculine**	**Feminine**
este	esta	estos	estas
ese	esa	esos	esas
aquel	aquella	aquellos	aquellas

Possessive adjectives

Singular	Singular nouns	Plural nouns
1st person	mi hermano mi hermana	mis hermanos mis hermanas
2nd person	tu hermano tu hermana	tus hermanos tus hermanas
3rd person	su hermano su hermana	sus hermanos sus hermanas

Plural	Singular nouns	Plural nouns
1st person	nuestro hermano nuestra hermana	nuestros hermanos nuestras hermanas
2nd person	vuestro hermano vuestra hermana	vuestros hermanos vuestras hermanas
3rd person	su hermano su hermana	sus hermanos sus hermanas

Appendix B

Verbs

Present tense (indicative)

Regular present tense		
hablar *(to speak)*	hablo hablas habla	hablamos habláis hablan
comer *(to eat)*	como comes come	comemos coméis comen
escribir *(to write)*	escribo escribes escribe	escribimos escribís escriben

Preterite tense (indicative)

hablar *(to speak)*	hablé hablaste habló	hablamos hablasteis hablaron
comer *(to eat)*	comí comiste comió	comimos comisteis comieron
escribir *(to write)*	escribí escribiste escribió	escribimos escribisteis escribieron

Present participle

The present participle is formed by replacing the *-ar* of the infinitive with *-ando* and the *-er* or *-ir* with *-iendo*.

hablar	hablando
comer	comiendo
vivir	viviendo

Progressive tenses

The present participle is used with the verbs *estar, continuar, seguir, andar* and some other motion verbs to produce the progressive tenses. They are reserved for recounting actions that are or were in progress at the time in question.

Present tense of stem-changing verbs

Stem-changing verbs are identified in this book by the presence of vowels in parentheses after the infinitive. If these verbs end in *-ar* or *-er*, they have only one change. If they end in *-ir*, they have two changes. The stem change of *-ar* and *-er* verbs and the first stem change of *-ir* verbs occur in all forms of the present tense, except *nosotros* and *vosotros*.

cerrar (ie) *(to close)*	e → ie	cierro cierras cierra	cerramos cerráis cierran

Verbs like **cerrar:** calentar *(to heat)*, comenzar *(to begin)*, despertar *(to wake up)*, despertarse *(to awaken)*, empezar *(to begin)*, encerrar *(to lock up)*, nevar *(to snow)*, pensar *(to think)*, recomendar *(to recommend)*, sentarse *(to sit down)*

contar (ue) (to tell)	o → ue	cuento cuentas cuenta	contamos contáis cuentan

Verbs like **contar:** acordar *(to agree)*, acordarse *(to remember)*, almorzar *(to have lunch)*, colgar *(to hang)*, costar *(to cost)*, demostrar *(to demonstrate)*, encontrar *(to find, to meet someone)*, probar *(to taste, to try)*, recordar *(to remember)*

jugar (ue) (to play)	u → ue	juego juegas juega	jugamos jugáis juegan

perder (ie) (to lose)	e → ie	pierdo pierdes pierde	perdemos perdéis pierden

Verbs like **perder:** defender *(to defend)*, descender *(to descend, to go down)*, encender *(to light, to turn on)*, entender *(to understand)*, extender *(to extend)*, tender *(to spread out)*

volver (ue) (to return)	o → ue	vuelvo vuelves vuelve	volvemos volvéis vuelven

Verbs like **volver:** devolver *(to return something)*, doler *(to hurt)*, llover *(to rain)*, morder *(to bite)*, mover *(to move)*, resolver *(to resolve)*, soler *(to be in the habit of)*, torcer *(to twist)*

pedir (i, i) (to ask for)	e → i	pido pides pide	pedimos pedís piden

Verbs like **pedir:** conseguir *(to obtain, to attain, to get)*, despedirse *(to say good-bye)*, elegir *(to choose, to elect)*, medir *(to measure)*, perseguir *(to pursue)*, repetir *(to repeat)*

sentir (ie, i) (to feel)	e → ie	siento sientes siente	sentimos sentís sienten

Verbs like **sentir:** advertir *(to warn)*, arrepentirse *(to regret)*, convertir *(to convert)*, convertirse *(to become)*, divertirse *(to have fun)*, herir *(to wound)*, invertir *(to invest)*, mentir *(to lie)*, preferir *(to prefer)*, requerir *(to require)*, sugerir *(to suggest)*

dormir (ue, u) (to sleep)	o → ue	duermo duermes duerme	dormimos dormís duermen

Another verb like **dormir:** morir *(to die)*

Present participle of stem-changing verbs

Stem-changing verbs that end in -*ir* use the second stem change in the present participle.

dormir (ue, u)	durmiendo
seguir (i, i)	siguiendo
sentir (ie, i)	sintiendo

Preterite tense of stem-changing verbs

Stem-changing verbs that end in *-ar* and *-er* are regular in the preterite tense. That is, they do not require a spelling change, and they use the regular preterite endings.

pensar (ie)	
pensé	pensamos
pensaste	pensasteis
pensó	pensaron

volver (ue)	
volví	volvimos
volviste	volvisteis
volvió	volvieron

Stem-changing verbs ending in *-ir* change their third-person forms in the preterite tense, but they still require the regular preterite endings.

sentir (ie, i)	
sentí	sentimos
sentiste	sentisteis
sintió	sintieron

dormir (ue, u)	
dormí	dormimos
dormiste	dormisteis
durmió	durmieron

Verbs with irregularities

The following charts provide some frequently used Spanish verbs with irregularities.

buscar *(to look for)*	
preterite	busqué, buscaste, buscó, buscamos, buscasteis, buscaron
Similar to:	explicar *(to explain)*, sacar *(to take out)*, tocar *(to touch, to play an instrument)*

dar *(to give)*	
present	doy, das, da, damos, dais, dan
preterite	di, diste, dio, dimos, disteis, dieron

decir *(to say, to tell)*	
present	digo, dices, dice, decimos, decís, dicen
preterite	dije, dijiste, dijo, dijimos, dijisteis, dijeron
present participle	diciendo

enviar *(to send)*	
present	envío, envías, envía, enviamos, enviáis, envían
Similar to:	esquiar *(to ski)*

estar *(to be)*	
present	estoy, estás, está, estamos, estáis, están
preterite	estuve, estuviste, estuvo, estuvimos, estuvisteis, estuvieron

hacer *(to do, to make)*	
present	hago, haces, hace, hacemos, hacéis, hacen
preterite	hice, hiciste, hizo, hicimos, hicisteis, hicieron

ir *(to go)*	
present	voy, vas, va, vamos, vais, van
preterite	fui, fuiste, fue, fuimos, fuisteis, fueron
present participle	yendo

leer (to read)

preterite	leí, leíste, leyó, leímos, leísteis, leyeron
present participle	leyendo

llegar (to arrive)

preterite	llegué, llegaste, llegó, llegamos, llegasteis, llegaron
Similar to:	colgar (to hang), pagar (to pay)

oír (to hear, to listen)

present	oigo, oyes, oye, oímos, oís, oyen
preterite	oí, oíste, oyó, oímos, oísteis, oyeron
present participle	oyendo

poder (to be able)

present	puedo, puedes, puede, podemos, podéis, pueden
preterite	pude, pudiste, pudo, pudimos, pudisteis, pudieron
present participle	pudiendo

poner (to put, to place, to set)

present	pongo, pones, pone, ponemos, ponéis, ponen
preterite	puse, pusiste, puso, pusimos, pusisteis, pusieron

querer (to love, to want)

present	quiero, quieres, quiere, queremos, queréis, quieren
preterite	quise, quisiste, quiso, quisimos, quisisteis, quisieron

saber (to know)

present	sé, sabes, sabe, sabemos, sabéis, saben
preterite	supe, supiste, supo, supimos, supisteis, supieron

salir (to go out, to leave)

present	salgo, sales, sale, salimos, salís, salen

ser (to be)

present	soy, eres, es, somos, sois, son
preterite	fui, fuiste, fue, fuimos, fuisteis, fueron

tener (to have)

present	tengo, tienes, tiene, tenemos, tenéis, tienen
preterite	tuve, tuviste, tuvo, tuvimos, tuvisteis, tuvieron

traer (to bring)

present	traigo, traes, trae, traemos, traéis, traen
preterite	traje, trajiste, trajo, trajimos, trajisteis, trajeron
present participle	trayendo

venir (to come)	
present	vengo, vienes, viene, venimos, venís, vienen
preterite	vine, viniste, vino, vinimos, vinisteis, vinieron
present participle	viniendo

ver (to see, to watch)	
present	veo, ves, ve, vemos, veis, ven
preterite	vi, viste, vio, vimos, visteis, vieron

Appendix C

Numbers

Cardinal numbers 0–1.000

0—cero	13—trece	26—veintiséis	90—noventa
1—uno	14—catorce	27—veintisiete	100—cien/ciento
2—dos	15—quince	28—veintiocho	200—doscientos,-as
3—tres	16—dieciséis	29—veintinueve	300—trescientos,-as
4—cuatro	17—diecisiete	30—treinta	400—cuatrocientos,-as
5—cinco	18—dieciocho	31—treinta y uno	500—quinientos,-as
6—seis	19—diecinueve	32—treinta y dos	600—seiscientos,-as
7—siete	20—veinte	33—treinta y tres, etc.	700—setecientos,-as
8—ocho	21—veintiuno	40—cuarenta	800—ochocientos,-as
9—nueve	22—veintidós	50—cincuenta	900—novecientos,-as
10—diez	23—veintitrés	60—sesenta	1.000—mil
11—once	24—veinticuatro	70—setenta	
12—doce	25—veinticinco	80—ochenta	

Ordinal numbers

1—primero,-a (primer)	5—quinto,-a	8—octavo,-a
2—segundo,-a	6—sexto,-a	9—noveno,-a
3—tercero,-a (tercer)	7—séptimo,-a	10—décimo,-a
4—cuarto,-a		

Appendix D

Syllabification

Spanish vowels may be weak or strong. The vowels *a, e* and *o* are strong, whereas *i* (and sometimes *y*) and *u* are weak. The combination of one weak and one strong vowel or of two weak vowels produces a diphthong, two vowels pronounced as one.

A word in Spanish has as many syllables as it has vowels or diphthongs.

> al gu nas
> lue go
> pa la bra

A single consonant (including *ch, ll, rr*) between two vowels accompanies the second vowel and begins a syllable.

> a mi ga
> fa vo ri to
> mu cho

Two consonants are divided, the first going with the previous vowel and the second going with the following vowel.

> an tes
> quin ce
> ter mi nar

A consonant plus *l* or *r* is inseparable except for *rl, sl* and *sr*.

> ma dre
> pa la bra
> com ple tar
> Car los
> is la

If three consonants occur together, the last, or any inseparable combination, accompanies the following vowel to begin another syllable.

> es cri bir
> som bre ro
> trans por te

Prefixes should remain intact.

> re es cri bir

Appendix E

Accentuation

Words that end in *a, e, i, o, u, n* or *s* are pronounced with the major stress on the next-to-the-last syllable. No accent mark is needed to show this emphasis.

> octubre
> refresco
> señora

Words that end in any consonant except *n* or *s* are pronounced with the major stress on the last syllable. No accent mark is needed to show this emphasis.

> escribir
> papel
> reloj

Words that are not pronounced according to the above two rules must have a written accent mark.

> lógico
> canción
> después
> lápiz

An accent mark may be necessary to distinguish identical words with different meanings.

> dé/de
> qué/que
> sí/si
> sólo/solo

An accent mark is often used to divide a diphthong into two separate syllables.

> día
> frío
> Raúl

Vocabulary Spanish / English

All active words introduced in *NAVEGANDO 1* appear in this end vocabulary. The number and letter following an entry indicate the lesson in which an item is first actively used. Additional words and expressions are included for reference and have no number. Obvious cognates and expressions that occur as passive vocabulary for recognition only have been excluded from this end vocabulary.

Abbreviations:
d.o. direct object
f. feminine
i.o. indirect object
m. masculine
pl. plural
s. singular

A

a to, at, in *2B; a caballo* on horseback *3A; a crédito* on credit *9B; a pie* on foot *3A; a propósito* by the way *1A; ¿a qué hora?* at what time? *2B; a veces* sometimes, at times *5B; a ver* let's see, hello (telephone greeting)

abierto,-a open *4A*

abran: see *abrir*

el **abrazo** hug *6B*

abre: see *abrir*

la **abreviatura** abbreviation

el **abrigo** coat *8A*

abril April *5B*

abrir to open *5A; abran (Uds.* command) open; *abre (tú* command) open

la **abuela** grandmother *4A*

el **abuelo** grandfather *4A*

aburrido,-a bored, boring *4B*

acabar to finish, to complete, to terminate *8A; acabar de* (+ infinitive) to have just *8A*

el **aceite** oil *6A*

la **aceituna** olive

el **acento** accent *1A*

la **acentuación** accentuation

aclarar to make clear, to explain

la **actividad** activity *5A*, exercise

el **acuerdo** accord; *de acuerdo* agreed, okay *3B*

adiós good-bye *1A*

el **adjetivo** adjective; *adjetivo posesivo* possessive adjective

¿adónde? (to) where? *3A*

adoptar to adopt

adornar to decorate *8A*

el **adverbio** adverb

los **aeróbicos** aerobics *7A*

el **aeropuerto** airport

la **agencia** agency; *agencia de viajes* travel agency

agosto August *5B*

el **agricultor** farmer

el **agua** *f.* water *3B; agua mineral* mineral water *3B*

el **aguacate** avocado *8B*

ahora now *3B; ahora mismo* right now *7A*

ahorrar to save *9B*

el **ajedrez** chess *7A*

el **ajo** garlic *8B*

al to the *3A; al lado de* next to, beside *6B*

alegre happy, merry, lively

el **alfabeto** alphabet

el **álgebra** algebra

algo something, anything *8A*

el **algodón** cotton *9A*

alguien someone, anyone, somebody, anybody *9A*

algún, alguna some, any *9A*

alguno,-a some, any *9A*

allá over there *6A*

allí there *2B*

la **almeja** clam

el **almuerzo** lunch *2B*

aló hello (telephone greeting) *2B*

alquilar to rent *7A*

alterna alternate (*tú* command)

alternen alternate (*Uds.* command)

alto,-a tall, high *4B*

amable kind, nice *4A*

amarillo,-a yellow *2B*

ambiguo,-a ambiguous

la **América** America; *América Central* Central America; *América del Sur* South America

americano,-a American *7A; el fútbol americano* football *7A*

el **amigo,** la **amiga** friend *2A; amigo/a por correspondencia* pen pal

el **amor** love *5A*

anaranjado,-a orange (color) *9A*

andino,-a Andean, of the Andes Mountains

el **anillo** ring *9B*

anteayer the day before yesterday *5B*

anterior preceding

antes de before *7A*

añade: see *añadir*

añadir to add *8B; añade (tú* command) add

el **año** year *5B; Año Nuevo* New Year's Day *5B; ¿Cuántos años tienes?* How old are you? *1A; tener* (+ number) *años* to be (+ number) years old *5A*

apagar to turn off *7A*

el **apartamento** apartment

el **apellido** last name, surname

el **apodo** nickname

aprender to learn
apropiado,-a appropriate
apunta: see *apuntar*
apuntar to point; *apunta (tú command)* point (at); *apunten (Uds. command)* point (at)
apunten: see *apuntar*
apurado,-a in a hurry *4A*
aquel, aquella that (far away) *6A*
aquellos, aquellas those (far away) *6A*
aquí here *1A; Aquí se habla español.* Spanish is spoken here.
el **árbol** tree; *árbol genealógico* family tree
el **arete** earring *9B*
la **Argentina** Argentina *1A*
arreglar to arrange, to straighten, to fix *8A*
arroba (@) at *(the symbol (@) used for e-mail addresses) 2B*
el **arroz** rice *8B*
el **arte** art *2B*
el **artesanía** handicrafts, artisanry
el **artículo** article *5A*
el **artista** artist
el **ascensor** elevator *9B*
la **asignatura** subject
la **aspiradora** vacuum *7A; pasar la aspiradora* to vacuum *8A*
el **Atlántico** Atlantic Ocean
la **atracción** attraction
aunque although
el **autobús** bus *3A*
la **avenida** avenue *3B*
aventurero,-a adventurous
el **avión** airplane *3A*
¡ay! oh! *2A*
ayer yesterday *5B*
la **ayuda** help
ayudar to help *6A*
el **azafrán** saffron
los **aztecas** Aztecs
el **azúcar** sugar *6A*
azul blue *2B*

B

bailar to dance *4B*
bajo,-a short (not tall), low *4B; planta baja* floor level *6B*
balanceado,-a balanced
el **baloncesto** basketball
el **banco** bank *3A*
el **baño** bathroom *6B; traje de baño* swimsuit *9A*

barato,-a cheap *9B*
el **barco** boat, ship *3A*
barrer to sweep *8A*
el **barril** barrel
basado,-a based
el **básquetbol** basketball *7A*
el **basquetbolista, la basquetbolista** basketball player *7B*
bastante rather, fairly, sufficiently; enough, sufficient *9B*
la **basura** garbage *8A*
la **bebida** drink
el **béisbol** baseball *4B*
la **biblioteca** library *3A*
la **bicicleta** bicycle, bike *3A*
bien well *1B*
bienvenido,-a welcome
la **billetera** wallet *9B*
la **biología** biology *2B*
blanco,-a white *2B*
la **blusa** blouse *2B*
la **boda** wedding
el **bolígrafo** pen *2A*
Bolivia Bolivia *1A*
el **bolo** ball; *jugar a los bolos* to bowl
el **bolso** handbag, purse *9B*
bonito,-a pretty, good-looking, attractive *4A*
borra: see *borrar*
el **borrador** eraser *2A*
borrar to erase; *borra (tú command)* erase; *borren (Uds. command)* erase
borren: see *borrar*
la **bota** boot *9A*
el **brazo** arm *9A*
buen good (form of *bueno* before a *m., s.* noun) *7B*
bueno well, okay (pause in speech) *3B;* hello (telephone greeting)
bueno,-a good *4B; buena suerte* good luck; *buenas noches* good night *1B; buenas tardes* good afternoon *1B; buenos días* good morning *1B*
la **bufanda** scarf *9B*
buscar to look for *5A*

C

el **caballero** gentleman
el **caballo** horse *3A; a caballo* on horseback *3A*

la **cabeza** head *9A*
cada each, every *5A*
el **café** coffee *8B*
la **cafetería** cafeteria
la **caja** cashier's desk *9B*
el **calcetín** sock *2B*
el **calendario** calendar
la **calidad** quality *9B*
caliente hot *4A*
la **calle** street *3B*
el **calor** heat *6B; hace calor* it is hot *7B; tener calor* to be hot *6B*
calvo,-a bald *4B*
la **cama** bed *8A*
el **camarón** shrimp
cambiar to change, to exchange *9B*
el **cambio** change *9B; en cambio* on the other hand *7B*
caminar to walk *3A*
el **camión** truck *3A;* bus (Mexico); *en camión* by truck *3A*
la **camisa** shirt *2B*
la **camiseta** jersey, polo, t-shirt *2B*
la **canción** song *5A*
canoso,-a white-haired *4B*
cansado,-a tired *4A*
el **cantante, la cantante** singer *3B*
cantar to sing *4B*
la **cantidad** quantity
la **capital** capital *1A*
el **capitán** captain
el **capítulo** chapter
la **cara** face
la **característica** characteristic, trait; *características de personalidad* personality traits; *características físicas* physical traits
¡caramba! wow! *5A*
cariñoso,-a affectionate *4A*
el **carnaval** carnival
la **carne** meat *8B*
caro,-a expensive *9B*
la **carrera** career, race
el **carro** car *3A; en carro* by car *3A*
la **carta** letter *6B,* playing card *7A*
la **casa** home, house *4A; en casa* at home
el **casete** cassette *5A*
casi almost *7A*
catorce fourteen *1A*
el **CD** CD (compact disc) *2B*
la **cebolla** onion *8B*
celebrar to celebrate *5B*

el **censo** census
el **centavo** cent
el **centro** downtown, center *3B; centro comercial* shopping center, mall *9A*
cerca (de) near *3A*
cero zero *1A*
cerrado,-a closed *4A*
cerrar (ie) to close *6A; cierra (tú* command) close; *cierren (Uds.* command) close
el **cesto de papeles** wastebasket *2A*
chao bye
la **chaqueta** jacket *9A*
charlando talking, chatting
la **chica** girl *2A*
el **chico** boy *2A*, man, buddy
Chile Chile *1A*
el **chisme** gossip *6B*
el **chocolate** chocolate *8B*
el **chorizo** sausage (seasoned with red peppers) *8B*
el **ciclismo** cycling
cien one hundred *1B*
la **ciencia** science
ciento one hundred (when followed by another number) *5B*
cierra: see *cerrar*
cierren: see *cerrar*
cinco five *1A*
cincuenta fifty *1B*
el **cine** movie theater *3A*
el **cinturón** belt *9B*
la **ciudad** city *3A*
la **civilización** civilization
el **clarinete** clarinet
¡claro! of course! *3A*
la **clase** class *2A*
el **clima** climate
el **coche** car; *en coche* by car
la **cocina** kitchen *6A*
cocinar to cook *8A*
el **cognado** cognate
el **colegio** school *2B*
colgar (ue) to hang *8A*
el **collar** necklace *9B*
Colombia Colombia *1A*
la **colonia** colony
el **color** color *2B*
combinar to combine *9A*
el **comedor** dining room *6A*
comer to eat *3B; dar de comer* to feed *8A*
cómico,-a comical, funny *4B*

la **comida** food *3B*, dinner
como like, since, as
¿cómo? how?, what? *1A; ¿Cómo?* What (did you say)? *2B; ¿Cómo está (Ud.)?* How are you (formal)? *1B; ¿Cómo están (Uds.)?* How are you *(pl.)? 1B; ¿Cómo estás (tú)?* How are you (informal)? *1B; ¡Cómo no!* Of course! *3B; ¿Cómo se dice...?* How do you say...? *2A; ¿Cómo se escribe...?* How do you write (spell)...? *1A; ¿Cómo se llama (Ud./él/ella)?* What is (your/his/her) name? *1A; ¿Cómo te llamas?* What is your name? *2A*
comodidad comfort
cómodo,-a comfortable *6B*
el **compañero**, la **compañera** classmate, partner *5A*
comparando comparing
la **competencia** competition
completa: see *completar*
completar to complete; *completa (tú* command) complete
la **compra** purchase *4B; ir de compras* to go shopping *4B*
comprar to buy *4B*
comprender to understand *2A; comprendo* I understand *2A*
comprendo: see *comprender*
la **computación** computer science *2B*
la **computadora** computer (machine) *2B*
común common
con with *1A; con (mucho) gusto* I would be (very) glad to *1B; con permiso* excuse me (with your permission), may I *1B*
el **concierto** concert *3B*
la **conjunción** conjunction
conmigo with me *9B*
conquistar to conquer
conseguir (i, i) to obtain, to attain, to get
la **contaminación** contamination, pollution; *contaminación ambiental* environmental pollution
contar (ue) to tell (a story) *9A; cuenta (tú* command) tell; *cuenten (Uds.* command) tell; to count

contento,-a happy, glad *4A; estar contento,-a (con)* to be satisfied (with) *4A*
contesta: see *contestar*
contestar to answer *4B; contesta (tú* command) answer; *contesten (Uds.* command) answer
contesten: see *contestar*
el **contexto** context
contigo with you *(tú) 9B*
continúa: see *continuar*
continuar to continue *7B; continúa (tú* command) continue; *continúen (Uds.* command) continue
continúen: see *continuar*
la **contracción** contraction
el **control remoto** remote control *7A*
copiar to copy *7B*
la **corbata** tie *9A*
correcto,-a right, correct
el **corredor**, la **corredora** runner *7B*
el **correo** mail; *correo electrónico* e-mail *2B*
correr to run *6B*
la **cortesía** courtesy
corto,-a short (not long) *9B*
la **cosa** thing *6A*
la **costa** coast
Costa Rica Costa Rica *1A*
costar (ue) to cost *7A*
crear to create
el **crédito** credit *9B; a crédito* on credit *9B; la tarjeta de crédito* credit card *9B*
creer to believe
el **crucero** cruise ship
cruzar to cross
el **cuaderno** notebook *2A*
¿cuál? which?, what?, which one? *(pl. ¿cuáles?)* which ones? *2B*
la **cualidad** quality
cualquier any
cuando when *6B*
¿cuándo? when? *3A*
¿cuánto,-a? how much? *2B (pl. ¿cuántos,-as?)* how many? *2B; ¿Cuántos años tienes?* How old are you? *1A; ¿Cuánto (+* time expression) *hace que (+* present tense of verb)...? How long...? *7A*

cuarenta forty *1B*

el **cuarto** quarter *1B*, room, bedroom *6B*; *cuarto de baño* bathroom; *menos cuarto* a quarter to, a quarter before *1B*; *y cuarto* a quarter after, a quarter past *1B*

cuarto,-a fourth *7B*

cuatro four *1A*

cuatrocientos,-as four hundred *5B*

Cuba Cuba *1A*

los **cubiertos** silverware *6A*

la **cuchara** tablespoon *6A*

la **cucharita** teaspoon *6A*

el **cuchillo** knife *6A*

cuenta: see *contar*

cuenten: see *contar*

el **cuero** leather *9B*

el **cuerpo** body *9A*

cuidar to take care of

el **cumpleaños** birthday *5B*; *¡Feliz cumpleaños!* Happy birthday! *5B*

cumplir to become, to become (+ number) years old, to reach *5B*; *cumplir años* to have a birthday *5B*

la **dama** lady

las **damas** checkers *7A*

dar to give *7A*; *dar de comer* to feed *8A*; *dar un paseo* to go for a walk, to go for a ride *7B*; *dé* (*Ud.* command) give

de from, of *1A*; *de acuerdo* agreed, okay *3B*; *¿de dónde?* from where? *1A*; *¿De dónde eres?* Where are you from? *1A*; *de la mañana* in the morning, A.M. *1B*; *de la noche* at night, P.M. *1B*; *de la tarde* in the afternoon, P.M. *1B*; *de nada* you are welcome, not at all *1B*; *de todos los días* everyday *6A*; *¿de veras?* really? *5B*; *¿Eres (tú) de...?* Are you from...? *1A*

dé: see *dar*

deber should, to have to, must, ought (expressing a moral duty) *6A*

décimo,-a tenth *7B*

decir to tell, to say *6B*; *¿Cómo se dice...?* How do you say...?

2A; *di* (*tú* command) say, tell; *díganme* (*Uds.* command) tell me; *dime* (*tú* command) tell me; *¿Qué quiere decir...?* What is the meaning (of)...? *2A*; *querer decir* to mean *6B*; *quiere decir* it means *2A*; *se dice* one says *2A*

el **dedo** finger, toe *9A*

dejar to leave *8A*

del of the, from the *3A*

delgado,-a thin *4B*

demasiado too (much) *9B*

la **democracia** democracy

el **dentista,** la **dentista** dentist *3A*

el **departamento** department *9A*

el **dependiente,** la **dependienta** clerk *9B*

el **deporte** sport *5A*

el **deportista,** la **deportista** athlete *7B*

desaparecido,-a missing

el **desastre** disaster

el **desayuno** breakfast

describe (*tú* command) describe

descubrir to discover

desde since, from *6B*

desear to wish

el **deseo** wish

la **despedida** farewell

después afterwards, later, then *6A*; *después de* after *7A*

di: see *decir*

el **día** day *2B*; *buenos días* good morning *1B*; *de todos los días* everyday *5A*; *todos los días* every day *5A*

el **diálogo** dialog

diario,-a daily

dibuja: see *dibujar*

dibujar to draw, to sketch *7A*; *dibuja* (*tú* command) draw; *dibujen* (*Uds.* command) draw

dibujen: see *dibujar*

el **dibujo** drawing, sketch *6B*

diciembre December *5B*

el **dictado** dictation

diecinueve nineteen *1A*

dieciocho eighteen *1A*

dieciséis sixteen *1A*

diecisiete seventeen *1A*

diez ten *1A*

la **diferencia** difference

diferente different

difícil difficult, hard *4B*

diga hello (telephone greeting)

dígame tell me, hello (telephone greeting)

díganme: see *decir*

dime: see *decir*

el **dinero** money *5A*

la **dirección** address *2B*; *dirección de correo electrónico* e-mail *2B*

el **director,** la **directora** director

dirigir to direct

el **disco** disc *2B*; *disco compacto (CD)* compact disk *2B*

disfrutar to enjoy

diskette diskette *2B*

divertido,-a fun *4A*

doblar to fold *8A*

doce twelve *1A*

el **doctor,** la **doctora** doctor

el **dólar** dollar

domingo Sunday *2B*; *el domingo* on Sunday

don title of respect used before a man's first name

donde where *6B*

¿dónde? where? *1A*

doña title of respect used before a woman's first name

dormir (ue, u) to sleep *7A*

dos two *1A*

doscientos,-as two hundred *5B*

Dr. abbreviation for *doctor*

Dra. abbreviation for *doctora*

durante during

el **DVD** DVD (digital video disc) *5A*; *el reproductor de DVDs* DVD player *5A*

e and (used before a word beginning with *i* or *hi*) *6B*

la **ecología** ecology

el **Ecuador** Ecuador *1A*

la **edad** age

el **edificio** building *3B*

la **educación física** physical education

el **efectivo** cash *9B*; *en efectivo* in cash *9B*

egoísta selfish *4B*

el **ejemplo** example; *por ejemplo* for example

el **the** (*m., s.*) *2A*

él he *2A*; him (after a preposition) *4B*; *Él se llama....* His name is.... *2A*

eléctrico,-a electric

electrónico, -a electronic *2B*

El Salvador El Salvador *1A*

ella she *2A*; her (after a preposition) *4B*; *Ella se llama....* Her name is.... *2A*

ellos,-as they *2A*; them (after a preposition) *4B*

empatados: see *empate*

el **empate** tie; *los partidos empatados* games tied

empezar (ie) to begin, to start *6A*

en in, on, at *2A*; *en* (+ vehicle) by (+ vehicle) *3A*; *en cambio* on the other hand *7B*; *en casa* at home; *en efectivo* in cash *9B*; *en resumen* in short

encantado,-a delighted, the pleasure is mine *3A*

encender (ie) to light, to turn on (a light) *6A*

encontrar (ue) to find

la **encuesta** survey, poll

enero January *5B*

el **énfasis** emphasis

el **enfermero,** la **enfermera** nurse

enfermo,-a sick *4A*

la **ensalada** salad *3B*

enseñar to teach, to show

entero,-a whole

entonces then *6A*

entrar to go in, to come in *5A*

entre between, among

la **entrevista** interview

enviar to send *7B*

el **equipo** team *7A*; *equipo de sonido* sound system, stereo *5A*

equivocado mistaken; *número equivocado* wrong number *2B*

eres: see *ser*

es: see *ser*

escalar to climb

la **escalera** stairway, stairs *6B*; *escalera mecánica* escalator *9B*

la **escena** scene

escoger to choose *8B*; *escogiendo* choosing

escogiendo: see *escoger*

escriban: see *escribir*

escribe: see *escribir*

escribir to write *6B*; *¿Cómo se escribe...?* How do you write (spell)...? *1A*; *escriban* (*Uds.* command) write; *escribe* (*tú* command) write; *se escribe* it is written *1A*

el **escritorio** desk *2A*

escucha: see *escuchar*

escuchar to listen (to) *4B*; *escucha* (*tú* command) listen; *escuchen* (*Uds.* command) listen

escuchen: see *escuchar*

la **escuela** school *3A*

ese, esa that *6A*

eso that (neuter form)

esos, esas those *6A*

el **espacio** space

España Spain *1A*

el **español** Spanish (language) *2B*

español, española Spanish

especial special *6A*

especializado,-a specialized

el **espectáculo** showcase

la **esposa** wife, spouse *4A*

el **esposo** husband, spouse *4A*

el **esquiador,** la **esquiadora** skier *7B*

esquiar to ski *7B*

está: see *estar*

establecieron settled down

la **estación** season *7B*

el **estadio** stadium

el **Estado Libre Asociado** Commonwealth

los **Estados Unidos** United States of America *1A*

están: see *estar*

estar to be *2B*; *¿Cómo está (Ud.)?* How are you (formal)? *1B*; *¿Cómo están (Uds.)?* How are you (pl.)? *1B*; *¿Cómo estás (tú)?* How are are you (informal)? *1B*; *está nublado,-a* it's cloudy *7B*; *está soleado,-a* it's sunny *7B*; *están* they are *1B*; *estar contento,-a (con)* to be satisfied (with) *4A*; *estar en oferta* to be on sale *9B*; *estar listo,-a* to be ready *7B*; *estás* you (informal) are *1B*; *estoy* I am *1B*

estás: see *estar*

este well, so (pause in speech)

este, esta this *6A*; *esta noche* tonight *7A*

el **estéreo** stereo

estos, estas these *6A*

estoy: see *estar*

la **estructura** structure

estudia: see *estudiar*

el **estudiante,** la **estudiante** student *2A*

estudiar to study *2B*; *estudia* (*tú* command) study; *estudien* (*Uds.* command) study

estudien: see *estudiar*

el **estudio** study

la **estufa** stove *6A*

estupendo,-a wonderful, marvellous *7A*

el **examen** exam, test *2B*

excelente excellent *7B*

el **éxito** success

explica: see *explicar*

la **explicación** explanation

explicar to explain; *explica* (*tú* command) explain

el **explorador,** la **exploradora** explorer

la **exportación** exportation

exportador, exportadora exporting

expresar to express

la **expresión** expression

la **extensión** extension

fácil easy *4B*

la **falda** skirt *2B*

falso,-a false

la **familia** family *4A*

famoso,-a famous

fantástico,-a fantastic, great *3A*

el **favor** favor; *por favor* please *1B*

favorito,-a favorite *3B*

febrero February *5B*

la **fecha** date *5B*

felicitaciones congratulations

feliz happy *(pl. felices) 5B*; *¡Feliz cumpleaños!* Happy birthday! *5B*

femenino,-a feminine

feo,-a ugly *4B*

el **ferrocarril** railway, railroad

la **fiesta** party *3A*

la **filosofía** philosophy

el **fin** end *5A*; *fin de semana* weekend *5A*

la **física** physics *6A*

la **flauta** flute

la **flor** flower *7B*

la **florcita** small flower

la **forma** form
la **foto(grafía)** photo *4A*
la **frase** phrase, sentence
el **fregadero** sink *6A*
la **fresa** strawberry *8B*
el **fresco** cool *7B; hace fresco* it is cool *7B*
fresco,-a fresh, chilly *8B*
los **frijoles** beans *3B*
el **frío** cold *4A; hace frío* it is cold *7B; tener frío* to be cold *6B*
frío,-a cold *4A*
la **fruta** fruit *8B*
fue: see *ser*
fuerte strong
el **fútbol** soccer *4B; fútbol americano* football *7A*
el **futbolista,** la **futbolista** soccer player *7B*
el **futuro** future

G

la **gana** desire *6B; tener ganas de* to feel like *6B*
ganados: see *ganar*
ganar to win; *los partidos ganados* games won
el **garaje** garage *6B*
el **gato,** la **gata** cat *5A*
el **género** gender
generoso,-a generous *4B*
la **gente** people *8A*
la **geografía** geography
la **geometría** geometry
el **gerundio** present participle
el **gesto** gesture
el **gimnasio** gym
la **gira** tour
el **gobernador,** la **gobernadora** governor
gordo,-a fat *4B*
la **grabadora** tape recorder *5A*
gracias thanks *1B; muchas gracias* thank you very much *1B*
el **grado** degree *7B*
gran big (form of *grande* before a *m., s.* noun)
grande big *3B*
gris gray *2B*
el **grupo** group; *grupo musical* musical group
el **guante** glove *9A*
guapo,-a good-looking, attractive, handsome, pretty *4A*
Guatemala Guatemala *1A*

el **guía,** la **guía** guide
Guinea Ecuatorial Equatorial Guinea *1A*
el **guisante** pea *8B*
la **guitarra** guitar
gusta: see *gustar*
gustar to like, to be pleasing to *4B; me/te/le/nos/vos/les gustaría...* I/you/he/she/it/we/they would like... *6B*
gustaría: see *gustar*
el **gusto** pleasure, delight, taste *3A; con (mucho) gusto* I would be (very) glad to *1B; el gusto es mío* the pleasure is mine *3A; ¡Mucho gusto!* Glad to meet you! *1A; Tanto gusto.* So glad to meet you. *3A*

H

la **habichuela** green bean *8B*
la **habitación** room, bedroom
el **habitante,** la **habitante** inhabitant
habla: see *hablar*
hablar to speak *2B; habla (tú command)* speak; *hablen (Uds. command)* speak; *Se habla español.* Spanish is spoken.
hablen: see *hablar*
hace: see *hacer*
hacer to do, to make *3B; ¿Cuánto (+ time expression) hace que (+ present tense of verb)...?* How long...? *7A; hace buen (mal) tiempo* the weather is nice (bad) *7B; hace fresco* it is cool *7B; hace frío (calor)* it is cold (hot) *7B; hace (+ time expression) que* ago *7A; hace sol* it is sunny *7B; hace viento* it is windy *7B; hacer aeróbicos* to do aerobics *7A; hacer falta* to be necessary, to be lacking *8B; hacer un viaje* to take a trip *5A; hacer una pregunta* to ask a question *3B; hagan (Uds. command)* do, make; *haz (tú command)* do, make; *haz el papel* play the part; *hecha* made
hagan: see *hacer*
el **hambre** hunger *6B; tener hambre* to be hungry *6B*
hasta until, up to, down to *1A;*

hasta la vista so long, see you later; *hasta luego* so long, see you later *1A; hasta mañana* see you tomorrow *1B; hasta pronto* see you soon *1B*
hay there is, there are *2A; hay neblina* it is misting *7B; hay sol* it is sunny *7B*
haz: see *hacer*
hecha: see *hacer*
el **helado** ice cream *8B*
la **hermana** sister *4A*
el **hermano** brother *4A*
el **hielo** ice *7B; patinar sobre hielo* to ice skate *7B*
la **hija** daughter *4A*
el **hijo** son *4A*
hispano,-a Hispanic
hispanohablante Spanish-speaking
la **historia** history *2B*
la **hoja** sheet; *hoja de papel* sheet of paper; leaf
hola hi, hello *1A*
el **hombre** man *9A*
Honduras Honduras *1A*
la **hora** hour *1B; ¿a qué hora?* at what time? *2B; ¿Qué hora es?* What time is it? *1B*
el **horario** schedule *2B*
el **horno microondas** microwave oven *6A*
horrible horrible *4B*
el **hotel** hotel *3A*
hoy today *3B*
el **huevo** egg *8B*

I

la **idea** idea *5B*
ideal ideal *4B*
ignorar to not know
la **imaginación** imagination
imaginar to imagine; *imagina (tú command)* imagine
el **impermeable** raincoat *9A*
importante important *4B*
importar to be important, to matter *8B*
la **impresora (láser)** (laser) printer *2B*
los **incas** Incas
incluir to include
indefinido,-a indefinite
la **independencia** independence
indica: see *indicar*

la **indicación** cue
indicado,-a indicated
indicar to indicate; *indica*
 (*tú* command) indicate
indígena native
el **informe** report
el **inglés** English (language) *2B*
el **ingrediente** ingredient *8B*
inicial initial
inmenso,-a immense
la **inspiración** inspiration
inteligente intelligent *4B*
interesante interesting *4B*
interrogativo,-a interrogative
el **invierno** winter *7B*
la **invitación** invitation
invitar to invite
ir to go *3A; ir a* (+ infinitive)
 to be going to (do something)
 3B; ir de compras to go
 shopping *4B; ¡vamos!* let's go!
 3A; ¡vamos a (+ infinitive)!
 let's (+ infinitive)! *3B; vayan*
 (*Uds.* command) go to; *ve*
 (*tú* command) go to
la **isla** island

el **jamón** ham *8B*
el **jardín** garden *8A*
la **jirafa** giraffe
los **jeans** jeans, blue jeans *2B*
joven young *5B*
la **joya** jewel *9B*
el **juego** game
jueves Thursday *2B; el jueves*
 on Thursday
el **jugador,** la **jugadora**
 player *7B*
jugar (ue) to play *4B, jugar a*
 (+ sport/game) *4B*
el **jugo** juice *3B*
julio July *5B*
junio June *5B*
junto,-a together *8A*

el **kilo (kg.)** kilogram *8B*

la the *(f., s.) 2A;* her, it, you
 (d.o.) 5A; a la...
 at...o'clock *2B*
el **lado** side *6B; al lado (de)* next
 to, beside *6B; por todos lados*
 everywhere *7B*

la **lámpara** lamp *6A*
la **lana** wool *9A*
la **langosta** lobster
lanzar to throw
el **lápiz** pencil *(pl. lápices) 2A*
largo,-a long *9B*
las the *(f., pl.) 2A;* them, you
 (d.o.) 5A; a las... at...o'clock *2B*
la **lástima** shame; *¡Qué lástima!*
 What a shame! *5A*
la **lata** can *8B*
el **lavaplatos** dishwasher *6A*
lavar to wash *8A*
le (to, for) him, (to, for) her,
 (to, for) it, (to, for) you
 (formal)*(i.o.) 3A*
lean: see *leer*
la **lección** lesson
la **leche** milk *8A*
la **lechuga** lettuce *8B*
la **lectura** reading
lee: see *leer*
leer to read *3B; lean (Uds.*
 command) read; *lee (tú*
 command) read
lejos (de) far (from) *3A*
la **lengua** language
lento,-a slow *4B*
les (to, for) them, (to, for) you
 (pl.)(i.o.) 3A
la **letra** letter
levantarse to get up, to rise;
 levántate (tú command) get up;
 levántense (Uds. command)
 get up
levántate: see *levantarse*
levántense: see *levantarse*
la **libertad** liberty, freedom
la **libra** pound
libre free *4A*
la **librería** bookstore *5A*
el **libro** book *2A*
el **líder** leader
limitar to limit
limpiar to clean *8A*
limpio,-a clean *4A*
lindo,-a pretty *9B*
la **lista** list *7A*
listo,-a ready *7B,* smart *8A;*
 estar listo,-a to be ready *7B; ser*
 listo,-a to be smart *8A*
la **literatura** literature
llama: see *llamar*
llamar to call, to telephone *5A;*
 ¿Cómo se llama (Ud./él/ella)?
 What is (your/his/her) name?

2A; ¿Cómo te llamas? What is
 your name? *1A; llamaron* they
 called (preterite of *llamar*); *me*
 llamo my name is *1A; se*
 llaman their names are; *te*
 llamas your name is *1A;*
 (Ud./Él/Ella) se llama....
 (Your [formal]/His/Her)
 name is.... *2A*
llamaron: see *llamar*
llamas: see *llamar*
llamo: see *llamar*
llegar to arrive *8A; llegó* arrived
 (preterite of *llegar*)
llegó: see *llegar*
llevar to wear *2B;* to take, to
 carry *5A*
llover (ue) to rain *7B*
la **lluvia** rain *7B*
lo him, it, you *(d.o.) 5A; lo que,*
 that which *6B; lo siento* I am
 sorry *1B*
loco,-a crazy *4A*
lógicamente logically
lógico,-a logical
los the *(m., pl.) 2A;* them, you
 (d.o.) 5A
luego then, later, soon *1A;*
 hasta luego so long, see you
 later *1A*
el **lugar** place *7B*
lunes Monday *2B; el lunes* on
 Monday
la **luz** light *(pl. luces) 6A*

la **madrastra** stepmother
la **madre** mother *4A*
maduro,-a ripe *8B*
el **maestro** teacher, master; *La*
 práctica hace al maestro.
 Practice makes perfect.
el **maíz** corn *8B*
mal badly *1B;* bad *7B*
la **maleta** suitcase *5A*
malo,-a bad *4B*
la **mamá** mother, mom
la **manera** manner, way
la **mano** hand *9A*
el **mantel** tablecloth *6A*
la **mantequilla** butter *6A*
la **manzana** apple *8B*
mañana tomorrow *1B; hasta*
 mañana see you tomorrow *1B;*
 pasado mañana the day after
 tomorrow *5B*

la **mañana** morning *1B; de la mañana* A.M., in the morning *1B; por la mañana* in the morning *7A*

el **mapa** map *2A*

la **maravilla** wonder, marvel

mariachi popular Mexican music and orchestra

el **marisco** seafood, shellfish

marrón brown *9A*

martes Tuesday *2B; el martes* on Tuesday

marzo March *5B*

más more, else *4A; el/la/los/las (+ noun) más (+ adjective)* the most *(+ adjective) 8B; lo más (+ adverb) posible* as *(+ adverb + noun)* as possible *8B; más (+ noun/adjective/ adverb) que* more *(+ noun/ adjective/adverb)* than *8B*

masculino,-a masculine

las **matemáticas** mathematics *2B*

el **material** material *9B*

máximo,-a maximum *7B*

maya Mayan

los **mayas** Mayans

mayo May *5B*

mayor older, oldest *5B,* greater, greatest *8B*

la **mayúscula** capital letter *1A*

me (to, for) me *(i.o.) 4B;* me *(d.o.) 5A;* me llaman they call me; me llamo my name is *1A*

mecánico,-a mechanic *9B; la escalera mecánica* escalator *9B*

la **medianoche** midnight *1B; Es medianoche.* It is midnight. *1B*

mediante by means of

las **medias** pantyhose, nylons *9A*

el **médico,** la **médica** doctor *3A*

medio,-a half; *y media* half past *1B*

medio tiempo (trabajo) part-time (work)

el **mediodía** noon; *Es mediodía.* It is noon. *1B*

mejor better *8B; el/la/los/las mejor/mejores (+ noun)* the best *(+ noun) 8B*

menor younger, youngest *5B,* lesser, least *8B*

menos minus, until, before, to (to express time) *1B,* less *8B; el/la/los/las (+ noun) menos (+ adjective)* the least *(+ adjective + noun) 8B; lo menos (+ adverb) posible* as *(+ adverb)* as possible *8B; menos (+ noun/adjective/ adverb) que* less *(+ noun/ adjective/adverb)* than *8B; por lo menos* at least

mentir (ie, i) to lie

la **mentira** lie *6B*

el **menú** menu *3B*

el **mercado** market *8B*

el **merengue** merengue (dance music)

el **mes** month *5B*

la **mesa** table *6A; poner la mesa* to set the table *6A; recoger la mesa* to clear the table *8A*

el **mesero,** la **mesera** food server *3B*

el **metro** subway *3A*

mexicano,-a Mexican

México Mexico *1A*

mi my *2A; (pl. mis)* my *4A*

mí me *4B;* (after a preposition) *4B*

el **miedo** fear *6B; tener miedo de* to be afraid of *6B*

el **miembro** member, part

mientras que while

miércoles Wednesday *2B; el miércoles* on Wednesday

mil thousand *5B*

mínimo,-a minimum *7B*

la **minúscula** lowercase *1A*

el **minuto** minute *7A*

mío,-a my, mine; *el gusto es mío* the pleasure is mine *3A*

mira: see *mirar*

mirar to look (at) *4B; mira (tú* command) look *2B;* hey, look (pause in speech); *miren (Uds.* command) look; hey, look (pause in speech)

miren: see *mirar*

mismo right (in the very moment, place, etc.) *7A; ahora mismo* right now *7A*

mismo,-a same *7A*

el **misterio** mystery

la **mochila** backpack *2A*

el **modelo** model

moderno,-a modern

el **momento** moment *3B*

el **mono** monkey

montar to ride *5A; montar en patineta* to skateboard *7B*

morado,-a purple *9A*

moreno,-a brunet, brunette, dark-haired, dark-skinned *4B*

la **moto(cicleta)** motorcycle *3A*

la **muchacha** girl, young woman *1A*

el **muchacho** boy, guy *1A*

muchísimo very much, a lot

mucho much, a lot of, very much *4A*

mucho,-a much, a lot of, very *3B; (pl. muchos,-as)* many *3B; con (mucho) gusto* I would be (very) glad to *1B; muchas gracias* thank you very much *1B; ¡Mucho gusto!* Glad to meet you! *1A*

la **mujer** woman *9A*

el **mundo** world; *todo el mundo* everyone, everybody

la **muralla** wall

el **museo** museum *3B*

la **música** music *2B*

muy very *1B*

la **nación** nation

nacional national

nada nothing *9A; de nada* you are welcome, not at all *1B*

nadar to swim *4B*

nadie nobody *9A*

la **naranja** orange *3B*

natal birth

la **Navidad** Christmas *5B*

la **neblina** mist *7B; hay neblina* it is misting *7B*

necesitar to need *2B*

negativo,-a negative

el **negocio** business; *el hombre de negocios* businessman; *la mujer de negocios* businesswoman

negro,-a black *2B*

nervioso,-a nervous *4A*

nevar (ie) to snow *7B*

ni not even *5B; ni...ni* neither...nor *9A*

Nicaragua Nicaragua *1A*

la **nieta** granddaughter *4A*

el **nieto** grandson *4A*

la **nieve** snow *7B*

ningún, ninguna none, not
  any *9A*
ninguno,-a none, not any *9A*
niño,-a child
no no *1A*
la **noche** night *1B; buenas noches*
  good night *1B; de la noche* P.M.,
  at night *1B; esta noche* tonight
  7A; por la noche at night *6B*
el **nombre** name
el **norte** north
nos (to, for) us *(i.o.) 4B;*
  us *(d.o.) 5A*
nosotros,-as we *2A;* us (after a
  preposition) *4B*
la **nota** grade
la **noticia** news
novecientos,-as nine
  hundred *5B*
noveno,-a ninth *7B*
noventa ninety *1B*
la **novia** girlfriend
noviembre November *5B*
el **novio** boyfriend
nublado,-a cloudy *7B; está
  nublado* it is cloudy *7B*
nuestro,-a our *4A*
nueve nine *1A*
nuevo,-a new *2A; el Año Nuevo*
  New Year's Day *5B*
el **número** number *2B; número de
  teléfono/de fax/de teléfono
  celular* telephone/fax/cellular
  telephone number *2B, número
  equivocado* wrong number *2B*
nunca never *4A*

o or *2B; o...o* either...or *9A*
la **obra** work, play
ochenta eighty *1B*
ocho eight *1A*
ochocientos,-as eight
  hundred *5B*
octavo,-a eighth *7B*
octubre October *5B*
ocupado,-a busy, occupied *4A*
ocupar to occupy
la **odisea** odyssey
la **oferta** sale *9B; estar en oferta* to
  be on sale *9B*
oficial official
la **oficina** office *3A*
oigan hey, listen (pause in
  speech)

oigo hello (telephone
  greeting)
oír to hear, to listen *8A; oigan*
  hey, listen (pause in speech);
  oigo hello (telephone
  greeting); *oye* hey, listen
  (pause in speech) *3B*
la **olla** pot, saucepan *8A*
olvidar to forget *8B*
la **omisión** omission
once eleven *1A*
el **opuesto** opposite
la **oración** sentence
el **orden** order
la **organización** organization
el **órgano** organ
el **oro** gold *9B*
os (to, for) you (Spain,
  informal, *pl., i.o.*), you (Spain,
  informal, *pl., d.o.*)
el **otoño** autumn *7B*
otro,-a other, another *(pl.
  otros,-as) 4A; otra vez* again,
  another time *6A*
oye hey, listen (pause in
  speech) *3B*

el **Pacífico** Pacific (Ocean)
el **padrastro** stepfather
el **padre** father *4A; (pl. padres)*
  parents
la **paella** paella (traditional
  Spanish dish with rice, meat,
  seafood and vegetables) *8B*
pagar to pay *9B*
la **página** page *2A*
el **país** country *1A*
la **palabra** word *2A; palabra
  interrogativa* question word;
  palabras antónimas
  antonyms, opposite words
el **pan** bread *6A*
Panamá Panama *1A*
la **pantalla** screen *2B*
el **pantalón** pants *2B*
el **pañuelo** handkerchief, hanky
  9B
la **papa** potato *8B*
el **papá** father, dad
los **papás** parents
el **papel** paper *2A,* role; *haz el
  papel* play the role; *la hoja de
  papel* sheet of paper
para for, to, in order to *3A*

el **paraguas** umbrella *9B*
el **Paraguay** Paraguay *1A*
parecer to seem *8B*
la **pared** wall *2A*
la **pareja** pair, couple
el **pariente, la pariente**
  relative *4A*
parientes políticos in-laws
el **parque** park *3A*
el **párrafo** paragraph
la **parte** part
el **partido** game, match *4B;
  partidos empatados* games tied;
  partidos ganados games won;
  partidos perdidos games lost
pasado,-a past, last *5B; pasado
  mañana* the day after
  tomorrow *5B*
pásame: see *pasar*
pasar to pass, to spend (time)
  5A, to happen, to occur; *pásame*
  pass me *6A; pasar la aspiradora*
  to vacuum *8A; ¿Qué te pasa?*
  What is wrong with you?
el **pasatiempo** pastime, leisure
  activity *7A*
la **Pascua** Easter
el **paseo** walk, ride, trip *7B; dar
  un paseo* to go for a walk, to go
  for a ride *7B*
el **patinador, la patinadora**
  skater *7B*
patinar to skate *4B; patinar
  sobre ruedas* to in-line skate *4B;
  patinar sobre hielo* to ice
  skate *7B*
el **patio** courtyard, patio, yard *6B*
pedir (i, i) to ask for, to order,
  to request *6B; pedir perdón* to
  say you are sorry *6B; pedir
  permiso (para)* to ask for
  permission (to do something)
  6B; pedir prestado,-a
  to borrow *6B*
la **película** movie, film *5A*
pelirrojo,-a red-haired *4B*
la **pelota** ball
pensar (ie) to think, to intend,
  to plan *6A; pensar de* to think
  about (i.e., to have an opinion)
  6A; pensar en to think about
  (i.e., to focus one's thoughts
  on) *6A; pensar en*
  (+ infinitive) to think about
  (doing something)

peor worse *8B; el/la/los/las peor/peores* (+ noun) the worst (+ noun) *8B*

pequeño,-a small *6B*

perder (ie) to lose; *los partidos perdidos* games lost

perdidos: see *perder*

perdón excuse me, pardon me *1B; pedir perdón* to say you are sorry *6B*

perezoso,-a lazy

perfecto,-a perfect *9B*

el **perfume** perfume *9B*

el **periódico** newspaper *2A*

el **periodista**, la **periodista** journalist, reporter

el **período** period

la **perla** pearl *9B*

el **permiso** permission, permit *7A; con permiso* excuse me (with your permission), may I *1B; pedir permiso (para)* to ask for permission (to do something) *6B*

permitir to permit *7A*

pero but *3B*

el **perro**, la **perra** dog *5A*

la **persona** person *8A*

personal personal; *el pronombre personal* subject pronoun

el **Perú** Peru *1A*

el **pescado** fish *3B*

el **petróleo** oil

el **piano** piano *4B*

el **pie** foot *9A; a pie* on foot *3A*

la **pierna** leg *9A*

el **pijama** pajamas *9A*

la **pimienta** pepper (seasoning) *6A*

el **pimiento** bell pepper *8B*

pintar to paint

la **pirámide** pyramid

la **piscina** swimming pool *6B*

el **piso** floor *6B; el primer piso* first floor *6B*

la **pista** clue

la **pizarra** blackboard *2A*

la **planta** plant *6B; planta baja* ground floor *6B*

la **plata** silver *9B*

el **plátano** banana *8B*

el **plato** dish, plate *6A; plato de sopa* soup bowl *6A*

la **playa** beach *4A*

la **plaza** plaza, public square *3B*

poco,-a not very, little, few *6B; un poco* a little (bit) *5A*

poder (ue) to be able *7A*

políticamente politically

el **pollo** chicken *3B*

poner to put, to place *6A;* to turn on (an appliance); *poner la mesa* to set the table *6A*

popular popular *4A*

un **poquito** a very little (bit)

por for *4A,* through, by *6B,* in *7A,* along *7B; por ejemplo* for example; *por favor* please *1B; por la mañana* in the morning *7A; por la noche* at night *6B; por la tarde* in the afternoon *7A; por teléfono* by telephone, on the telephone *6B; por todos lados* everywhere *7B; por lo general* generally

¿por qué? why? *3A*

porque because *3A*

la **posibilidad** possibility

la **posición** position, place

el **póster** poster

el **postre** dessert *6A*

la **práctica** practice *5A; La práctica hace al maestro.* Practice makes perfect.

el **precio** price *8B*

preferir (ie, i) to prefer *6A*

la **pregunta** question *3B; hacer una pregunta* to ask a question *3B*

preguntar to ask *3B*

el **premio** award, prize

la **preparación** preparation

preparar to prepare *8A*

el **preparativo** preparation

la **preposición** preposition

presenciar to witness

la **presentación** introduction

presentar to introduce, to present; *le presento a* let me introduce you (formal, *s.*) to *3A; les presento a* let me introduce you (*pl.*) to *3A; te presento a* let me introduce you (informal, *s.*) to *3A*

presente present

presento: see *presentar*

prestado,-a on loan *6B; pedir prestado,-a* to borrow *6B*

prestar to lend *8A*

la **primavera** spring *7B*

primer first (form of *primero* before a *m., s.* noun) *6B; el primer piso* first floor *6B*

primero,-a first *5B*

primero first (adverb) *5A*

el **primo**, la **prima** cousin *4A*

principal main

la **prisa** rush, hurry, haste *6B; tener prisa* to be in a hurry *6B*

el **problema** problem *3A*

produce produces

el **producto** product

el **profesor**, la **profesora** teacher *2A; el profe* teacher

el **programa** program, show *7A*

prometer to promise *9A*

el **pronombre** pronoun; *pronombre personal* subject pronoun

el **pronóstico** forecast

pronto soon, quickly *1B; hasta pronto* see you soon *1B*

la **pronunciación** pronunciation

el **propósito** aim, purpose; *A propósito* by the way *1A*

próximo,-a next

la **publicidad** publicity

público,-a public

la **puerta** door *2A*

Puerto Rico Puerto Rico *1A*

pues thus, well, so, then (pause in speech) *3B*

la **pulsera** bracelet *9B*

el **punto** point, dot (*term used in Internet addresses*) *2B*

la **puntuación** punctuation

el **pupitre** desk *2A*

Q

que that, which *5A; lo que* what, that which *6B; más* (+ noun/adjective/adverb) *que* more (+ noun/adjective/adverb) than *8B; que viene* upcoming, next *5A*

¡qué (+ adjective)! how (+ adjective)! *4A*

¡qué (+ noun)! what a (+ noun)! *5A*

¿qué? what? *2A; ¿a qué hora?* at what time? *2B; ¿Qué comprendiste?* What did you understand?; *¿Qué hora es?* What time is it? *1B; ¿Qué quiere* *decir...?* What is the meaning (of)...? *2A; ¿Qué tal?* How are you? *1B; ¿Qué te pasa?* What is wrong with you?; *¿Qué temperatura hace?* What is the temperature? *7B; ¿Qué (+ tener)?* What is wrong with (someone)? *6B; ¿Qué tiempo hace?* How is the weather? *7B*

quedar to remain, to stay *9A; quedarle bien a uno* to fit, to be becoming *9A*

el **quehacer** chore *8A*

el **quemador de discos compactos (CDs)** compact disc (CD) burner *5A*

querer (ie) to love, to want, to like *6A; ¿Qué quiere decir...?* What is the meaning (of)...? *2A; querer decir* to mean *6B; quiere decir* it means *2A; quiero* I love *4A;* I want *3A*

querido,-a dear *6B*

el **queso** cheese *8B*

¿quién? who? *2A; (pl. ¿quiénes?)* who? *3A*

quiere: see *querer*

quiero: see *querer*

la **química** chemistry

quince fifteen *1A*

quinientos,-as five hundred *5B*

quinto,-a fifth *7B*

quisiera would like

quizás perhaps *8A*

R

la **radio** radio (broadcast) *4B;* el *radio* radio (apparatus)

rápidamente rapidly *5B*

rápido,-a rapid, fast *4B*

el **rascacielos** skyscraper

el **ratón** mouse (pl. *ratones*) *2B*

la **razón** reason

real royal

la **realidad** reality

la **receta** recipe *8A*

recibir to receive *9B*

el **recibo** receipt *9B*

recoger to pick up *8A; recoger la mesa* to clear the table *8A*

recordar (ue) to remember *7A*

redondo,-a round

el **refresco** soft drink, refreshment *3B*

el **refrigerador** refrigerator *6A*

el **regalo** gift *9B*

regañar to scold

regatear to bargain, to haggle

la **regla** ruler *2A*

regresar to return, to go back

regular average, okay, so-so, regular *1B*

relacionado,-a related

el **reloj** clock, watch *2A*

remoto,-a remote *7A*

repasar to reexamine, to review

el **repaso** review

repetir (i, i) to repeat *6B; repitan (Uds.* command) repeat; *repite (tú* command) repeat

repitan: see *repetir*

repite: see *repetir*

reportando reporting

el **reproductor** player *5A; reproductor de CDs* CD player *5A; reproductor de DVDs* DVD player *5A; reproductor de MP3* MP3 player *5A*

la **República Dominicana** Dominican Republic *1A*

resolver (ue) to resolve, to solve

responder to answer

la **respuesta** answer

el **restaurante** restaurant *3A*

el **resultado** result

el **resumen** summary; *en resumen* in short

la **reunión** meeting

la **revista** magazine *2A*

rico,-a rich

el **riel** rail

el **río** river

el **ritmo** rhythm

rojo,-a red *2B*

la **ropa** clothing *2B; ropa interior* underwear *9A*

rosado,-a pink *9A*

rubio,-a blond, blonde *4B*

la **rutina** routine

S

sábado Saturday *2B; el sábado* on Saturday

saber to know *3B; sabes* you know *3B; sé* I know *2A*

sabes: see *saber*

el **sacapuntas** pencil sharpener *2A*

sacar to take out *8A; sacar fotos* to take photographs

la **sal** salt *6A*

la **sala** living room *6B*

salir to go out *4A*

la **salsa** salsa (dance music)

la **salud** health

el **saludo** greeting

el **salvavidas** lifeguard

la **sangre** blood

el **santo** saint's day; *Todos los Santos* All Saints' Day

el **saxofón** saxophone

se *¿Cómo se dice...?* How do you say...? *2A; ¿Cómo se escribe...?* How do you write (spell)...? *1A; ¿Cómo se llama (Ud./él/ella)?* What is (your/his/her) name? *2A; se considera* it is considered; *se dice* one says *2A; se escribe* it is written *1A; Se habla español.* Spanish is spoken.; *se llaman* their names are; *(Ud./Él/Ella) se llama....* (Your [formal]/His/Her) name is.... *2A*

sé: see *saber*

sea: see *ser*

la **sed** thirst *6B; tener sed* to be thirsty *6B*

la **seda** silk *9A*

seguir (i, i) to follow, to continue, to keep on; *sigan (Uds.* command) follow; *sigue (tú* command) follow

según according to

el **segundo** second *7B*

segundo,-a second *7A*

seguro,-a safe

seis six *1A*

seiscientos,-as six hundred *5B*

selecciona select (*tú* command)

la **selva** jungle; *selva tropical* tropical rain forest

la **semana** week *5A; el fin de semana* weekend *5A; Semana Santa* Holy Week

sentarse (ie) to sit (down); *siéntate (tú* command) sit (down); *siéntense (Uds.* command) sit (down)

sentir (ie, i) to be sorry, to feel sorry, to regret *6A; lo siento* I am sorry *1B*

señalar to point to, to point at, to point out; *señalen (Uds.* command) point to

señalen: see *señalar*

el **señor** gentleman, sir, Mr. *1B*

la **señora** lady, madame, Mrs. *1B*

la **señorita** young lady, Miss *1B*

septiembre September *5B*

séptimo,-a seventh *7B*

ser to be *2A; eres* you are *1A; ¿Eres (tú) de...?* Are you from...? *1A; es* you (formal) are, he/she/it is *1B; es la una* it is one o'clock *1B; Es medianoche.* It is midnight. *1B; Es mediodía.* It is noon. *1B; fue* you (formal) were, he/she/it was (preterite of *ser*) *5B; ¿Qué hora es?* What time is it? *1B; sea* it is; *son* they are *1B; son las* (+ number) it is (+ number) o'clock *1B; soy* I am *1A*

serio,-a serious

la **servilleta** napkin *6A*

sesenta sixty *1B*

setecientos,-as seven hundred *5B*

setenta seventy *1B*

sexto,-a sixth *7B*

si if *5A*

sí yes *1A*

siempre always *3B*

siéntate: see *sentarse*

siéntense: see *sentarse*

siento: see *sentir*

siete seven *1A*

sigan: see *seguir*

el **siglo** century *7A*

los **signos de puntuación** punctuation marks

sigue: see *seguir*

siguiente following; *lo siguiente* the following

la **silabificación** syllabification

el **silencio** silence

la **silla** chair *2A*

el **símbolo** symbol

similar alike, similar

simpático,-a nice, pleasant *3A*

sin without *8B*

sintético,-a synthetic *9B*

la **situación** situation

sobre on, over, on top of *2B*, about; *patinar sobre hielo* to ice skate *7B; patinar sobre ruedas* in-line skate *4B*

la **sobrina** niece *4A*

el **sobrino** nephew *4A*

el **sol** sun *7B; hace sol, hay sol* it is sunny *7B*

solamente only

soleado,-a sunny *7B; está soleado* it is sunny *7B*

solo, -a alone

sólo only, just *8A*

el **sombrero** hat *9A*

son: see *ser*

el **sondeo** poll

el **sonido** sound; *equipo de sonido* sound system *5A*

la **sopa** soup *6A*

la **sorpresa** surprise *5A*

soy: see *ser*

Sr. abbreviation for *señor 1B*

Sra. abbreviation for *señora 1B*

Srta. abbreviation for *señorita 1B*

su, sus his, her, its, your (*Ud./Uds.*), their *4A*

suave smooth, soft

el **subdesarrollo** underdevelopment

subir to climb, to go up, to go upstairs, to take up, to bring up, to carry up *8A*

el **suceso** happening

sucio,-a dirty *4A*

el **sueño** sleep *6B; tener sueño* to be sleepy *6B*

el **suéter** sweater *9A*

el **supermercado** supermarket *8A*

el **sur** south

el **sustantivo** noun

T

tal such, as, so; *¿Qué tal?* How are you? *1B*

el **tamal** tamale

el **tamaño** size *9B*

también also, too *3A*

el **tambor** drum

tampoco either, neither *2B*

tan so *5A; tan* (+ adjective/ adverb) *como* (+ person/item) as (+ adjective/adverb) as (+ person/item) *8B*

tanto,-a so much *3A; tanto,-a* (+ noun) *como* (+ person/ item) as much/many (+ noun) as (+ person/item) *8B; tanto como* as much as *8B; Tanto gusto.* So glad to meet you. *3A*

la **tapa** tidbit, appetizer

la **tarde** afternoon *1B; buenas tardes* good afternoon *1A; de la tarde* P.M., in the afternoon *1B; por la tarde* in the afternoon *7A;* late

la **tarea** homework *4B*

la **tarjeta** card *9B; tarjeta de crédito* credit card *9B*

el **taxi** taxi *3A*

la **taza** cup *6A*

te (to, for) you (*i.o.*) *3A;* you (*d.o.*) *5A; ¿Cómo te llamas?* What is your name? *1A; te llamas* your name is *1A*

el **teatro** theater *3B*

el **teclado** keyboard *2B*

el **teléfono** telephone *2B; el número de teléfono* telephone number *2B; por teléfono* by the telephone, on the telephone *6B*

la **telenovela** soap opera *7A*

la **televisión** television *4B; ver la televisión* to watch television *4B*

el **televisor** television set *7A*

el **tema** theme, topic

la **temperatura** temperature *7B; ¿Qué temperatura hace?* What is the temperature? *7B*

temprano early *5B*

el **tenedor** fork *6A*

tener to have *5A; ¿Cuántos años tienes?* How old are you? *1A; ¿Qué* (+ *tener*)? What is wrong with (person)? *6B; tener calor* to be hot *6B; tener frío* to be cold *6B; tener ganas de* to feel like *6B; tener hambre* to be hungry *6B; tener miedo de* to be afraid *6B; tener* (+ number) *años* to be (+ number) years old *5A; tener prisa* to be in a hurry *6B; tener que* to have to *6A; tener sed* to be thirsty *6B; tener sueño* to be sleepy *6B; tengo* I have *1A; tengo* (+ number) *años* I am (+ number) years old *1A; tiene* it has; *tienes* you have *1A*

tengo: see *tener*

el **tenis** tennis *4B*

el **tenista,** la **tenista** tennis player *7B*

tercer third (form of *tercero* before a *m., s.* noun) *7B*

tercero,-a third *7B*
terminar to end, to finish *2B*
ti you (after a preposition) *4B*
la **tía** aunt *4A*
el **tiempo** time *4A*, weather *7B*, verb tense; *Hace buen (mal) tiempo.* The weather is nice (bad). *7B*; *¿Qué tiempo hace?* How is the weather? *7B*
la **tienda** store *3B*
tiene: see *tener*
tienes: see *tener*
el **tío** uncle *4A*
típico,-a typical
el **tipo** type, kind
la **tiza** chalk *2A*
toca: see *tocar*
tocar to play (a musical instrument) *4B*, to touch; *toca (tú* command) touch; *toquen (Uds.* command) touch
todavía yet *7A*, still *7B*
todo,-a all, every, whole, entire *4A*; *de todos los días* everyday *6A*; *por todos lados* everywhere *7B*; *todo el mundo* everyone, everybody; *todos los días* every day *5A*
todos,-as everyone, everybody
tolerante tolerant
tomar to take *3A*, to drink, to have *3B*
el **tomate** tomato *8B*
tonto,-a silly *4B*
el **tópico** theme
toquen: see *tocar*
trabajar to work *8A*; *trabajando en parejas* working in pairs
el **trabajo** work *8A*
traer to bring *8A*
el **traje** suit *9A*; *traje de baño* swimsuit *9A*
el **transporte** transportation *3A*
tratar (de) to try (to do something)
trece thirteen *1A*
treinta thirty *1B*
el **tren** train *3A*
tres three *1A*
trescientos,-as three hundred *5B*
triste sad *4A*
el **trombón** trombone

la **trompeta** trumpet
tu your (informal) *2B; (pl. tus)* your (informal) *4A*
tú you (informal) *1A*
la **tumba** tomb
el **turista,** la **turista** tourist

u or (used before a word that starts with *o* or *ho*) *6B*
Ud. you (abbreviation of *usted*) *1B*; you (after a preposition) *4B; Ud. se llama....* Your name is.... *2A*
Uds. you (abbreviation of *ustedes*) *1B*; you (after a preposition) *4B*
último,-a last
un, una a, an, one *2A*
único,-a only, unique *4A*
unido,-a united
la **universidad** university
uno one *1A*
unos, unas some, any, a few *2A*
el **Uruguay** Uruguay *1A*
usar to use *9B*
usted you (formal, *s.*) *1B*; you (after a preposition) *4B*
ustedes you (*pl.*) *1B*; you (after a preposition) *4B*
la **uva** grape *8B*

las **vacaciones** vacation *9A*
Vallenato a combination of African, European and Colombian folkloric sounds
¡vamos! let's go! *3A; ¡vamos a (+ infinitive)!* let's (+ infinitive)! *3B*
varios,-as several
el **vaso** glass *6A*
vayan: see *ir*
ve: see *ir*
veinte twenty *1A*
veinticinco twenty-five *1B*
veinticuatro twenty-four *1B*
veintidós twenty-two *1B*
veintinueve twenty-nine *1B*
veintiocho twenty-eight *1B*
veintiséis twenty-six *1B*
veintisiete twenty-seven *1B*

veintitrés twenty-three *1B*
veintiuno twenty-one *1B*
vender to sell *9A*
Venezuela Venezuela *1A*
vengan: see *venir*
venir to come *5B; vengan (Uds.* command) come
la **ventana** window *2A*
ver to see, to watch *3B; a ver* let's see, hello (telephone greeting); *ver la televisión* to watch television *4B*
el **verano** summer *4A*
el **verbo** verb
verdad true
la **verdad** truth *6B*
¿verdad? right? *3A*
verde green *2B*
la **verdura** greens, vegetables *8B*
ves: see *ver*
el **vestido** dress *9A*
la **vez** time *(pl. veces) 5B; a veces* at times, sometimes *5B;* (number +) *vez/veces al/a la* (+ time expression) (number +) time(s) per (+ time expression) *7A; otra vez* again, another time *6A*
viajar to travel *6A*
el **viaje** trip *5A; hacer un viaje* to take a trip *5A; la agencia de viajes* travel agency
la **vida** life *7A*
el **videojuego** video game *7A*
viejo,-a old *5B*
el **viento** wind *7B; hace viento* it is windy *7B*
viernes Friday *2B; el viernes* on Friday
el **vinagre** vinegar *8B*
la **vista** view; *hasta la vista* so long, see you later
vivir to live *4A*
el **vocabulario** vocabulary
la **vocal** vowel; *vocales abiertas* open vowels; *vocales cerradas* closed vowels
el **voleibol** volleyball *7A*
volver (ue) to return, to go back, to come back *7A*
vosotros,-as you (Spain, informal, pl.) *1B*

vuestro,-a,-os,-as your (Spain, informal, *pl.*)

y and *1A; y cuarto* a quarter past, a quarter after *1B; y media* half past *1B*

ya already *6A; ¡ya lo veo!* I see it!

yo I *1A*

la **zanahoria** carrot *8B*

el **zapato** shoe *2B; zapato bajo* flats *9A; zapato de tacón* high-heel shoe *9A*

Vocabulary English / Spanish

A

a un, una *1B*; *a few* unos, unas *1B*; *a lot (of)* mucho *4B*, muchísimo
about sobre
accent el acento *1A*
activity la actividad *5A*
to add añadir *8B*
address la dirección *2B*
to adopt adoptar
aerobics los aeróbicos *7A*; *to do aerobics* hacer aeróbicos *7A*
affectionate cariñoso,-a *4A*
afraid asustado,-a; *to be afraid of* tener miedo de *6B*
after después de *7A*
afternoon la tarde *1B*; *good afternoon* buenas tardes *1A*; *in the afternoon* de la tarde *1B*; por la tarde *7A*
afterwards después *7A*
again otra vez *6A*
age la edad
agency la agencia; *travel agency* agencia de viajes
ago hace (+ *time expression*) que *7A*
agreed de acuerdo *3B*
airplane el avión *3A*; *by airplane* en avión *3A*
airport el aeropuerto
algebra el álgebra
all todo,-a *4A*
almost casi *7A*
alone solo,-a
along por *7B*
already ya *6A*
also también *3A*
alternate alterna (*tú command*); alternen (*Uds. command*)
although aunque
always siempre *3B*
American americano,-a *7A*
an un, una *2A*

and y *1A*; e *(used before a word beginning with i or hi)* *6B*
another otro,-a *2A*; *another time* otra vez *4B*
answer la respuesta
to answer contestar *4B*
any unos, unas *2A*; alguno,-a, algún, alguna *8A*, cualquier
anybody alguien *9A*
anyone alguien *9A*
anything algo *9A*
apartment el apartamento
apple la manzana *8B*
April abril *5B*
Argentina la Argentina *1A*
arm el brazo *9A*
to arrange arreglar *8A*
to arrive llegar *8A*
art el arte *2B*
article el artículo *5A*
artist el artista, la artista
as tal *1B*, como; *as (+ adverb) as possible* lo más/menos (+ *adverb*) posible *8B*; *as (+ adjective/adverb) as (+ person/item)* tan (+ *adjective/adverb*) como (+ *person/item*) *8B*; *as much/many (+ noun) as (+ person/item)* tanto,-a (+ *noun*) como (+ *person/item*) *8B*; *as much as* tanto como *8B*
to ask preguntar *3B*; *to ask a question* hacer una pregunta *3B*; *to ask for* pedir (*i, i*) *6B*; pedir permiso (para) *to ask for permission (to do something)* *6B*
at en; *(@) symbol for e-mail address* arroba *2B*; *at home* en casa *9B*; *at night* de la noche *1B*, por la noche *6B*; *at... o'clock* a la(s)... *2B*; *at times* a veces *5B*; *at what time?* ¿a qué hora? *2B*
athlete el deportista, la deportista *7B*
to attain conseguir *(i, i)*

attractive bonito,-a, guapo,-a *4A*
August agosto *5B*
aunt la tía *4A*
autumn el otoño *7B*
avenue la avenida *3B*
average regular *1B*
avocado el aguacate *8B*
award el premio

B

backpack la mochila *2A*
bad malo,-a *4B*
bald calvo,-a *4B*
ball pelota, bola; *to bowl* jugar a los bolos
banana el plátano *8B*
bank el banco *3A*
to bargain regatear
baseball el béisbol *4B*
basketball el básquetbol *7A*, el baloncesto; *basketball player* el basquetbolista, la basquetbolista *7B*
bathroom el baño *6B*, el cuarto de baño
to be ser *2A*; *to be able to* poder (*ue*) *7A*; *to be afraid of* tener miedo de *6B*; *to be hot* tener calor *6B*; *to be hungry* tener hambre *6B*; *to be important* importar *8B*; *to be in a hurry* tener prisa *6B*; *to be lacking* hacer falta *8B*; *to be necessary* hacer falta *8B*; *to be (+ number) years old* tener (+ *number*) años *5A*; *to be pleasing to* gustar *4B*; *to be ready* estar listo,-a *7B*; *to be satisfied (with)* estar contento,-a (con) *4A*; *to be sleepy* tener sueño *6B*; *to be smart* ser listo,-a *8A*; *to be sorry* sentir *6A*; *to be thirsty* tener sed *6B*
beach la playa *4A*
beans los frijoles *3B*
because porque *3A*

to become cumplir *5B*; *to become (+ number) years old* cumplir (+ *number*) años *5B*

bed la cama *8A*

bedroom el cuarto *6B*, la habitación

before antes de *7A*

to begin empezar *(ie) 6A*

to believe creer

belt el cinturón *9B*

beside al lado (de) *6B*

best mejor *8B*; *the best (+ noun)* el/la/los/las mejor/mejores (+ *noun*) *8B*

better mejor *8B*

between entre

bicycle la bicicleta *3A*

big grande *3B*, gran *(form of grande before a m., s. noun)*

bike la bicicleta *3A*

biology la biología *2B*

birthday el cumpleaños *5B*; *Happy birthday!* ¡Feliz cumpleaños! *5B*; *to have a birthday* cumplir años *5B*

black negro,-a *2B*

blackboard la pizarra *2A*

blond, blonde rubio,-a *4B*

blouse la blusa *2B*

blue azul *2B*; *blue jeans* los jeans *2B*

boat el barco *3A*

body el cuerpo *9A*

Bolivia Bolivia *1A*

book el libro *2A*

bookstore la librería *5A*

boot la bota *9A*

bored aburrido,-a *4B*

boring aburrido,-a *4B*

to borrow pedir prestado,-a *6B*

boy el chico *2A*, el muchacho *1A*

boyfriend el novio

bracelet la pulsera *9B*

bread el pan *6A*

breakfast el desayuno

to bring traer *8A*

to bring up subir *8A*

brother el hermano *4A*

brown marrón *9A*

brunet, brunette moreno,-a *4B*

building el edificio *3B*

bus el autobús *3A*

busy ocupado,-a *4A*

but pero *3B*

butter la mantequilla *6A*

to buy comprar *4B*

by por *4A*; *by (+ vehicle)* en (+ *vehicle*) *3A*; *by telephone* por teléfono *6B*; *By the way* A propósito; *by means of* mediante

C

cafeteria la cafetería

calendar el calendario

to call llamar *5A*

can la lata *8B*

capital la capital *1A*

car el carro *3A*, el coche; *by car* en carro *3A*, en coche

card la tarjeta *9B*; *credit card* tarjeta de crédito *9B*; *playing card* la carta *7A*

carrot la zanahoria *8B*

to carry llevar *5A*; *to carry up* subir *8A*

cash el efectivo *9B*; *in cash* en efectivo *9B*

cash register la caja *9B*

cassette el casete *5A*

cat el gato, la gata *5A*

CD el CD, el disco compacto *2B*; *CD player* el reproductor de CDs *5A*; *CD burner* el quemador de CDs *5A*

to celebrate celebrar *5B*

census el censo

center el centro *3B*; *shopping center* centro comercial *9A*

century el siglo *7A*

chair la silla *2A*

chalk la tiza *2A*

change el cambio *9B*

to change cambiar *9B*

cheap barato,-a *9B*

checkers las damas *7A*

cheese el queso *8B*

chemistry la química

chess el ajedrez *7A*

chicken el pollo *3B*

child niño,-a

Chile Chile *1A*

chilly fresco,-a *7B*

chocolate el chocolate *8B*

to choose escoger *8B*

chore el quehacer *8A*

Christmas la Navidad *5B*

city la ciudad *3A*

clam la almeja

clarinet el clarinete

class la clase *2A*

classmate el compañero, la compañera *5A*

clean limpio,-a *4A*

to clean limpiar *8A*

clerk el dependiente, la dependienta *9B*

to climb subir *8A;* escalar

clock el reloj *2A*

to close cerrar *(ie) 6A*

closed cerrado,-a *4A*

clothing la ropa *2B*

cloudy nublado,-a *7B*; *it is cloudy* está nublado *7B*

coat el abrigo *8A*

coffee el café *8B*

cold frío,-a *4A*; el frío *4A*; *it is cold* hace frío *7B*; *to be cold* tener frío *6B*

Colombia Colombia *1A*

color el color *7B*

to combine combinar *9A*

to come venir *5B*; *to come back* volver *(ue) 7A*; *to come in* entrar *5A*

comfort comodidad

comfortable cómodo,-a *6B*

comical cómico,-a *4B*

common común

compact disc el disco compacto (CD) *2B*; *CD player* el reproductor de discos compactos (CDs) *5A*; *CD burner* el quemador de discos compactos (CDs) *5A*

competition la competencia

to complete completar, acabar *8A*

computer la computadora *2B*

computer science la computación *2B*

concert el concierto *3B*

congratulations felicitaciones

to conquer conquistar

to continue continuar *7B*, seguir *(i, i)*

to cook cocinar *8A*

cool el fresco *7B*; *it is cool* hace fresco *7B*

to copy copiar *7B*

corn el maíz *8B*

to cost costar *(ue) 7A*

Costa Rica Costa Rica *1A*

cotton el algodón *9A*

to count contar

country el país *1A*

couple la pareja

courtyard el patio *6B*

cousin el primo, la prima *4A*

crazy loco,-a *4A*

to create crear
credit el crédito 9B; *credit card* la tarjeta de crédito 9B; *on credit* a crédito 9B
to cross cruzar
Cuba Cuba 1A
cup la taza 6A
cycling ciclismo

dad el papá
to dance bailar 4B
dark obscuro,-a; *dark-haired, dark-skinned* moreno,-a 4B
date la fecha 5B
daughter la hija 4A
day el día 2B; *every day* todos los días 6A; *the day after tomorrow* pasado mañana 5B; *the day before yesterday* anteayer 5B
dear querido,-a 5B
December diciembre 5B
to decorate adornar 8A
degree el grado 7B
delighted encantado,-a 3A
dentist el dentista, la dentista 3A
department el departamento 9A
desire la gana 6B
desk el escritorio, el pupitre 2A
dessert el postre 6A
difficult difícil 4B
dinner la comida 6A
to direct dirigir
director el director, la directora
dirty sucio,-a 4A
disaster el desastre
disc el disco 2B; *compact disc (CD)* el disco compacto 2B; *CD player* el reproductor de discos compactos (CDs) 5A; *CD burner* el quemador de discos compactos (CDs) 5A
to discover descubrir
dish el plato 6A
dishwasher el lavaplatos 6A
diskette el diskette 2B
to do hacer 3B; *to do aerobics* hacer aeróbicos 7A
doctor el médico, la médica 3A, el doctor, la doctora
dog el perro, la perra 5A
dollar el dólar

Dominican Republic la República Dominicana 1A
door la puerta 2A
dot punto 2B
downtown el centro 3B
to draw dibujar 7A
drawing el dibujo 6B
dress el vestido 9A
drink el refresco 3B, la bebida
to drink tomar 3B
drum el tambor
during durante
DVD el DVD 5A; *DVD player* el reproductor de DVDs 5A

E

e-mail correo electrónico 2B
each cada 5A
early temprano 5B
earring el arete 2B
Easter la Pascua
easy fácil 4B
to eat comer 3B
Ecuador el Ecuador 1A
egg el huevo 8B
eight ocho 1A
eight hundred ochocientos, -as 5B
eighteen dieciocho 1A
eighth octavo,-a 7B
eighty ochenta 1B
either tampoco 2B; *either...or* o...o 9A
electric eléctrico,-a 6A
electronic electrónico,-a 2B
elevator el ascensor 9B
eleven once 1A
El Salvador El Salvador 1A
else más 4A
end el fin 5A
to end terminar 2B
English el inglés *(language)* 2B
to enjoy disfrutar
enough bastante 9B
to erase borrar
eraser el borrador 2A
escalator la escalera mecánica 9B
every todo,-a 4A, cada 5A; *every day* todos los días 5A
everybody todo el mundo, todos,-as
everyday de todos los días 5A
everyone todo el mundo, todos,-as
everywhere por todos lados 7B

exam el examen 5A
example el ejemplo; *for example* por ejemplo
excellent excelente 7B
to exchange cambiar 9B
excuse me perdón, con permiso 1B
expensive caro,-a 9B
to explain explicar, aclarar
explanation la explicación

face cara
fairly bastante
family la familia 4A; *family tree* el árbol genealógico
famous famoso,-a
fantastic fantástico,-a 3A
far (from) lejos (de) 3A
fast rápido,-a 4B
fat gordo,-a 4B
father el padre 4A
favorite favorito,-a 3B
fear el miedo 6B; *to be afraid of* tener miedo de 6B
February febrero 5B
to feed dar de comer 8A
to feel like tener ganas de 6B
to feel sorry sentir (ie) 6A
few poco,-a 6A
fifteen quince 1A
fifth quinto,-a 7B
fifty cincuenta 1B
film la película 5A
to find encontrar (ue)
finger el dedo 9A
to finish terminar 2B, acabar 8A
first primero,-a 5B, primer *(form of primero before a m., s. noun)* 6B, primero *(adverb)* 5B; *first floor* el primer piso 6B
fish el pescado 3B
to fit quedarle bien a uno 9A
five cinco 1A
five hundred quinientos,-as 5B
to fix arreglar 8A
floor el piso 6B; *first floor* el primer piso 6B; *ground floor* la planta baja 6B
flower la flor 7B
flute la flauta
to fold doblar 8A
to follow seguir (i, i); *the following* lo siguiente
food la comida 3B; *food server* el mesero, la mesera 3B

foot el pie *9A*; *on foot* a pie *3A*
football el fútbol americano *7A*
for por, para *3A*; *for example* por ejemplo *1B*
to forget olvidar *8B*
fork el tenedor *6A*
forty cuarenta *1B*
four cuatro *1A*
four hundred cuatrocientos, -as *5B*
fourteen catorce *1A*
fourth cuarto,-a *7B*
free libre *4A*
fresh fresco,-a *8B*
Friday viernes *2B*; *on Friday* el viernes
friend el amigo, la amiga *2A*
from de *1A*, desde *6B*; *from the* de la/del (de + el) *3A*; *from where?* ¿de dónde? *1A*
fruit la fruta *8B*
fun divertido,-a *4A*
funny cómico,-a *4B*

G

game el partido *4B*, el juego
garage el garaje *6B*
garbage la basura *8A*
garden el jardín *8A*
garlic el ajo *8B*
generally generalmente
generous generoso,-a *4B*
geography la geografía
geometry la geometría
to get conseguir *(i, i)*
to get together reunir
gift el regalo *9B*
girl la chica *2A*, la muchacha *1A*
girlfriend la novia
to give dar *7A*
glad contento,-a *2A*; *Glad to meet you!* ¡Mucho gusto! *1A*; *I would be glad to* con (mucho) gusto *1A*; *So glad to meet you.* Tanto gusto. *1A*
glass el vaso *4B*
glove el guante *9A*
to go ir *3A*; *let's go!* ¡vamos! *3A*; *to be going to (do something)* ir a (+ *infinitive*) *3B*; *to go back* regresar, volver *(ue) 7A*; *to go in* entrar *5A*; *to go out* salir *4A*; *to go shopping* ir de compras *4B*; *to go up* subir *8A*; *to go upstairs* subir *8A*

gold el oro *9B*
good bueno,-a *4B*, buen (*form of* bueno *before a m., s. noun*) *7B*; *good afternoon* buenas tardes *1B*; *good luck* buena suerte; *good morning* buenos días *1B*; *good night* buenas noches *1B*
good-bye adiós *1A*
good-looking guapo,-a *4A*, bonito,-a *4A*
gossip el chisme *6B*
grade la nota, la calificación
granddaughter la nieta *4A*
grandfather el abuelo *4A*
grandmother la abuela *4A*
grandson el nieto *4A*
grape la uva *8B*
gray gris *2B*
great fantástico,-a *3A*
greater mayor *8B*
greatest mayor *8B*
green verde *2B*
green bean la habichuela *8B*
greens la verdura *8B*
group el grupo; *musical group* grupo musical
Guatemala Guatemala *1A*
guitar la guitarra
guy el muchacho *1A*
gym el gimnasio

H

half medio,-a; *half past* y media *1B*
ham el jamón *8B*
hand la mano *9A*; *on the other hand* en cambio *7B*
handbag el bolso *9B*
handkerchief el pañuelo *9B*
handsome guapo,-a *4A*
to hang colgar *(ue) 8A*
to happen pasar
happy contento,-a *4A*, feliz (*pl.* felices) *5B*, alegre; *Happy birthday!* ¡Feliz cumpleaños! *5B*
hard difícil *4B*
hat el sombrero *9A*
to have tomar *3B*, tener *5A*; *to have a birthday* cumplir años *5B*; *to have just* acabar de (+ *infinitive*) *8A*; *to have to* deber, tener que *6A*
he él *2A*
head la cabeza *9A*
health la salud
to hear oír *8A*

heat el calor *6B*
hello hola *1A*; *hello (telephone greeting)* aló *2B*, diga, oigo
help la ayuda
to help ayudar *6A*
her su, sus *4A*; la *(d.o.) 5A*; le *(i.o.) 1A*; *(after a preposition)* ella *4B*
here aquí *1A*
hey mira, miren, oye, oigan
hi hola *1A*
him lo *(d.o.) 5A*; le *(i.o.) 3A*; *(after a preposition)* él *4B*
his su, sus *4A*
hispanic hispano,-a
history la historia *2B*
hockey el hockey
home la casa *4A*; *at home* en casa
homework la tarea *4B*
Honduras Honduras *1A*
horrible horrible *4B*
horse el caballo *3A*; *on horseback* a caballo *3A*
hot caliente *4A*; *it is hot* hace calor *7B*; *to be hot* tener calor *6B*
hotel hotel *3A*
hour la hora *1B*
house la casa *4A*
how? ¿cómo? *1A*; *How are you?* ¿Qué tal? *1B*; *How are you (formal)?* ¿Cómo está (Ud.)? *1B*; *How are you (informal)?* ¿Cómo estás (tú)? *1B*; *How are you (pl.)?* ¿Cómo están (Uds.)? *1B*; *How do you say...?* ¿Cómo se dice...? *2A*; *How do you write (spell)...?* ¿Cómo se escribe...? *1A*; *How is the weather?* ¿Qué tiempo hace? *7B*; *How long...?* ¿Cuánto (+ *time expression*) hace que (+ *present tense of verb*)...? *7A*; *how many?* ¿cuántos,-as? *2B*; *how much?* ¿cuánto,-a? *2B*; *How old are you?* ¿Cuántos años tienes? *1A*
how (+ adjective)! ¡qué (+ *adjective*)! *4A*
hug el abrazo *6B*
hunger el hambre *f. 6B*
hungry: to be hungry tener hambre *6B*
hurry la prisa *6B*; *in a hurry* apurado,-a *4A*; *to be in a hurry* tener prisa *6B*
husband el esposo *4A*

I

I yo *1A*
ice el hielo *7B*; *to ice skate* patinar sobre hielo *7B*
ice cream el helado *8B*
idea la idea *5B*
ideal ideal *4B*
if si *5A*
to **imagine** imaginar
important importante *4B*
in en *2A*, por *4A*
in-laws los parientes políticos
ingredient el ingrediente *8B*
in order to para *3A*
intelligent inteligente *4B*
to **intend** pensar *(ie) 6A*
interesting interesante *4B*
to **introduce** presentar *3A*; *let me introduce you (formal, s.) to* le presento a *3A*; *let me introduce you (informal, s.) to* te presento a *3A*; *let me introduce you (pl.) to* les presento a *3A*
invitation la invitación
to **invite** invitar
island la isla
it la *(d.o.)*, lo *(d.o.) 5A*
its su, sus *4A*

J

jacket la chaqueta *9A*
January enero *5B*
jeans los jeans *2B*
jersey la camiseta *2B*
jewel la joya *9B*
juice el jugo *3B*
July julio *5B*
June junio *5B*
just sólo

K

to **keep on** seguir *(i, i)*
keyboard el teclado *2B*
kilogram el kilo (kg.)
kind amable *4A*, el tipo
kitchen la cocina *6A*
knife el cuchillo *6A*
to **know** saber *3B*

L

lady la señora, Sra. *1B*, la dama; *young lady* la señorita *1B*
lamp la lámpara *6A*
language la lengua, el idioma
last pasado,-a *5B*, último,-a

late tarde
later luego *1A*, después *6A*; *see you later* hasta luego *1A*, hasta la vista
lazy perezoso,-a
to **learn** aprender
leather el cuero *9B*
to **leave** dejar *8A*
leg la pierna *9A*
to **lend** prestar *8B*
less menos *8B*; *less (+ noun/ adjective/adverb) than* menos (+ *noun/adjective/adverb*) que *8B*; *the least (+ adjective + noun)* el/la/los/las (+ *noun*) menos (+ *adjective*) *8B*
let's (+ infinitive)! ¡vamos a (+ *infinitive*)! *3B*
let's go! ¡vamos! *3A*
letter la carta *6B*, la letra; *capital letter* la mayúscula *1A*; *lowercase letter* la minúscula *1A*
lettuce la lechuga *8B*
library la biblioteca *3A*
lie la mentira *6B*
to **lie** mentir *(ie, i)*
life la vida *7A*
light la luz *(pl. luces) 6A*
to **light** encender *(ie) 6A*
like como
to **like** gustar *4B*; querer *6A*; *I/you/he/she/it/we/they would like...* me/te/le/nos/vos/les gustaría... *6B*
list la lista *7A*
to **listen (to)** escuchar *4B*
little poco,-a *6B*; *a little (bit)* un poco *5A*; *a very little (bit)* un poquito
to **live** vivir *4A*
living room la sala *6B*
lobster la langosta
long largo,-a *9B*
to **look (at)** mirar *4B*; *to look for* buscar *3A*
to **lose** perder *(ie)*
love el amor *5A*
to **love** querer *6A*
lunch el almuerzo *2B*

M

magazine la revista *2A*
to **make** hacer *3B*
mall el centro comercial *9A*
man el hombre *9A*
many mucho,-a *3B*

map el mapa *2A*
March marzo *5B*
market el mercado *8B*
match el partido *4B*
material el material *9B*
mathematics las matemáticas *2B*
to **matter** importar *8B*
maximum máximo,-a *7B*
May mayo *5B*
me me *(i.o.) 4B*; me *(d.o.) 5A*; *they call me* me llaman; *(after a preposition)* mí
to **mean** querer decir *6B*; *it means* quiere decir *2A*; *What is the meaning (of)...?* ¿Qué quiere decir...? *2A*
meat la carne *8B*
mechanic mecánico,-a *9B*; la escalera mecánica *9B*
menu el menú *3B*
Mexico México *1A*
microwave oven horno microondas *6A*
midnight la medianoche *1B*; *It is midnight.* Es medianoche. *1B*
milk la leche *8A*
mine mío,-a; *the pleasure is mine* el gusto es mío *3A*
minimum mínimo,-a *7B*
minus menos *1B*
minute el minuto *7A*
Miss la señorita, Srta. *1B*
mist la neblina *7B*
mistaken equivocado
modern moderno,-a
mom la mamá
moment el momento *3B*
Monday lunes *2B*; *on Monday* el lunes
money el dinero *5A*
month el mes *5B*
more más *4A*; *more (+ noun/ adjective/adverb) than* más (+ *noun/adjective/adverb*) que *8B*
morning la mañana *1B*; *good morning* buenos días *1B*; *in the morning* de la mañana *1B*, por la mañana *7A*
most: the most (+ adjective + noun) el/la/los/las (+ *noun*) más (+ *adjective*) *8B*
mother la madre *4A*
motorcycle la moto(cicleta) *3A*

mouse ratón (*pl.* ratones) *2B*
movie la película *5A*; *movie theater* el cine *3A*
Mr. el señor, Sr. *1B*
Mrs. la señora, Sra. *1B*
much mucho,-a, mucho *4B*; *very much* muchísimo
museum el museo *3B*
music la música *2B*
must deber *6A*
my mi *2A, (pl. my)* mis *4A*; *my name is* me llamo *1A*

N

name el nombre; *last name* el apellido; *my name is* me llamo *1A*; *their names are* se llaman; *What is your name?* ¿Cómo te llamas? *2A*; *What is (your/his/her) name?* ¿Cómo se llama (Ud./él/ella)? *1A*; *(Your [formal]/His/Her) name is....* (Ud./Él/Ella) se llama.... *2A*; *your name is* te llamas *1A*
napkin la servilleta *6A*
near cerca (de) *3A*
necklace el collar *9B*
to need necesitar *2B*
neither tampoco *2B*; *neither...nor* ni...ni *9A*
nephew el sobrino *4A*
nervous nervioso,-a *4A*
never nunca *4A*
new nuevo,-a *2A*; *New Year's Day* el Año Nuevo *5B*
news la noticia
newspaper el periódico *2A*
next próximo,-a, que viene *5A*; *next to* al lado (de) *6B*
Nicaragua Nicaragua *1A*
nice simpático,-a *3A*, amable *4A*; *the weather is nice* hace buen tiempo *7B*
nickname el apodo
niece la sobrina *4A*
night la noche *1B*; *at night* de la noche *1B*, por la noche *6B*; *good night* buenas noches *1B*
nine nueve *1A*
nine hundred novecientos, -as *5B*
nineteen diecinueve *1A*
ninety noventa *1B*
ninth noveno,-a *7B*
no no *1A*
nobody nadie *9A*

none ninguno,-a, ningún, ninguna *9A*
noon el mediodía; *It is noon.* Es mediodía. *1B*
north el norte
not: not any ninguno,-a, ningún, ninguna *9A*; *not even* ni *5B*; *not very* poco,-a *6B*
notebook el cuaderno *2A*
nothing nada *9A*
November noviembre *5B*
now ahora *2B*; *right now* ahora mismo *7A*
number el número *2B*; *telephone/fax/cellular telephone number* número de teléfono/ de fax/de teléfono celular *2B*; *wrong number* número equivocado *2B*

O

to obtain conseguir *(i, i)*
occupied ocupado,-a *4A*
to occur pasar
October octubre *5B*
of de *1A*; *of the* de la/del (de + el) *1A*
of course! ¡claro! *3A*, ¡Cómo no! *3B*
office la oficina *3A*
official oficial
oh! ¡ay! *2A*
oil el aceite *6A*, el petróleo
okay de acuerdo *3B*, regular *1B*; *(pause in speech)* bueno *3B*
old viejo,-a *5B*; *How old are you?* ¿Cuántos años tienes? *1A*; *to be (+ number) years old* tener (+ number) años *5A*
older mayor *5B*
oldest el/la mayor *5B*
on en *2A*, sobre *2B*; *on credit* a crédito *9B*; *on foot* a pie *3A*; *on loan* prestado,-a *6B*; *on the other hand* en cambio *7B*; *on the telephone* por teléfono *6B*
one un, una, uno *2A*
one hundred cien *1B*; *(when followed by another number)* ciento *5B*
onion la cebolla *8B*
only único,-a *4A*, sólo *8A*, solamente
open abierto,-a *4A*
to open abrir *5A*

or o *2B*, u *(used before a word that starts with o or ho)* *6B*; *either...or* o...o *9A*
orange la naranja *3B*; anaranjado,-a *(color)* *9A*
to order pedir *(i, i)* *6B*
organ el órgano
other otro,-a *4A*
ought deber *6A*
our nuestro,-a *4A*
over sobre *2B*; *over there* allá *6A*

P

paella la paella *8B*
page la página *2A*
pair la pareja
pajamas el pijama *9A*
Panama Panamá *1A*
pants el pantalón *2B*
pantyhose las medias *9A*
paper el papel *2A*; *sheet of paper* la hoja de papel
Paraguay el Paraguay *1A*
pardon me perdón *1B*
parents los padres *2A*, los papás
park el parque *3A*
part-time (work) medio tiempo (trabajo)
partner el compañero, la compañera *5A*
party la fiesta *3A*
to pass pasar *5A*; *pass me* pásame *6A*
past pasado,-a *5B*; *half past* y media *1B*
pastime el pasatiempo *7A*
patio el patio *6B*
to pay pagar *9B*
pea el guisante *8B*
pearl la perla *9B*
pen el bolígrafo *2A*
pencil el lápiz (*pl.* lápices) *2A*; *pencil sharpener* el sacapuntas *2A*
people la gente *8A*
pepper la pimienta *(seasoning)* *6A*; *bell pepper* el pimiento *8B*
perfect perfecto,-a *9B*
perfume el perfume *9B*
perhaps quizás *8A*
permission el permiso *7A*; *to ask for permission (to do something)* pedir permiso (para) *6B*
permit el permiso *7A*
to permit permitir *7A*

person la persona *7A*
personal personal
Perú el Perú *1A*
philosophy la filosofía
photo la foto(grafía) *4A*
physics la física *6A*
piano el piano *4B*
to pick up recoger *8A*
pink rosado,-a *9A*
place el lugar *7B*, la posición
to place poner *6A*
to plan pensar *(ie) 6A*
plant la planta *6B*
plate el plato *6A*
to play jugar *(ue) 4B; (a musical instrument)* tocar *4B; (+ a sport/game)* jugar a *4B*
player el jugador, la jugadora *7B; CD player* el reproductor de CDs *5A; DVD player* el reproductor de DVDs *5A; MP3 player* el reproductor de MP3 *5A*
playing card la carta *7A*
plaza la plaza *3B*
pleasant simpático,-a *3A*
please por favor *1B*
pleasure el gusto *3A; the pleasure is mine* encantado,-a, el gusto es mío *3A*
plural el plural
point el punto
to point apuntar; *to point to (at, out)* señalar
politically políticamente
pollution la contaminación ambiental
polo la camiseta *2B*
popular popular *4A*
pot la olla *8A*
potato la papa *8B*
pound la libra
practice la práctica *5A*
to prefer preferir *(ie, i) 6A*
to prepare preparar *8A*
pretty bonito,-a *2A*, guapo,-a *2A*, lindo,-a *8B*
price el precio *8B*
printer (laser) la impresora (láser) *2B*
problem el problema *3A*
program el programa *7A*
to promise prometer *9A*
public público,-a; *public square* la plaza *3B*
Puerto Rico Puerto Rico *1A*

purchase la compra *4B*
purple morado,-a *9A*
purpose el propósito
purse el bolso *9B*
to put poner *6A*

quality la calidad *9B*
quarter el cuarto *1B; a quarter after, a quarter past* y cuarto *1B; a quarter to, a quarter before* menos cuarto *1B*
question la pregunta *3B; to ask a question* hacer una pregunta *3B*
quickly pronto *1B*

R

radio (broadcast) la radio *4B;* el radio
rain la lluvia *7B*
to rain llover *(ue) 7B*
raincoat el impermeable *9A*
rapid rápido *4B*
rapidly rápidamente *5B*
rather bastante *9B*
to reach cumplir *5B*
to read leer *3B*
reading la lectura
ready listo,-a *7B; to be ready* estar listo,-a *7B*
really? ¿de veras? *5B*
receipt el recibo *9B*
to receive recibir *9B*
recipe la receta *8B*
red rojo,-a *2B*
red-haired pelirrojo,-a *4B*
refreshment el refresco *3B*
refrigerator el refrigerador *2B*
to regret sentir *(ie, i) 6A*
regular regular *1B*
relative el pariente, la pariente *4A*
to remain quedar *9A*
remains restos
to remember recordar *(ue) 7A*
remote remoto,-a *7A; remote control* el control remoto *7A*
to rent alquilar *7A*
to repeat repetir *(i, i) 6B*
report el informe
reporter el periodista, la periodista
to request pedir *(i,i) 6B*
to resolve resolver *(ue)*
restaurant el restaurante *3A*

to return volver *(ue) 4A*, regresar
to review repasar
rice el arroz *8B*
ride el paseo *7B; to go for a ride* dar un paseo *7B*
to ride montar *5A*
right correcto,-a; *right now* ahora mismo *7A*
right? ¿verdad? *3A*
ring el anillo *9B*
ripe maduro,-a *8B*
river el río
room el cuarto *6B; dining room* el comedor *6A; living room* la sala *6B*
ruler la regla *2A*
to run correr *6B*
runner el corredor, la corredora *7B*
rush la prisa *6B*

S

sad triste *4A*
safe seguro,-a
saint's day el santo; *All Saints' Day* Todos los Santos
salad la ensalada *3B*
sale la oferta *9B; to be on sale* estar en oferta *9B*
salt la sal *6A*
same mismo,-a *7A*
satisfied: *to be satisfied (with)* estar contento,-a (con) *4A*
Saturday sábado *2B; on Saturday* el sábado
saucepan la olla *8A*
sausage el chorizo *(seasoned with red peppers) 8B*
to save ahorrar *9B*
saxophone el saxofón
to say decir *6B; How do you say...?* ¿Cómo se dice...? *2A; one says* se dice *2A; to say you are sorry* pedir perdón *6B*
scarf la bufanda *9B*
schedule el horario *2B*
school el colegio *2B*, la escuela *3A*
science la ciencia
to scold regañar
screen la pantalla *2B*
season la estación *7B*
second el segundo *7B;* segundo,-a *7A*
to see ver *3B; I see it!* ¡ya lo veo!; *let's see* a ver; *see you later*

hasta la vista, hasta luego *1A*; *see you soon* hasta pronto *1B*; *see you tomorrow* hasta mañana *1B*; *you see* ves

to seem parecer *8B*

selfish egoísta *4B*

to sell vender *9A*

to send enviar *7B*

sentence la oración, la frase

September septiembre *5B*

settled down establecieron

seven siete *1A*

seven hundred setecientos,-as *5B*

seventeen diecisiete *1A*

seventh séptimo,-a *7B*

seventy setenta *1B*

several varios,-as

shame la lástima; *What a shame!* ¡Qué lástima! *5A*

she ella *2A*

sheet la hoja; *sheet of paper* hoja de papel

ship el barco *3A*

shirt la camisa *2B*

shoe el zapato *2B*; *high-heel shoe* zapato de tacón *9A*; *low-heel shoe* zapato bajo *8A*

short bajo,-a *(not tall) 4B*, corto,-a *(not long) 9B*; *in short* en resumen

should deber *6A*

show el programa *7A*

to show enseñar

shrimp el camarón

sick enfermo,-a *4A*

side el lado *6B*

silk la seda *9A*

silly tonto,-a *4B*

silver la plata *9B*

silverware los cubiertos *6A*

since desde *6B*, como

to sing cantar *4B*

singer el cantante, la cantante *3B*

sink el fregadero *6A*

sir el señor, Sr. *1B*

sister la hermana *4A*

six seis *1A*

six hundred seiscientos,-a *5B*

sixteen dieciséis *1A*

sixth sexto,-a *7B*

sixty sesenta *1B*

size el tamaño *9B*

to skate patinar *4B*; *to ice skate* patinar sobre hielo *7B*; *to in-line skate* patinar sobre ruedas *4B*

to skateboard montar en patineta *7B*

skater el patinador, la patinadora *7B*

sketch el dibujo *6B*

to sketch dibujar *7A*

to ski esquiar *7B*

skier el esquiador, la esquiadora *7B*

skirt la falda *2B*

skyscraper el rascacielos

sleep el sueño *6B*

to sleep dormir *(ue, u) 7A*

slow lento,-a *4B*

small pequeño,-a *6B*

smart listo,-a *8A*; *to be smart* ser listo,-a *8A*

smooth suave

snow la nieve *7B*

to snow nevar *(ie) 7B*

so tal, tan *5A*

soap opera la telenovela *7A*

soccer el fútbol *4B*; *soccer player* el futbolista, la futbolista *7B*

sock el calcetín *2B*

soft suave; *soft drink* el refresco *3B*

so long hasta luego *1A*

to solve resolver *(ue)*

some unos, unas *2A*; alguno,-a, algún, alguna *9A*

somebody alguien *9A*

someone alguien *9A*

something algo *9A*

sometimes a veces *5B*

son el hijo *4A*

song la canción *5A*

soon luego *1A*, pronto *1B*; *see you soon* hasta pronto *1B*

sorry: *I am sorry* lo siento *1B*; *to feel sorry* sentir *(ie, i) 6A*; *to say you are sorry* pedir perdón *6B*

so-so regular *1B*

sound system el equipo de sonido *5A*

soup la sopa *6A*; *soup bowl* el plato de sopa *6A*

south el sur

Spain España *1A*

Spanish el español *(language) 2B*, español, española; *Spanish-speaking* hispanohablante

to speak hablar *2B*

special especial *6A*

to spend (time) pasar *5A*

sport el deporte *5A*

spouse el esposo, la esposa *4A*

spring la primavera *7B*

stadium el estadio

stairway la escalera *6B*

to start empezar *(ie) 6A*

to stay quedar *9A*

stepfather el padrastro

stepmother la madrastra

stereo el estéreo

still todavía *7B*

store la tienda *3B*

stove la estufa *6A*

to straighten arreglar *8A*

strawberry la fresa *8B*

street la calle *3B*

strong fuerte

student el estudiante, la estudiante *2A*

study el estudio

to study estudiar *2B*

subject la asignatura *8A*

subway el metro *3A*

such tal

sufficient bastante *9B*

sufficiently bastante

sugar el azúcar *6A*

suit el traje *9A*

suitcase la maleta *5A*

summer el verano *4A*

sun el sol *7B*

Sunday domingo *2B*; *on Sunday* el domingo

sunny soleado,-a *7B*; *it is sunny* está soleado *7B*, hay sol *7B*, hace sol *7B*

supermarket el supermercado *8B*

surprise la sorpresa *5A*

sweater el suéter *9A*

to sweep barrer *8A*

to swim nadar *4B*

swimming pool la piscina *6B*

swimsuit el traje de baño *9A*

synthetic sintético,-a *9B*

table la mesa *6A*; *to clear the table* recoger la mesa *8A*; *to set the table* poner la mesa *6A*

tablecloth el mantel *6A*

tablespoon la cuchara *6A*

to take tomar *3A*, llevar *5A*; *take turns* alterna *(tú command)*;

alternen (Uds. *command*); *to take a trip* hacer un viaje 5A; *to take out* sacar 8A; *to take up* subir 8A

tall alto,-a 4B

tape recorder la grabadora 5A

taste gusto

to taste probar

to teach enseñar

teacher el profesor, la profesora 2A

team el equipo 7A

teaspoon la cucharita 6A

telephone el teléfono 2B; *by the telephone, on the telephone* por teléfono 6B; *telephone number* el número de teléfono 2B; *cellular telephone number* número de teléfono celular

to telephone llamar 5A

television la televisión 4B; *to watch television* ver la televisión 4B

television set el televisor 7A

to tell decir 6B; *(a story)* contar (ue) 9A; *tell me* dígame (Ud. *command*)

temperature la temperatura 7B; *What is the temperature?* ¿Qué temperatura hace? 7B

ten diez 1A

tennis el tenis 4B

tennis player el tenista, la tenista 7B

tenth décimo,-a 7B

to terminate acabar 8A

test el examen 2B

than: more (+ noun/ adjective/adverb) than más (+ *noun/adjective/adverb*) que 8B

thanks gracias 1B; *thank you very much* muchas gracias 1B

that que 5A, ese, esa 6A, *(far away)* aquel, aquella 6A, *(neuter form)* eso; *that which* lo que 6B

the el *(m., s.)* 2A, la *(f., s.)* 2A, las *(f., pl.)* 2A, los *(m., pl.)* 2A; *to the* al 3A

theater el teatro 3B

their su, sus 4A

them les *(i.o.)* 3A; los/las *(d.o.)* 5A; *(after a preposition)* ellos,-as 4B

theme el tema, el tópico

then luego 1A, después 6A, entonces 6A; *(pause in speech)* pues 3B

there allí 2A; *there is, there are* hay 2A; *over there* allá 6A

these estos, estas 6A

they ellos,-as 2A; *they are* son 2A; *they were* fueron

thin delgado,-a 4B

thing la cosa 6A

to think pensar *(ie)* 6A; *to think about (i.e., to have an opinion)* pensar de 6A; *to think about (i.e., to focus one's thoughts)* pensar en 6A; *to think about (doing something)* pensar en (+ *infinitive*)

third tercero,-a,tercer *(form of tercero before a m., s. noun)* 7B

thirst la sed 6B; *to be thirsty* tener sed 6B

thirteen trece 1A

thirty treinta 1B

this este *(m., s.)*, esta *(f., s.)* 6A

those esos, esas 6A, *(far away)* aquellos, aquellas 6A

thousand mil 5B

three tres 1A

three hundred trescientos,-as 5B

through por 6B

to throw lanzar

Thursday jueves 2B; *on Thursday* el jueves

thus pues 3B

tie la corbata 9A

time el tiempo 4A, la vez (pl. veces) 5B; *at times, sometimes* a veces 5B; *at what time?* ¿a qué hora? 2B; *(number +) time(s) per (+ time expression)* (number +) vez/veces al/a la (+ *time expression*) 7A; *What time is it?* ¿Qué hora es? 1B

tired cansado,-a 4A

to a 2B

today hoy 3B

toe el dedo 9A

together junto,-a

tomato el tomate 8B

tomorrow mañana 1B; *see you tomorrow* hasta mañana 1B; *the day after tomorrow* pasado mañana 5B

tonight esta noche 7A

too también 3A, *too (much)* demasiado 9B

to touch tocar

train el tren 3A

transportation el transporte 3A

to travel viajar 6A

tree el árbol; *family tree* árbol genealógico

trip el paseo 7B, el viaje 5A; *to take a trip* hacer un viaje 5A

trombone el trombón

truck el camión

trumpet la trompeta

truth la verdad 6B

to try (to do something) tratar (de)

t-shirt la camiseta 2B

Tuesday martes 2B; *on Tuesday* el martes

to turn off apagar 7A

to turn on encender *(ie)* 6A, poner

twelve doce 1A

twenty veinte 1A

twenty-eight veintiocho 1B

twenty-five veinticinco 1B

twenty-four veinticuatro 1B

twenty-nine veintinueve 1B

twenty-one veintiuno 1B

twenty-seven veintisiete 1B

twenty-six veintiséis 1B

twenty-three veintitrés 1B

twenty-two veintidós 1B

two dos 1A

two hundred doscientos,-as 5B

typical típico, -a

ugly feo,-a 4B

umbrella el paraguas 9B

uncle el tío 4A

to understand comprender 2A; *I understand* comprendo 2A

underwear la ropa interior 9A

unique único,-a 4A

united unido,-a

United States of America los Estados Unidos 1A

university la universidad

until hasta 1A, *(to express time)* menos 1B

upcoming que viene 5A

Uruguay el Uruguay 1A

us nos *(i.o.)* 4B; nos *(d.o.)* 5A; *(after a preposition)* nosotros 4B
to use usar 9B

vacation las vacaciones 9A
vacuum la aspiradora 7A; *to vacuum* pasar la aspiradora 8A
vegetable la verdura 8B
Venezuela Venezuela 1A
verb el verbo
very muy, mucho,-a 3B; *very much* mucho, muchísimo 4A; *not very* poco,-a 6B
video game el videojuego 7A
vinegar el vinagre 8B
volleyball el voleibol 7A

walk el paseo 7B; *to go for a walk* dar un paseo 7B; *to walk* caminar 3A
wall la pared 2A, la muralla
wallet la billetera 9B
to want querer 6A
to wash lavar 8A
wastebasket el cesto de papeles 2A
watch el reloj 2A
to watch ver 3B; *to watch television* ver la televisión
water el agua *f.* 4B; *mineral water* agua mineral 3B
way la manera; *By the way* A propósito 1A
we nosotros 2A
to wear llevar 2B
weather el tiempo 7B; *How is the weather?* ¿Qué tiempo hace? 7B; *the weather is nice (bad)* hace buen (mal) tiempo 7B
Wednesday miércoles 2B; *on Wednesday* el miércoles
week la semana 5A
weekend el fin de semana 5A
welcome bienvenido,-a; *you are welcome* de nada 1B
well bien 1B; *(pause in speech)* bueno, este, pues 3B

what a (+ noun)! ¡qué (+ *noun*)! 5A
what? ¿qué? 2A, ¿cuál? 2B; *at what time?* ¿a qué hora? 2B; *What is the meaning (of)...?* ¿Qué quiere decir...? 2A; *What is the temperature?* ¿Qué temperatura hace? 7B; *What is wrong with (someone)?* ¿Qué (+ *tener*)? 6B; *What is wrong with you?* ¿Qué te pasa?; *What is your name?* ¿Cómo te llamas? 2A; *What is (your/his/her) name?* ¿Cómo se llama (Ud./él/ella)? 1A; *What time is it?* ¿Qué hora es? 1B
when cuando 6B
when? ¿cuándo? 3A
where donde 6B
where? ¿dónde? 1A; *from where?* ¿de dónde? 1A; *(to) where?* ¿adónde? 3A
which que 5A; *that which* lo que 6B
which? ¿cuál? 2B; *which one?* ¿cuál? 2B; *which ones?* ¿cuáles? 2B
white blanco,-a 2B
white-haired canoso,-a 4B
who? ¿quién? 2A, *(pl.)* ¿quiénes? 3A
whole entero,-a
why? ¿por qué? 3A
wife la esposa 4A
to win ganar; *games won* los partidos ganados
wind el viento 7B; *it is windy* hace viento 7B
window la ventana 2A
winter el invierno 7B
to wish desear
with con 1A; *with me* conmigo 9B; *with you* (tú) contigo 9B
without sin 8B
to witness presenciar
woman la mujer 9A
wonderful estupendo,-a 7A
wool la lana 9A
word la palabra 2A
work el trabajo 8A, la obra

to work trabajar 8A
world el mundo
worse peor 8B
worst: the worst (+ noun) el/la/los/las peor/peores 8B
wow! ¡caramba! 5A
to write escribir 6B; *How do you write...?* ¿Cómo se escribe...? 1A; *it is written* se escribe 1A

yard el patio 6B
year el año 5B; *New Year's Day* el Año Nuevo 5B; *to be (+ number) years old* tener (+ *number*) años 5A
yellow amarillo,-a 8A
yes sí 1A
yesterday ayer 5B; *the day before yesterday* anteayer 5B
yet todavía 7A
you tú *(informal)* 1A, usted (Ud.) *(formal, s.)* 1B, ustedes (Uds.) *(pl.)* 1B, vosotros,-as *(Spain, informal, pl.)* 1B; *(after a preposition)* ti 4B, usted (Ud.), ustedes (Uds.), vosotros,-as 1B; la, lo, *(d.o.)* 5A, las, los, *(d.o.)* 5A, te *(d.o.)* 6A, os *(Spain, informal, pl., d.o.)*, le *(formal, i.o.)*, les *(pl., i.o.)* 1A, os *(Spain, informal, pl., i.o.)*, te *(i.o.)* 3A; *Are you from...?* ¿Eres (tú) de...? 1A; *you are* eres 1A; *you (formal) are* es 1B; *you (pl.) were* fueron
young joven 5B; *young lady* la señorita 1B; *young woman* la muchacha 3A
younger menor 5B
youngest el/la menor 5B
your tu *(informal)* 2B, tus *(informal, pl.)* 4A, su, sus (Ud./Uds.) 4A, vuestro,-a,-os, -as *(Spain, informal, pl.)*

zero cero 1A

Index

Page references followed by "A" refer to *Navegando 1A*; those followed by "B" refer to *Navegando 1B*.

Credits

Acknowledgments

The authors wish to thank the many people of the Caribbean Islands, Central America, South America, Spain, and the United States who assisted in the photography used in the textbook and videos. Also helpful in providing photos and materials were the National Tourist Offices of Argentina, Chile, Costa Rica, Colombia, Ecuador, Guatemala, the Dominican Republic, Honduras, Mexico, Nicaragua, Panamá, Perú, Puerto Rico, Spain, and Venezuela.

Photo Credits

Anderson, Jennifer J.: 77 (tl), 138 (l), 165 (tl), 183 (l, c)
AP / Wide World Photos: 86, 130 (c, r), 183 (r)
Bechara Baruque, Omar; Eye Ubiquitous / CORBIS: 23 (tl)
Béjar Latonda, Mónica: 4 (tl, tc, tr), 12 (tl, tc, tr), 22 (l, c, r), 30 (l, c, r), 36 (l), 48 (l, c, r), 54 (l, c, r), 68 (l, c, r), 76 (l, c, r), 84 (l), 96 (tl, tc, tr), 106 (l, c, r), 107 (l), 116 (l, c, r), 117, 126 (l, c, r), 130 (l), 142 (l, c, r), 152 (tl, tc, tr), 164 (l, c, r), 172 (tl, tc, tr), 178 (l), 198 (l), 200, 201
Charlier, Claude / CORBIS: 96 (b)
Chilean Ministry of Tourism (Ministerio de Turismo de Chile): v (t), 69 (tr)
Corbis Royalty-Free: v (b), 4 (bl, bc, br), 5 (pearl in shell), 19 (l, r), 39 (l, r), 44–45, 47 (#1, #5), 51 (#1, #2), 53, 56, 57 (t), 63 (t), 65 (r), 68 (b), 69 (tl), 73, 75 (A, B, E), 79 (Modelo, #3, #5, #6), 80, 103, 105 (Activity 19, C), 108, 112, 113 (l, r), 120, 122, 143 (b), 153 (tr), 160 (r), 172 (c), 177, 179 (r), 191 (b), 193 (b), 203 (l, r)
Corporación Nacional de Turismo-Colombia: 23 (tr)
Creatas Images: 153 (tl)
Cummins, Jim / CORBIS: 78
DigitalVision: 48 (b)
Duomo / CORBIS: 75 (D)
Englebert, Victor: iv (r), viii (r, b), xvi (l), 18 (t, b), 23 (c), 26, 31 (t), 32, 34 (b), 36 (r), 37 (l), 49 (b), 51 (#4), 57 (bl), 87 (c), 107 (r), 160 (l), 178 (c, r), 189 (c, l, r), 193 (t), 205 (tl)
Federación Argentina de Pato: 64 (l, r)
Fisher, Peter M. / CORBIS: vii (b), 138–139
Francisco, Timothy: 31 (b), 51 (#3), 159, 176, 185 (r), 188 (l, c, r), 195 (l, c, r)
Franken, Owen / CORBIS: 87 (t)
Fried, Robert: vi (l), viii (l), 12 (b), 31 (c), 49 (t), 54 (b), 55 (tr), 63 (b), 69 (b), 72, 77 (b), 92–93, 97 (tl, b), 105 (A), 119, 123, 137 (l, r), 152 (b), 165 (tr), 173 (tr, b), 179 (l), 181 (l, r), 186 (l), 186–187, 192 (r), 193 (r), 195 (tr), 198 (ct, cb), 199 (tr, br), 205 (br)

Goldberg, Beryl: 13 (t), 17 (tl), 24, 61, 147 (r), 148, 185 (l), 192 (l), 195 (tl, b), 198 (r), 199 (tl, bl), 205 (c)
Haas, Ken / eStock Photo: 191 (t)
Hutchinson, Justin / CORBIS: 50
Kaufman, Ronnie / CORBIS: 70
Lewine, Rob / CORBIS: 25
Look GMBH / eStock Photo: 40
Luxner, Larry: 172 (b)
LWA-Stephen Welstead / CORBIS: 167
MAPS.com / CORBIS: 5 (map of Venezuela)
Massimo Mastrorillo / CORBIS: 55 (b)
Mug Shots / CORBIS: 105 (B)
Pelaez, José Luis, Inc. / CORBIS: 144
Peterson, Chip and Rosa María de la Cueva: ix (r), 5 (l: Caracas; tr: oil derricks), 6, 13 (b), 44 (l), 47 (#2, #4), 49 (c), 71, 79 (#1), 98, 102, 147 (l), 173 (tl), 182
Pierini, Javier / CORBIS: 55 (tl)
Pitamitz, Sergio / CORBIS: vii (t), 143 (t)
Rangel, Francisco: 47 (#3), 57 (br), 154
Reuters NewMedia Inc. / CORBIS: 5 (cacao beans)
Rowell, Galen / CORBIS: 83
Sanger, David: 132, 133 (b)
Savage, Chuck / CORBIS: 35
Schaefer, Norbert / CORBIS: 105 (D)
Schafer, Kevin / CORBIS: 84 (r)
Simson, David: iv (l), vi (r), xvi–1, 12 (c), 29, 34 (t), 37 (r), 47 (#6), 58, 65 (l), 77 (tr), 79 (#2, #4), 81, 97 (tr), 100, 131 (l, r), 133 (t), 153 (b), 158, 161 (l, c, r), 166, 205 (tc)
Smith, Ford / CORBIS: 92 (l)
Smith, Johnathan; Cordaiy Photo Library Ltd. / CORBIS: 8
Stewart, Tom / CORBIS: 87 (b)
Stockbyte Images: 75 (C, F)
Tourist Office of Spain: ix (l), 127 (t, c, b), 135 (t, b)
Uripos / eStock Photo: 99